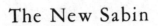

The New Sabin

The New Sabin;
Books Described by Joseph Sabin and His
Successors, Now Described Again on the
Basis of Examination of Originals,
and Fully Indexed by Title, Subject,
Joint Authors, and Institutions and Agencies

by

Lawrence S. Thompson

Entries 1–2484

Volume I

The Whitston Publishing Company
Troy, New York
1974

To John Cook Wyllie,

1908-1968

PREFACE

The late John Cooke Wyllie was a sort of an apostle of the rare book in America. His breviary was Joseph Sabin's *Dictionary of Books Relating to America,* and he dreamed of expanding it to a point at which it would dwarf the *National Union Catalog* in sheer bulk. He printed for very limited distribution six entries of a type which he conceived to be the ideal Sabin. For example, Sabin 3966, *The Battle of Fort Sumter and First Victory of the Southern Troops, April 13th, 1861* (Charleston, 1861), is a seven-page folder containing the front wrapper of the McGregor copy and the title page photographed over graph paper, a facsimile of the folding map over graph paper, a copy of the printed card for the Library of Congress copy, some 500 words of general comment, some 250 words of a discussion of the authorship, a nearly 200-word commentary on the collation of the two editions, locations, references, and auction records. Mr. Wyllie once suggested to the writer of this preface that a new Sabin could be done in this style by twenty-six dedicated bibliographers, each taking one letter of the alphabet. This writer immediately volunteered to take the letter X.

Sabin should not and cannot be done again in the style originally conceived by Sabin and carried on by his successors. To include every printed record of a public hanging in the United States, every annual report of street railway companies in South America, every folder for riverboat excursions, or, in our own time, every multilithed report of a government-subsidized scientific experiment (Sabin included them for the last century) would be overwhelming, and, indeed, considerably less useful than national bibliographies. Instead, bibliographies of imprints on a regional basis, of places, persons, and subjects, and of library holdings are considerably more practical and more likely to be created.

Libraries are being created today by the large microform publishers, who are assembling collections that could never be brought together in the original formats by any person or agency starting out in our time. The major microform publisher in the field of Americana is the Lost Cause Press of Louisville. The catalog of its collection of some 5,000 items on *The Southern Black in Slavery and Freedom* has already been published by Whitston. All of the titles in the latter catalog existed before Sabin was completed and were eligible for inclusion, yet less than half actually appear in Sabin. The same is true of other Lost Cause Press series such as those of western Americana (using Wagner-Camp as a point of departure), nineteenth-century American literature, and Kentuckiana. Book catalogs of all will ultimately be published, possibly integrated in the present series. The columns of serials such as the *Papers* of the Bibliographical Society of America, *Proof, Studies in Bibliography,* and *American Notes and Queries* are open to bibliographers who will make contributions comparable to Mr. Wyllie's essay on *The Battle of Fort Sumter.*

The value of the present Sabin Redivivus cannot be credited to the Lost Cause Press, Whitston, or the compiler, except for their initiative. The responsibility lies with Mr. Eastman and his useful shutters and lenses which

reproduce faithfully most aspects of books, above
all the text, and with Herbert Putnam, who in-
sisted on printing and distributing widely catalog cards with adequate subject and other secon-
dary entries in most cases. This volume repre-
sents books which have been seen by the compiler
in the original or one film, and the entries are
copies of the descriptive portions of Library of
Congress cards for the most part. The entries
in Sabin often left much to be desired, even
when adequately descriptive, from the standpoint
of the convenience of readers who are enslaved
to library catalogs in the Anglo-American tradition. The greatest value of the present work
is the subject index, combined with all other
useful entries such as those for joint authors,
issuing agencies, sub-titles, etc. To pluck out
of Sabin everything on the Virginia and Kentucky
Resolutions, the Battle of Perryville, or the
Star Route Scandal is simply not practical. The
index to this volume, which will be cumulative
in future volumes, makes a subject approach to
American history through books recorded in Sabin
a practical matter. All items will be numbered
serially, and the author alphabet will start over
in each volume. In future cumulations of the
index there will be entries for the authors.

Adequate subject indexes are needed even for
bibliographical works which are based on meticu-
lously careful examination of original works by
a skilled bibliographer. Thus one or more of
the future volumes in this new Sabin will include the novels in the Lyle Wright bibliograph-
ies--all eligible for inclusion in Sabin and a
large proportion of them already there. The
subject indexing of fiction has concerned many
bibliographers. Thus there is one woefully
inadequate study of fiction dealing with the
War Between the States. The present writer's
study of *The Kentucky Novel*, compiled with

iii

the late Algernon D. Thompson and published in
1953, would have been a better work if Wright
had been available with a subject index at the time.

While the organization of the present work
has been fixed by the first volume (i.e., new
alphabets in each volume with cumulative indexes
in each volume), there is the possibility of
alteration of scope. It is likely that future
volumes will include the product of other microform publishers, notably that of General Micro-
film Company of Cambridge, Massachusetts, with
its series of Canadiana, American genealogy,
Mexicana, and American biography, but with nota-
tion of the location of the negative. It should
be noted that the important *National Register
of Microform Masters* (first edition, 1972) has
no subject index (unlike the card file of micro-
forms owned by the Library of Congress itself)
and that descriptive entries could not be brought
up to the quality of Library of Congress entries due to the great variety of sources. Thus,
the plans for the present set will supplement
the *National Register* insofar as Americana is
concerned. Since the scope of this work is
subject to change insofar as its utility to
scholarship may be improved, the publisher and
the compiler will welcome any suggestions.

Lawrence S. Thompson

Lexington, Kentucky

August 1973

A

1   A   , G.
        The young travellers in South America:
     or, A popular introduction to the his-
     tory and resources of that interesting
     and important region. By G. A. ...
     London, J. Macrone, 1835.
        vii, [1], 292 p.   20 1/2 cm.

2   Aa, Pieter van der, 1659-1733.
        Naaukeurige versameling der gedenk-
     waardigste zee en landreysen na Oost en
     West-Indiën ... beginnende met het jaar
     1246. en eyndigende op dese tijd ...
     Leyden, P. vander Aa, 1707.
        28 v. in 29.   plates, maps.   18 cm.

3   Abbad y Lasierra, Iñigo, 1745-1813.
        Historia geográfica, civil y politica
     de la isla de S. Juan Bautista de Puer-
     to Rico. Dala á luz don Antonio Valla-
     dares de Sotomayor. Madrid, Impr. de
     A. Espinosa, 1788.
        1 p. l., 103 p.   21 1/2 cm.

4   Abbot, Abiel, 1770-1828.
        A discourse delivered at Plymouth
     December 22, 1809, at the celebration
     of the 188th anniversary of the land-
     ing of our forefathers in that place.
     By Abiel Abbot, A.M., pastor of the
     First church in Beverly. Boston:
     Printed by Greenough and Stebbins,
     1810.
        28 p.   23 1/2 cm.

5   Abbot, Abiel, 1770-1828.
        An eulogy on the illustrious life
     and character of George Washington;
     delivered before the inhabitants of
     the town of Haverhill, on his birth
     day, 1800, at the request of their
     committee. By Abiel Abbot. And the

invaluable last address of President
Washington to the citizens of the United States, the legacy of the Father of
his country ... Haverhill. [Mass.]
Printed by [S]eth H. Moore. [1800]
  27, 21 p.   22 cm.

6   Abbot, Abiel, 1765-1859, *comp*.
      A genealogical register of the des-
cendants of George Abbot, of Andover;
George Abbot, of Rowley; Thomas Abbot,
of Andover; Arthur Abbot, of Ipswich;
Robert Abbot, of Branford, Ct.--and
George Abbot, of Norwalk, Ct. Comp.
by Rev. Abiel Abbot, D. D. and Rev.
Ephraim Abbot. Boston, J. Munroe and
company, 1847.
   xx, 197 p.   23 1/2 cm.

7   Abbot, Abiel, 1765-1859.
      History of Andover, from its settle-
ment to 1829. By Abiel Abbot, A. M.
Andover [Mass.] Flagg and Gould, 1829.
   204 p.   19 cm.

8   Abbot, Abiel, 1770-1828.
      Letters written in the interior of
Cuba, between the mountains of Arcana,
to the east, and of Cusco, to the west,
in the months of February, March,
April, and May, 1828. By the late Rev.
Abiel Abbot ... Boston, Bowles and
Dearborn, 1829.
   xv, 256 p.   21 cm.

9   Abbott, Jacob, 1803-1879.
      American history, by Jacob Abbott.
New York, Sheldon & co.; Boston, Gould
& Lincoln [1860-65]
   8 v.   front, illus., pl., port.,
maps.   18 cm.

10   [Abbott, Jacob] 1803-1879.
      New England, and her institutions.
By one of her sons. Boston, J. Allan
& co., 1835.

11   Abbott, John Stevens Cabot, 1805-1877.
            History of Hernando Cortez. By John
        S. C. Abbott ... New York, Harper &
        Brothers, 1855.
            5 p. l., [13]-348 p. incl. 12 pl.,
        3 maps.   16 1/2 cm.

12   Abbott, John Stevens Cabot, 1805-1877.
            History of King Philip, sovereign
        chief of the Wampanoags. Including
        the early history of the settlers of
        New England. By John S. C. Abbott ...
        New York, Harper & brothers, 1857.
            viii, [9]-410 p. incl. plates, front.
        17 cm.

13   Abbott, John Stevens Cabot, 1805-1877.
            ... The life of Christopher Colum-
        bus. by John S.C. Abbott ...   New
        York, Dodd & Mead [1875]
            1 p. l., 345 p.   front., pl.   18 1/2
        cm.

14   Abbott, John Stevens Cabot, 1805-1877.
            South and North; or, Impressions re-
        ceived during a trip to Cuba and the
        South. By John S. C. Abbott ... New
        York, Abbey & Abbot, 1860.
            352 p.   19 cm.

15   Abbott, Simon C   1826-1858, *comp.*
            A record of births, marriages and
        deaths, in Worcester, Vermont, from
        October 21, 1813, to June 18, 1858.
        Alphabetically arranged. By Simon
        C. Abbott. Montpelier, E.P. Walton,
        printer, 1858.
            31 p.   15 1/2 cm.

16   Abbring, Hermanus Johannes, 1787-1874.
            Weemoedstoonen uit de geschiedenis
        van mijn leven, of, Mijne reis naar
        Curaçao, en vlugtige beschouwingen
        van dat eiland gedurende mijn tienjarig
        verblijf op hetzelve. Door H. J.

Abbring. Groningen, W. van Boekeren, 1834.
6 p. 1., 205 p.   23 1/2 cm.

17   Abdy, Edward Strutt, 1791-1846.
American whites and blacks, in reply to a German orthodermist. By E.S. Abdy ... London, C. Gilpin, 1842.
50 p.   21 cm.

18   Abdy, Edward Strutt, 1791-1846.
Journal of a residence and tour in the United States of North America, from April, 1833, to October, 1834. By E. S. Abdy ...   London, J. Murray, 1835.
3 v.   19 1/2 cm.

19   Abeille, J
Essai sur nos colonies, et sur le rétablissement de Saint Domingue, ou considérations sur leur legislation, admininistration, commerce et agri-culture.   Par Mr. J. Abeille ... Paris, Chomel, 1805.
2 p. ℓ., xiii, 154 p., 1 ℓ.   20 cm.

20   Abercrombie, James, 1758-1841.
A sermon, preached in Christ church and St. Peter's, Philadelphia: on Wednesday, May 9, 1798.   Being the day appointed by the President, as a day of fasting, humiliation, and pray-er, throughout the United States of North America.   By James Abercrombie ...   Philadelphia: Printed by John Ormrod, no. 41, Chesnut-street [1798]
38 p.   22 cm.

21   Abert, John James, 1788-1863.
Reply of Col. Abert and Mr. Markoe to the Hon. Mr. Tappan, of the United States Senate.   Washington, W.Q. Force, print., 1843.
18 p.   23 1/2 cm.

22   Abingdon, Willoughby Bertie, *4th earl of*,
          1740-1799.
            Thoughts on the Letter of Edmund
          Burke, esq; to the sheriffs of Bristol,
          on the affairs of America. By the
          Earl of Abingdon, Oxford, Printed for
          W. Jackson [1777]
            64 p.   21 1/2 cm.

23   Abrahall, Chandos Hoskyns.
            Arctic enterprise. A poem in seven
          parts. By Chandos Hoskyns Abrahall
          ... London, Hope & co., 1856.
            4 p. 1., 216 p.   20 cm.

24   [Abreu de Galindo, Juan de]
            The history of the discovery and con-
          quest of the Canary islands: tr. from
          a Spanish manuscript, lately found in
          the island of Palma. With an enquiry
          into the origin of the ancient inhabi-
          tants. To which is added, A descrip-
          tion of the Canary islands, including
          the modern history of the inhabitants,
          and an account of their manners, cus-
          toms, trade, &c. By George Glas.
          London, R. and J. Dodsley [etc.] 1764.
            4 p. 1., viii, 368 p. 3 maps.   29 cm.

25   An account of the French settlements in
          North America: shewing from the lat-
          est authors, the towns, ports, islands,
          lakes, rivers, &c. of Canada, claimed
          and improved by the French king. By a
          gentleman. To which is added an appen-
          dix, giving a more particular and exact
          account of Quebec, with its inhabitants
          and their manner of living. By P.
          Charlevoix. Boston: Printed and sold
          by Rogers and Fowle in Queen-street
          next to the prison. 1746 [Boston,
          1937]
            facsim.: 26 p.   24 cm.

26   An account of the Spanish settlements in

America. In four parts ... To which
is annexed, a succinct account of the
climate, produce, trade, manufactures,
&c. of old Spain. Illustrated with a
map of America. Edinburgh, Printed by
A. Donaldson and J. Reid for the author
[etc.] 1762
    xvi, 512 p.   fold. map   21 cm.

27   Achenbach, Hermann.
    Tagebuch meiner reise nach den
Nordamerikanischen freistaaten, oder:
Das neue Kanaan ... Von Hermann
Achenbach ... Düsseldorf, Gedruckt
auf kosten des verfassers, bei J.
Wolf, 1835.
    2 v. front., fold. map 22 cm.

28   Achenwall, Gottfried, 1719-1772.
    Einige anmerkungen über Nord-Amerika
und über dasige grosbrittannische
colonien. Aus mündlichen nachrichten
des Herrn B. Franklins verfasst von
hrn. d. Gottfried Achenwall. Nebst ...
John Wesleys schrift von den
streitigkeiten mit den colonien in
Amerika. Helmstedt, J.H. Kühnlin,
1777.
    27 (*i.e.* 72) p.   19 cm.

29   Acosta, Joaquin, 1799-1852.
    Compendio histórico del descubri-
miento y colonización de la Nueva
Granada en el siglo décimo sexto ...
Paris, Impr. de Beau, 1848.
    xvi, 400 p. 4 pl. 8 c.

30   Acrelius, Israel. 1714-1800.
    Beskrifning om de swenska församl-
lingars forna och närwarande tilstand,
uti det sä kallade Nya Swerige, sedan
Nya Nederland, men nu för tiden Pen-
sylvanien, samt nästliggande orter wid
alfwen [!] De la Ware, Wäst-Yersey
och New-Castle county uti Norra America; utgifwen af Israel Acrelius ...

Stockholm, Tryckt hos Harberg &
Hesselberg, 1759.
    10 p. 1., 533, [1] p.   19 1/2 x
16 cm.

31   Acuña, Cristóbal de, *b.* 1597.
        Nvevo descvbrimiento del gran rio
    de las Amazonas. Por el padre Chris-
    toval de Acuña ... Al qval fve, y se
    hizo por orden de Su Magestad, el año
    de 1639. Por la provincia de Qvito
    en los reynos del Perù ... Madrid,
    Impr. del reyno, 1641.
        6 p. 1., 46 numb. 1.   20 cm.

32   Adair, James, *trader with the Indians.*
        The history of the American Indians;
    particularly those nations adjoining
    to the Missisippi [!] East and West
    Florida, Georgia, South and North Caro-
    lina, and Virginia: containing an ac-
    count of their origin, language, man-
    ners, religious and civil customs,
    laws, form of government, punishments,
    conduct in war and domestic life,
    their habits, diet, agriculture, manu-
    factures, diseases and method of cure
    ... With observations on former his-
    torians, the conduct of our colony
    governors, superintendents, mission-
    aries, &c. Also an appendix, contain-
    ing a description of the Floridas, and
    the Missisippi [!] lands, with their
    productions--the benefits of coloniz-
    ing Georgiana, and civilizing the In-
    dians--and the way to make all the
    colonies more valuable to the mother
    country ... By James Adair ... Lon-
    don, E. and C. Dilly, 1777.
        6 p. 1., 464 p. front. (fold. map)
    27 1/2 x 22 cm.

33   Adam, William, *b.* 1799.
        Genealogy of the Adam family, by
    William Adam ... Albany, J. Munsell,

1848.
16 p.   22 cm.

34   Adams, Amos, 1728-1775.
         A concise historical view of the dif-
      ficulties, hardships, and perils which
      attended the planting and progressive
      improvements of New England. With a
      particular account of its long and
      destructive wars, expensive expedi-
      tions, &c. By Amos Adams ... Boston
      printed; London, Reprinted for E. and
      C. Dilly, 1770.
         2 p. 1., 68 p.   20 cm.

35   Adams, Amos, 1728-1775.
         Songs of victory directed by human
      compassion, and qualified with Chris-
      tian benevolence; in a sermon deliv-
      ered at Roxbury, October 25, 1759.
      On the general thanksgiving, for the
      success of His Majesty's arms, "more
      particularly, in the reduction of Que-
      bec, the capital of Canada." By Amos
      Adams ... Boston, Printed and sold
      by Edes and Gill, 1759.
         29 p.   21 cm.

36   Adams, Charles Baker, 1814-1853.
         ... Catalogue of shells collected
      at Panama, with notes on their synon-
      ymy, station, and geographical distri-
      bution. By C. B. Adams ... Read be-
      fore the Lyceum of natural history,
      May 10th, 1852. New York, R. Craig-
      head, printer, 1852.
         viii, [5]-334 p., 1 1. 28 x 22 cm.

37   Adams, Charles Baker, 1814-1853.
         Contributions to conchology: con-
      ducted by C. B. Adams ... v. 1: Oct.
      1849-Nov. 1852. New York, London
      [etc.] H. Baillière [1849-52]
         iv. 258 p.   22 cm.

38   Adams, Charles Francis, 1807-1886.

An address delivered before the members of the schools, and the citizens of Quincy, July 4, 1856. By Charles Francis Adams. Boston, Little, Brown and company, 1856.
36 p.   24 cm.

39   Adams, Charles Francis, 1807-1886.
An address on the occasion of opening the new town hall, in Braintree, July 29, 1858. By Charles Francis Adams. Boston, W. White, printer, 1848.
86 p.   23 1/2 cm.

40   [Adams, Charles Francis] 1807-1886.
Reflections upon the present state of the currency in the United States. Boston, Printed by E. Lincoln, 1837.
34 p.   22 1/2 cm.

_41   Adams, Charles Francis, 1807-1886.
Texas and the Massachusetts resolutions. By Charles Francis Adams. Boston, Eastburn's press, 1844.
54 p.   22 cm.

42   Adams, Charles Francis, 1807-1886.
What makes slavery a question of national concern? A lecture, delivered, by invitation, at New York, January 30, at Syracuse, February 1, 1885. By Charles Francis Adams. Boston, Little, Brown, and co., 1855.
46 p.   24 cm.

43   Adams, Daniel, 1773-1864.
An oration, sacred to the memory of Gen. George Washington. Delivered at Leominster, Feb. 22, 1800. By Daniel Adams, M. B. ... Leominster, Mass., Printed by Adams & Wilder, 1800.
25 p. 24 cm.

44   Adams, Eliphalet, 1677-1753.
God sometimes answers his people, by

terrible things in righteousness. A
discourse occasioned by that awful
thunder-clap which struck the meeting-
house in N. London, Aug. 31st. 1735.
At what time one was killed outright
and diverse others much hurt and wound-
ed, yet graciously & remarkably pre-
served, together with the rest of the
congregation, from immediate death.
As it was delivered (Sept. 7th.) the
Lord's Day following. By Eliphalet
Adams, M. A. and pastor of the church
there ... N. London, Printed & sold
by T. Green, 1735.
2 p. l., vi, 46 p. 15 1/2 cm.

45   Adams, Francis Colburn.
Justice in the bye-ways. A tale of
life. By F Colburn Adams ... New
York, Livermore & Rudd; [etc., etc.]
1856.
vi, [5]-439 p. 19 1/2 cm.

46   Adams, Francis Colburn.
Manuel Pereira; or, The sovereign
rule of South Carolina. With views of
southern laws, life, and hospitality.
By F. C. Adams ... Washington, Buell
& Blanchard, 1853.
1 p. l., 302 p. 18 1/2 cm.

47   Adams, Francis Colburn.
The story of a trooper. With much
of interest concerning the campaign
on the Peninsula, not before written.
By F. Colburn Adams ... New York,
Dick & Fitzgerald, 1865.
2 p. l., [3]-616 p. 19 1/2 cm.

48   Adams, Francis Colburn.
Uncle Tom at home. A review of the
reviewers and repudiators of Uncle
Tom's cabin by Mrs. Stowe. By F.C.
Adams ... Philadelphia, W. P. Hazard,

1853.
vi, 7-142 p.   19 cm.

49   Adams, George Washington, d. 1829.
        An oration delivered at Quincy, on
      the fifth of July, 1824, by George
      Washington Adams. Boston, Printed by
      E. Lincoln, 1824.
        24 p.   20 1/2 cm.

50   Adams, Hannah, 1755-1831.
        A dictionary of all religions and
      religious denominations, Jewish, heath-
      en, Mahometan and Christian, ancient
      and modern. With an appendix, con-
      taining a sketch of the present state
      of the world, as to population, reli-
      gion, toleration, missions, etc., and
      the articles in which all Christian
      denominations agree. By Hannah Adams
      ... Fourth ed., with corrections and
      large additions. Published by James
      Eastburn and company, at the Literary
      rooms, corner of Broadway and Pine
      street, N. York; and by Cummings and
      Hilliard, no. 1, Cornhill, Boston,
      1817.
        4 p. l., [5]-376 p.   22 cm.

51   Adams, Hannah, 1755-1831.
        A memoir of Miss Hannah Adams, writ-
      ten by herself. With additional not-
      ices, by a friend. Boston, Gray and
      Bowen, 1832.
        iv, 110 p. front. (port.)   19 1/2
      cm.

52   Adams, Hannah, 1755-1831.
        A narrative of the controversy be-
      tween the Rev. Jedidiah Morse, D. D.
      and the author. By Hannah Adams.
      Boston: Sold by Cummings and Hilliard,
      Bradford and Read, and Isaiah Thomas.
      jun. Marlboro street. 1814. John
      Eliot, printer.
        viii, 31, 3 p.   24 1/2 cm.

53   Adams, Hannah, 1755-1831.
            A summary history of New-England,
        from the first settlement at Plymouth,
        to the acceptance of the federal Con-
        stitution. Comprehending a general
        sketch of the American war. By Han-
        nah Adams ... Dedham [Mass.] Print-
        ed for the author, by H. Mann and
        J.H. Adams, 1799.
            513, [3] p.   22 cm.

54   Adams, Hannah, 1755-1831.
            A view of religions, in two parts.
        Pt. I. Containing an alphabetical
        compendium of the various religious
        denominations, which have appeared in
        the world, from the beginning of the
        Christian era to the present day. Pt.
        II. Containing a brief account of the
        different schemes of religion now
        embraced among mankind. The whole
        collected from the best authors, an-
        cient and modern. By Hannah Adams
        ... The 3d ed., with large additions
        ... Published according to act of
        Congress. Boston, Printed by and for
        Manning & Loring, proprietors, No. 2,
        Cornhill, Boston. October, 1801.
            xxxv, [37]-504 p.   22 cm.

55   Adams, John, 1704-1740.
            Poems on several occasions, origin-
        al and translated. By the late Rev-
        erend and learned John Adams, M.A.
        ... Boston, Printed for D. Gookin,
        in Marlborough-street, over against
        the Old South meeting house. 1745.
            4 p. 1., 176 p.   15 1/2 cm.

56   [Adams, John] *pres. U.S.*, 1735-1826,
            comp.
            A collection of state-papers, rela-
        tive to the first acknowledgment
        of the sovereignty of the United
        States of America, and the reception
        of their minister plenipotentiary, by

their high mightinesses the States
general of the United Netherlands.
To which is prefixed, the political
character of John Adams, ambassador
plenipotentiary ... By an American.
Likewise, An essay on canon and feu-
dal law, by John Adams, esq.   London,
Printed for J. Fielding [etc.] 1782.
    2 p. l., 100 p.   21 1/2 cm.

57   Adams, John, *pres. U.S.*, 1735-1826.
        The correspondence of John Adams,
    esquire, late president of the United
    States of America; concerning the
    British doctrine of impressment; and
    many interesting things which occurr-
    ed during his administration: Orig-
    inally published in the Boston pa-
    triot. Baltimore: Published at the
    office of the Evening post, by H.
    Niles.--September 15, 1809.   G. Dob-
    bin and Murphy, printers.
        72 p.   22 1/2 cm.

58   Adams, John, *pres. U.S.*, 1735-1826.
        Correspondence of the late Presi-
    dent Adams. Originally published in
    the Boston patriot. In a series of
    letters ... Boston, Everett and
    Munroe, 1809 [10]
        iv, 572 p.   21 1/2 cm.

59   [Adams, John, *pres. U.S.*] 1735-1826.
        Discourses on Davila. A series of
    papers, on political history. Written
    in the year 1790, and then published
    in the Gazette of the United States.
    By an American citizen ... Boston,
    Printed by Russell and Cutler, 1805.
        248 p.   22 cm.

60   Adams, John, *pres. U.S.*, 1735-1826.
        Four letters: being an interesting
    correspondence between those eminently
    distinguished characters, John Adams,
    late president of the United States;

and Samuel Adams, late governor of
Massachusetts. On the important subject of government. Boston, Printed
for Adams & Rhoades, 1802.
iv. [5]-32 p. 20 1/2 cm.

61   Adams, John, *pres.* U.S., 1735-1826.
The inadmissible principles, of the
King of England's proclamation, of
October 16, 1807--considered. By the
late President Adams. (Originally
published in the Boston patriot.)
Boston: Printed by Everett & Munroe,
1809.
20 p. 21 1/2 cm.

62   Adams, John, *pres.* U.S., 1735-1826.
Letters of John Adams, addressed to
his wife. Ed. by his grandson, Charles
Francis Adams ... Boston, C.C. Little
and J.Brown, 1841.
2 v. front. (port.) 17 1/2 cm.

63   Adams, John, *pres.* U.S., 1735-1826.
The works of John Adams, second
president of the United States; with
a life of the author, notes and illustrations, by his grandson Charles
Francis Adams ... Boston, Little,
Brown and company [etc.] 1850-56 [v.
1, '56]
10 v. fronts (v. 1-2, 5, 7-10)
plates, ports, facsims. (part fold.)
22 1/2 cm.

64   Adams, John, 1750?-1814.
The flowers of modern travels; being elegant, entertaining and in-
structive extracts, selected from the
works of the most celebrated travellers ... Intended chiefly for
young people of both sexes. By the
Rev. John Adams ... Boston: Printed
for John West, No. 75, Cornhill, 1797.
2 v. 17 1/2 cm.

65   Adams, John Greenleaf, 1810-1887.
       Our country, and its claims upon
us.   An oration delivered before the
municipal authorities and citizens of
Providence, July 4, 1863.   By Rev.
John G. Adams.   Providence, Knowles,
Anthony & co., city printers, 1863.
       30 p.   25 cm.

66   Adams, John Quincy, *pres. U.S.*, 1767-
       1848.
       An address delivered at the request
of a committee of the citizens of
Washington: on the occasion of reading the Declaration of independence,
on the fourth of July, 1821.   By John
Quincy Adams.   Washington, Printed by
Davis and Force, 1821.
       31 p.   22 1/2 cm.

67   Adams, John Quincy, *pres. U.S.*, 1767-
       1848.
       Address of John Quincy Adams, to his
constituents of the Twelfth congressional district, at Braintree, September 17th, 1842 ...   Boston, J.H. Eastburn, printer, 1842.
       63 p.   23 cm.

68   Adams, John Quincy, *pres. U.S.*, 1767-
       1848.
       An address, to the members of the
Massachusetts charitable fire society,
at their annual meeting, May 28, 1802.
By John Quincy Adams ...   Boston,
Printed by Russell and Cutler, 1802.
       25 p., 1 l.   20 1/2 cm.

69   [Adams, John Quincy] *pres. U.S.*, 1767-
       1848.
       American principles.   A review of
Works of Fisher Ames, compiled by a
number of his friends.   First published in the Boston patriot ...   Boston: Published by Everett and

Munroe ..... 1809.
56 p.   22 cm.

70   Adams, John Quincy, *pres. U.S.*, 1767-
      1848.
      Argument of John Quincy Adams, be-
      fore the Supreme court of the United
      States, in the case of the United
      States, appellants, *vs.* Cinque, and
      others, Africans, captured in the
      schooner Amistad, by Lieut. Gedney,
      delivered on the 24th of February and
      1st of March, 1841. With a review of
      the case of the Antelope, reported in
      the 10th, 11th and 12th volumes of
      Wheaton's Reports. New York, S.W.
      Benedict, 1841.
      135 p.   21 1/2 cm.

71   Adams, John Quincy, *pres. U.S.*, 1767-
      1848.
      Correspondence between John Quincy
      Adams, president of the United States,
      and several citizens of Massachusetts
      concerning the charge of a design to
      dissolve the union alleged to have
      existed in that state. To which are
      now added additional papers, illustra-
      tive of the subject. Washington,
      Printed and sold by J. Elliot, 1829.
      69 p.   21 1/2 cm.

72   Adams, John Quincy, *pres. U.S.*, 1767-
      1848.
      The duplicate letters, the fisher-
      ies and the Mississippi. Documents
      relating to transactions at the nego-
      tiation of Ghent. Collected and pub.
      by John Quincy Adams, one of the com-
      missioners of the United States at
      that negotiation. Washington, Print-
      ed by Davis and Force, 1822.
      256, [2] p., 1 l.   23 cm.

73   Adams, John Quincy, *pres. U.S.*, 1767-
      1848.

An eulogy: on the life and character of James Monroe, fifth president
of the United States. Delivered at
the request of the corporation of the
city of Boston, on the 25th of August,
1831. By John Quincy Adams ... Boston, J.H. Eastburn, city printer, 1831.
100 p. 24 cm.

74   Adams, John Quincy, *pres. U.S.*, 1767-
1848.
The jubilee of the Constitution. A
discourse delivered at the request of
the New York historical society, in
the city of New York, on Tuesday, the
30th of April, 1839; being the fiftieth anniversary of the inauguration
of George Washington as president of
the United States, on Thursday, the
30th of April, 1789 ... By John Quincy Adams. New York, S. Colman, 1839.
136 p. front. 24 cm.

75   Adams, John Quincy, *pres. U.S.*, 1767-
1848.
A letter to the Hon. Harrison Gray
Otis, a member of the Senate of Massachusetts, on the present state of
our national affairs: with remarks
upon Mr. Pickering's Letter to the
governor of the commonwealth. By
John Quincy Adams. Boston: Published by Oliver and Munroe. 1808.
32 p. 21 1/2 cm.

76   Adams, John Quincy, *pres. U.S.*, 1767-
1848.
Letters from John Quincy Adams to
constituents of the Twelfth congressional district in Massachusetts. To
which is added his speech in Congress,
delivered February 9, 1837. Boston,
I. Knapp, 1837.
72 p. 18 cm.

77   Adams, John Quincy, *pres. U.S.*, 1767-
      1848.
          Lives of celebrated statesmen, by
      John Quincy Adams, LL. D., with a
      sketch of the author, by the Rev.
      Charles W. Upham. New York, W.H.
      Graham, 1846.
          105 p.   24 1/2 cm.

78   Adams, John Quincy, *pres. U.S.*, 1767-
      1848.
          The lives of James Madison and
      James Monroe, fourth and fifth presi-
      dents of the United States. By John
      Quincy Adams. With historical notices
      of their administrations. Boston,
      Phillips, Sampson & co.; Buffalo,
      G.H. Derby and co., 1850.
          1 p. l., viii, [9]-432 p.   20 cm.

79   Adams, John Quincy, *pres. U.S.*, 1767-
      1848.
          An oration addressed to the citizens
      of the town of Quincy, on the Fourth
      of July, 1831, the fifty-fifth anni-
      versary of the independence of the
      United States of America. By John
      Quincy Adams. Boston, Richardson,
      Lord & Holbrook, 1831.
          40 p.   24 1/2 cm.

80   Adams, John Quincy, *pres. U.S.*, 1767-
      1848.
          An oration, delivered at Plymouth,
      December 22, 1802. At the anniver-
      sary commemoration of the first land-
      ing of our ancestors, at that place.
      By John Quincy Adams. [Pub. at the
      request of ... the Committee of the
      town of Plymouth ...] Boston, Print-
      ed by Russell and Cutler, 1802.
          31 p.   21 cm.

81   Adams, John Quincy, *pres. U.S.*, 1767-
      1848.
          An oration delivered before the

Cincinnati astronomical society, on
the occasion of laying the corner
stone of an astronomical observatory,
on the 10th of November, 1843. By
John Quincy Adams. Cincinnati, Printed by Shepard & co., 1843.
72 p. 23 cm.

82   Adamson, John, 1787-1855.
Bibliotheca lusitana; or Catalogue
of books and tracts, relating to the
history, literature, and poetry, of
Portugal: forming part of the library of John Adamson ... Newcastle
on Tyne, Printed by T. and J. Hodgson,
1836.
iv, 115 p. illus. 19 1/2 cm.

83   Adamson, Thomas.
A reply to "Considerations and
arguments, proving the inexpediency
of an international copyright law, by
John Campbell." By Thomas Adamson.
New York, Bartlett & Welford, 1844.
20 p. 22 1/2 cm.

84   Addey, Markinfield.
"Little Mac," and how he became a
great general: a life of George
Brinton McClellan, for young Americans. By Markinfield Addey ... New
York, J.G. Gregory, 1864.
1 p. 1., 352 p. 5 pl. (incl. front.
ports) 18 cm.

85   Addey, Markinfield.
"Stonewall Jackson." The life and
military career of Thomas Jonathan
Jackson, lieutenant-general in the
Confederate army. By Markinfield
Addey ... New York, C.T. Evans;
Chicago, J.R. Walker; [etc., etc.]
1863.
240 p. front. (port.) 19 cm.

86   Addoms, Jonas Smith, *fl.* 1792.

An inaugural dissertation on the
malignant fever, which prevailed in
the city of New York during the
months of August, September, and
October, in the year 1791. Submitted to the examination of the Rev.
William Linn, D. D. P. T., president; and to the trustees and facul-
ty of Queen's college, New-Jersey; for
the degree of doctor of medicine ...
By Jonas Smith Addoms, of New-York
... New-York: Printed by T. and J.
Swords, no. 27, William-street.
1792.
 3 p. 1., [5]-37 p.   19 cm.

87   Address of Democratic members of Con-
      gress to the Democracy of the Unit-
      ed States. [Washington, L. Towers
      & co., printers, 1864]
       8 p.   22 cm.

88   An address of members of the House of
      representatives, of the Congress of
      the United States, to their consti-
      tuents, on the subject of the war
      with Great Britain. Windsor [Vt.]:
      Printed by Thomas M. Pomeroy. 1812.
       30 p.   25 cm.

89   Address of the Free constitutionalists
      to the people of the United States.
      [2d ed.] Boston, Thayer & Eldridge,
      1860.
       54 p.   22 cm.

90   Address to Christians throughout the
      world. By the clergy of the Confed-
      erate states of America. [London,
      Strangeways and Walden, printers,
      1862?]
       16 p.   22 cm.

91   An address to the merchants of Great-
      Britain: or, A review of the con-
      duct of the administration, with

regard to our trade and navigation:
shewing how the trading interest
have been impos'd upon by the enemies of the ministry: with a justi-
fication of the convention concluded between Great-Britain and Spain.
By a merchant retir'd. London, Printed for J. Roberts [1738?]
  2 p. 1., 50 p.   23 cm.

92   An address to the people of America, on
      the prospect of war with France.
      Recommended to the perusal, of the
      people of Great Britain, by a true
      friend to his country. 1798 [Lon-
      don, 1798]
         16 p.   21 cm.

93   An address to the people of Great-Bri-
      tain in general, the members of Par-
      liament, and the leading gentlemen of
      opposition in particular, on the pres-
      ent crisis of American politics.
      Bristol [Eng.] Printed by T. Cocking,
      and sold by the booksellers of Bristol
      and Bath, and by F. Newbery, London,
      1776.
         2 p. 1., v, 79 p.   21 cm.

94   An address to the people of the American
      states who choose electors .... to the
      people of the states who choose the
      legislators who appoint electors ....
      to the legislators who appoint elec-
      tors .... and to the electors of presi-
      dent and vice-president of the Unit-
      ed States. To which is added, a
      short sketch of the biography of Gen.
      George Clinton, and several essays,
      which have appeared in the Washington
      expositor and other papers, on the
      subject of the ensuing election of
      president and vice-president. Wash-
      ington city, 1808.
         11, 2-54 p.   17 1/2 cm.

95   An address to the representatives in
       Parliament, upon the state of the
       nation ... London, Printed for J.
       Almon, 1779.
         38 p.   21 1/2 cm.

96   An address to the Republicans and peo-
       ple of New-York, Pennsylvania, and
       Virginia. Upon the state of presi-
       dential parties. By a citizen of
       New-York. September, 1824. New
       York, Printed by W. Grattan, 1824.
         23 p.   21 cm.

97   Adelung, Johann Christoph, 1732-1806.
         Mithridates, oder Allgemeine
       sprachenkunde, mit dem Vater unser
       als sprachprobe in bey nahe fünf
       hundert sprachen und mundarten ...
       Berlin, Vossische buchhandlung,
       1806-17.
         4 v.   21 1/2 cm.

98   Adger, John Bailey, 1810-1899.
         A review of reports to the legisla-
       ture of S.C., on the revival of the
       slave trade. By John B. Adger. From
       the April number of the Southern
       Presbyterian review. Columbia, S.C.,
       Press of R.W. Gibbes, 1858.
         cover-title, 36 p.   23 cm.

99   Adirondack iron and steel company, *New
       York*.
         The Adirondack iron and steel com-
       pany, New-York ... New York, W.E. &
       J. Sibell, 1854.
         47 p.   ilus., 3 fold. maps (incl.
       front.) tables.   22 1/2 cm.

100   Adlam, Samuel, 1798-1880.
         The First church in Providence,
       not the oldest of the Baptists in Amer-
       ica, attempted to be shown by S.
       Adlam ... Newport, Cranston &

Norman's power press, 1850.
28 p.   23 cm.

101   Adlard, George.
        The Sutton-Dudleys of England and
    the Dudleys of Massachusetts in New
    England. From the Norman conquest
    to the present time. By George Ad-
    lard. New York, Printed for the
    author, 1862.
        6 p. 1., xvi, 160 p.   illus.,
    plates, geneal. tables.   23 1/2 cm.

102   Administration dissected. In which the
    grand national culprits, are laid
    open for the public inspection. Lon-
    don, Printed for J. Barker, 1779.
        vii, 302 p.   21 1/2 cm.

103   Adolphus, John, 1768-1845.
        The history of England, from the
    accession of King George the Third,
    to the conclusion of peace in the
    year one thousand seven hundred and
    eighty-three. By John Adolphus ...
    4th ed., rev. by the author. London,
    Printed for T. Cadell and W. Davies,
    1817.
        3 v.   22 1/2 cm.

104   Aengemerckte voorvallen op de vredens
    articulen met Portugael. Anno 1663.
    [n.p., 1663]
        15 p.   19 x 15 cm.

105   Affaires de l'Angleterre et de l'Amér-
    ique. [t. 1-15] Anvers, 1776-[79]
        15 v. in 17.   tables.   20 1/2 cm.

106   African servitude: when, why, and by
    whom instituted, By whom, and how
    long, shall it be maintained? Read
    and consider ... New York, Davies
    & Kent, 1860.
        54 p., 1 1.   22 1/2 cm.

23

107   Agassiz, Louis, 1887-1873.
        Contributions to the natural his-
        tory of the United States of America.
        By Louis Agassiz ... Boston, Little,
        Brown, and company; London, Trübner
        & co., 1857-62.
        4 v.   illus., 77 pl. (4 col., 2
        fold)   33 cm.

108   Agassiz, Louis, 1807-1873.
        Lake Superior: its physical char-
        acter, vegetation, and animals, com-
        pared with those of other and simi-
        lar regions. By Louis Agassiz. With
        a narrative of the tour, by J. Elliot
        Cabot. And contributions by other
        scientific gentlemen ... Boston,
        Gould, Kendall and Lincoln, 1850.
        x, [2], [9]-428 p.   front., illus.,
        plates, map.   22 1/2 cm.

109   Agassiz, Louis, 1807-1873.
        On extraordinary fishes from Calif-
        ornia, constituting a new family. By
        L. Agassiz. Extracted from the Ameri-
        can journal of science and arts, vol.
        xvi, 2^d ser. Nov. 1863. New Haven,
        Printed by B.L. Hamlen, 1853.
        12 p.   23 cm.

110   Agnew, John Holmes, 1804-1865.
        Reply to Professor Tayler Lewis'
        review of Rev. Henry J. Van Dyke's
        sermon on Biblical slavery; also, to
        his other articles on the same sub-
        ject, published in "The World." By
        J. Holmes Agnew. New York, D. Apple-
        ton and company, 1861.
        63 p.   22 cm.

111   Agüero, Pedro de, 1821-
        Biografías de Cubanos distinguidos.
        Por P. de Agüero ... I.   Don José
        Antonio Saco. Lóndres, Impr. de
        W. & A. Webster, 1858.
        83 p.   front. (port.)   25 cm.

112   Aiken, John
          Labor and wages, at home and abroad:
      in a series of newspaper articles,
      by John Aiken. Lowell, D. Bixby &
      co., 1849.
          28 p., 1 1.   22 1/2 cm.

113   Aiken, Peter Freeland.
          A comparative view of the constitu-
      tions of Great Britain and the Unit-
      ed States of America, in six lectures.
      By P.F. Aiken ... London, Longman
      and co.; [etc., etc.] 1842.
          viii, 192 p.   18 cm.

114   Aiken, Solomon, 1758-1833.
          An address to federal clergymen,
      on the subject of the war proclaimed
      by the Congress of the United States,
      June 18, 1812, against the United
      Kingdom of Great-Britain and Ireland.
      By Solomon Aiken ... Boston, Printed
      for the author. 1813.
          85 p.   31 cm.

115   Aikin, John, 1747-1822.
          Annals of the reign of King George
      the Third; from its commencement in
      the year 1760, to the general peace
      in the year 1815. By John Aiken ...
      London, Longman, Hurst, Rees, Orme,
      and Brown, 1816.
          2 v.   22 cm.

116   Aikman, William, 1824-1909.
          The future of the colored race in
      America: being an article in the
      Presbyterian quarterly review of July,
      1862. By William Aikman ... New
      York, A.D.F. Randolph, 1862.
          35 p.   23 1/2 cm.

117   Aikman, William, 1824-1909.
          Government and administration: a
      sermon preached on the Sabbath suc-
      ceeding the secession riots in New

York city, July 19, 1863, by William
Aikman ... Wilmington [Del.] H.
Eckel, printer, 1863.
    cover-title, 12 p.   19 cm.

118   Ainsworth, William Harrison, 1805-1882.
        John Law, the projector [a novel]
      By William Harrison Ainsworth. Lon-
      don, Chapman and Hall, 1864.
        3 v.   19 1/2 cm.

119   Aislabie, John, 1670-1742.
        The case of the Right Honble John
      Aislabie, esq. ... [London] Printed
      for J. Roberts [1721?]
        2 p. l., 3-42 (*i.e.* 38)p.   23 cm.

120   Alamán, Lucas, 1792-1853, *defendant*.
        Proceso instructivo formado por la
      sección del Gran jurado de la Cámara
      de diputados del Congreso general, en
      averiguacion de los delitos de que
      fueron acusados los ex-ministros d.
      Lucas Alaman, d. Rafael Mangino, d.
      José Antonio Facio y d. José Ignacio
      Espinosa. Se imprime de orden de la
      Cámara. México, Impreso por I.
      Cumplido, 1833.
        2 p. l., 255, [6] p.   20 cm.

121   The alarm bell, no. 1. By a constitu-
      tionalist. New York, Baker & Godwin,
      1863.
        16 p.   23 1/2 cm.

122   [Albenino, Nicolao de] 1514?-
        Verdadera ‖ relacion: de lo
      sussedido ‖ en los Reynos e prouin- ‖
      cias del peru / dede la yda ‖ ellos del
      vi Rey Blasco ‖ nuñes vela / hasta
      el des ‖ barato y muerte de gon ‖ calo
      Picarro. [Sevilla, J. de Leon, 1549]
      [Boston, 1924]
        facsim.: 160 l.   18 1/2 cm.   [Ameri-
      cana series; photostat reproductions

by the Massachusetts historical society. no. 123]

123   Alberdi, Juan Bautista, 1810-1884.
       Organizacion política y económica
de la Confederación argentina ... por
d. Juan Bautista Albcrdi ... Nueva
ed. oficial, corr. y rev. por el
autor. Besanzon, Impr. de J. Jacquin,
1856.
       xvii, 870 p., 1 1.   21 1/2 cm.

124   Alberti, Leandro, 1479-1552.
       Descrittione di tvtta Italia, di
F. Leandro Alberti. Bolognese, nella
quale si contiene il sito di essa,
l'origine, & le signorie delle citta,
& de' castelli; co' nomi antichi, &
moderni; i costumi de popoli, & le
conditioni de paesi. Et di più gli
huomini famosi, che l'hanno illustrata;
i monti i laghi. i fiumi, le fontane,
i bagni, le minere, & tutte l'opere
marauigliose in lei dalla natura pro-
dotte. Aggiuntaui la descrittione di
tutte l'isole, all' Italia apparten-
enti, co' suoi disegni, collocati a
i luoghi loro, con ordine bellissimo.
Con le sve tavole copiosissime. Nuo-
uamente ristampata. & con somma
diligenza reuista, & corretta. Vinegia, A. Salicato, 1588.
       34 p. 1., 495, 100 numb. 1., [9] p.
7 fold. maps.   21 1/2 cm.

126   Albertus *Magnus, bp. of Ratisbon.*
       Habes in hac pagina, Amice lector,
Alberti Magni Germani pri̅cipis phil-
osophi, De natura locorum Librum mira
eruditione, & singulari fruge refertu̅,
& iam primum summa dilige̅tia reuisum,
in luce̅ aeditum, quem leges dilige̅-
tius, vel si Cosmographia vel Physica
profecisse te volueris. [*Colophon:*
Argentorati. Ex Aedibus Matthiae
Sehurerij, Mense Ianuario. M.D. XV.

27

Duetu Leonhardi, & Lucae Alantse
fratrum]
3 p. l., xliii numb. l.   21 cm.

127   Albro, John Adams, 1799-1866.
The life of Thomas Shepard. By
John A. Albro ... Boston, Massachusetts Sabbath school society, 1847.
vi, [7]-324 p.   19 cm.

128   Alcedo, Antonio de, 1736-1812.
The geographical and historical
dictionary of America and the West
Indies. Containing an entire trans-
lation of the Spanish work of Colonel
Don Antonio de Alcedo ... with
large additions and compilations
from modern voyages and travels, and
from original and authentic information. By G.A. Thompson ... London,
Printed for J. Carpenter; [etc., etc.]
1812-15.
5 v. fold. tab.   28 x 22 cm.
--Atlas to Thompson's Alcedo; or,
Dictionary of America & West Indies;
collated with all the most recent
authorities, and composed chiefly
from scarce and original documents,
for that work, by A. Arrowsmith ...
London, Printed by G. Smeeton, 1816.
2 p. l., 5 fold. maps.   64 x 53
cm.

129   [Alcoforado, Francisco]
Relation historique de la découverte de l'isle de Madère. Traduit
de portugais. Paris, C. Barbin,
1671.
8 p. l., 185 p.   14 1/2 cm.

130   Alcott, Louisa May, 1832-1888.
Hospital sketches. By L. M. Alcott ... Boston, J. Redpath, 1863.
102 p.   17 x 11 1/2 cm.

131   Alcott, Louisa May, 1832-1888.
On picket duty, and other tales.

28

By L.M. Alcott. Boston, J. Redpath;
New York, H. Dexter, Hamilton & co.
[1864]
    96 p.   16 1/2 cm.

132   Alden, Ebenezer, 1788-1881.
    The early history of the medical
profession in the county of Norfolk,
Mass. An address delivered before
the Norfolk district medical society ... May 10, 1853. By Ebenezer
Alden ... Pub. by request of the
society. From the Boston medical
and surgical journal. Boston, S.K.
Whipple & co., 1853.
    48 p.   23 cm.

133   Alden, Joseph, 1807-1885.
    The science of government in con-
nection with American institutions.
By Joseph Alden ... New York, Sheldon and company, 1866.
    248 p.   19 1/2 cm.

134   Alden, Timothy, 1771-1839.
    An account of sundry missions per-
formed among the Senecas and Mun-
sees; in a series of letters. With
an appendix. By Rev. Timothy Alden ... New-York, Printed by J.
Seymour, 1827.
    180 p.   front. (port.)   15 cm.

135   Alden, Timothy, 1771-1839.
    An account of the several relig-
ious societies in Portsmouth, New-
Hampshire, from their first establishment and of the ministers of
each, to the first of January, 1805.
By Timothy Alden, jun. ... Boston:
Printed by Munroe, Francis, & Parker,
Shakspeare's Head, no. 4 Cornhill,
1808.
    40 p.   22 1/2 cm.

136   Alden, Timothy, 1771-1839.

A collection of American epitaphs
and inscriptions, with occasional
notes. By Rev. Timothy Allen ...
New York [S. Marks, printer] 1814.
5 v. fronts. (v 2-5 ports.)   14
1/2 cm.

137   Alden, Timothy, 1771-1839.
         The glory of America. A century
sermon delivered at the South church,
in Portsmouth, Newhampshire, IV January, MDCCCI. Together with a number of historical notes, and an appendix, containing an account of the
newspapers printed in the state. By
Timothy Alden, jun. ... Portsmouth,
Printed by W. Treadwell and co., 1801.
         47, [5] p.   22 cm.

138   Alden, Timothy, 1771-1839.
         A sermon, delivered at the South
church in Portsmouth, on the v January, M,DCCC. Occasioned by the sud-
den and universally lamented death
of George Washington ... By Timothy
Alden, jun. ... Portsmouth, (New-
Hampshire,) Printed at the United
States' oracle-office, by Charles
Peirce, January, 1800.
         24 p.   20 cm.

139   Alegre, Francisco Javier, 1729-1788.
         Historia de la Compañía de Jesus
en Nueva-España, que estaba escri-
biendo el p. Francisco Javier Alegre
al tiempo de su expulsión. Publicala
para probar la utilidad que prestará
a la America mexicana la solicitada
reposición de dicha Compañía, Carlos
Maria de Bustamante ... Mexico,
Impr. de J.M. Lara, 1841-42.
         3 v. 3 port.   22 cm.

140   Alexander, Alexander, *fl*. 1825.
         The life of Alexander Alexander:
written by himself, and ed. by John

Howell. Edinburgh, W. Blackwood;
[etc., etc.] 1830.
   2 v. front. (port.)   18 cm.

141   Alexander, Archibald, 1772-1851.
      Biographical sketches of the found-
   er, and principal alumni of the Log
   college. Together with an account
   of the revivals of religion, under
   their ministry. Collected and ed. by
   A. Alexander, D.D. Princeton, N.J.,
   Printed by J.T. Robinson, 1845.
      369 p.   19 cm.

142   Alexander, Archibald, 1772-1851.
      A discourse occasioned by the burn-
   ing of the theatre in the city of
   Richmond, Virginia, on the twenty-
   sixth of December, 1811. By which
   awful calamity a large number of
   lives were lost. Delivered in the
   Third Presbyterian church, Philadelphia, on the eighth day of January,
   1812, at the request of the Virginia
   students attached to the medical
   class, in the University of Pennsylvania. By A. Alexander, D.D. Philadelphia, Printed by John Woldwood
   Scott, No. 147 Chestnut-street, for
   Daniel Wilson, M.D. 1812.
      iv p., 1 l., [7]-28 p.   23 cm.

143   Alexander, Caleb, 1755-1828.
      A sermon: occasioned by the death
   of His Excellency George Washington,
   lieutenant general of the American
   army, and late president of the United States. Who departed this life,
   December 14, 1799, aet. 68 ... By
   Caleb Alexander, A.M., pastor of the
   church in Mendon ... Printed by
   Samuel Hall, no. 53, Cornhill, Boston. 1800.
      23 p.   21 1/2 cm.

144   Alexander, Charles A.

The fall of Aztalan, and other
poems. By A. Alexander, esq. Washington, W.M. Morrison, 1839.
79 p.   24 x 14 1/2 cm.

145   Alexander, George William, 1802-1890.
Letters on the slave-trade, slav-
ery, and emancipation; with a reply
to objections made to the liberation
of the slaves in the Spanish colonies; addressed to friends on the continent of Europe, during a visit to
Spain and Portugal. By G.W. Alexander. London, C. Gilpin [etc.] 1842.
xvi, 176 p.   16 cm.

146   Alexander, George William, 1802-1890.
Liberté immédiate et absolue, ou
esclavage. Observations sur le
rapport de m. de due de Broglie,
président de la commission instituée
par décision royale du 26 mai 1840,
pour l'examen des questions relatives
à l'esclavage et à la constitution
politique des colonies françaises;
adressées à tous les français amis
de la liberté et de l'humanité par
Geo. W. Alexander et John Scoble ...
Paris, Firmin Didot frères, 1844.
2 p. l., 55 p.   23 cm.

147   Alexander, *Sir* James Edward, 1803-1885.
L'Acadie; or, Seven years' explora-
tions in British America. By Sir
James E. Alexander ... London, H.
Colburn, 1849.
2 v.   fronts., 1 illus., plates,
maps,   19 cm.

148   Alexander, James Waddell, 1804-1859.
The life of Archibald Alexander, D.D., first
professor in the Theological seminary, at Princeton, New Jersey. By
James W. Alexander, D.D. New-York,
C. Scribner, 1854.
xi, 700 p.   front. (port) 23 1/2 cm.

32

149   Alexander, John Henry, 1812-1867, *ed.*
        Index to the Calendar of Maryland
        state-papers, comp. under direction
        of John Henry Alexander ... Balti-
        more, J.S. Waters, 1861.
        xiv p., 1 l., 66 p.   24 cm.

150   Alexander, J[ohn] H[enry] 1812-1867.
        International coinage for Great
        Britain and the United States: a
        note inscribed to the Hon. James A.
        Pearce, by J.H. Alexander, esq.   Bal-
        timore, Printed by J.D. Toy, 1855.
        iv, 20 p.   fold, tab.   22 cm.

151   Alexandria, Va.   Citizens.
        Letter from the mayor of the town
        of Alexandria, in the District of
        Columbia, inclosino [!] sundry reso-
        lutions of the citizens of the town
        and county of Alexandria, expressive
        of their disapprobation of a motion
        now depending before the House, to
        recede to the states of Virginia &
        Maryland, respectively, the jurisdic-
        tion of such parts of the said Dis-
        trict as are without the limits of
        the city of Washington ... Washing-
        ton city: Printed by William Duane
        and son.   1804.
        6 p.   21 cm.

152   Alfieri, Vittorio, 1749-1803.
        L'America libera: odi di Vittorio
        Alfieri da Asti ...   Kehl, Co'
        caratteri di Baskerville, 1784.
        44 p.   26 cm.

153   Alfonso, Pedro Antonio.
        Memorias de un Matancero.   Apuntes
        para la historia de la isla de Cuba,
        con relación á la ciudad de San Cárlos
        y San Severino de Matanzas ...   Por D.
        Pedro Antonio Alfonso.   Matanzas,
        Marsal y c[a]., 1854.
        232 [8] p. fold. map.   19 1/2 cm.

154   Alger, William Rounseville, 1822-1905.
          The genius and posture of America.
       An oration delivered before the citi-
       zens of Boston, July 4, 1857, by
       William Rounseville Alger. With pref-
       ace and appendix. Boston, Office
       Boston daily bee, 1857.
          60 p.   23 1/2 cm.

155   Alger, William Rounseville, 1822-1905.
          The genius and posture of America.
       An oration delivered before the citi-
       zens of Boston, July 4, 1857, by
       William Rounseville Alger. Boston,
       J.E. Farwell and company, printers
       to the city, 1864.
          53 p.   23 1/2 cm.

156   Alger, William Rounseville, 1822-1905.
          Inferences from the pestilence and
       the fast: a discourse preached in
       the Mount Pleasant Congregational
       church, Roxbury, Mass., August 3,
       1849, by Rev. William R. Alger. Pub-
       lished by request. Boston, W. Cros-
       by and H.P. Nichols, 1849.
          30 p.   22 cm.

157   Alger, William Rounseville, 1822-1905.
          Public morals: or, The true glory
       of a state. A discourse delivered
       before the executive and legislative
       departments of the government of
       Massachusetts, at the annual election,
       Wednesday, Jan. 1, 1862. By Rev.
       William Rounseville Alger. Boston,
       W. White, printer to the state, 1862.
          55 p.   21 1/2 cm.

158   The Allegheny magazine, or Repository of
       useful knowledge ...   v. 1; July 1816-
       June 1817. Meadville, Press of T.
       Atkinson, 1816-[17]
          vi, 7 -304 p.   21 cm.

159   Allegheny college, *Meadville, Pa.*

34

By-laws, and system of education, established at Allegheny college in Meadville, Pa. Pub. by order of the trustees. Meadville, J.C.G. Kennedy, printer, 1834.
15 p. 17 1/2 cm.

160   Allen, Andrew, 1740-1825.
The claim and answer with the subsequent proceedings in the case of Andrew Allen, esquire, against the United States. Under the sixth article of the treaty of amity, commerce, and navigation, between His Britannic Majesty and the United States of America. Philadelphia: Printed by James Humphreys, opposite the Bank of the U.S., 1799.
50 p. 24 1/2 x 20 cm.

161   Allen, Ethan, 1738-1789.
Allen's captivity, being a Narrative of Colonel Ethan Allen, containing his voyages, travels, &c., interspersed with political observations. Written by himself. Boston, O.L. Perkins, 1845.
126 p. incl. front. 15 cm.

162   Allen, Ethan, 1737-1789.
A concise refutation of the claims of New-Hampshire and Massachusetts-Bay, to the territory of Vermont; with occasional remarks on the long disputed claim of New-York to the same. Written by Ethan Allen and Jonas Fay, esq'rs. and pub. by order of the governor and Council of Vermont. Bennington, the first day of January, 1780. Joseph Fay, sec'ry. Hartford, Printed by Hudson and Goodwin [1780]
29 p. 19 cm.

163   Allen, Ethan, 1738-1789.
Ethan Allen's Narrative of the

35

capture of Ticonderoga, and of his captivity and treatment by the British. Written by himself. 5th ed., with notes. Burlington [Vt.] C. Goodrich and S.B. Nichols, 1849 [c1838]
50 p. 22 1/2 cm.

164 Allen, Ethan, 1738-1789.
A narrative of Col. Ethan Allen's captivity, from the time of his being taken by the British, near Montreal, on the 25th day of September, in the year 1775, to the time of his exchange, on the 6th day of May, 1778. Containing his voyages and travels, with the most remarkable occurrences respecting himself, and many other continental prisoners ... particularly the destruction of the prisoners at New-York, by General Sir William Howe, in the years 1776 and 1777; interspersed with some political observations. Written by himself, and now published for the information of the curious in all nations ... To which are now added a considerable number of explanatory and occasional notes, together with an index ... Walpole, N.H. Published by Thomas & Thomas. From the press of Charter & Hale. 1807.
xi, [13]-158 p. 17 1/2 cm.

165 Allen, Ethan, 1738-1789.
A narrative of Col. Ethan Allen's captivity. Written by himself. 4th ed., with notes. Burlington [Vt.] C. Goodrich, 1846.
120 p. 18 1/2 cm.

166 Allen, Ethan, 1738-1789.
A narrative of the captivity of Col. Ethan Allen, from the time of his being taken by the British, near Montreal, on the 25th day of September,

in the year 1775, to the time of his
exchange, on the 6th day of May,
1778. Containing his voyages and
travels, with the most remarkable
occurrences respecting himself, and
many other continental prisoners ...
particularly the destruction of the
prisoners at New-York, by General
Sir William Howe, in the years 1776
and 1777; interspersed with some political observations. Written by
himself ... Albany: Published by
Pratt & Clark, printed by Moses
Pratt, jun. no. 162, Lion-street,
1814.
    iv, [5]-144 p.   18 1/2 cm.

167   Allen, Ethan, 1796-1879.
    Clergy in Maryland of the Protes-
tant Episcopal church since the independence of 1783, by Rev. Ethan Allen ... Baltimore, J.S. Waters, 1860.
    106 p.   24 cm.

168   Allen, Ethan, 1796-1879.
    A discourse prepared for the nation-
al fast day June 1st, 1865, on account of the murder of our late president, and preached at St. Thomas'
church. Homestead, Baltimore county,
M^d. By Ethan Allen ... Baltimore,
Printed by Wm. K. Boyle, 1865.
    12 p.   19 cm.

169   Allen, Ethan, 1796-1879.
    Historical notices of St. Ann's
parish in Ann Arundel county, Maryland, extending from 1649 to 1857
... By the Rev. Ethan Allen ...
Baltimore, J.B. Des Forges, 1857.
    131 p.   19 cm.

170   Allen, Ethan, 1796-1879.
    Maryland toleration; or, Sketches
of the early history of Maryland,
to the year 1650 ... By the Rev.

Ethan Allen ... Baltimore, J.S.
Waters, 1855.
64 p.   21 cm.

171   Allen, Ethan, 1796-1879.
Who were the early settlers of
Maryland: a paper read before the
"Maryland historical society," at
its meeting held Thursday evening,
October 5, 1865. By the Rev. Ethan
Allan, D.D. Baltimore, Printed at
the office of the Am. quar. church
review, New Haven, Conn., 1866.
18 p.   23 1/2 cm.

172   [Allen, George] 1792-1883.
Resistance to slavery every man's
duty. A report on American slavery,
read to the Worcester central association, March 2, 1847. Boston. W.
Crosby & H.P. Nichols, 1847.
40 p.   24 cm.

173   [Allen, George] 1792-1883.
Thoughts on "the excitement" in reply to a Letter to Hon. Edward Everett ... Worcester, Printed by M.W.
Grout, 1833.
44 p.   21 cm.

174   Allen, Harrison, 1841-1897.
... Monograph of the bats of North
America. By H. Allen ... Washington,
Smithsonian institution, 1864.
xxii, 85 p.   illus.   23 1/2 cm.

175   [Allen, Ira] 1751-1814.
A concise summary of the second
volume of the Olive Branch, a book
containing an account of Governor
Chittenden's giving written instructions to Gen. Ira Allen in 1795, to
purchase military stores in Europe,
for the militia of the state of Vermont, of his purchase of 24 brass
field pieces, 20,000 muskets ... in

France, of his being captured by an
English 74 gun ship, with consequences resulting therefrom. To
which is subjoined, General Allen's
circular letter, on the subject of a
ship canal of commerce, and the ad-
vantage of British America in pre-
serving peace between Great Britain
and the United States. Including
General Allen's memorials to the Senate of the United States, of February, 1805, and December, 1806 ...
Philadelphia, Printed for the author,
1807.
    24 p.   22 cm.

176   Allen, Ira, 1751-1814.
    Miscellaneous remarks, on the pro-
ceedings of the state of New-York,
against the state of Vermont, &c.
By Ira Allen. Hartford, Printed by
Hannah Watson, near the Great bridge,
1777.
    13 p.   21 cm.

177   Allen, Ira, 1751-1814.
    The natural and political history
of the state of Vermont, by Ira Allen. 1798.
    (*In* Vermont historical society.
Collections. Montpelier, 1870.
23 1/2 cm.)

178   Allen, Ira, 1751-1814.
    Particulars of the capture of the
ship Olive Branch laden with a cargo
of arms, &c., the property of Major-
General Ira Allen, destined for supplying the militia of Vermont and
captured by His Britannic Majesty's
ship of war, Audacious; together
with the proceedings and evidence
before the High Court of Admiralty
of Great Britain. London, Printed
by J.W. Myers, 1798-1805.
    2 v.   21-24 cm.

179   [Allen, James] 1739-1808.
        The Poem which the Committee of
        the town of Boston had voted unani-
        mously to be published with the late
        oration; with Observations relating
        thereto; together with some very per-
        tinent Extracts from an ingenious
        Composition never yet published.
        Boston: Printed and Sold by E. Rus-
        sell, at his Printing-Office, near
        Dr. Gardiner's, in Marlborough-
        Street. 1772.
        30 p.   22 1/2 cm.

180   Allen, James, 1809-1837.
        Narrative of the life of James
        Allen, alias George Walton, alias
        Jonas Pierce, alias James H. York,
        alias Burley Grove, the highwayman.
        Being his death-bed confession, to
        the warden of the Massachusetts state
        prison. Boston, Harrington & co.,
        1837.
        32 p.   22 cm.

181   [Allen, John] *fl.* 1764, *supposed author.*
        The American alarm, or The Boston-
        ian plea, for the rights, and liber-
        ties, of the people. Humbly ad-
        dressed to the King and Council; and
        to the constitutional sons of liber-
        ty, in America. By the British Bos-
        tonian. Boston, Printed by D. Knee-
        land, and N. Davis, in Queen street
        and sold M.DCC.LNNIII.
        35, 8, 9, 16 p.   17 1/2 cm.

182   Allen, John, 1763-1812.
        Speech of John Allen, esqr., in the
        House of representatives, Friday,
        the 20th day of April, 1798. Rela-
        tive to employing the armed vessels
        as convoys. Philadelphia, W. Cobbett,
        1798.
        v, [7]-32 p.   20 1/2 cm.

183   Allen, Joseph, 1772-1806.
          An oration on the character of the
       late Gen. George Washington: pro-
       nounced before the inhabitants of
       the town of Western, on Saturday the
       22d of February, 1800. By Joseph
       Allen, jun. esq. Printed at the re-
       quest of said town. Printed at
       Brookfield, Massachusetts, By E.
       Merriam & Co., March, 1800.
          12 p.   19 x 15 1/2 cm.

184   Allen, Joseph, 1790-1873.
          The day of small things. A cen-
       tennial discourse, delivered in North-
       borough, June 1, 1846, in commemora-
       tion of the organization of the First
       Congregational church in that place,
       and the ordination of their first
       minister, one hundred years ago.
       With an appendix. By Joseph Allen,
       the third minister in succession of
       said church ... Boston, W. Crosby
       and H.P. Nichols, 1846.
          64 p.   24 cm.

185   Allen, Joseph, 1810?-1864.
          Battles of the British navy, from
       A.D. 1000 to 1840. By Joseph Allen
       ... London, A.H. Baily & co., 1842.
          2 v. front., pl., port., fold.
       tab., diagr.   17 cm.

186   Allen, Joseph, 1810?-1864.
          Memoir of the life and services of
       Admiral Sir William Hargood ... com-
       piled from authentic documents, un-
       der the direction of Lady Hargood,
       by Joseph Allen ... Greenwich,
       Printed for private circulation only,
       by H.S. Richardson, 1841.
          xii p., 1 l., 296 p. front. (port.)
       illus., 2 pl.   25 cm.

187   Allen, Joseph Henry, 1820-1898.
          The public man. A discourse on

occasion of the death of Hon. John
Fairfield, delivered in Washington,
Dec. 26, 1847 ... Washington, T.
Barnard, printer, 1848.
27 p.   22 cm.

188   Allen, Joseph Henry, 1820-1898.
The statesman and the man. A dis-
course on occasion of the death of
Hon. John Quincy Adams, delivered in
Washington, Feb. 27, 1848, by Joseph
Henry Allen. Washington [D.C.] Print-
ed by J. and G.S. Gideon, 1848.
23 p.   21 cm.

189   Allen, Lewis Leonidas.
The island of Cuba; or, Queen of
the Antilles. By Rev. L. Leonidas
Allen ... Cleveland, Harris, Fairbanks & co., 1852.
26 p.   21 1/2 cm.

190   Allen, Lewis Leonidas.
Pencillings of scenes upon the Rio
Grande; originally pub. bu [!] the
Saint Louis American. By the Rev.
L.L. Allen. Late chaplain to the La.
volunteers in the United States services, upon the Rio Grande. [2d ed.,
enl. and improved] New York, 1848.
48 p.   19 1/2 cm.

191   Allen, Myron Oliver.
The history of Wenham, civil and
ecclesiastical, from its settlement
in 1639, to 1860. By Myron O. Allen,
M.D. Boston, Printed by Bazin &
Chandler, 1860.
vi p., 1 l., [13]-220 p.   19 1/2
cm.

192   Allen, Paul, 1775-1826.
A history of the American revolution; comprehending all the principal
events both in the field and in the
cabinet. By Paul Allen, esq. To

which are added the most important
resolutions of the Continental congress, and many of the most important letters of General Washington
... Baltimore: Printed for John
Hopkins . . . . . Thomas Murphy.
printer. 1819.
2 v.   24 cm.

193   Allen, Paul, 1775-1826.
      A history of the American revolu-
tion; comprehending all the principal
events both in the field and in the
cabinet. By Paul Allen, esq. To
which are added, the most important
resolutions of the Continental congress, and many of the most important letters of General Washington
... Baltimore, Printed for F. Betts,
1822.
2 v.   fronts. (ports.)   21 cm.

194   Allen, Paul, 1775-1826.
      An oration, on the necessity of
political union at the present day:
delivered at the Baptist meeting-
house, in Providence, at the commencement of Rhode-Island college, A.D.
1797. By Paul Allen ...   Providence:
Printed by Carter and Wilkinson, and
sold at their Book-Store, opposite
the Market. 1797.
8 p.   20 cm.

195   Allen, Richard, L   1808-1873.
      An analysis of the principal mineral
fountains at Saratoga Springs, embracing an account of their history;
their chemical and curative properties; together with general directions
for their use; also, some remarks upon
the natural history, and objects of
general interest in the county of
Saratoga, by R.L. Allen ...   New
York, Ross & Tousey, 1858.
113, [1]p.   plates.   15 1/2 cm.

196   Allen, Robert, *late of Peru*.
       An essay on the nature and meth-
       ods of carrying on a trade to the
       South-sea. By Robert Allen ...
       London, Printed, and sold by R.
       Mount, 1712.
       2 p. l., 37 p.   18 cm.

197   Allen, Wilkes, 1775-1845.
       The history of Chelmsford, from
       its origin in 1653, to the year 1820--
       together with an historical sketch of
       the church, and biographical notices
       of the four first pastors. To which
       is added a memoir of the Pawtuckett
       tribe of Indians. With a large ap-
       pendix. By Wilkes Allen ... Haver-
       hill: Printed by P.N. Green. 1820.
       192 p.   23 cm.

198   Allen, William, 1780-1873.
       The history of Norridgewock: com-
       prising memorials of the aboriginal
       inhabitants and Jesuit missionaries,
       hardships of the pioneers, biographi-
       cal notices of the early settlers, and
       ecclesiastical sketches. By William
       Allen ... Norridgewock [Me.] E.J.
       Peet, 1849.
       252 p.   plates. 18 cm.

199   [Allen, William] 1784-1868.
       Accounts of shipwreck and of other
       disasters at sea, designed to be
       interesting and useful to mariners,
       with an appendix, containing Dr.
       Rayson's address to seamen and a
       few prayers for their use. Comp.
       by a friend of seamen. Brunswick,
       Me., Printed by Joseph Griffin, 1823.
       xxiv, 335 p.   20 cm.

200   Allen, William, 1784-1868.
       An address, delivered at Northamp-
       ton, Mass., on the evening of Oct.
       29, 1854, in commemoration of the

close of the second century since the settlement of the town. By William Allen ... Northampton, Hopkins, Bridgman & company, 1855.
 56 p.   23 cm.

201   Allen, William, 1784-1868.
 An American biographical and historical dictionary, containing an account of the lives, characters, and writings of the most eminent persons in North America from its first discovery to the present time, and a summary of the history of the several colonies, and of the United States, by William Allen ... Cambridge [Mass.] W. Hilliard, 1809.
 viii, 632 p.   front. (port.) fold. tab.   22 cm.

202   Allen, William, 1784-1868.
 An American biographical and historical dictionary, containing an account of the lives, characters, and writings of the most eminent persons in North America from its first settlement, and a summary of the history of the several colonies and of the United States. By William Allen ... 2d ed.   Boston, W. Hyde & co., 1832.
 viii, 800 p.   24 cm.

203   Allen, William, 1784-1868.
 The American biographical dictionary: containing an account of the lives, characters, and writings of the most eminent persons deceased in North America from its first settlement. By William Allen ... 3d ed. Boston, J.P. Jewett and company; Cleveland, O., H.P.B. Jewett, 1857.
 ix, 905 p.   27 cm.

204   Allen, William, 1784-1868.
 Wunnissoo, or The vale of Hoosatunnuk, a poem, with notes. By

45

William Allen ...   Boston, J.P. Jewett and company; New York, Sheldon,
Blakeman & company: [etc., etc.] 1856.
   237 p.   front. (port.)   19 1/2 cm.

205   Allen, William, 1803-1879.
      Speech of Mr. Allen of Ohio on the
bill to separate the Government from
the banks. Delivered in the Senate
of the United States, February 20,
1838. Washington, Printed at the
Globe office, 1838.
   16 p.   23 cm.

206   Allen, William G.
      The American prejudice against col-
or. An authentic narrative, showing
how easily the nation got into an up-
roar. By W.G. Allen, a refugee from
American despotism. London, W. and
F.G. Cash; [etc., etc.] 1853.
   2 p. 1., 107 [1] p.   16 1/2 cm.

207   Allen, William Henry, 1808-1882.
      Eulogy on the character and ser-
vices of the late Daniel Webster, pronounced at the request of the Select
and Common councils of the city of
Philadelphia, January 18, 1853, by
William H. Allen ...   Philadelphia,
Crissy & Markley, printers, 1853.
   51 p.   23 cm.

208   Allen, William Henry, 1808-1882.
      Our country's mission in history.
An address delivered at the anniversary of the Philomathaean society of
Pennsylvania college, September 19,
1855. By William H. Allen ...   Philadelphia, T.K. and P.G. Collins, printers, 1855.
   38 p.   23 1/2 cm.

209   Allen, William Joshua, 1828-1901
      Speech of Hon. William J. Allen ...
upon the President's message, delivered

in the House of representatives, January 27, 1864.   Washington, Printed
at the office of "The Constitutional
union," 1864.
    14 p.   23 1/2 cm.

210   Alley, John Bassett, 1817-1896.
        Speech of Hon. John B. Alley, of
Mass., on the principles and purposes
of the Republican party.   Delivered
in the House of representatives of
the United States, Monday, April 30,
1860.   [Washington, 1860]
    8 p.   24 cm.

211   Allgemeine historie der reisen zu wasser
und lande: oder Sammlung aller
reisebeschreibungen, welche bis itzo
in verschiedenen sprachen von allen
volkern herausgegeben worden ... durch
eine gesellschaft gelehrter männer
im englischen zusammen getragen, und
aus demselben ins deutsche übersetzet
... Leipzig, Bey Arkstee und Merkus,
1747-74.
    21 v.   front., plates (part fold.)
maps (part fold) plans (part fold.)
25 cm.

212   Allibone, Samuel Austin, 1816-1889.
        A critical dictionary of English
literature, and British and American
authors, living and deceased, from the
earliest accounts to the middle of the
nineteenth century.   Containing thirty
thousand biographies and literary notices, with forty indexes of subjects.
By S. Austin Allibone ... Philadelphia, J.B. Lippincott & co. [etc.]
1858-71.
    3 v.   27 cm.

213   Allin, John, 1596-1671.
        The spouse of Christ coming out of
affliction, leaning upon her Beloved:
or, A sermon preached by Mr. John

Allin the late reverend pastor to
the Church of Christ at Dedham, at
the administration of the Lord's sup-
per. August 6, 1671. And may be useful to any Church of Christ, or true
believer in a state of affliction ...
Cambridge [Mass.] Printed by Samuel
Green: and are to be sold by John
Tappin of Boston, 1672.
2 p. ℓ., 26 p. 19 cm.

214 Alling, Jeremiah.
A register of the weather, or, An
account of the several rains, snow-
storms, depth of each snow,--hail and
thunder; with some account of the
weather each day, and some other
events worthy of notice, for the last
twenty-five years, ending March 31,
1810. From observations, taken most
of the time in Hamden, near New-Haven,
in Connecticut ... By Jeremiah Alling.
New Haven, Printed by O. Steele and
co., 1810.
84 p. 23 1/2 cm.

215 Allison, Joseph, 1819-1896.
An eulogy upon the life, character
and public services of General Zachary Taylor. Delivered at the Commissioners' hall, Spring Garden, July
29th, 1850. By Joseph Allison, esq.
... Philadelphia, J.H. Jones, printer, 1850.
24 p. 22 1/2 cm.

216 Allison, Patrick, 1740-1802.
A discourse, delivered in the
Presbyterian church, in the city of
Baltimore, the 22d of February, 1800.
--the day dedicated to the memory of
Gen. George Washington. By the Rev.
Patrick Allison, D.D. Baltimore,
Printed by W. Pechin--for the Editor
of the American. [1800]
24 p. 20 1/2 cm.

217   [Allsop, Thomas] 1795-1880.
        California and its gold mines: be-
        ing a series of recent communications
        from the mining districts, upon the
        present condition and future prospects
        of quartz mining; with an account of
        the richer deposits, and incidental
        notices of the climate, scenery, and
        mode of life in California. Edited by
        Robert Allsop ... London, Groombridge
        and sons, 1853.
        2 p. l., [3]-149 p. 16 cm.

218   Allston, Robert Francis Withers, 1801-
        1864.
        Report on the free school system in
        South-Carolina. By R.F.W. Allston,
        esq. Charleston, S.C., Miller &
        Browne, 1817.
        cover-title, 42 p. 22 1/2 cm.

219   Allyn, John, 1767-1833.
        A sermon, delivered at Plimouth,
        December 22, 1801, commemorative of
        the pious ancestry who first imigrat-
        ed [!] to that place, 1620. By John
        Allyn ... Boston: Printed by Mun-
        roe & Francis, Half-court square, back
        of the Post-office.--1802.
        35 p. 22 cm.

220   Allyn, John, 1767-1833.
        A sermon, preached in the audience
        of His Excellency Caleb Strong, esq.,
        governor, the other members of the
        executive, and the honorable legisla-
        ture of the commonwealth of Massa-
        chusetts, on the anniversary elec-
        tion, May 29, 1805. By John Allyn,
        Congregational minister of Duxborough.
        Boston: Printed for Young & Minns,
        printers to the state. 1805.
        37 p. 19 cm.

221   Almbert, Alfred d', 1813-1887.
        Flânerie parisienne aux États-Unis,

par Alfred d'Almbert. Paris. Librairie théâtrale. 1856.
2 p. l., 278 p., 1 l. 16 1/2 cm.

222   [Almon, John] 1737-1805
Anecdotes of the life of the Right
Hon. William Pitt, earl of Chatham,
and of the principal events of his
time. With his speeches in Parliament, from the year 1736 to the year
1778 ... 6th ed., cor. ... London,
Printed for L.B. Seeley, 1797.
3 v. 21 1/2 cm.

223   [Almon, John] 1737-1805.
Biographical, literary, and political anecdotes, of several of the
most eminent persons of the present
age. Never before printed. With an
appendix; consisting of original,
explanatory, and scarce papers. By
the author of Anecdotes of the late
Earl of Chatham ... London, T.N. Longman, and L.B. Seeley, 1797.
3 v. 22 1/2 cm.

224   [Almon, John] 1737-1805, *comp.*
A collection of interesting, authentic papers, relative to the dispute
between Great Britain and America; shewing the causes and progress of that
misunderstanding, from 1764 to 1775.
London, Printed for J. Almon, 1777.
280, [2] p., 1 l. 21 1/2 cm.

225   [Almon, John] 1737-1805.
The history of the late minority.
Exhibiting the conduct, principles,
and views of that party, during the
years 1762, 1763, 1764, and 1765.
London, Printed 1765, reprinted,
with additions, 1766.
x, [9]-332 p., 1 l. 21 cm.

226   Almon, John, 1737-1805.
Memoirs of John Almon, bookseller,

of Piccadilly. London, 1790.
3 p. 1., [9]-262 p. 22 cm.

227 Alsinet, José.
Nuevas utilidades de la quina,
demostradas, confirmadas, y añadidas,
por el Doct. D. Josef Alsinet ...
Se manifiesta el modo cómo cada uno
en su casa podra quitar el amargor
à la quina, sin perjuicio de su vir-
tud febrifuga. Madrid, En la impr.
de A. Muñóz del Valle, 1774.
9 p. 1., 168 [2] p. 15 cm.

228 Alsop, Richard, 1761-1815.
A poem, sacred to the memory of
George Washington, late president of
the United States and commander-in-
chief of the armies of the United
States, adapted to the 22nd of Feb-
ruary 1800. By Richard Alsop ...
Hartford: Printed by Hudson and
Goodwin. 1800. Tarrytown, N.Y.,
Reprinted, W. Abbatt, 1926.
(In The Magazine of history, with
notes and queries. Tarrytown, N.Y.,
1926. 26 1/2 cm.

229 [Alsop, Richard] 1761-1815.
The political green-house, for the
year 1798. Addressed to the readers
of the Connecticut courant, January
1st, 1799. Published according to
act of Congress. Hartford: Printed
by Hudson & Goodwin [1799]
24 p. 20 1/2 cm.

230 Alvarez, Francisco, *Asturian.*
Noticia del establecimiento y
población de las colonias inglesas
en la America Septentrional; religion,
orden de gobierno, leyes y costumbres
de sus naturales y habitantes;
calidades de su clima, terreno,
frutos, plantas y animales; y estado
de su industria, artes, comercio y

51

navegación: sacada de varios autores
por don Francisco Alvarez ... Madrid, A. Fernandez, 1778.
196 p.   21 cm.

231 Álvarez, José María, 1777-1820.
Instituciones de derecho real de
Castilla y de Indias, por el dr. d.
José María Álvarez ... Guatemala,
Impr. de I. Beteta, 1818-20.
4 v.   14 1/2 cm.

232 Alvord, Benjamin, 1813-1884.
Address before the Dialectic society of the Corps of cadets, in commemoration of the gallant conduct of the
nine graduates of the Military academy, and other officers of the United
States' army, who fell in the battles
which took place in Florida, on the
28th of December, 1835, and the 25th
of December, 1837; the former called
Dade's battle, the latter, the battle
of Okee-cho-bee. Delivered at West
Point, N.Y., on the 29th December,
1838. By Lieutenant Benjamin Alvord,
U. S. A. ... New York, Wiley & Putnam, 1839.
62 p.   22 cm.

233 Alvord, John Watson, 1807-1880.
Historical address, delivered in the
First Congregational church in Stam-
ford, Ct. at the celebration of the
second centennial anniversary of the
first settlement of the town. By
Rev. J.W. Alvord, Dec. 22d, 1841.
New York, S. Davenport, 1842.
40 p.   22 1/2 cm.

234 Amati, Giacinto, 1778-1850.
Viaggi di Cristoforo Colombo tratti
dall'opera; ricerche storico-critico-
scientifiche sulle origini, scoperte,
invenzioni, ecc. ecc. Dell'abate
don Giacinto Amati ... Aggiuntevi

storiche notizie ed illustrazioni
sopra le precedenti edizioni; con
carta geografica. Milano, Colle
stampe di G. Pirotta, 1830.
   70 p.   front. (fold. map)   23
1/2 cm.

235   America: a dramatic poem. New-York,
      A.D.F. Randolph, 1863.
      110 p.   19 1/2 cm.

236   America, an ode to the people of Eng-
      land ... London, Printed for J.
      Almon, 1776.
      1 p. l., 10 p.   26 x 20 1/2 cm.

237   America's appeal to the impartial world.
      Wherein the rights of the Americans,
      as men, British subjects, and as
      colonists; the equity of the demand,
      and of the manner in which it is
      made upon them by Great-Britain, are
      stated and considered. And, the
      opposition made by the colonies to
      acts of Parliament, their resorting
      to arms in their necessary defence,
      against the military armaments, em-
      ployed to enforce them, vindicated
      ... Hartford, Printed by E. Watson,
      1775.
      72 p.   18 1/2 cm.

238   American academy of arts and sciences,
      Boston.
      Memoirs of the American academy of
      arts and sciences. v. 1-4; new ser.,
      v. 1- Boston [etc.] 1785-19
      v. illus., plates (part col.)
      maps, facsims., tables, diagrs.   27-
      30 1/2 cm. *and* atlas. 25 1/2 x
      29 1/2 cm.

239   The American almanac and repository of
      useful knowledge, for ... 1830-61.
      v. 1-32. Boston, Gray and Bowen;
      [etc., etc., 1829]-61.

32 v. fold. maps. 18 - 19 1/2
cm.

240 The American annual eyclopaedia and
register of important events ... Embracing political, civil, military,
and social affairs; public documents;
biography, statistics, commerce, finance, literature, science, agriculture, and mechanical industry. v.
[1]-14; 1861-74. New York, D. Appleton and company, 1862-75.
14 v. illus., ports. 25 1/2 cm.

241 The American annual register; for the
years 1825/26 - 1832/33, or the
50th - 57th years of American independence. New York, G. & C. Carvill;
[etc., etc.] 1827-35.
8 v. 22 cm.

242 American antiquarian society, *Worcester,
Mass.*
Address to the members of the American antiquarian society; together
with the laws and regulations of the
institution, and a list of donations
to the Society since the last publication. Worcester, Printed by William
Manning, March, 1819.
38 p. 22 cm.

243 American antiquarian society, *Worcester,
Mass.*
Catalogue of the officers and members of the American antiquarian society. May, 1839. Worcester, Printed by T.W. & J. Butterfield, 1839.
15 p. 22 cm.

244 American antiquarian society, *Worcester,
Mass.*
Communication from the president
of the American antiquarian society
[Isaiah Thomas] to the members,
October 24th, 1814. [Published by

order of the society.] Together with
the laws of the society, as revised.
Worcester (Mass.) Printed by W.
Manning [1815]
   27, 8 p.   23 cm.

245 American association for the advancement
        of science.
        Report on the history and progress
     of the American coast survey up to the
     year 1858. By the committee of twen-
     ty appointed by the American associa-
     tion for the advancement of science,
     at the Montreal meeting, August, 1857.
     [n.p., 1858]

246 The American bee; a collection of enter-
     taining histories, selected from dif-
     ferent authors, and calculated for
     amusement and instructions. The 1st
     ed. Leominster [Mass.] Printed by
     and for Charles Prentiss. 1797.
        249 p.   18 cm.

247 American bureau of mines, *New York*.
        Union Pacific railroad. A geologi-
     cal & agricultural survey of 100
     miles west of Omaha. By the American
     bureau of mines. New York, American
     bureau of mines, 1866.
        44 p.   23 cm.

248 American destiny: what shall it be, Re-
     publican or Cossack? An argument ad-
     dressed to the people of the late Un-
     ion, North and South. New York, Pub.
     for the Columbian association, 1864.
        cover-title, 44 p.   22 1/2 cm.

249 American Ethnological Society.
        Transactions. v. 1- 3, pt. 1. New
     York, G.P. Putnam [etc.] 1945-53.
        3 v. illus., fold. maps.   24 cm.

250 The American gazette. Being a collec-
     tion of all the authentic addresses,

memorials, letters, &c. which relate
to the present disputes between Great
Britain and her colonies. Containing also many original papers never
before pub. no. 1-5; 1768-69. London, Printed for G. Kearsly, 1768-
69.
5 no. in 1 v.   21 cm.

251   The American gazetteer. Containing a
distinct account of all the parts of
the New world: their situation, climate, soil, produce, former and present condition; commodities, manufactures, and commerce. Together with
an accurate account of the cities,
towns, ports, bays, rivers, lakes,
mountains, passes, and fortifications
... London, Printed for A. Millar
[etc.] 1762.
3 v. fronts., fold. maps.   17 1/2
cm.

252   The American gift book; a perpetual
souvenir. New York, Derby & Jackson,
18.
v. plates.   19 cm.

253   The American's guide: comprising the
Declaration of independence; the Articles of confederation; the Constitution of the United States, and the
constitutions of the several states
composing the Union ... Philadelphia,
J.B. Lippincott & co., 1864.
657 p.   20 1/2 cm.

254   The American historical magazine. v. 1;
Jan.-June, 1836. [New Haven, W. Stor-
er, jr.] 1836.
1 v.   22 1/2 cm.

255   American historical society, *Washington,
D. C.*
Transactions of the American histori-
cal society; instituted at the city

of Washington, October 12, 1835. vol.
1. Washington, Printed by J. Gideon,
jr., 1839.
   [522] p. fold. pl. 25 1/2 cm.

256   The American in Algiers; or, The patriot
      of seventy-six in captivity. A poem,
      in two cantos ... New-York, Printed
      and sold by J. Buel, 1797.
         36 p. 18 1/2 cm.

257   American institute of instruction.
         The act of incorporation, constitu-
      tion and by-laws of the American in-
      stitute of instruction. Boston,
      Classic press, I.R. Butts [1831?]
         11 p. 20 cm.

258   American international relief committee,
      for the suffering operatives of Great
      Britain.
         Report. New York.
         v. 22 cm.

259   American journal of conchology. Ed. by
      George W. Tryon, jr. ... v. 1-7;
      Feb. 1865-May 1872. Philadelphia,
      G.W. Tryon, jr.; [etc., etc.] 1865-
      72.
         7 v. illus., plates (part col.)
      ports., tab. 22 1/2 cm.

260   The American journal of education. Ed.
      by Henry Barnard, L.L. D. v. 1-32;
      Aug. 1855-1882. Hartford, F. C.
      Brownell; [etc., etc.] 1856-82.
         32 v. illus., plates, ports. 22
      1/2 - 24 cm.

261   The American journal of education and
      college review; published monthly.
      v. 1-3; Aug. 1855-Apr. 1857. New
      York, N.A. Calkins; [etc., etc.]
      1856-[57]
         3 v. illus., ports. 23 cm.

262   The American journal of improvements in
       the useful arts, and mirror of the
       patent office in the United States ...
       v. 1- Jan. 1828- Ed. ... by I.L.
       Skinner. Washington, Printed by W.
       Greer, 1828-
         v. plates 24 cm.

263   The American kalendar; or, United States
       register ... London, J. Debrett, 17
         v. 25 1/2 cm.

264   The American keepsake, or Book for every
       American; containing the Declaration
       of independence, and signers names,
       Constitution of the United States,
       and ... amendments, Washington's
       inaugural address, first annual mes-
       sage, and his farewell address ...
       date of formation of state constitu-
       tions ... [etc.] To which is append-
       ed the new postage law of 1845, en-
       tire. Boston, E.L. Pratt, 1845.
         1 p. 1., [7]-76 p. front. (11
       port.) 19 cm.

265   American literary gazette and publishers'
       circular. v. 1-8, Sept. 1855 - Dec.
       1862; new ser., v. 1, Jan.-Apr. 1863;
       octavo ser., v. 1-18, May 1863-Jan.
       15, 1872. New York, Book publishers'
       association [etc.] 1855-63; Phila-
       delphia, G.W. Childs, 1863-72.
         27 v. 24-30 cm.

266   The American magazine, containing a mis-
       cellaneous collection of original and
       other valuable essays in prose and
       verse, and calculated both for instruc-
       tion and amusement. no. [1]-12; Dec.
       1787-Nov. 1788. New York, Printed by
       S. Loudon [etc., 1787-88]
         882 p. plates, plan. 22 1/2 cm.

267   The American magazine and monthly chron-
       icle for the British colonies. Vol.

I. containing from October 1757 to
October 1758 inclusive. By a society
of gentlemen ... Philadelphia, Printed by William Bradford [1757-58]
1 p. l., 654 + p. 21 cm.

268   The American magazine of wit; a collection of anecdotes, stories, and narratives, humorous, marvellous, witty,
queer, remarkable, and interesting.
Partly selected and partly original;
with plates. By a judge of the con-
vivial court of Dover, aided by a jury
of odd fellows ... New-York, Printed
by H.C. Southwick, 1808.
iv. [5]-353 p. fold. front., 2 pl.
28 cm.

269   American mechanics' magazine: containing useful original matter, on subjects connected with manufactures,
the arts and sciences: as well as
selections from the most approved
domestic and foreign journals. Conducted by associated mechanics. v.
1-2; Feb. 5, 1825-Feb. 11, 1826.
New-York, J.V. Seaman [etc.] 1825-
26.
2 v. in 1. illus. 22 cm.

270   The American mineralogical journal: being a collection of facts and observations tending to elucidate the
mineralogy and geology of the United
States of America ... Conducted by
Archibald Bruce ... v. 1; 1810. New-
York, Printed by Collins & co., 1814.
vi, 270, [2] p. plates. 24 cm.

271   The American monthly magazine and critical review. v. 1-4; May 1817-
Apr. 1819. New York, Pub. for H.
Biglow by Kirk & Mercein [etc.] 1817-
18.
4 v. 22 1/2 cm.

272   The American monthly review. v. 1-4;
        Jan. 1832-Dec. 1833. Cambridge,
        Hilliard and Brown: Boston, Hil-
        liard, Gray and co.: [etc., etc.]
        1832-33.
          4 v.   23 cm.

273   The American museum, or Universal maga-
        zine; containing, essays on agricul-
        ture--commerce--Manufactures--politics
        --morals--and manners. Sketches of
        national characters--natural and civ-
        il history--and biography. Law in-
        formation--public papers--intelli-
        gence. Moral tales--ancient and mod-
        ern poetry ... v. 1-[12] Jan. 1787-
        Dec. 1792. Philadelphia, Printed by
        Mathew Carey [etc.] 1787-92.
          12 v.   illus., pl., map.   20 1/2-
        22 1/2 cm.

274   The American musical miscellany: a col-
        lection of the newest and most ap-
        poved [!] songs, set to music ...
        Printed at Northampton, Massachus-
        etts. By Andrew Wright, for Daniel
        Wright and company. Sold by them,
        and by S. Butler, in Northampton:
        by I. Thomas, jun. in Worcester; by
        F. Barker, in Greenfield: and by the
        principal booksellers in Boston.--
        1798.
          xii. [13]-300 p.   16 1/2 cm.

275   American naval battles: being a com-
        plete history of the battles fought
        by the navy of the United States
        from its establishment in 1794 to
        the present time, including the wars
        with France, and with Tripoli, the
        late war with Great Britain and with
        Algiers, with an account of the at-
        tack on Baltimore, and of the battle
        of New Orleans. With twenty-one ...
        engravings ... Boston, J.J. Smith,
        jr., 1831.

2 p. l., [iii]-v, [7]-278 p., 1
l. illus., pl.   22 1/2 cm.

276   American naval battles; being a complete
      history of the battles fought by the
      navy of the United States, from its
      establishment in 1794 to the present
      time; including the wars with France
      and Tripoli; the late war with Great
      Britain, and with Algiers; with an
      account of the attack on Baltimore,
      and of the battle of New Orleans ...
      Boston, C. Gaylord, 1837.
         v. [7]-278 p., 1 l. illus., 2 pl.
      (incl. front.)   20 1/2 cm.

277   American notes and queries. v. 1, no.
      1-4; Jan. 1-Apr. 1, 1857. [Philadel-
      phia, W. Brotherhead, 1857]
         160 p.   22 1/2 cm.

278   American numismatic society.
         Constitution and by-laws of the
      American numismatic society. Adopt-
      ed September, 1858. New York, T.W.
      Strong, printer, 1858.
         8 p.   15 cm.

279   American oratory; or Selections from
      the speeches of eminent Americans
      [1775-1826] Comp. by a member of
      the Philadelphia bar. Philadelphia,
      E.C. & J. Biddle, 1853.
         viii, 531 p.   21 1/2 cm.

280   The American's own book, containing the
      Declaration of independence, with the
      lives of the signers; the Constitu-
      tion of the United States: the in-
      augural addresses and first annual
      messages of all the presidents from
      Washington to Pierce; the farewell ad-
      dresses of George Washington and An-
      drew Jackson; with a portrait and
      life of each president of the United
      States, to the present time. New

York, Leavitt & Allen, 1855.
vi, [7]-496 p. front. (port.)
19 1/2 cm.

281   American Pharmaceutical Association.
Proceedings of the ... annual meeting. [1st-59th]; 1852-1911. Philadelphia.
59 v. in 54. illus., ports., maps.
23 cm.

282   American philosophical society, *Philadelphia*.
Laws and regulations of the American philosophical society, held at
Philadelphia, for promoting useful
knowledge. Vide minutes of the society, of the 4th May, 1804. Philadelphia, Printed at the office of
the United States gazette, 1814.
36 p.   18 cm.

283   American philosophical society, *Philadelphia*.
Laws and regulations of the American philosophical society, held at
Philadelphia, for promoting useful
knowledge. Revised, and finally
adopted, June 21, 1833. Philadelphia, Printed by T. Kite & co., 1833.
46 p., 1 l.   20 1/2 cm.

284   American philosophical society, *Philadelphia*.
Laws and regulations of the American philosophical society, held at
Philadelphia, for promoting useful
knowledge, as finally amended and
adopted, December 16, 1859. Together with the chapter of the society,
and a list of its members. Philadelphia, J.C. Clark & son, printers,
1860.
80 p.   23 cm.

285   American philosophical society, *Philadelphia*.

Proceedings of the American philosophical society held at Philadelphia for promoting useful knowledge.
v. 1-   ; 1838/40-19   Philadelphia,
The Society, 1840-49.
 v. illus., plates (part col.)
photos., ports., maps, facsims.,
tables, diagrs.   23 - 24 1/2 cm.

286   American philosophical society, *Philadelphia*.
   Transactions of the American philosophical society, held at Philadelphia, for promoting useful knowledge.
Philadelphia, 1771-
   v. illus., plates (part col.) maps,
plans, tables, diagrs.   24 1/2 x
30 1/2 cm.

287   The American pioneer, a monthly periodi-
cal, devoted to the objects of the
Logan historical society; or, to col-
lecting and publishing sketches relative to the early settlement and suc-
cessive improvement of the country ...
v. 1-2; Jan. 1842-Oct. 1843. Cincinnati, O., J.S. Williams, 1842-43.
   2 v.   illus., plates, plans.   23
cm.

288   The American quarterly observer. v. 1-
3; July 1833-Oct. 1834. Boston,
Perkins & Marvin [etc.] 1833-34.
   3 v.   23 cm.

289   The American quarterly register.   v.
[1]-15;   July 1827-May 1843.   Boston
[etc.]
   15 v. in 9.   illus., ports.   23 -
25 cm.

290   American question ... A letter from a
calm observer, to a noble lord, on
the subject of the late declaration
relative to the Orders in council.
London, Printed by A.J. Valpy, 1812.

16 p.   21 1/2 cm.

291   The American question. Secession. Tar-
       iff. Slavery. Brighton, H. Taylor,
       1862.
          iv, [5]-73, [1] p.   18 cm.

292   ... American railway guide, and pocket
       companion for the United States ...
       together with a complete railway map.
       New York, C. Dinsmore.
          v. fold. maps.   14 cm.

293   The American register, or general reposi-
       tory of history, politics and sci-
       ence. v. 1-7; 1806/7-1810. Philadel-
       phia, C. & A. Conrad & co., Baltimore,
       Conrad, Lucas, & co.; [etc., etc.]
       1807-11.
          7 v.   23 cm.

294   The American register; or, Summary re-
       view of history, politics and litera-
       ture. v. 1-2. Philadelphia, T.
       Dobson, 1817.
          2 v.   23 cm.

295   The American remembrancer; or, An im-
       partial collection of essays, re-
       solves, speeches, &c. relative, or
       having affinity, to the treaty with
       Great Britain. Philadelphia, Print-
       ed by H. Tuckniss, for M. Carey,
       1795-[96]
          3 v.   21 1/2 cm.

296   American resistance indefensible. A ser-
       mon, preached on Friday December 13,
       1776, being the day appointed for a
       general fast ... By a country curate.
       London, Printed for H. Gardner, and
       sold by C. Parker [etc., 1777?]
          1 p. 1., [5]-26 p.   22 x 17 cm.

297   The American review, and literary jour-
       nal, for ... 1801-1802 ... v. 1-2.

New York, Printed by T. & J. Swords, 1801-1802.
    2 v.   23 cm.

298   American sketches; by a native of the
        United States ...   London, J. Miller,
        1827.
            xviii, 412 p.   20 cm.

299   American society for promoting national
        unity.
            American society for promoting na-
        tional unity ...   [Programme, consti-
        tution and proposed members]   New
        York, J.F. Trow, 1861.
            10, 6 p.   22 1/2 cm.

300   American society for the encouragement
        of domestic manufactures.
            Address of the American society for
        the encouragement of domestic manufac-
        tures, to the people of the United
        States.   New-York: Van Winkle, Wiley
        & co., Printers.   1817.
            32 p.   23 cm.

301   The American spectator, or Matrimonial
        preceptor.   A collection (with addi-
        tions and variations) of essays,
        epistles, precepts and examples,
        relating to the married state, from
        the most celebrated writers, ancient
        and modern.   Adapted to the state of
        society in the American republic ...
        Boston, D. West, 1797.
            xi, [13]-286 p.   front.   17 1/2
        cm.

302   The American star.   Being a choice col-
        lection of the most approved patri-
        otic & other songs.   Together with
        many original ones, never before pub-
        lished.   2d ed.   Richmond: Published
        by Peter Cottom, And for sale at his
        Bookstores in Richmond and Lynchburg,
        and by M. Carey & son, Philadelphia.

1817. [Shepherd & Pollard, printers, Richmond, Va.]
2 p. 1., [3]-215 p.   front.   14 cm.

303   American statistical association.
Collections of the American statistical association. v. 1. Boston, Printed for the Association, by T.R. Marvin, 1847.
3 p. 1., [v]-x p., 1 1., [9]-120 p., 1 1., [121]-596 p. incl. tables. 22 cm.

304   American statistical association.
Constitution and by-laws of the American statistical association. With a list of officers, fellows, and members, and an address. Boston, Printed by Perkins & Marvin, 1840.
24 p.   24 1/2 cm.

305   American statistical association.
Constitution and by-laws of the American statistical association. With a list of officers, fellows, and members, and an address. Boston, Press of T.R. Marvin, 1844.
24 p.   23 cm.

306   American telegraph magazine. v. 1, no. 1-6; Oct. 1852-July 1853. New York, D. Mann, 1852-53.
cover-title, 292 p.   23 1/2 cm.

307   American temperance union.
Permanent temperance documents. v. 1-3 ... New York, American temperance union, 1851-52 [v. 3, '51]
3 v.   21 1/2 cm.

308   American Thanksgiving dinner, at St. James' hall, London. Thursday, November 26th, 1863. London, W. Ridgway, 1863.
94 p.   21 cm.

309   American tract society, *Boston.*
        A brief history of the organization
    and work of the American tract socie-
    ty. Instituted in Boston, 1814. Bos-
    ton, American tract society, 1855.
    cover-title, 32 p. 18 cm.

310   The American traveller; being a new his-
    torical collection carefully compil-
    ed from original memoirs in several
    languages, and the most authentic
    voyages and travels, containing a
    compleat account of that part of the
    world, now called the West Indies,
    from its discovery by Columbus to
    the present time. Illustrated with
    the heads of the most eminent admir-
    als, commanders, and travellers,
    neatly engraved. To which is pre-
    fixed an introduction, shewing the
    rise, progress, and improvement of
    navigation, the use and properties
    of the loadstone, and an enquiry con-
    cerning the first inhabitants of Amer-
    ica. With an account of Admiral Ver-
    nons taking Porto Bello, Fort Chagre,
    and Carthagenna ... London, Printed
    and sold by J. Fuller, 1743.
        1 p. l., xiii, 11-398 p. 2 pl., 2
    port. (incl. front.) 18 cm.

312   American union commission.
        The American union commission; its
    origin, operations and purposes. Or-
    ganized to aid in the restoration of
    the Union upon the basis of freedom,
    industry, education, and Christian
    morality ... October, 1865. New
    York, Sanford, Harroun & co., print-
    ers, 1865.
    cover-title, 24 p. 22 1/2 cm.

313   The American union commission. Speeches
    of Hon. W. Dennison, postmaster-
    general, Rev. J.P. Thompson, D.D.,
    president of the commission, Col.

N.G. Taylor of east Tennessee, Hon.
J.R. Doolittle, U.S. Senate, Gen. J.
A. Garfield, M.C., in the Hall of
representatives, Washington, Feb.
12, 1865. New York, Printed by San-
ford, Harroun & co., 1865.
    43 p.   21 1/2 cm.

314   The American universal magazine.   v. 1-
       4; Jan. 2, 1797-Mar. 7, 1798. Phila-
       delphia, Printed for R. Lee [etc.,
       1797-98]
           4 v.   plates, ports.   21 1/2 cm.

315   The American wanderer, through various
       parts of Europe, in a series of let-
       ters to a lady (interspersed with
       a variety of interesting anecdotes)
       By a Virginian ...   London, J. Rob-
       son.   1783.
           xvi (i.e. xviii), 422 p.   21 1/2
       cm.

316   The American weekly messenger; or, Reg-
       ister of state papers, history and
       politics ...   v. 1-2; Sept. 25, 1813-
       Sept. 17, 1814.   Philadelphia, Print-
       ed for J. Conrad, 1814-15.
           2 v.   24 1/2 - 25 1/2 cm.

317   The American Whig review ...   v. 1-6,
       Jan. 1845 - Dec. 1847; v. 7-16
       (new ser., v. 1-10) Jan. 1848-Dec.
       1852.   New-York, Wiley and Putnam
       [etc.] 1845-52.
           16 v.   ports.   22 1/2 - 23 cm.

318   American wit and humor, illustrated by
       J. McLenan.   N[ew]Y[ork]Harper &
       bro's [C1859]
           2 pl 1., [7]-206 p.   illus.   24
       cm.

319   Americanus examined, and his principles
       compared with those of the approved
       advocates for America, by a

Pennsylvanian. Philadelphia, Printed
in the year 1774.
24 p.   19 1/2 cm.

320   Americus, *pseud.*
Thoughts for the times: addressed
to the considerate people of the northern states. By Americus ...   London, Printed for the author, 1862.
125 p.   25 cm.

321   Amerika, dargestellt durch sich selbst.
juny 1818-dec. 1820. Leipzig, G.J.
Göschen [1818-20]
3 v.   24 1/2 x 21 cm.

322   Amerikanisches magazin; oder Authen-
tische beitrage zur erdbeschreibung,
staatskunde und geschichte von Amerika, besonders aber der Vereinten
Staaten. Hrsg. von professor
Hegewisch in Kiel und professor Ebel-
ing in Hamburg. 1.bd. Hamburg,
C.E. Bohn [1795]-97.
4 pt. in 2 v.   fold, tab.   20 cm.

323   Ames, Fisher, 1758-1808.
The speech of Mr. Ames, in the
House of representatives of the United States, when in committee of the
whole, on Thursday, April 28, 1796,
in support of the following motion:
Resolved, That it is expedient to
pass the laws necessary to carry into effect the treaty lately concluded between the United States and the
king of Great-Britain. Philadelphia,
Printed by J. Fenno, 1796.
2 p. 1., 59 p.   21 1/2 cm.

324   Ames, Fisher, 1758-1808.
The speech of Mr. Ames, in the House
of representatives of the United
States, when in Committee of the
whole, on Thursday, April 28, 1796,
in support of the following motion:

Resolved, That it is expedient to
pass the laws necessary to carry into
effect the treaty lately concluded
between the United States and the
King of Great-Britain. [2d ed.] Boston, Printed by Jno. & J.N. Russell;
sold by them; and by William P. Blake
[1796]
52 p. 23 1/2 cm.

325   [Ames, Julius Rubens] 1801-1850.
"Liberty" ... [New York, American
anti-slavery society] 1837.
231 p. illus. 23 cm.

326   Ames, Nathaniel, 1708-1764.
An astronomical diary, or, An
almanack for the year of Our Lord
Christ 1747. Being the 3d year after
Bissextile, or leap year. And in the
twentieth year of the reign of Our
Most Gracious Sovereign King George
II. Wherein are contained the luna-
tions, eclipses of the luminaries,
aspects, sun and moon's rising &
setting, time of high water, courts,
spring tides, judgment of the weather, &c. Calculated for the meridian
of Boston, in New-England, lat. 42
deg. 25 min. north. By Nathanael
Ames ... Boston in New-England:
Printed by John Draper, for the booksellers [1746]
[16] p. 15 1/2 cm.

327   Amherst college.
Discourses and addresses at the
installation and inauguration of the
Rev. William A. Stearns, D.D., as
president of Amherst college, and
pastor of the college church. 2d ed.
Amherst, Printed by J.S. & C. Adams,
1855.
94 p. 23 cm.

328   Amherst college.

70

A plea for a miserable world. I.
An address, delivered at the laying
of the corner stone of the building
erecting for the charity institution
in Amherst, Massachusetts, August 9,
1820, by Noah Webster, esq. II. A
sermon, delivered on the same occasion, by Rev. Daniel A. Clark ...
III. A brief account of the origin
of the institution. Boston: Printed by Ezra Lincoln, no. 4, Suffolk
buildings, Congress street. 1820.
     48 p.   22 1/2 cm.

329   Amherst college.
          Triennial catalogue of Amherst
      college, including the officers of
      government and instruction, the alum-
      ni, and all others who have received
      honorary degrees. Amherst, Mass.,
      1828-78.
          18 v. in 6.   22 1/2 - 24 cm.

330   Amherst college. *Library*.
          Catalogue of Amherst college libra-
      ry. Amherst, Printed by W. Faxon,
      1855.
          iv, 177, [1] p.   23 1/2 cm.

331   [Amherst, Jeffery Amherst, *1st baron*]
          Commissary Wilson's orderly book.
      Expedition of the British and provin-
      cial army, under Maj. Gen. Jeffrey
      Amherst, against Ticonderoga and
      Crown point. 1759. Albany, N.Y.,
      J. Munsell; [etc., etc.] 1857.
          xi, 220 p.   front. (fold. map)
      22 1/2 x 19 cm.

332   Amicus reipublicae, *pseud*.
          An address to the public, contain-
      ing some remarks on the present polit-
      ical state of the American repub-
      licks, &c. By Amicus reipublicæ.
      Exeter [N.H.]: Printed and Sold, by
      Lamson and Ranlet, at their Office,

near the Treasurer's, [1786]
36 p.   20 1/2 cm.

333   Amory, Thomas Coffin, 1812-1889.
The argument of Thomas C. Amory,
against the proposed Metropolitan
police bill, before the Joint special
committee of the legislature, Monday,
March 16, 1863 ... Boston, J.E.
Farwell and company, printers to the
city, 1863.
31 p.   23 1/2 cm.

333   Amory, Thomas Coffin, 1812-1889.
Life of James Sullivan: with selections from his writings. By Thomas
C. Amory ... Boston, Phillips, Sampson, and company, 1859.
2 v. front. (port.)   23 cm.

334   Amos, Andrew, 1791-1860, *ed*.
Report of trials in the courts of
Canada, relative to the destruction
of the Earl of Selkirk's settlement
on the Red River: with observations.
By A. Amos ... London, J. Murray,
1820.
2 p. l., [vii]-xxx, [2], 388, iv
p. front. (fold. map)   22 1/2 cm.

335   Ampère, Jean Jacques Antoine, 1800-1864.
Promenade en Amérique: États-Unis--
Cuba--Mexique, par J.J. Ampère ...
Paris, Michel Lévy frères, 1855.
2 v.   22 cm.

336   Ampère, Jean Jacques Antoine, 1800-1864.
Promenade en Amérique; États-Unis--
Cuba--Mexique par J.J. Ampère ...
Nouv.éd. entièrement revue ... Paris,
Michel Lévy frères, 1860.
v.   22 cm.

337   Amphlett, William.
The emigrant's directory to the
western states of North America;

including a voyage out from Liverpool;
the geography and topography of the
whole western country, according to
its latest improvements; with instructions for descending the rivers Ohio
and Mississippi; also, a brief account of a new British settlement on
the headwaters of the Susquehanna, in
Philadelphia [!] By William Amphlett
... London, Longman, Hurst, Rees,
Orme, and Brown, 1819.
    viii, 208 p.   21 1/2 cm.

338   Ampzing, Samuel, 1591?-1632.
      West-Indische triumph-basvyne, tot
Godes ere, ende roem der Batavieren
gesteken, van wegen de veroveringe
der Spaensche silver-vlote van Nova
Hispania, inde baij van Matanca, door
de schepen vande geoctroijeerde West-
Indische compagnie, onder het beleyd
vande E. manhafte heren see-helden
Pieter Pieterszen Heyn, generael, ende
Heynrick Korneliszen Lonk, admirael,
geschied den 8. Sept. 1628. Door
Samvel Ampzing ... Haerlem, A Rooman,
1629.
      6 p, 1,, 44 p,   18 x 14 cm,

339   Amsterdams dam-praetje, van wat outs en
      wat nieuws. En wat vreemts. Tot
      Amsterdam, By Ian van Soest, 1649.
      [39] p.   20 1/2 cm.

340   Amsterdams tafel-praetje, van wat goets
      en wat quaets en wat noodichs. Gouda,
      I. Cornelisz, 1649.
      [31] p.   20 x 15 cm.

341   The amulet: a tale of Spanish California.
      London, Longmans, Green, and co.,
      1865.
      ix, 273, [1] p.   17 1/2 cm.

342   The Analectic magazine ... Comprising
      original reviews, biography, analytical

abstracts of new publications, trans-
lations from French journals, and selections from the most esteemed British reviews. v. 1-14, 1813-19; new
ser., v. 1-2,1820. Philadelphia, M.
Thomas [etc.] 1813-20.
   16 v. illus., plates (part col.)
ports., plans, facsim.   21 1/2 - 22
1/2 cm.

343   Anania, Giovanni Lorenzo d'.
         L'vniversale fabrica del mondo,
      overo Cosmografia dell'ecc. Gio.
      Lorenzo d'Anania, diuisa in quattro
      trattati ... Di nuouo ornata con le
      figure delle quattro parti del mondo
      in rame: et dal medesimo auttore con
      infinite aggiuntioni per ogni parte
      dell'opera ampliata ... Venetia,
      Presso il Muschio: ad instanza di A.
      San Vito di Napoli, 1582.
         28 p. 1., 402 p.   4 double maps.
      23 cm.

344   Anburey, Thomas.
         Anburey's reisen im inneren Amerika.
      Aus dem englischen übersetzt van
      Georg Forster. [Berlin, Vossische
      buchhandlung, 1792]
         ix, [1], 444 p. pl., fold. map,
      fold. plan.   21 cm.

345   [Anburey, Thomas]
         Travels through the interior parts
      of America. In a series of letters.
      By an officer ... London, Printed
      for W. Lane, 1789.
         2 v. front. (fold. map) 5 pl.
      (part fold.) fold. plan, 8 facsim,
      on 1 1.   21 cm.

346   [Anburey, Thomas]
         Travels through the interior parts
      of America; in a series of letters.
      By an officer. A new ed. ... London,
      Printed for W. Lane, 1791.

2 v. plates (part fold.) fold.
map, fold. plan. 22 cm.

347 [Anburey, Thomas]
Voyages dans les parties intér-
ieures de l'Amérique, pendant le
cours de la derniere guerre, par un
officier de l'armée royale. Tr. de
l'anglois ... Paris, Briand, 1790.
2 v. 19 cm.

348 Anderde discovrs. by forma van messieve.
Daer in kortelijck ende grondich
verthoondt wort. de nootwendicheyt
der Oost ende West Indische navigatie
... Worden daerom alle getrouwe
patriotten, des vaderlants ...
vermaendt, om tot dese, nu nieuwe
geoctroyeerde West-Indiaensche compagnie mildclijck te contribueren ...
[Amsterdam?] 1622.
24 p. 18 1/2 cm.

349 Andover theological seminary. *Library*.
Catalogue of the library belonging
to the theological institution in
Andover. Andover, Printed by Flagg
and Gould, 1819.
161 p. 24 cm.

350 Andover theological seminary. *Library*.
Catalogue of the library of the
Theol. seminary in Andover, Mass. By
Oliver A. Taylor, M.A. Andover, Print-
ed by Gould & Newman, 1838.
viii, [9]-531 p. 23 1/2 cm.

351 André, John, 1751-1780.
The cow chace, a poem in three
cantos. By Major John André ...
Albany, N.Y., J. Munsell, 1866.
69 p. fold. map. 22 1/2 cm.

352 André, John, 1751-1780.
The cow chase: an heroick poem,
in three cantos. Written at New

York, 1780, by the late Major André,
with explanatory notes, by the editor
... London, J. Fielding, 1781.
    1 p. l., [5]-32 p.   26 cm.

353   André, John, 1751-1780, *defendant*.
        Minutes of a court of inquiry, upon
    the case of Major John André, with
    accompanying documents, published in
    1780 by order of Congress. With an
    additional appendix containing copies
    of the papers found upon Major André
    when arrested, and other documents re-
    lating to the subject. Albany, J.
    Munsell, 1865.
        iv. 86 p. front. (port.)   22 cm.

354   André, John, 1751-1780, *defendant*.
        Proceedings of a board of general
    officers, held by order of His Excel-
    lency Gen. Washington, commander in
    chief of the army of the United States
    of America. Respecting Major John
    André, adjutant general of the Brit-
    ish army. September 29, 1780. Phila-
    delphia, Printed by F. Bailey, 1780.
        1 p. l., 21 p.   20 cm.

355   Andreana. Containing the trial, execu-
    tion and various matter connected
    with the history of Major John André,
    adjutant general of the British army
    in America, A.D. 1780. Philadelphia,
    H.W. Smith, 1865.
        3 p. l., [3]-67, [4] p. 9 port.,
    3 facsim. (1 fold.)   31 1/2 cm.

356   Andrews, Charles.
        The prisoners' memoirs, or, Dartmoor
    prison; containing a complete and
    impartial history of the entire cap-
    tivity of the Americans in England,
    from the commencement of the late war
    between the United States and Great
    Britain, until all prisoners were re-
    leased by the treaty of Ghent. Also,

a particular detail of all occurrences
relative to that horrid massacre at
Dartmoor, on the fatal evening of the
6th of April, 1815. The whole carefully comp. from the journal of Charles
Andrews, a prisoner in England, from
the commencement of the war, until
the release of all the prisoners ...
New York, Printed for the author, 1815.
vii, [9]-283 p. fold. front. 19
cm.

357 Andrews, Charles C.
The history of the New-York African
free-schools, from their establishment in 1787, to the present time;
embracing a period of more than forty
years: also a brief account of the
successful labors, of the New-York
manumission society: with an appendix ... By Charles C. Andrews ...
New York, Printed by M. Day, 1830.
2 p. l., [7]-148 p. front. 18
1/2 cm.

358 [Andrews, Charles Wesley] 1807-1875.
An apology. The Protestant Episcopal society for the promotion of evangelical knowledge: its origin, constitution, tendencies and work; submitted to the impartial judgment of
the members of the Protestant Episcopal church. New York. Printed by
J.A. Gray, 1854.
44 p. 21 1/2 cm.

359 Andrews, Joseph.
Journey from Buenos Ayres, through
the provinces of Cordova, Tucuman,
and Salta, to Potosi, thence by the
deserts of Caranja to Arica, and
subsequently to Santiago de Chili and
Coquimbo, undertaken on behalf of the
Chilian and Peruvian mining association, in the years 1825-26. By Captain Andrews ... London, J. Murray,

1827.
2 v.   19 1/2 cm.

360   Andrews, Rufus F.
Letter of Rufus F. Andrews, lately
surveyor of the port of New York, to
Thurlow Weed ...   New York, 1864.
14 p.   19 cm.

361   Andrews, Sidney.
The South since the war, as shown
by fourteen weeks of travel and observation in Georgia and the Carolinas.
By Sidney Andrews.   Boston, Ticknor
and Fields, 1866.
viii, 400 p.   18 cm.

362   Andrews, W   S.
Andrews' illustrations of the West
Indies ...   London, Day and son [1861]
2 v. in 1.   plates (part col.)
27 1/2 x 37 1/2 cm.

363   Andros, Thomas, 1759-1845.
The grand era of ruin to nations
from foreign influence.   A discourse,
delivered before the Congregational
society in Berkley, Nov. 26, 1812 ...
By Thomas Andros, A.M.   Boston, S.T.
Armstrong, 1812.
18 p.   24 cm.

364   Andros, Thomas, 1759-1845.
The old Jersey captive: or, A narrative of the captivity of Thomas Andros ... on board the old Jersey prison ship at New York, 1781.   In a series of letters to a friend ...   Boston, W. Peirce, 1833.
80 p.   14 1/2 cm.

365   Andueza, José María de.
Isla de Cuba, pintoresca, histórica
política, literaria, mercantil é
industrial.   Recuerdos, apuntes,
impresiones de dos épocas.   Por don

J.M. de Andueza.   Ed. ilustrada.
Madrid, Boix, 1841.
    vii, 182 p., 1 l.   plates.   26
1/2 cm.

366   Anecdotes   secrètes sur la révolution
      du 18 fructidor; et nouveaux mémoires
      des déportés à la Guiane, écrits par
      eux-mêmes: contenant des lettres
      du général Murinais, de Barthélemy,
      de Tronçon Du Coudray, de Laffond
      Ladebat, de de La Rue, &c.   Relation
      des événemens qui suivirent à la
      Guiane l'évasion de Pichegru, Ramel,
      &c.--Tableau des prisons de Rochefort,
      par Richer-Sérisy.--Narration de la
      captivité et de l'évasion de Sir
      Sidney Smith de la prison du Temple.--
      Mémoire de Barbé Marbois, &c., &c.
      Faisant suite au Journal de général
      Ramel.   2. éd., rev., cor. et augm.
      Paris, Giguet et co; Londres, J.
      Wright [etc.] 1799.
         2 p. 1., 215 p.   21 cm.

367   Anent the North American continent ...
      London, W. Ridgway, 1864.
         15 [1] p.   21 cm.

368   Anent the United States and Confederate
      States of North America ...   London,
      J. Ridgway, 1862.
         7 p.   21 1/2 cm.

369   Angelis, Pedro de.
         Biografía del Señor general Arenales
      y juicio sobre la Memoria histórica
      de su segunda campaña a la Sierra del
      Perú en 1821 ...   Por Pedro de Angelis.
      Buenos-Aires, Imprenta de la independen-
      cia, 1832.
         17 p.   21 1/2 cm.

370   Angelis, Pedro de, 1784-1859.
         Coleccion de obras y documentos
      relativos a la historia antigua y

moderna de las provincias del Rio de
la Plata. Ilustrados con notas y
disertaciones por Pedro de Angelis.
Buenos-Aires, Imprenta del estado,
1836-37.
　6 v. mounted pl., tables (part
fold.) diagrs. 31 cm.

371　　Angelis, Pedro de, 1784-1859.
　　　Historical sketch of Pepys' island
in the south Pacific [*i.e.* Atlantic]
ocean: from the work on the Rio de
la Plata, by P. de Angelis. Buenos-
Aires, 1842.
　9, xvii p. 1 pl. 23 cm.

372　　Angelis, Pedro de.
　　　Memoria histórica sobre los dere-
chos de soberania y dominio de la
Confederación Argentina a la parte
austral del continente americano,
comprendida entre las costas del
oceano Atlantico y la Gran Cordillera
de los Andes, desde la boca del Rio
de la Plata hasta el cabo de Hornos,
inclusa la isla de Los Estados, la
Tierra del Fuego, y el estrecho de
Magallanes en toda su extensión. Por
D. Pedro de Angelis ... Buenos-Aires,
1852.
　54, lviii p. 25 1/2 cm.

373　　Anghiera, Pietro Martire d', 1455-1526.
　　　De nouo orbe, or The historie of
the West Indies, contayning the actes
and aduentures of the Spanyardes,
which haue conquered and peopled those
countries, inriched with varietie of
pleasant relation of the manners, ceremonies, lawes, gouernments, and
warres of the Indians. Comprised in
eight decades. Written by Peter Martyr a Millanoise of Angleria ...
Whereof threè, haue beene formerly
translated into English, by R. Eden,
whereunto the other fiue, are newly

added by ... M. Lok ... London,
Printed for Thomas Adams, 1612.
6 p. 1., 318 numb. 1.   20 cm.

374   Anghiera, Pietro Martire d', 1455-1526.
De nvper ‖ svb D. Carolo reper-
‖ tis insulis, simulqz, incolarum ‖
moribus, R. Petri Marty- ‖ ris,
enchiridion, Domi- ‖ næ Margaritæ,
Diui ‖ Max. Caes. filiæ ‖ dicatum.
‖ Basileae, anno ‖ M.D.XXI.
43 p.   20 1/2 cm.

375   Anghiera, Pietro Martire d', 1455-1526.
The Decades of the newe worlde or
west India ... Wrytten in the Latine
tounge by Peter Martyr of Angleria,
and translated into Englysshe by
Rycharde Eden.
(*In* Eden, Richard, ed. The Decades
of the newe worlde or west India ...
Londini, 1555.   19 cm.)

376   Anghiera, Pietro Martire d', 1455-1526.
Petri Martyris ab Angleria,
Mediolanen. oratoris clarissimi.
Fernandi & Helisabeth Hispaniarum
quondam regum à consilijs, de rebus
oceanicis & obre nouo decades tres:
quibus quicquid de inuentis nuper
terris traditum, nouarum rerum
cupidum lectorem retinere possit,
copiose, fideliter, cruditeqz, docetur.
Eivsdem praeterea Legationis baby-
lonicae libri tres ... Basileae,
apud Ioannem Bebelium, M.D.XXXIII.
12 p. 1., 92 numb. 1.   30 1/2 cm.

377   Angier, Joseph.
A eulogy, on the occasion of the
death of William Henry Harrison, late
president of the United States: de-
livered at Milton, May 14, 1841.
By Joseph Angier, minister of the
First parish in Milton. Boston, W.H.S.
Jordan, 1841.

32 p.   23 1/2 cm.

378   Anglo-Californian, *pseud.*
The national crisis. A letter to
the Hon. Milton S. Latham, senator
from California ... by Anglo-Californian ... San Francisco, Towne & Bacon,
printers, 1861.
cover-title, 21 p.   23 cm.

379   Annaes maritimos e coloniaes. Publica-
ção mensal redigida sob a direcção
da Associação maritima e colonial.
[1.]-- ser.; nov. 1840- Lisboa,
Imprensa nacional, 1840--
v. plates, maps, plans, tab.   21
cm.

380   The annals of administration. Containing the genuine history of Georgiana
the queen-mother, and Prince Coloninus
her son. A biographical fragment.
Written about the year 1575. Inscribed, by the proprietor of the authentic
papers, to Edmund Burke, esq. London,
Printed for J. Bew, MDCCLXXV.
viii, 27 p.   21 1/2 cm.

381   Anneke, Fritz.
Der zweite freiheitskampf der
Vereinigten Staaten von Amerika. Von
Fritz Anneke ... Erster band. Mit
drei uebersichtskärtchen. Frankfurt
am Main, J.D. Sauerländer, 1861.
viii, [iii]-vii, 368 p.   3 fold.
maps.   17 1/2 cm.

382   Anspach, Frederick Rinehart, 1815-1867.
A discourse pronounced on Sabrath
[!] evening, July 4, 1852, in the
Lutheran church of Hagerstown, on the
death of Henry Clay, by the Rev. F.R.
Anspach, A.M. Hagerstown, Printed
by Mittag & Sneary, 1852.
12 p.   22 1/2 cm.

383   Anspach, Lewis Amadeus.
            Geschichte und beschreibung
        von Newfoundland und der küste =
        Labrador, von C. [!] A. Anspach. Aus
        dem englischen übersetzt. Mit zwei
        charten. Weimar, Im verlage des Gr.
        H.S. priv. landes-industrie-comptoirs,
        1822.
            x, 272 p. fold. maps.   21 cm.

384   Anspach, Lewis Amadeus.
            A history of the island of Newfound-
        land: containing a description of
        the island, the Banks, the fisheries
        and trade of Newfoundland and the
        coast of Labrador. London, 1819.
            xxviii, 512 p. 2 fold. maps.   24
        cm.

385   Anspach, Lewis Amadeus.
            A summary of the laws of commerce
        and navigation, adapted to the pres-
        ent state, government, and trade of
        the island of Newfoundland. By the
        Rev. Lewis Amadeus Anspach ... Lon-
        don, Printed for the author, by Heney
        and Haddon, 1809.
            2 p. l., xv, [17]-140 p.   22 1/2
        cm.

386   Ansted, David Thomas, 1814-1880.
            The gold-seeker's manual; being a
        practical and instructive guide to
        all persons emigrating to the newly-
        discovered gold regions of California.
        By David T. Ansted ... New-York, D.
        Appleton & company; [etc., etc.]
        1849.
            96 p.   18 cm.

387   Ansted, David Thomas, 1814-1880.
            Scenery, science and art; being
        extracts from the note-book of a
        geologist and mining engineer. By
        Professor D.T. Ansted ... London,
        J. Van Voorst, 1854.

viii, 323 p. illus., 4 col. pl.
(incl. front.)   22 cm.

388   Anthoine de Saint-Joseph, Fortuné, 1794-
      1853.
          Concordance entre les codes civils
      étrangers et le Code Napoléon. 2.
      éd., entièrement refondue et augm.
      de la concordance de la législation
      civile de plus de quarante pays, par
      m. Anthoine de Saint-Joseph ...
      Ouvrage terminé et pub. par m. A. de
      Saint-Joseph son fils ... Paris,
      Cotillon, 1856.
          4 v.   24 cm.

389   Anthon, George Christian, 1820-1877.
          Narrative and documents connected
      with the displacement of the profes-
      sor of the Greek language and litera-
      ture in the University of the city of
      New York, April 2d, 1851; by George
      C. Anthon, A.M. New York, J.R. Win-
      ser, printer, 1851.
          72 p.   22 1/2 cm.

390   Anthon, Henry, 1795-1861.
          Parish annals. A sermon giving
      historical notices of St. Mark's
      church in the Bowery, N.Y., (from
      A.D. 1795 to A.D. 1845) Delivered
      in said church, May 4, 1845. By
      Henry Anthon ... Published by the
      request of the vestry. New-York,
      Stanford and Swords, 1845.
          4 p. l., [5]-58 p. 1 illus.   22
      1/2 cm.

391   Anthon, Henry, 1795-1861.
          The subject and spirit of the Chris-
      tian minister. A sermon, preached
      by request in St. Peter's church,
      twentieth-street, New-York, on Palm
      Sunday, April 1st, 1849. Being the
      Sunday after the decease of the Rev.
      Hugh Smith, D.D. ... By Henry

Anthon ... New-York, Stanford &
Swords, 1849.
22 p.   22 1/2 cm.

392   Anthon, John, 1784-1863.
An oration delivered before the
Washington benevolent society and
the Hamilton society in the city of
New-York, on the fourth of July, 1812.
By John Anthon, esq. Published by
the Washington benevolent society. New-
York: Printed by Largin & Thompson,
no. 5 Burling-slip. 1812.
22 p.   23 cm.

393   Anthony, Elliott, 1827-1898.
Is a constitutional convention a
legislature? Speech of Hon. Elliott
Anthony, delegate from (Chicago),
Cook Co., delivered in the Constitutional convention of Illinois, February 12, 1862 ... [Springfield,
Ill., 1862]
13 p.   21 cm.

394   Anticipation continued. Containing the
substance of the speech intended to
be delivered from the t----------e
to both h-----s of P--r---m---t, on
the opening of the ensuing session.
To which is added, a sketch of the
debate which will take place in the
H----e of l----ds on the motion for an
address and amendment ... London,
Printed for the editor, and sold by
J. Bew, 1779.
viii, [9]-57 p.   21 1/2 cm.

395   Anticipation of marginal notes on the
declaration of government of the
9th of January, 1813. In the American National intelligencer ... London, Printed by A.J. Valpy, 1813.
iv, 31 p.   22 1/2 cm.

396   Antidote to the merino-mania now

progressing through the United States:
or, The value of the merino breed,
placed by observation and experience,
upon a proper basis ... Printed and
sold by J. & A.Y. Humphreys, 'Change-
walk, corner of Second and Walnut-
streets. Philadelphia. 1810.
iv, [5]-52 p.   22 cm.

397   Antigua and the Antiguans: a full account of the colony and its inhabitants from the time of the Caribs to
the present day, interspersed with
anecdotes and legands. Also, an impartial view of slavery and the free
labour systems; the statistics of the
island, and biographical notices of
the principal families ... London,
Saunders and Otley, 1844.
2 v.   21 x 12 1/2 cm.

398   Antoine, Antoine, *de Saint-Gervais,* 1776-
1836.
Histoire des émigrés français,
depuis 1789, jusqu'en 1828. Par A.
Antoine (de Saint-Gervais) ... Paris,
L.F. Hivert, 1828.
3 v.   21 cm.

399   Antonio, Nicolás, 1617-1684.
Bibliotheca hispana nova; sive,
Hispanorum scriptorum qui ab anno
MD. ad MDCLXXXIV. floruere notitia.
Auctore d. Nicolao Antonio, Hispalen-
si ... nunc primum prodit, recog-
nita emendata aucta ab ipso auctore.
[Tomus 1.-2.] Matriti, J. de Ibarra,
1783-88.
2 v.   36 cm.

400   Antonio, Nicolás, 1617-1684.
Bibliotheca hispana vetus, sive,
Hispani scriptores qui ab Octaviani
Augusti aevo ad annum Christi M.D.
floruerunt. Auctore d. Nicolao
Antonio Hispalensi ... Curante

Francisco Perezio Bayerio qui et
prologum, & auctoris vitae epitomen,
& notulas adiecit ... Matriti, apud
viduam et heredes D.J. Ibarrae, 1788.
2 v. front., port., fold. facsim.
36 cm.

401 [Antrobus, Benjamin] *d.* 1715.
Some buds and blossoms of piety,
also, some fruit of the spirit of love,
which directs to the Divine wisdom.
Being a collection of several papers,
written by a young man, some of them
in the time of his apprenticeship,
some of them at several times since,
and the latter part of them in his
late confinement, by a writ De excom-
municato capiendo ... To which sub-
joyned is a Tripple plea, touching
law, physick and divinitie, formerly
printed and subscribed T.C. Also,
some Lines written by J.C. London,
Printed and sold by Andrew Sowle,
1684.
3 p. 1., 76 (*i.e.* 72) p. 19 1/2
cm.

402 Antúnez y Acevedo, Rafael.
Memorias históricas sobre la
legislación, y gobierno del comercio
de los españoles con sus colonias en
las Indias occidentales, recopiladas
por el sr. d. Rafael Antúnez y Acevedo
... Madrid, En la imprenta de Sancha,
M.DCC.XCVII.
2 p. 1., xv, 1 , 330 p., 1 1.,
cv p. 21 cm.

403 Apes, William, *b.* 1798.
Eulogy on King Philip, as pronounced at the Odeon, in Federal street,
Boston, by the Rev. William Apes,
an Indian ... Boston, The author,
1836.
60 p. incl. front. 18 cm.

404   Apes, William, *b*. 1798.
        Indian nullification of the uncon-
        stitutional laws of Massachusetts,
        relative to the Marshpee tribe: or,
        The pretended riot explained. By Wil-
        liam Apes, an Indian and preacher of
        the gospel. Boston, Press of J.
        Howe, 1835.
        168 p. incl. front.   17 1/2 cm.

405   Apes, William, *b*. 1798.
        A son of the forest. The experi-
        ence of William Apes, a native of the
        forest. Comprising a notice of the
        Pequod tribe of Indians. Written by
        himself. New-York. The author,
        1829.
        216 p.   14 1/2 cm.

406   Apianus, Petrus, 1495-1552.
        Cosmographicus liber Petri Apiani
        mathematici studiose collectus.
        [Landshutae, impensis P. Apiani,
        1524]
        4 p. l., 104, [6] p.   illus.,
        tables, diagrs.   21 x 15 1/2 cm.

407   Apianus, Petrus, 1495-1552.
        Cosmographicvs liber Petri Apiani
        mathematici, iam denuo integritati
        restitutus per Gemmam Phrysium.
        Item eiusdem Gemmae Phrysij Libellus
        de locorum describendorum ratione,
        & de eorum distantijs inueniendis,
        nunq̃ ante hac visus. Vaeneunt
        [Antuerpiae] in Pingui gallina per
        Arnoldum Birckman [1533]
        66 numb. l.   illus., tables,
        diagrs.   20 1/2 x 15 1/2 cm.

408   Apollonius, Levinus, *16th cent.*
        Dritte theil Der Newen welt. Des
        peruuischen königreichs, welches
        das mechtigste vnd fruchtbareste
        est, vnder allen andern landtschafften
        oder prouintzen des indianischen

nidergängischen reichs: wie vnd
durch welche personen dasselbig zum
ersten erfunden, vnd was sich von
der ersten erfindung an, biss auff
vnsere jetzige zeit, für schröckliche
krieg vnd blutuergiessungen, eyns
theils gegen den peruuischen einwohnern, andertheils zwischen den spanis-
chen landtpflägern vnd vögten, allein
von wegen ehrgeytzes vnd eygennutzes
verloffen vnd zugetragen haben. Auch
von derselbige völckern sitten, regiment, aberglauben, ceremonien,
gottesdienst, gebrauch in essen vnd
trincken, handthierungen, gewerb-
schafften vnd vnerschöpfflichen
goldtgruben vnd reichthumben, so in
diesem königreich gefunden werden.
Item, von der Frantzosen schiffarth
in die landtschafft Floridam, vnd
ihrer schröcklichen niderlag die sie
von den Spaniern im jar M.D.I.XV.
darinn erlitten. Mit angehenckter
supplication an könig Carol den IX.
in Franckreich, der erschlagnen
Frantzosen witwen, waysen, verwandten
vnd einwohnern in der landtschafft
Florida, darinn sie ihr vnschuld gegen
den Spaniern vor Königlicher May,
gründtlich erkläret vnd geoffenbaret.
Alles durch glaubwürdige personen,
vnd fürnemblich durch den hochber-
hümbten geschichtschreiber Levinvm
Apollonivm Gandobrvganum, in latein-
ischer sprach wahrhafftig beschrieben, vnd zum theil selbs persönlich
erfahren. Erst jetz aber auss dem
latein ... mit höchstem fleiss vnd
mühe verteutschet, durch Nicolaum
Höniger ... Getruckt zu Basel.
[Colophon: Getruckt, zu Basel, durch
Sebastian Henricpetri, im jar ...
M.D.LXXXIII ...]
     6 p. l., ccccvi, [2] p. incl.
double plan. 33 1/2 cm.

409   An apology for the times: a poem, ad-
        dressed to the King ... London, J.F.
        and C. Rivington; [etc., etc.] 1778.
          2 p. l., 72 p.   27 cm.

410   An appeal to the conservative men of all
        parties. The presidential question.
        An important question--shall the sub-
        ject of slavery forever prevent all
        useful legislation, or shall it be
        settled by the doctrine of non-inter-
        vention? ... The state debt. Profli-
        gate legislation ... [n.p., 1860]
          16 p.   23 1/2 cm.

411   An appeal to the government and Congress
        of the United States, against the
        depredations committed by American
        privateers, on the commerce of nations
        at peace with us. By an American
        citizen ... New York, Printed for
        the booksellers, 1819.
          viii, [9]-100 p.   22 1/2 cm.

412   An appeal to the people of the North.
        [Louisville, Ky., Hanna & co.,
        printers? 1861]
          16 p.   22 cm.

413   Appendix to a late Essay, on the rights
        and duties of nations relative to
        fugitives, &c., being a key to uni-
        versal demonstration: discovered
        and illustrated in a "supplementary"
        argument. By "our writers ..."
        56th American ed., enl. and carefully
        rev. and cor. from the last London
        ed. To which is added, The embargo
        [on common sense] "taken off." By
        us ... Boston, Printed by D. Car-
        lisle, 1808.
          32 p.   21 cm.

414   Appleton, Jesse, 1772-1819.
          Addresses by Rev. Jesse Appleton,
        D.D., late president of Bowdoin

college. Delivered at the annual
commencements, from 1808 to 1818;
with a sketch of his character. Brunswick [Me.] Joseph Griffin, printer,
1820.
     xxxi, 176 p.   20 1/2 cm.

415   Appleton, Jesse, 1772-1819.
      The immensity of God. A sermon
delivered to the Congregational society in Hampton, November 14, 1797;
at the dedication of their new house,
for public worship. By Jesse Appleton, A.M., minister of the Congregational church in Hampton ... Newburyport: Printed by Edmund M. Blunt--
1797.
     32 p.   21 cm.

416   Appleton, Jesse, 1772-1819.
      A sermon, delivered at Brunswick,
April 13, 1815, appointed as a day
of national thanksgiving, by the
President of the United States, on account of the peace recently established between this country and Great
Britain, by Jesse Appleton ... Hallowell [Me.] Printed by E. Goodale,
1815.
     24 p.   21 cm.

417   Appleton, Jesse, 1772-1819.
      A sermon preached at Boston, at
the annual election, May 25, 1814. Before His Excellency Caleb Strong, esq.,
governor, His Honor William Phillips,
esq., lieutenant governor, the honorable Council, and the legislature of
Massachusetts. By Jesse Appleton,
D.D., president of Bowdoin college.
Boston: Printed by Russell, Cutler
and co. for Benjamin Russell ...
printer to the state, 1814.
     2 p. 1., [3]-29 p.   24 cm.

418   Appleton, William Sumner, 1840-1903.

Some descendants of William Adams
of Ipswich, Mass. By W.A. Appleton.
Boston, D. Clapp & son, 1881.
1 p. l., 8 p., 1 l. 25 cm.

419 Apthorp, East, 1732 *or* 3-1816.
Considerations on the institution
and conduct of the Society for the
propagation of the gospel in foreign
parts, by East Apthorp, M.A., missionary at Cambridge ... Boston,
New-England: Printed by Green &
Russell, in Queen-street, and Thomas
& John Fleet, in Cornhill, MDCCLXIII.
24 p. 22 1/2 cm.

420 Arago, Jacques Étienne Victor, 1790-
1855.
Deux océans, par M. Jacques Arago
... Paris, Librairie théatrale,
1854.
2 v. 18 1/2 cm.

421 Arago, Jacques Étienne Victor, 1790-
1855.
Narrative of a voyage round the
world, in the Uranie and Physicienne
corvettes, commanded by Captain Freycinet, during the years 1817, 1818,
1819, and 1820; on a scientific expe-
edition undertaken by order of the
French government. In a series of
letters to a friend, by J. Arago
... To which is prefixed, the report made to the Academy of sciences,
on the general results of the expedition. London, Treuttel & Wurtz,
Treuttel, jun. & Richter, 1823.
vi p., 1 l., xxvii, 3 p., 1 l.,
297, 3 p. incl. front. (map)
tables. plates. 28 x 21 1/2 cm.

422 Arago, Jacques Étienne Victor, 1790-
1855.
Promenade autour du monde pendant
les années 1817, 1818, 1819 et 1820,

sur les corvettes du roi l'Uranie et
la Physicienne, commandées par M.
Freycinet, par J⁵. Arago, dessinateur
de l'expédition ... Paris, Leblanc,
1822.
2 v. tables. 20 1/2 cm.

423 Arago, Jacques Étienne Victor, 1790-
1855.
Souvenirs d'un aveugle. Voyage
autour du monde par m. J. Arago,
ouvrage enrichi de soixante dessins
et de notes scientifiques ... Paris,
Hortet et Ozanne, 1839-40.
5 v. fronts. (v. 1, 3-4) 73 pl.
(incl. ports.) 23 1/2 cm.

424 [Arango y Núñez del Castillo, José de]
1765-1851.
Nadie se asuste por la segunda
y ultima esplicación mia sorbe [!]
la Independencia de la isla de Cuba.
Habana, Impr. fraternal de los Diaz
de Castro, 1821.
42 p. 19 cm.

425 Araujo e Silva, Domingos de, 1834--
Diccionario historico e geographico
da provincia de S. Pedro ou Rio
Grande do Sul contendo a historia e
a descripção da provincia em relação
aos tres reinos da natureza ... por
Domingos de Araujo e Silva ... Rio
de Janeiro, E. & H. Laemmert, 1865.
vii, 192 p. 22 cm.

426 Archdale, John, 1642?-1717.
A new description of that fertile
and pleasant province of Carolina:
with a brief account of its discovery and settling, and the government
thereof to this time ... By John
Archdale ... London--Printed in
1707.
(In Carroll, B.R. Historical
collections of South Carolina ...

New-York, 1836.   22 cm. v. 2, p.
[85]-120)

427   Archenholz, Johann Wilhelm von, 1743-
            1812.
            Histoire de flibustiers, tr. de
        l'allemand de Mr. J.W. d'Archenholtz;
        avec un avant-propos et quelques
        notes du traducteur. Paris, Henrichs,
        1804.
            xvi, 355 p.   21 cm.

428   Archenholz, Johann Wilhelm von, 1743-
            1812.
            The history of the pirates, free-
        booters, or buccaneers of America.
        Tr. from the German of J.M. [!] von
        Archenholtz, by George Mason ... Lon-
        don, Printed for J. Stratford, and T.
        and R. Hughes, 1807.
            xiv, 240 p.   19 cm.

429   Archer, Armstrong.
            A compendium of slavery, as it
        exists in the present day in the
        United States of America. To which
        is prefixed, a brief view of the
        author's descent from an African king
        on one side, and from the celebrated
        Indian chief Powhattan on the other;
        in which he refers to the principal
        transactions and negotiations between
        this noble chief and the English
        colony under the famous Captain Smith,
        on the coast of Virginia, in the year
        1608, as well as to his still more
        illustrious daughter, the Princess
        Pocahontas, who excited so much inter-
        est in England. By Armstrong Archer.
        London, The author. 1844.
            iv. 68 p.   front.   17 cm.

430   Archer, William Segar, 1789-1855.
            Speech of Mr. Archer, of Virginia,
        on the tariff bill, delivered in the
        House of representatives of the United

States, April 26, 1820. [Washington, 1820.]
21 p.   18 cm.

431   Archer, William Segar, 1789-1855.
Speech of Mr. Archer, on the proposition to amend the Constitution of the United States, respecting the election of president and vice president. Delivered in the House of representatives, February 20, 1826. [Washington, 1826]
39 p.   18 cm.

432   ... Archivo americano y espiritu de la prensa del mundo. Buenos Aires, Impr. de la Independencia, 18.
v.   23 1/2 - 32 1/2 cm.

433   Arctic miscellanies. A souvenir of the late polar search. By the officers and seamen of the expedition. 2d ed. London, Colburn and co., 1852.
2 p. l., [vii]-xxiv, 347, [1] p. col. front., illus.   22 cm.

434   Arctic rewards and their claimants. London, T. Hatchard, 1856.
31 p.   21 1/2 cm.

435   Arcturus, a journal of books and opinion ...   v. 1-3; Dec. 1840 - May 1842. New York, B.G. Trevett [etc.] 1841-42.
3 v.   pl., port.   22 1/2 cm.

436   Arenales, José Ildefonso Alvarez de, 1798-1862.
Memoria histórica sobre las operaciones e incidencias de la división libertadora, a las órdenes del Gen. D. Juan Antonio Alvarez de Arenales, en su segunda campaña a la sierra del Peru, en 1821. Por José Arenales ... Buenos-Ayres, Imprenta de la Gaceta mercantil, 1832.

3 p. l., [iii]-xv, [2], 247, [4]
p., 1 l. front. (port.) 2 fold.
maps, fold. tab. 20 cm.

437 Arenales, José Ildefonso Alvarez de,
1798-1862.
Noticias históricas y descriptivas
sobre el gran pais del Chaco y rio
Bermejo; con observaciones relativas
á un plan de navegación y colonización
que se propone. Por José Arenales
... Buenos Aires, Impreso en la
impr. de Hallet y ca., 1833.
1 p. l., v, 421 p., 1 l. fold.
map. 20 1/2 cm.

438 Arey, Henry W.
The Girard college and its founder: containing the biography of Mr.
Girard, the history of the institution, its organization and plan of
discipline, with the course of education, forms of admission of pupils,
description of the buildings, &c.
&c., and the will of Mr. Girard. By
Henry W. Arey ... Philadelphia, C.
Sherman, printer, 1852.
85 p., 1 l. front. (port.) pl.
19 1/2 cm.

439 Arfwedson, Carl David, 1806-1881.
De colonia Nova Svecia in Americam
borealem deducta historiola ...
Upsaliae, excudebant Regiae aca-
demiae typographi [1825]
2 p. l., 34 p. fold. map. 24 1/2
x 20 1/2 cm.

440 Arfwedson, Carl David, 1806-1881.
Förenta Staterna och Canada, ären
1832, 1833 och 1834, af C.D. Arfwedson ... Stockholm, L.J. Hjerta, 1835.
2 v. 15 cm.

441 Arfwedson, Carl David, 1806-1881.
The United States and Canada, in

1832, 1833, and 1834. By C.D.
Arfwedson ... London, R. Bentley,
1834.
2 v. fronts. 22 cm.

442 Arlach, H   de T   d'.
Souvenirs de l'Amérique Centrale,
par H. de T. d'Arlach ... Paris,
Charpentier, 1850.
168 p. 23 cm.

443 Armistead, Wilson, 1819?-1868.
... 'A cloud of witnesses' against
slavery and oppression. Containing
the acts, opinions, and sentiments of
individuals and societies in all ages.
Selected from various sources and for
the most part chronologically arranged, by Wilson Armistead ... London,
W. Tweedie [etc] 1853.
154 p. 17 1/2 cm.

444 Armistead, Wilson, 1819?-1868.
Memoirs of James Logan; a distinguished scholar and Christian legis-
lator; founder of the Loganian library at Philadelphia; secretary of the
province of Pennsylvania; chief justice ... including several of his letters and those of his correspondents,
many of which are now first printed
from the original mss. collated and
arranged for the purpose; by Wilson
Armistead ... London, C. Gilpin,
1851.
vi, [7]-192 p. front. (port.) pl.
19 cm.

445 Armistead, Wilson, 1819?-1868.
A tribute for the Negro; being a
vindication of the moral, intellec-
tual, and religious capabilities of
the coloured portion of mankind;
with particular reference to the
African race. Illustrated by numerous biographical sketches, facts,

anecdotes, etc. ... By Wilson Armistead. Manchester, W. Irwin; American agent, W. Harned, New York; [etc., etc.] 1848.
xxxv, 564 p. front., plates, ports., facsims. 23 1/2 cm.

446 Armitage, John, 1807-1856.
The history of Brazil, from the period of the arrival of the Braganza family in 1808, to the abdication of Don Pedro the Frist in 1831. Comp. from state documents and other original sources. Forming a continuation to Southey's history of that country. By John Armitage, esq. ... London, Smith, Elder and co., 1836.
2 v. fronts. (ports) 22 cm.

447 Armitage, Thomas, 1819-1896.
The past, present, and future of the United States. A discourse, delivered by Rev. Thomas Armitage, pastor of the Fifth avenue Baptist church, on Thanksgiving day, Nov. 27, and repeated by request, December 18, 1862. New York, T. Holman, 1862.
31 p. 23 cm.

448 [Armroyd, George]
A connected view of the whole internal navigation of the United States; natural and artificial, present and prospective: corrected and improved from the edition of 1826, and much enlarged, from authentic materials, down to the present time. With a sheet map, and numerous engraved profiles ... The map ... is projected, on a reduced scale, from Tanner's ... map of the United States ... By a citizen of the United States. Philadelphia, Pub. by the author, printed by Lydia R. Bailey, 1830.
1 p. 1., viii, [9]-617 p. front.

(fold. map) fold. diagrs. 23 1/2
cm.

449   Armstrong, *Sir* Alexander, 1818-1899.
        A personal narrative of the dis-
      covery of the northwest passage;
      with numerous incidents of travel
      and adventure during nearly five
      years' continuous service in the
      Arctic regions while in search of
      the expedition under Sir John Frank-
      lin. By Alex. Armstrong ... late
      surgeon and naturalist of H.M.S.
      'Investigator.' London, Hurst and
      Blackett, 1857.
        xxii, [2], 616 p. col. front.,
      fold. map.   22 cm.

450   Armstrong, Edward.
        An address, delivered at Chester,
      before the Historical society of
      Pennsylvania, on the 8th of Novem-
      ber, 1851, by Edward Armstrong ...
      In celebration of the one hundred
      and sixty-ninth anniversary of the
      landing of William Penn at that
      place. Philadelphia, J. Penington,
      1852.
        36 p., 1 l.   25 cm.

451   Armstrong, George Dodd, 1813-1899.
        The Christian doctrine of sla-
      very. By Geo. D. Armstrong, D.D.,
      pastor of the Presbyterian church
      of Norfolk, Va. ... New York, C.
      Scribner, 1857.
        vi, 7-147 p.   19 cm.

452   Armstrong, George Dodd, 1813-1899.
        The summer of the pestilence. A
      history of the ravages of the yellow
      fever in Norfolk, Virginia, A.D.
      1855. By George D. Armstrong ...
      Philadelphia, J.B. Lippincott & co.,
      1856.
        192 p.   17 cm.

453   Armstrong, John J.
         An oration delivered at Flushing,
       Long Island, Fourth of July, 1862.
       By John J. Armstrong ... New York,
       Printed by E.O. Jenkins, 1862.
         24 p.   23 cm.

454   Armstrong, John J.
         An oration delivered at Queens,
       (Jamaica) L.I. on July 4th, 1861,
       by John J. Armstrong ... Jamaica,
       L.I., J.J. Brenton, printer, 1861.
         28 p.   22 1/2 cm.

455   Armstrong, Koscluszko.
         Review of T.L. McKenney's narra-
       tive of the causes which, in 1814,
       led to General Armstrong's resigna-
       tion of the war office. By Koscius-
       zko Armstrong. New York, R. Craig-
       head. printer, 1846.
         20 p.   23 cm.

456   Armstrong, Lebbeus, 1775-1860.
         The signs of the times; comprised
       in ten lectures, designed to show
       the origin, nature, tendency, and
       alliances of the present popular
       efforts for the abolition of capi-
       tal punishment. By the Rev. Lebbeus
       Armstrong. New York, R. Carter,
       1848.
         1 p. l., [ix]-xx, [21]-312 p.
       19 1/2 cm.

457   Armstrong, Lebbeus, 1775-1860.
         The temperance reformation: its
       history, from the organization of the
       first temperance society to the adop-
       tion of the liquor law of Maine,
       1851; and the consequent influence
       of the promulgation of that law on
       the political interest of the state
       of New York, 1852. By Rev. Lebbeus
       Armstrong ... New York, Boston
       [etc.] Fowlers and Wells, 1853.

xvi, [17]-408 p.   19 1/2 cm.

458   Armstrong, Lebbeus, 1775-1860.
       ... William Morgan, abducted and
murdered by masons, in conformity
with masonic obligations; and masonic measures, to conceal that outrage
against the laws; a practical comment on the sin of Cain.   Illustrated and proved in a sermon, by
Lebbeus Armstrong ...   delivered in
Edinburgh, Saratoga County, Sept.
12, 1831 ...   New York, Printed by
L.D. Dewey & co., 1831.
       32 p.   1 illus.   23 1/2 cm.

459   Armstrong, Robert.
       The influence of climate and other
agents, on the human constitution,
with reference to the causes and
prevention of disease among seamen;
with observations on fever in general
and an account of the epidemic fever
of Jamaica, by Robert Armstrong ...
London, Longman, Brown, Green and
Longman; [etc., etc.] 1843.
       xv, 207, [1] p.   22 cm.

460   Armstrong, Robert G.
       Memoir of Hannah Hobbie; or,
Christian activity, and triumph in
suffering.   By Rev. Robert G. Armstrong ...   New-York, American tract
society [1837?]
       2 p. l., [3]-255 p.   pt.   15 1/2
cm.

461   [Armstrong, William]
       Stocks and stock-jobbing in Wall-
street, with sketches of the brokers,
and fancy stocks.   Containing a full
account of the nature of all kinds
of stocks and securities ... by a
reformed stock gambler.   New-York,
New-York published company, 1848.
       39, [1] p.   23 cm.

101

462   The Army and Navy chronicle and scientific repository. v. 1-3 (no. 1-77); Jan. 12, 1843-June 27, 1844. Washington, W. Force.
        3 v. in 1. illus. 27 cm.

463   The Army & navy official gazette. Containing reports of battles; also, important orders of the War department, record of courts-martial, etc. Published by authority of the War department. v. 1-2; July 7, 1863-June 27, 1865. Washington city, Printed at the office of J.C. Rives [etc.] 1864-65.
        2 v. pl., maps. 30 cm.

464   The army hymn-book. 2d ed. Richmond. Va., Presbyterian committee of publication, 1864.
        128 p. 11 1/2 cm.

465   Arnaud, Achille, 1826-
        Abraham Lincoln; sa naissance, sa vie, sa mort avec un récit de la guerre d'Amérique d'après les documents les plus authentiques, par Achille Arnaud ... Paris, Charlieu frères et Huillery, 1865.
        96 p. incl. illus., ports, map, plan. 29 1/2 cm.

466   Arnold, Benedict, 1741-1801, *defendant*.
        Proceedings of a general court martial for the trial of Major General Arnold. With an introduction, notes, and index. New York, Priv. print., 1865.
        xxix p., 1 l., 182 p. 31 1/2 x 24 1/2 cm.

467   Arnold, Benedict, 1741-1801, *defendant*.
        Proceedings of a general court martial of the line, held at Raritan,

in the state of New-Jersey, by order of His Excellency George Washington, esq., general and commander
in chief of the army of the United
States of America, for the trial of
Major General Arnold, June 1, 1779.
Major General Howe, president, Pub.
by order of Congress. Philadelphia,
Printed by F. Bailey, 1780.
55 p. 33 cm.

468   Arnold, Charles Henry.
The new and impartial universal
history of North and South America,
from the earliest accounts to the
ratification of the provisional articles of peace ... By Charles Henry
Arnold ... London, A. Hogg [1790?]
xi, [25]-282 p. front. 18 cm.

469   Arnold, Isaac Newton, 1815-1884.
Congressional legislation. Speech
of Hon. Isaac N. Arnold, July 14,
1864. [n.p., 1864]
16 p. 21 1/2 cm.

470   Arnold, Isaac Newton, 1815-1884.
The history of Abraham Lincoln,
and the overthrow of slavery. By
Isaac N. Arnold ... Chicago, Clarke
& co., 1866.
xvi, 17-736 p. front. (port.)
23 cm.

471   Arnold, Isaac Newton, 1815-1884.
The power, duty, and necessity of
destroying slavery in the rebel
states. Speech of Hon. Isaac N.
Arnold, of Illinois. Delivered in
the House of representatives, January 6, 1864. [Washington] Towers,
printers [1864]
cover-title, 8 p. 23 1/2 cm.

472   Arnold, Isaac Newton, 1815-1884.
Reconstruction: liberty the

cornerstone, and Lincoln the archi-
tect. Speech of Hon. Isaac N. Arnold, of Illinois. Delivered in the
House of representatives, March 19,
1864. 2d ed. Washington, Printed
by L. Towers & co., 1864.
    14 p.   22 1/2 cm.

473   Arnold, Isaac Newton, 1815-1884.
        Ship canal from the Mississippi to
    Lake Michigan. Speech of Hon. Isaac
    N. Arnold ... delivered in the House
    of representatives of the United
    States, Jan. 15, 1863. [Washington,
    L. Towers & co., printers, 1863]
        cover-title, 8 p.   23 cm.

474   Arnold, Josias Lyndon, 1768-1796.
        Poems. By the late Josias Lyndon
    Arnold, esq; of St. Johnsbury (Ver-
    mong) formerly of Providence, and a
    tutor in Rhode-Island college. Print-
    ed at Providence, by Carter and Wil-
    kinson, and sold at their book-store,
    opposite the Market. 1797.
        xii, [13]-141 p.   18 cm.

475   Arnold, Samuel George, 1806-1891, *ed*.
        Biographical sketches of distin-
    guished Jerseymen. By S.G. Arnold
    ... Trenton, N.J., Press of the Em-
    porium, 1845.
        80 p.   20 1/2 cm.

476   Arnold, Samuel George, 1806-1891.
        The life of George Washington,
    first president of the United States,
    by S.G. Arnold ... Rev. by the edi-
    tors. New-York, Pub. by T. Mason
    and G. Lane, for the Sunday school
    union of the Methodist Episcopal
    church, 1840.
        228 p.   14 1/2 cm.

477   Arnold, Samuel Greene, 1821-1886.
        History of the state of Rhode

Island and Providence plantations.
By Samuel Greene Arnold ... New
York [etc.] D. Appleton & co., 1859-
60.
  2 v. pl., fold. maps. 24 cm.

478 Arnold, Samuel Greene, 1821-1880.
      The spirit of Rhode Island his-
     tory. A discourse, delivered before
     the Rhode-Island historical society
     on the evening of Monday January 17,
     1853. By Hon. Samuel Greene Arnold
     ... Providence, G.H. Whitney, 1853.
       32 p.   23 cm.

479 Arnold, Seth S.
      A sermon, preached at Alstead, on
     the first Sabbath in January, 1826.
     With historical sketches of the
     town. By Seth S. Arnold, A.M., pas-
     tor of the 1st Congregational church
     and society ... Alstead, N.H., New-
     ton and Tufts, 1826.
       48 p.   21 cm.

480 Arnould, Ambroise Marie, 1750?-1812.
      Système maritime et politique des
     Européens, pendant le dix-huitieme
     siècle; fonde sur leurs traités de
     paix, de commerce et de navigation.
     Par le citoyen Arnould ... Paris,
     Impr. d'A. Bailleul, an v--1797.
       2 p. l., viii, 341, [3] p.   19
     1/2 cm.

481 Arrington, Alfred W. 1810-1867.
      The rangers and regulators of the
     Tanaha; or, Life among the lawless.
     A tale of the republic of Texas.
     By Charles Summerfield (A.W. Arring-
     ton) ... New York, R.M. De Witt
     [^c1856]
       xi, [13]-397 p.   incl. front.
     plates.   18 1/2 cm.

482 Arróniz, Marcos, d. 1858 or 9.

... Manual de historia y crono-
logía de Méjico, arreglado por
Marcos Arróniz. Paris, Rosa y Bouret,
1858.
vi p., 1 1., [9]-126 p.   16 cm.

483   Arróniz, Marcos, *d.* 1858 *or* 9.
... Manual del viajero en Méjico,
ó Compendio de la historia de la
ciudad de Méjico, con la descripción
é historia de sus templos, conventos,
edificios públicos, las costumbres
de sus habitantes, etc., y con el
plan de dicha ciudad. Por Marcos
Arróniz. Paris, Rosa y Bouret, 1858.
vi, [7]-208 p.   fold. plan.
16 cm.

484   Arthur, Timothy Shay, 1809-1885.
The history of Georgia, from its
earliest settlement to the present
time. By T.S. Arthur and W.H. Carpenter. Philadelphia, Lippincott,
Grambo & co., 1852.
1 p. 1., [5]-331 p.   17 1/2 cm.

485   Arthur, Timothy Shay, 1809-1885.
The history of Kentucky, from its
earliest settlement to the present
time. By T.S. Arthur and W.H. Carpenter. Philadephia, Lippincott,
Grambo & co., 1852.
1 p. 1., 5-316 p.   18 cm.

486   Arthur, Timothy Shay, 1809-1885.
The history of Virginia, from its
earliest settlement to the present
time. By T.S. Arthur and W.H.
Carpenter. Philadelphia, Lippincott,
Grambo & co., 1852.
[3]-332 p.   17 cm.

487   Arthur, Timothy Shay, 1809-1885.
Home lights and shadows. By T.S.
Arthur ... New York, C. Scribner,
1853.

2 p. l., iv, [7]-376 p. front.
17 1/2 cm.

488   Arthus, Gotthard, 1570-1630?
Historia Indiae Orientalis, ex
variis avctoribvs collecta, et ivxta
seriem topographicam regnorum,
prouinciarum & insularum, per Africae,
Asiaeque littora, ad extremos vsque
Iaponios deducta ... Avctore m.
Gotardo Arthvs ... Coloniae Agrip-
pinae, symptibvs Vvilhelmi Lutzen-
kirch, 1608.
9 p. l., 616 p. 16 cm.

489   Articles of agreement, for carrying on
an expedition, by Hudson's streights,
for the discovery of a north-west passage to the western and southern ocean
of America. Dated March 30, 1745.
London: Printed in the year 1745.
[Boston, 1940]
facsim.: 16 p. 27 1/2 cm.

490   Asbury, Francis, 1745-1816.
The journal of the Rev. Francis
Asbury, bishop of the Methodist Episcopal church, from August 7, 1771,
to December 7, 1815 ... New York,
N. Bangs and T. Mason, 1821.
3 v. 22 cm.

491   [Ash, Thomas] *fl. 1682, supposed author.*
Carolina; or A description of the
present state of that country, and
the natural excellencies thereof;
namely, the healthfulness of the air,
pleasantness of the place, advantages and usefulness of those rich
commodities there plentifully abound-
ing ... Pub. by T.A., gent., clerk
on board His Majesties ship the Richmond, which was sent out in the year
1680, with particular instructions
to enquire into the state of that
country by His Majesties special

command, and return'd this present year, 1682. London, Printed for W. C., and to be sold by Mrs. Grover, 1682. [New-York, 1836]
(*In* Carroll, Bartholomew R. Historical collections of South Carolina. New-York, 1836. 22 1/2 cm. v. 2, p. [59]-84)

492   Ashe, Thomas, 1770-1835.
A commercial view, and geographical sketch, of the Brasils in South America, and of the island of Madeira ... serving as a guide to the commercial world ... By T. Ashe, esq. ... London, Allen & co., 1812.
2 p. 1., 160 p.   21 1/2 cm.

493   Ashe, Thomas, 1770-1835.
Memoirs and confessions of Captain Ashe ... London, H. Colburn, 1815.
3 v.   18 cm.

494   Ashe, Thomas, 1770-1835.
Memoirs of mammoth, and various other extraordinary and stupendous bones, of incognita, or non-descript animals, found in the vicinity of the Ohio, Wabash, Illinois, Mississippi, Missouri, Osage, and Red rivers, &c. &c. Published for the information of those ladies and gentlemen, whose taste and love of science tempt them to visit the Liverpool museum. By Th. Ashe ... Liverpool, Printed by G.F. Harris, 1806.
12, 60 p.   23 cm.

495   Asher, Adolf, 1800-1853.
Bibliographical essay on the collection of voyages and travels edited and published by Levinus Hulsius and his successors, at Nuremberg and Francfort from anno 1598 to 1660. By A. Asher. Berlin, A. Asher, 1839.

2 p. l., 118 p.   23 cm.

496   Asher, Jeremiah, *b*. 1812.
        Incidents in the life of the Rev.
        J. Asher, pastor of Shiloh (colour-
        ed) Baptist church, Philadelphia,
        U.S.   With an introduction by Wil-
        son Armistead ...   London, C. Gilpin,
        1850.
        2 p. l., 80 p.   17 cm.

497   Ashley, Chester, 1790-1848.
        Speech of Hon. C. Ashley, of Arkan-
        sas, on the Oregon question.   Deliv-
        ered in the Senate of the United
        States, Friday, April 3, 1846.   Wash-
        ington, Printed at the office of
        Blair and Rives, 1846.
        16 p.   21 1/2 cm.

498   Ashley, James Monroe, 1824-1896.
        The rebellion--its causes and con-
        sequences.   A speech delivered by Hon.
        J.M. Ashley, at College hall in the
        city of Toledo, Tuesday evening, Nov.
        26, 1861.   Toledo, Pelton and Wag-
        goner, printers, 1861.
        16 p.   23 1/2 cm.

499   Ashley, James Monroe, 1824-1896.
        Success of the Calhoun revolution:
        the Constitution changed and slavery
        nationalized by the usurpations of
        the Supreme court.   Speech of Hon.
        James M. Ashley, of Ohio.   Delivered
        in the U.S. House of representatives,
        May 29, 1860.   Washington, D.C.,
        Buell & Blanchard, printers, 1860.
        30 p.   22 1/2 cm.

500   Ashley, John, *d*. 1751.
        Memoirs and considerations concern-
        ing the trade and revenues of the
        British colonies in America ...   By
        John Ashley ...   London, Printed for
        C. Corbett [etc.] 1740-43.

2 v.   20 1/2 cm.

501   [Ashley, John] *d*. 1751.
           Some observations on a direct ex-
       portation of sugar from the British
       Islands; with answers to Mr. Toriano's
       objections to it.   In a letter from a
       gentleman in Barbadoes, to his friend
       in London.   London, 1735.
           23 p.   22 1/2 cm.

502   Ashmun, George, 1804-1870.
           Speech of Mr. Geo. Ashmun, of Mass.,
       on the Mexican war.   Delivered in the
       House of representatives of the U.S.,
       Feb. 4, 1847.   Washington, J. & G.S.
       Gideon, printers, 1847.
           16 p.   24 cm.

503   Ashmun, Jehudi, 1794-1828.
           History of the American colony in
       Liberia, from December 1821 to 1823.
       By J. Ashmun.   Comp. from the authen-
       tic records of the colony.   Washing-
       ton city, Printed by Way & Gideon,
       1826.
           42 p.   front. (fold. map)   22 1/2
       cm.

504   The aspect of the times: a political
       poem, and other pieces.   By a native
       of Newark.   Newark: Printed by Hull
       & Bartlett, for the author, 1831.
           vi, [7]-[73] p., 1 l.   13 1/2
       x 10 1/2 cm.

505   Aspinwall, Thomas, 1786-1876.
           Remarks on the Narraganset patent.
       Read before the Massachusetts histori-
       cal society, June, 1862, by Thomas
       Aspinwall.   2d ed.   Providence, S.S.
       Rider & brother, 1865.
           40 p.   25 1/2 x 15 cm.

506   Asplund, John, *d*. 1807.
           The annual register of the Baptist

denomination, in North-America; to
the first of November, 1790. Containing an account of the churches
and their constitutions, ministers,
members, associations, their plan and
sentiments, rule and order, proceedings and correspondence. Also remarks upon practical religion. Humbly offered to the public, by John
Asplund. [n.p., 1792]
iv, 5-57, 69-70 p.   21 1/2 x 16
1/2 cm.

507   Assall, Friedrich Wilhelm.
Nachrichten über die früheren
einwohner von Nordamerika und ihre
denkmäler, gesammelt von Friedrich
Wilhelm Assall ... Hrsg. mit einem
vorberichte von Franz Joseph Mone ...
Mit einem atlas von 12 steintafeln.
Heidelberg, A. Osswald, 1827.
xvi, 160 p.   19 1/2 cm.

508   The assassination and history of the
conspiracy, a complete digest of
the whole affair from its inception
to its culmination, sketches of the
principal characters, reports of the
obsequies, etc. ... Cincinnati, J.
R. Hawley & co., 1865.
3 p. l., v-xi, 21-163 p.   front.,
plates, ports.   22 1/2 cm.

509   Association of American geologists and
naturalists.
Reports of the first, second, and
third meetings of the Association
of American geologists and naturalists, at Philadelphia, in 1840 and
1841, and at Boston in 1842. Embracing its proceedings and transactions.
Boston, Gould, Kendall & Lincoln,
1843.
viii, [9]-544 p.   illus., xxi (*i.
e.* 19) pl. (part double; incl. maps)
25 cm.

510   Association of Franklin medal scholars,
        Boston.
           The association of Franklin medal
        scholars. Printed for the associa-
        tion from the Annual report of the
        school committee for 1857. Boston,
        G.C. Rand & Avery, 1858.
           40 p.   illus.   23 cm.

511   Asti, Felice.
           Memoria o dissertazione sopra la
        nuova china china del regno di S.
        Fè nell'America Meridionale cioe'
        alcune riflessioni sopra la mede-
        sima fatte dal dottore Don Felice
        Asti ... 2.ed. dall'autore cor-
        retta, ed arricchita di addizioni
        con due lettere di Vicenzo Dandolo
        ... Venezia, M. Fenzo, 1791.
           91 p.   2 pl.   27 1/2 cm.

512   Astié, Jean Frédéric, 1822-1894.
           Histoire de la république des
        États-Unis depuis l'établissement
        des premières colonies jusqu'à
        l'élection du président Lincoln
        (1620-1860) par J.-F. Astié; précé-
        dée d'une préface par M. Éd. Laboulaye
        ... Paris, Grassart, 1865.
           2 v.   21 1/2 cm.

513   Astor library, *New York*.
           The act of incorporation and by-
        laws of the Trustees of the Astor
        library. New York, Sibell & Mott,
        1849.
           8 p.   21 1/2 cm.

514   Astor library, *New York*.
           Alphabetical index to the Astor
        library, or catalogue, with short
        titles, of the books now collected
        and of the proposed accessions, as
        submitted to the trustees ... Jan.
        1851. New York, R. Craighead, print-
        er, 1851.

iv. 446 p.   23 cm.

515   Astor library, *New York*.
       Catalogue of books in the Astor
       library relating to the languages
       and literature of Asia, Africa, and
       the Oceanic islands. New York,
       Astor library autographic press, 1854.
       4 p. 1., 424 p.   24 cm.

516   Astor library, *New York*.
       Catalogue or alphabetical index
       of the Astor library. In two parts.
       Part I. Authors and books ... New
       York, R. Craighead, printer, 1857-61.
       4 v.   26 cm.

517   Astor library, *New York*.
       A concise classified list of the
       most important works on bibliography,
       being those selected in this depart-
       ment for the Astor library. New
       York, R. Craighead, printer, 1849.
       iv, 30 p.   22 cm.

518   Astor library, *New York*.
       List of periodicals & transac-
       tions of societies, taken in at
       the Astor library 1855. [New York,
       1855]
       26 p.   24 cm.

519   Atcheson, Nathaniel, 1771-1825.
       American encroachments on British
       rights; or, Observations on the im-
       portance of the British North Ameri-
       can colonies and on the late treaties
       with the United States: with remarks
       on Mr. Baring's examination; and a
       defence of the shipping interest
       from the charge of having attempted to
       impose on Parliament ... By Nathan-
       iel Atcheson ... London, J. Butter-
       worth [etc.] 1808.
       xiii, [1], cxiii, 250 p.   2 maps
       (1 fold.) tables (1 fold.)   22 cm.

113

520   [Atcheson, Nathaniel] 1771-1825.
        A compressed view of the points
        to be discussed, in treating with
        the United States of America; A.D.
        1814. With an appendix and two
        maps ... London, Printed for J.M.
        Richardson, 1814.
        2 p. l., 39, [1] p. 2 fold. maps.
        23 1/2 cm.

521   Atchison, David Rice, 1807-1886.
        Speech of Hon. D.R. Atchison, of
        Missouri, on the Oregon question. De-
        livered in the Senate of the United
        States, March 12, 1846. [Washington,
        D.C., 1846]
        8 p.   24 cm.

522   Atkins, John, 1685-1757.
        A voyage to Guinea, Brasil, and
        the West-Indies ... London, C. Ward
        and R. Chandler, 1735.
        xxv, 2, 19-265 p.   20 cm.

523   Atkinson, Archibald, 1792-1872.
        Speech of Mr. Atkinson, of Vir-
        ginia, on the Oregon question. De-
        livered in the House of Representa-
        tives, February 7, 1846. Washing-
        ton, Printed at the Union office,
        1846.
        8 p.   23 cm.

524   Atkinson, Christopher William.
        A historical and statistical ac-
        count of New-Brunswick, B.N.A., with
        advice to emigrants. By the Rev.
        W. Christopher Atkinson ... 3d ed.,
        greatly improved and cor. ... Edin-
        burgh, Printed by Anderson & Bryce,
        1844.
        xvi, [13]-284 p. incl. illus.,
        pl. fold. map. 16 1/2 cm.

525   [Atkinson, Edward] 1827-1905.
        Cheap cotton by free labor: by a

cotton manufacturer. Boston, A.
Williams & co., 1861.
52 p. incl. tables. 23 cm.

526 Atkinson, Edward, 1827-1905.
Report to the Boston board of
trade on the cotton manufacture of
1862. [Boston, 1863]
cover-title, 21 p. fold. map.
23 1/2 cm.

527 Atkinson, John.
The hermit, or An account of Francis Adam Joseph Phyle, a native of
Switzerland, who lived without the
use of fire for upwards of twenty-
two years, in a small cave, in the
midst of a wood, near Mount-Holly,
in Burlington county, New-Jersey;
and was found dead therein, in the
year 1780. In a series of letters,
from Baltus Hiltzhimer to Melchoir
Miller. Interspersed with some observations of the author, and sentiments of celebrated men. 2d ed.
New Jersey. Published by John Atkinson. Printed by John Bioren, no.
88, Chestnut-street, Philadelphia.
1811.
108 p. 14 cm.

528 Atkinson, William King.
An oration; delivered at Dover,
New-Hampshire, on the fourth of
July, 1791. Being the fifteenth
anniversary of American independence
... By William King Atkinson. Dov-
er, N.H., Printed by E. Ladd, 1791.
23 p. 19 x 16 cm.

529 The Atlantic club-book: being sketches
in prose and verse, by various writers ... New York, Harper and brothers, 1834.
2 v. 19 1/2 cm.

530   The Atlantic navigator: being a nauti-
       cal description of the coasts of
       France, Spain and Portugal, the west
       coast of Africa, the coasts of Brazil
       and Patagonia, the islands of the
       Azores, Madeiras, Canaries and Cape
       Verdes, and of the detached shoals
       & dangers reported to exist in the
       Atlantic; to this is added a general
       review of the winds, tides, currents,
       &c., a description of the principal
       harbours on the coast of North Ameri-
       ca, and an account of the most advan-
       tageous tracks across the Atlantic.
       4th ed., materially improved and en-
       larged. London, J. Imray and son,
       1854.
         2 p. l., [iii]-xii, vi, 532 p.

531   [Atlantic telegraph company, *London*]
         The Atlantic telegraph. A history
       of preliminary experimental proceed-
       ings, and a descriptive account of
       the present state & prospects of the
       undertaking. Published by order of
       the directors of the Company. July,
       1857. London, Jarrold and sons,
       1857.
         69 p. fold. front., illus., pl.
       24 cm.

532   The Atlantic telegraph: its history,
       from the commencement of the under-
       taking in 1854, to the sailing of the
       "Great Eastern" in 1866. Accompan-
       ied with a familiar explanation of the
       theory of telegraphy; a chronologi-
       cal summary of the progress of the
       art; and a tabular list of the sub-
       marine cables now in operation; also
       an account of the leading submarine
       and land lines in progress and pro-
       jected ... London, Bacon and co.,
       1866.
         iv, [5]-116, [2] p. illus., fold.
       pl., 3 port., 2 fold. maps (incl.

front.)   19 1/2 cm.

533   Atlantis. Zeitschrift für leben und
        literatur in England und Amerika.
        Hrsg. von Dr. Karl Elze ...   1.-2.
        bd.; jahrg. 1853-54. Dessau,
        Gebrüder Katz. 1853-54.
            2 v.   24 1/2 cm.

534   Atlee, Edwin Pitt, 1799-1836.
            An address, delivered before the
        Female anti-slavery society of Phila-
        delphia, in the session room of the
        Second Presbyterian church ... in
        the first month, (January,) 1834.
        By E.P. Atlee, M.D. To which is
        added an appendix. Philadelphia,
        Printed by T.K. Collins & co., 1834.
            27 p.   21 cm.

535   Atlee, Washington Lemuel, 1808-1878.
            Memoir of William R. Grant, M.D.,
        late professor of anatomy in the
        Medical department of Pennsylvania
        college. With a notice of his theory
        of the foetal circulation. Read to
        the College of physicians of Phila-
        delphia. March 2, 1853. By Washing-
        ton L. Atlee, M.D. Written and print-
        ed by order of the College. Phila-
        delphia, Lippincott, Grambo, and
        co., 1853.
            22 p.   front. (port.) 1 illus.
        24 cm.

536   Atson, William.
            Heart whispers; or, A peep behind
        the family curtain, interspersed with
        sketches of a tour through nine south-
        ern states. Contained in a series
        of letters to his wife ... Philadel-
        phia, H. Cowperthwait & co., 1859.
            xvi, 25-368 pp.   12 cm.

537   An attempt to elucidate the pernicious
        consequences of a deviation from the

117

principles of the Orders in council.
London, S. Tipper. 1809.
1 p. l., 76 p.   21 1/2 cm.

538   Atterbury, John Guest, 1811-1887.
God in civil government, a discourse preached in the First Presbyterian church, New Albany, Nov. 27,
1862, by the Rev. John G. Atterbury
... New Albany [Ind.] G.R. Beach,
printer, 1862.
16 p.   21 1/2 cm.

539   Atwater, Caleb, 1778-1867.
The general character, present and
future prospects of the people of
Ohio. An address delivered at the
United States' court house, during
the term of the United States' circuit court, in Columbus, Ohio, December, 1826. By Caleb Atwater ...
Columbus, Printed by P.H. Olmsted &
co., 1827.
21, [1] p.   23 1/2 cm.

540   Atwater, Caleb, 1778-1867.
A history of the state of Ohio,
natural and civil. By Caleb Atwater ... 1st ed. Cincinnati, Stero-
typed by Glezen & Shepard [c1838]
403 p.   22 cm.

541   Atwater, Caleb, 1778-1867.
Remarks made on a tour to Prairie
du Chien; thence to Washington city,
in 1829. By Caleb Atwater. Columbus, (O.) Printed by Jenkins and
Grover, 1831.
vii, 296 p.   17 cm.

542   Atwater, Caleb, 1778-1867.
Writings of Caleb Atwater. Columbus [O.] The author, printed by
Scott and Wright, 1833.
7, [1] p., 1 l., [9]-408 p.   incl.
illus., 10 pl.   20 cm.

543   Atwater, Jesse.
        Considerations, on the approaching
       dissolution, of the United States
       bank. In a series of numbers, by
       Jesse Atwater. New-Haven, Sidney's
       press, 1810.
           22 p.   21 1/2 cm.

544   Atwood, Edward Sumner, 1833-1888.
        In memoriam. Discourses in commem-
       oration of Abraham Lincoln, president
       of the United States, delivered in
       the South church, Salem, April 16th,
       and June 1st, 1865, by the pastor,
       Rev. E.S. Atwood. Salem, Printed at
       the office of the Salem gazette, 1865.
           cover-title, 31 p.   22 1/2 cm.

545   Atwood, Thomas, d. 1793.
        The history of the island of
       Dominica. Containing a description of
       its situation, extent, climate, moun-
       tains, rivers, natural productions, &c.
       &c. Together with an account of the
       civil government, trade, laws, customs,
       and manners of the different inhabi-
       tants of that island. Its conquest
       by the French, and restoration to
       the British dominions. By Thomas At-
       wood. London, Printed for J. John-
       son, 1791.
           vii, 285 p.   8 cm.

546   [Atwood, William] d. 1705?
        The case of William Atwood, esq;
       by the late King William ... consti-
       tuted chief justice of the province
       of New York in America, and judge of
       the admiralty there, and in neighbor-
       ing colonies. With a true account of
       the government and people of that prov-
       ince; particularly of Bayard's fac-
       tion, and the treason for which he
       and Hutchins stand attainted; but
       reprieved before the Lord Cornbury's
       arrival, upon acknowledging their

offences, and begging pardon ...
London, 1703.
1 p. 1., 23 p.   33 1/2 x 21 cm.

547   Aucaigne, Félix, *d.* 1914.
L'alliance russo-américaine, par
Félix Aucaigne. 2.éd. Paris, E.
Dentu, 1863.
32 p.   24 cm.

548   Auchinleck, Gilbert.
A history of the war between Great
Britain and the United States of
America. During the years 1812, 1813,
and 1814. By G. Auchinleck ... Tor-
onto, Maclear & co., 1855.
vii, [3]-408.iii p. incl. illus.,
maps.   24 1/2 cm.

549   Audubon, John James, 1785-1851.
A synopsis of the birds of North
America. By John James Audubon ...
Edinburgh, A. and C. Black; [etc.,
etc.] 1839.
xii, 359, [1] p.   22 1/2 cm.

550   Auger, Édouard.
Voyage en Californie, 1852-1853.
Paris, L. Hachette, 1854.
238 p.   18 cm.

551   Aughey, John Hill, *b.* 1828.
The iron furnace: or, Slavery and
secession. By Rev. John H. Aughey,
a refugee from Mississippi ...
Philadelphia, W.S. & A. Martien, 1863.
206 p. front. (port.) 2 pl.   18
cm.

552   Austin, Arthur Williams, 1807-1884.
A memorandum concerning the Charlestown post-office. By Arthur W. Austin ... [Charlestown, Mass., 1835]
23 p.   23 cm.

553   Austin, Benjamin, 1752-1820.

Constitutional republicanism, in opposition to fallacious federalism; as published occasionally in the Independent chronicle, under the signature of Old-South. To which is added, a prefatory address to the citizens of the United States, never before published. By Benjamin Austin, jun. ... Boston: Printed for Adams & Rhoades, editors of the Independent Chronicle. 1803.
327 p.   23 cm.

554   [Austin, Benjamin] 1752-1820.
Observations on the pernicious practice of the law. As published occasionally in the Independent chronicle, in the year 1786, and republished at the request of a number of respectable citizens. With an address never before published. Corrected and amended. By Honestus [*pseud.*] With remarks on the rights of jury as judges of law and evidence. Boston, Printed by True & Weston, 1819.
60 p.   23 cm.

555   Austin, David, 1760-1831.
A discourse, delivered on occasion of the death of George Washington, late president, general, and commander in chief of the forces of the United States of America, in compliance with the request of the mayor, aldermen, and Common-council of the borough of Elizabeth, December 25, 1799.
Also, sketches of a running discourse, delivered to the Union brigade, on the same occasion, at their cantonment on Green Brook, in compliance with a request from Colonel Smith, the commanding officer, December 26, 1799. With an address to the throne of grace, offered at the door of the tabernacle of the cantonment on Green Brook, February 22, the

birth-day of our national luminary.
By David Austin, jun. New-York,
Printed by G.F. Hopkins, 1800.
    iv, [5]-35, [1] p. pl.   21 x
17 cm.

556   Austin, David, 1760-1831.
        The national "barley cake," or,
the "rock of offence" into a "glorious holy mountain:" in discourses
and letters. By David Austin ...
Submitted. Washington, District of
Columbia: Printed by Way and Groff,
north E street. January 14, A.D.
1802.
        80 p.   23 1/2 cm.

557   Austin, Ivers James, 1808-1889.
        An address delivered before the
corps of cadets of the United States
military academy. By Ivers J. Austin ... June, 1842. New York,
Wiley and Putnam, 1842.
        18 p.   22 cm.

558   Austin, Ivers James, 1808-1889.
        Argument of Ivers J. Austin, coun-
sel for the remonstrants from Watertown, against the petition for the
incorporation of the town of Bel-
mont, before the joint standing committee on towns. Boston, Printed by
A. Mudge and son, 1857.
        1 p. l., 58 p., 1 l. fold. map.
24 cm.

559   Austin, Ivers James, 1808-1889.
        An oration delivered by request
of the city authorities before the
citizens of Boston, on the sixty
third anniversary of American independence, July 4, 1839. By Ivers
James Austin. Boston, J.H. Eastburn, city printer, 1839.
        36 p.   24 cm.

560   Austin, James Trecothick, 1784-1870.
            The life of Elbridge Gerry. With
        contemporary letters. To the close
        of the American revolution. By James
        T. Austin. Boston, Wells and Lilly,
        1828-29.
            2 v.   front. (port.)   22 cm.

561   Austin, James Trecothick, 1784-1870.
            An oration, delivered on the
        Fourth of July, 1829, at the celebra-
        tion of American independence, in the
        city of Boston. By James T. Austin.
        Boston, J.H. Eastburn, city printer,
        1829.
            26 p.   24 cm.

562   Austin, James Trecothick, 1784-1870.
            An oration, pronounced at Lexing-
        ton, Mass., in commemoration of the
        independence of the United States of
        America, and the restoration of peace.
        4th July, 1815. By James T. Austin
        ... Boston: Printed by Rowe and
        Hooper, at the Yankee office, 1815.
            21 p.   21 cm.

563   [Austin, James Trecothick] 1784-1870.
            Remarks on Dr. Channing's Slavery.
        By a citizen of Massachusetts. Bos-
        ton, Russell, Shattuck and co., and
        J.H. Eastburn, 1835.
            48 p.   24 1/2 cm.

564   [Austin, Moses] 1761-1821.
            A summary description of the lead
        mines in Upper Louisiana. Also, an
        estimate of their produce for three
        years past. City of Washington: A.
        and G. Way, printers. 1804.
            22 p.   22 cm.

565   Austin, Samuel, 1760-1830.
            An address, pronounced in Worces-
        ter, (Mass.) on the Fourth of July,
        1825, being the forty-ninth anniver-

sary of the independence of the
United States, before an assembly
convened for the purpose of celebrat-
ing this event religiously. By
Samuel Austin... Worcester, Printed
by W. Manning [1825?]
   23 p.   24 cm.

566   Austin, Samuel, 1760-1830.
       [The apology of patriots, or The
heresy of the friends of the Washington peace policy defended. A sermon, preached in] Worcester, Massachusetts, on the day of the national
fast, Thursday, August 20, 1812.
Observed in compliance with the rec-
ommendation of James Madison, president of the United States; and in
consequence of the declaration of war
against Great-Britain. By Samuel
Austin, D.D. Pub. by request. Worcester, Printed by I. Sturtevant,
1812.
       32 p.   22 cm.

567   Austin, Samuel, 1760-1830.
       An oration, pronounced at Worcester,
on the Fourth of July, 1798; the anni-
versary of the independence of the
United States of America. By Samuel
Austin, A.M. Worcester, Printed by
Leonard Worcester, 1798.
       38 p.   21 1/2 cm.

568   Austin, Stephen Fuller, 1793-1836.
       An address delivered by S.F. Aus-
tin of Texas, to a very large audi-
ence of ladies and gentlemen in the
Second Presbyterian church, Louisville, Kentucky, on the 7th of March,
1836. Lexington, J. Clarke & co.,
printers, 1836.
       30 p.   17 1/2 cm.

569   Austin, William, 1778-1841.

124

An oration, pronounced at Charlestown, at the request of the Artillery
company, on the seventeenth of June;
being the anniversary of the battle
of Bunker Hill, and of that company
... By William Austin, A.B. Charlestown [Mass.] Printed by Samuel
Etheridge, 1801.
29 p.   19 1/2 cm.

570   An authentic journal of the siege of
the Havana. By an officer. To
which is prefixed, a plan of the
siege of the Havana, shewing the
landing, encampments, approaches,
and batteries of the English army.
With the attacks and stations of
the fleet. London, Printed for T.
Jefferys [etc.] 1762.
1 p. 1., [5]-44 p. front. (fold.
map)   19 1/2 cm.

571   An authentic narrative of facts relating to the exchange of prisoners
taken at the Cedars; supported by
the testimonies and depositions of
His Majesty's officers, with several
original letters and papers. Together with remarks upon the report and
resolves of the American Congress
on that subject. London, Printed for
T. Cadell, 1777.
2 p. 1., 50 p.   23 cm.

572   Authentic papers from America: submitted to the dispassionate consideration of the public. London, Printed for T. Becket, 1775.
1 p. 1., 33 p.   20 cm.

573   Authentic papers relating to the expedition against Carthagena: being the
resolutions of the councils of war;
both of sea and land-officers respec-
tively, at sea and on shore: also
the resolutions of the general council

of war, composed of both sea and
land-officers, held on board the
Princess Carolina, &c. With copies
of the letters which passed between
Admiral Vernon and General Wentworth; and also between the governor of Carthagena and the admiral.
London, Printed for L. Raymond, and
sold by J.M., 1744.
   2 p. 1., 100 p.   20 1/2 cm.

574   Authentic papers relative to the expedition against the Charibbs, and the
sale of lands in the island of St.
Vincent.   London, Printed for J.
Almon, 1773.
   83 p.   26 cm.

575   An authentic register of the British
successes; being a collection of
all the extraordinary and some of
the ordinary gazettes, from the taking of Louisbourgh, July 26, 1758,
by the honourable Admiral Boscawen
and Gen. Amhurst [!]; to the defeat
of the French, fleet under M. Con-
flans, Nov. 21, 1759, by Sir Edward
Hawke.   To which is added, a particular account of M. Thurot's defeat,
by Captain John Elliott.   London,
Printed for G. Kearsly, 1760.
   vi, 126 p.   19 1/2 x 11 1/2 cm.

576   Avalle,   *habitant cultivateur de
Saint-Domingue.*
   Tableau comparatif des productions
des colonies françaises aux Antilles,
avec celles des colonies anglaises,
espagnoles et hollandiases; de l'année 1787 à 1788.   Suivi de l'établissement et mouvement d'une sucre-
rie, pendant le cours d'une année
... Par le citoyen Avalle, habitant
cultivateur de Saint-Domingue.
Paris, Goujon fils [etc., 1799]
   3 p. 1., [v]-vii p., 2 1., [6],

73 p.   xii tab. (partly fold.) fold.
plan, 25 1/2 x 20 1/2 cm.

577   Avé-Lallemant, Robert Christian Bert-
hold, 1812-1884.
Reise durch Nord-Brasilien in jahre
1859. Von dr. Robert Avé-Lallemant.
Leipzig, F.A. Brockhaus, 1860.
2 v. in 1.   21 cm.

578   Avé-Lallemant, Robert Christian Bert-
hold, 1812-1884.
Reise durch Süd-Brasilien im jahre
1858. Von dr. Robert Avé-Lallemant
... Leipzig, F.A. Brockhaus, 1859.
2 v.   21 cm.

579   Avery, David, 1746-1818.
The Lord is to be praised for the
triumphs of His power. A sermon,
preached at Greenwich, in Connecticut, on the 18th of December 1777.
Being a general thanksgiving through
the United American states. By David Avery ... Norwich Conn.:   Printed by Green & Spooner, 1778.
47 p.   18 1/2 cm.

580   Aves, Thomas, *defendant*.
Case of the slave-child, Med. Report of the arguments of counsel,
and of the opinion of the court, in
the case of Commonwealth vs. Aves;
tried and determined in the Supreme
judicial court of Massachusetts.
Boston, I. Knapp, 1836.
40 p.   22 cm.

581   [Avezac-Macaya, Armand d'] 1800-1875.
Martin Hylacomylus Waltzemuller,
ses ouvrages et ses collaborateurs.
Voyage d'exploration et de décou-
vertes à travers quelques épîtres
dédicatoires, préfaces et opuscules
en prose et en vers du commencement
du XVIe siècle: notes, causeries

et digressions bibliographiques et autres, par un géographe bibliophile. Paris, Challamel aîné, 1867.
vi, 176 p.   22 cm.

582   Avezac-Macaya, Armand d', 1800-1875.
Les voyages de Améric Vespuce au compte de l'Espagne, et les mesures itinéraires employées par les marins espagnols et portugais des XVe et XVIe siècles ... Revue critique de deux opuscules intitulés: I. Vespuce et son premier voyage, II. Examen de quelques points de l'histoire géographique du Brésil. Communication à la Société de géographie de Paris dans sa séance du 16 juillet 1858, par M. d'Avezac ... Paris, Impr. de L. Martinet, 1858.
2 p. l., 188 p.   25 cm.

583   Avila, Francisco de, *Franciscan*.
Arte de la lengua mexicana, y breves platicas de los mysterios de n. santa fee catholica, y otras para exortación de su obligación, á los Indios. Compuesto por el P.F. Francisco de Avila ... En Mexico, Por los herederos de la viuda de M. de Ribera Calderõ, 1717.
13 p. l., 37 numb. l.   14 x 10 cm.

584   [Avity, Pierre d', *sieur de Montmartin*] 1573-1635.
Les estats, empires, et princi-pavtez dv monde, representez par la description des pays, moeurs des habitans, richesses des prouinces, les forces, le gouuernement, la religion, et les princes qui ont gouuerné chacun estat, auec l'origine de toutes les religions, et de tous les cheualiers et ordres militaires. Par le s.^{r} D.T.V.Y. gentilhõme ord^{re}. de la chambre du roy. A.S. Omer,

Chez Charles Boscard, imprimeur, 1614.
    10 p. 1., 1104, 59, [1] p.   21 cm.

585   ... Away in the wilderness; or, Life among the Red Indians and fur-traders of North America. With four coloured illustrations. New York, D. Appleton & co., 1865.
    177 p. col. front., col. plates. 15 1/2 cm.

586   Awful calamities: or, The shipwrecks of December, 1839, being a full account of the dreadful hurricanes of Dec. 15, 21 & 27, on the coast of Massachusetts... comprising also a particular relation of the shipwreck of the following vessels: Barque Lloyd, brigs Pocahontas, Ridcout and J. Palmer, and schs. Deposite, Catharine Nichols and Miller. And also of the dreadful disasters at Gloucester. 5th ed. Boston, Press of J. Howe, 1840.
    24 p. 1 illus. 21 cm.

587   Ayers, Elisha.
    A journal of travel, by Elisha Ayers, esq., formerly Gen. Taylor's school-master, now of Preston, Conn., who traveled a number of years in different parts of the United States, including anecdotes, remarks, adventures, criticism, geography, mineralogy, history, curiosities, antiquities, poetry, observations, etc., etc. [Preston] The author, 1847.
    52 p. 22 1/2 cm.

588   [Ayscough, Samuel] 1745-1804.
    Remarks on The letters from an American farmer; or, A detection of the errors of Mr. J. Hector St. John; pointing out the pernicious tendency of these letters to Great

Britain. London, Printed for J.
Fielding, 1783.
1 p. l., 26 p.   20 1/2 cm.

589   Azara, Félix de, 1746-1821.
        Apuntamientos para la historia
natural de los páxaros del Paragüay
y Rio de la Plata, escritos por Don
Félix de Azara ...   Madrid, Impr.
de la viuda de Ibarra [etc.] 1802-
05.
        3 v.   21 cm.

590   Azara, Felix de, 1746-1821.
        Apuntamientos para la historia
natural de los quadrúpedos del Paragüay y Rio de la Plata, escritos por
Don Felix de Azara ...   Madrid, En
la impr. de la viuda de Ibarra, 1802.
        2 v.   22 cm.

591   Azara, Félix de, 1746-1821.
        Correspondencia oficial e inedita
sobre la demarcación de limites entre
el Paraguay y el Brasil, por d. Félix
de Azara, primer comisario de la
tercera división.   1.ed.   Buenos-
Aires, Imprenta del estado.   1836.
        1 p. l., ii, [3]-68, ii p.   33 cm.

592   Azara, Félix de, 1746-1821.
        Descripción é historia del Paraguay
y del Rio de la Plata.   Obra póstuma
de don Félix de Azara ...   La publica
su sobrino y heredero el señor don
Agustín de Azara, marqués de Nibbiano
... bajo la direccion de don Basilio
Sebastian Castellanos de Losada ...
Madrid, Impr. de Sanchiz, 1847.
        2 v.   port., fold. tab.   22 1/2
cm.

593   Azara, Félix de, 1746-1821.
        Diario de la navegación y recono-
cimiento del rio Tebicuari.   Obra
postuma de d. Félix de Azara.   1.ed.

Buenos-Aires, Imprenta del estado,
1836.
1 p. l., v, 47 p.   33 cm.

594   Azara, Félix de, 1746-1821.
Diario de un reconocimiento de las
guardias y fortines, que guarnecen
la línea de frontera de Buenos-Aires,
para ensancharla, por D. Félix de
Azara ... [1796] 1. ed. Buenos-
Aires, Imprenta del estado, 1837.
1 p. l., iv, [3]-49 p.   33 cm.

595   Azara, Félix de, 1746-1821.
Informes de D. Félix de Azara,
sobre varios proyectos de colonizar
el Chaco. 1.ed. Buenos-Aires,
Imprenta del estado, 1836.
1 p. l., vi, [3]-16 p.   33 cm.

596   Azara, Félix de, 1746-1821.
Memorias sobre el estado rural del
Rio de la Plata en 1801; demarcación
de límites entre el Brasil y el
Paraguay á últimos del siglo XVIII,
é informes sobre varios particulares
de la América Meridional española.
Escritos postumos de Don Félix de
Azara ... Los publica su sobrino
Don Agustin de Azara, marqués de
Nibbiano ... bajo la dirección de
Don Basilio Sebastian Castellanos
de Losada ... Madrid, Impr. de
Sanchiz, 1847.
viii, 232 p. port.   21 1/2 cm.

597   Azara, Felix de, 1746-1821.
The natural history of the quad-
rupeds of Paraguay and the river La
Plata: tr. from the Spanish of Don
Félix de Azara. With a memoir of
the author, a physical sketch of
the country, and numerous notes; by
W. Perceval Hunter ... v. 1. Edinburgh, A. & C. Black; [etc., etc.]
1838.

xxxii, 340 p.   front. (fold. map)
23 1/2 cm.

598   Azara, Félix de, 1746-1821.
        Voyages dan l'Amérique Méridionale,
par don Félix de Azara ... depuis
1781 jusqu'en 1801; contenant la
description géographique, politique
et civile du Paraguay et de la rivière de la Plata; l'histoire de la
découverte et de la conquête de
ces contrées; des détails nombreux
sur leur histoire naturelle, et sur
les peuples sauvages qui les habitent ... Publiés d'après les manu-
scrits de l'auteur, avec une notice
sur sa vie et ses écrits par C.A.
Walckenaer; enrichis de notes par
G. Cuvier ... Suivis de L'histoire
naturelle des oiseaux du Paraguay et
de la Plata, par le même auteur,
traduite d'après l'original espagnol,
et augmentée d'un grand nombre de
notes par m. Sonnini: accompagnés
d'un atlas de vingt-cinq planches
... Paris, Dentu, 1809.
        4 v. fold. tab.   20 1/2 cm.

                          B

599   Babbidge, Charles.
        The claims of Congregational
churches. A centennial address: being a plea in vindication of the
rights of the First church of
Christ in Pepperell, Mass. Delivered Feb. 9, 1847. By Charles Babbidge
... Boston, W. Crosby and H.P.
Nichols, 1847.
        44 p.   22 1/2 cm.

600   Babbitt, Benjamin B.
        A sermon, before the first annual
convention of the Church union of
the Protestant Episcopal church, in

the diocese of Massachusetts, delivered in St. Paul's church, Tuesday,
May 19, 1863, by Rev. Benjamin B.
Babbitt ... Together with the constitution, plan of operation and organization of the Church union. Boston, Printed for the Church union,
by T.R. Marvin & son, 1863.
   31, [1] p.   23 1/2 cm.

601   Babbitt, Elijah, 1796-1887.
   Organization of the House. Speech
of Hon. Elijah Babbitt, of Penn. Delivered in the House of representatives, January 20, 1860. [Washing-
ton, Buell & Blanchard, printers,
1860]
   8 p.   24 cm.

602   Babbitt, Elijah, 1796-1887.
   Speech of Hon. Elijah Babbitt, of
Pennsylvania, on the confiscation of
rebel property. Delivered in the
House of representatives, May 22,
1862. [Washington, L. Towers & co.,
printers, 1862]
   8 p.   21 cm.

603   Babcock, George R.   d. 1876.
   ... Remarks of Mr. Babcock, of
Erie, on the Roman Catholic church
property bill: in the Senate, June
24, 1853, upon the motion to strike
out the enacting clause of the bill.
Albany, Cuyler & Henly, printers,
1853.
   12 p.   24 cm.

604   Babcock, Samuel Brazer, 1807-1873.
   A discourse on the death of President Lincoln, preached in the Ortho-
dox Congregational church, in Dedham,
by the Rev. Samuel B. Babcock ...
April 19, 1865. Dedham, Mass.,
Printed by J. Cox, jr., 1865.
   16 p.   23 1/2 cm.

605   Babson, John James, 1809-1886.
        History of the town of Gloucester,
        Cape Ann, including the town of Rock-
        port. By John J. Babson. Gloucester
        [Mass.] Procter brothers, 1860.
        xi, 610 p. illus., plates, fold.
        map.   23 1/2 cm.

606   Bach, Moriz.
        Descripción de la nueva provincia
        de Otuquis en Bolivia. 2 ed. corr.
        y aumentada. Buenos Aires, Imprenta
        argentina, 1843.
        25 p., 1 l.   29 1/2 cm.

607   Bache, Alexander Dallas, 1806-1867.
        Additional notes of a discussion of
        tidal observations made in connection
        with the coast survey at Cat Island,
        Louisiana. By Prof. A.D. Bache. ...
        New Haven, Printed by B.L. Hamlen,
        1852.
        15 p. incl. tables.   23 1/2 cm.

608   Bache, Franklin, 1792-1864.
        Observations and reflections on the
        penitentiary system. A letter from
        Franklin Bache, M.D., to Roberts
        Vaux. Philadelphia, J. Harding,
        printer, 1829.
        13 p.   23 cm.

609   Bache, William, 1811--
        Historical sketches of Bristol
        Borough, in the county of Bucks,
        anciently known as "Buckingham:"
        being the second chartered borough
        in Pennsylvania; commencing with
        its colonial settlement, in 1681,
        and closing with the year 1853. By
        William Bache. Bristol, Pa. [W.
        Bache, printer] 1853.
        60 p.   20 cm.

610   Bachiller y Morales, Antonio, 1812-
        1889.

Antigüedades americanas. Noticias
que tuvieron los Europeos de la
América ántes del descubrimiento
de Cristobal Colón, recogidas por
A. Bachiller y Morales ... Habana,
Oficina del Faro industrial, 1845.
133, 3 p. illus., map. 21 cm.

611   Bachiller y Morales, Antonio, 1812-
       1889.
       Apuntes para la historia de las
       letras y de la instrucción pública
       de la isla de Cuba, por Antontio
       Bachiller y Morales ... Habana, Impr.
       de P. Massana [etc.] 1859-61.
       3 v.   21 cm.

612   Bachiller y Morales, Antonio, 1812-1889.
       Elogio del Señor Don José de
       Arango y Castillo, uno de los
       fundadores de la Real sociedad
       económica de la Habana. Escrito
       por D.A. Bachiller y Morales. Haba-
       na, Impr. del Tiempo, 1852.
       13 p.   22 1/2 cm.

613   Bachiller y Morales, Antonio, 1812-
       1889.
       Prontuario de agricultura general,
       para el uso de los labradores i
       hacendados de la isla de Cuba, por
       Antonio Bachiller y Morales (edición
       ilustrada con láminas.) Habana,
       Impr. de Barcina, 1856.
       vi, 405 [6] p. illus.   24 cm.

614   Back, Sir George, 1796-1878.
       Narrative of an expedition in
       H.M.S. Terror, undertaken with a
       view to geographical discovery on
       the Arctic shores, in the years 1836-
       7, by Captain Back ... London, J.
       Murray, 1838.
       vii, 456 p. front., plates. fold.
       map.   21 cm.

615   Back, *Sir* George, 1796-1878.
          Voyage dans les régions arctiques,
       à la recherche du capitaine Ross, en
       1834 et 1835; et reconnaissance du
       Thlew-ee-choh, maintenant Grande
       Rivière Back; par le capitaine Back
       ... traduit par M.P. Cazeaux ...
       Paris, A. Bertrand, 1836.
          2 v.   fold. map.   21 1/2 cm.

616   Backus, Azel, 1765-1817.
          An inaugural discourse, delivered
       in the village of Clinton, December 3,
       1812, by the Rev. Azel Backus, D.D.,
       on the day of his induction into the
       office of president of Hamilton col-
       lege.   Utica, Printed by I. Merrell,
       1812.
          20 p.   21 cm.

617   Backus, Isaac, 1724-1806.
          All true ministers of the gospel
       are called into that work by the spe-
       cial influences of the Holy Spirit.
       A discourse shewing the nature and
       necessity of an internal call to
       preach the everlasting gospel ...   To
       which is added, Some short account
       of the experiences and dying testimony
       of Mr. Nathanael Shepherd.   By Isaac
       Backus, preacher of the gospel, Bos-
       ton: Printed by Fowle in Ann Street,
       near the Town-Dock, 1754.
          xiii, 15-115, [1] p.   20 cm.

618   [Backus, Isaac] 1724-1806.
          An appeal to the public for relig-
       ious liberty, against the oppressions
       of the present day ...   Boston: Print-
       ed by John Boyle in Marlborough-
       street, 1773.
          62 p.   19 cm.

619   Backus, Isaac, 1724-1806.
          The doctrine of sovereign grace
       opened and vindicated: and also the

consistency and duty of declaring
divine sovereignty, and mens impo-
tency, while yet we address their
consciences with the warnings of
truth, and calls of the Gospel. By
Isaac Backus, pastor of a church in
Middleborough ... Providence, Rhode-
Island: Printed by John Carter, at
Shakespear's Head, 1771.
1 p. l., [5]-71, xii p. 20 cm.

620   Backus, Isaac, 1724-1806.
Government and liberty described;
and ecclesiastical tyranny exposed.
By Isaac Backus, pastor of a church
in Middleborough ... Massachusetts-
state: Boston; Printed by Powars
and Willis, and sold by Phillip Freeman, in Union-street [1778]
20 p. 20 cm.

621   Backus, Isaac, 1724-1806.
A history of New-England, with particular reference to the denomination of Christians called Baptists
... Collected from the most authentic records and writings, both ancient
and modern. By Isaac Backus, pastor
of the first Baptist church in Mid-
[d]leborough ... Boston: Printed
by Edward Draper, at his Printing-
Office in Newbury-Street: and sold
by Phillip Freeman, in Union-Street.
1777-96.
3 v. 19 1/2 - 22 cm.

622   [Backus, Isaac] 1721-1806.
Policy, as well as honesty, forbids
the use of secular force in religious
affairs. Massachusetts-state: Boston: Printed by Draper and Folsom,
and sold by Phillip Freeman, in Union-
street. M.DCC.LXXXIX.
26 p. 20 cm.

623   Backus, Joseph, *b.* 1667.

The proclamation of the Honourable Joseph Jenks dep. governour,
answered; and the proceedings of a
justice's court held at Norwich, July
26, 1725 therein refer'd to, vindicated. By Joseph Backus, esq. [New
London?] Printed for the author:
sold at several of the booksellers
shops in Boston, and N. London. 1726.
1 pl l., 32 p. 17 cm.

624 Backus, Simon.
A dissertation on the right and
obligation of the civil magistrate to
take care of the interest of religion,
and provide for its support; in which
the arguments in confirmation of said
right and obligation, both from reason
and the Sacred Scriptures, are ad-
duced: the usual objections examined,
--together with several corollaries deduced from the subject. By Simon
Backus, A.M. Middletown [Conn.]:
Printed by T.&J.B. Dunning. 1804.
[Copy-right secured according to Act
of Congress.]
v, 34 p. 23 cm.

625 [Bacon, Anthony]
A short address to the government,
the merchants, manufacturers, and
the colonists in America, and the
sugar islands, on the present state of
affairs. By a member of Parliament.
London, Printed for G. Robinson, 1775.
2 p. l., 40 p. 20 1/2 cm.

626 Bacon, *Mrs.* Eliza Ann (Munroe)
Memoir of Rev. Henry Bacon. By
Mrs. E. A. Bacon ... Boston, A.
Tompkins, 1857.
vi, [11]-361 p. front. (port.)
20 cm.

627 Bacon, George Washington, 1830-1921.
Abraham Lincoln geschetst in zijn

leven en daden. Naar het Engelsch,
van G.W. Bacon. Amsterdam, J. Leen-
dertz, 1865.
    2 p. 1., 89 p., 1 1.   20 cm.

628   Bacon, George Washington.
       Bacon's descriptive handbook of
America ... By George Washington
Bacon ... and William George Larkins
... London and New York, G.W. Bacon
and co. [1866]
    viii, 392 p. col. front., illus.,
pl., maps (partly fold.)   19 1/2
cm.

629   Bacon, George Washington.
       Life and speeches of President
Andrew Johnson. Embracing his early
history, political career, speeches,
proclamations, etc. With a sketch
of the secession movement, and his
course in relation thereto; also his
policy as president of the United
States. By G.W. Bacon ... London,
Bacon and co. [1865]
    iv p., 1 1., 106 p.   19 1/2 cm.

630   Bacon, James, *fl*. 1795.
       The American Indian; or, Virtues
of nature. A play. In three acts.
With notes. Founded on an Indian
tale. By James Bacon ... London,
Printed for the author, by Messrs.
Harrison and co., 1795.
    5 p. 1., ix xvi, [2], 11 p.   21
cm.

631   Bacon, John, 1738-1820.
       Illustrations illustrated. Con-
taining a brief reply to some part of
the Illustrations, annexed to a
piece, intituled, Letters of friend-
ship, &c. By John Bacon, A.M. Hartford: Printed by Hudson & Goodwin.
M.DCC.LXXXI.
    iv, [5]-31 p.   19 cm.

632   Bacon, John, 1738-1820.
       A sermon preached September 29th,
1771. By John Bacon ... The next
Lord's day after he was installed,
and the Reverend Mr. John Hunt ...
ordained, colleague pastors of the
South church in Boston. Boston,
Printed by Kneeland and Adams, 1772.
35 p.   20 1/2 cm.

633   Bacon, Leonard, 1802-1881.
       An address before the New England
society of the city of New York, on
forefathers' day, December 22, 1838.
By Leonard Bacon ... New York, E.
Collier, 1839.
46 p., 1 l.   24 cm.

634   Bacon, Leonard, 1802-1881.
       A commemorative discourse, on the
completion of fifty years from the
founding of the theological seminary
at Andover. By Leonard Bacon ...
Andover, Printed by W.F. Draper, 1858.
46 p.   21 1/2 cm.

635   Bacon, Leonard, 1802-1881.
       A discourse on the early constitu-
tional history of Connecticut, delivered before the Connecticut historical society, Hartford, May 17, 1843.
By Leonard Bacon ... Hartford, Case,
Tiffany & Burnham, printers, 1843.
24 p.   23 cm.

636   Bacon, Leonard, 1802-1881.
       A historical discourse delivered
at Worcester, in the Old south meeting house, September 22, 1863; the
hundredth anniversary of its erection.
By Leonard Bacon ... With introductory remarks by Hon. Ira M. Barton ...
And an appendix. Worcester, Printed
by E.R. Fiske, 1863.
106 p. front.   23 1/2 cm.

637   Bacon, Leonard, 1802-1881.
            The jugglers detected. A discourse
        delivered by request, in the Chapel
        street, church, New Haven, December
        30, 1860, by Leonard Bacon, pastor
        of the First church. With an appen-
        dix. New Haven, T.H. Pease, 1861.
            39 p.   22 1/2 cm.

638   Bacon, Leonard, 1802-1881.
            Reply to Professor Parker, by Rev.
        Leonard Bacon ... [New Haven,
        1863]
            1 p. l., p. 191-258.   23 cm.

639   [Bacon, Leonard] 1802-1881.
            Review of pamphlets on slavery and
        colonization. First published in
        the Quarterly Christian spectator;
        for March, 1833. 2d separate ed. New-
        Haven, A.H. Maltby; Boston, Pierce
        and Parker, 1833.
            24 p.   22 cm.

640   Bacon, Leonard, 1802-1881.
            Sketch of the life and public
        services of Hon. James Hillhouse of
        New Haven; with a notice of his son,
        Augustus Lucas Hillhouse. By Rev.
        Leonard Bacon, D.D. New Haven, 1860.
            46, [557]-572 p.   front. (port.)
        23 cm.

641   Bacon, Leonard, 1802-1881.
            Slavery discussed in occasional
        essays, from 1833 to 1846. By Leon-
        ard Bacon ... New York, Baker and
        Scribner, 1846.
            x p., 1 l., [13]-247 p.   19 1/2
        cm.

642   Bacon, Leonard, 1802-1881.
            Thirteen historical discourses,
        on the completion of two hundred years,
        from the beginning of the First
        church in New Haven, with an appendix

By Leonard Bacon ... New Haven,
Durrie & Peck; New York, Gould, Newman & Saxton, 1839.
viii, 400 p. front. (port.) 23
1/2 cm.

643 Bacon, Leonard Woolsey, 1830-1907.
An historical discourse, on the
two hundredth anniversary of the
founding of the Hopkins grammar
school, New Haven, Connecticut. Delivered before the "Hopkins grammar
school association," July 24th,
1860, by Leonard Woolsey Bacon. With
notes and an appendix. Pub. by request of the Association. New Haven,
Printed by T.J. Stafford, 1860.
70 p. 23 1/2 cm.

644 Bacon, *Mrs*. Lydia B (Stetson) 1786-
1853.
Biography of Mrs. Lydia B. Bacon.
Written for the Massachusetts Sabbath school society, and approved by
the committee of publication. Boston, Massachusetts Sabbath school
society [c1856]
348 p. 19 1/2 cm.

645 Bacon, Oliver N.
A history of Natick, from its
first settlement in 1651 to the
present time; with notices of the
first white families, and also an
account of the centennial celebration, Oct. 16, 1851, Rev. Mr. Hunt's
address at the consecration of Dell
Park cemetery, &c. ... By Oliver
N. Bacon ... Boston, Damrell &
Moore, printer, 1856.
2 p. l., [3]-261 p. front.,
plates, ports. 24 1/2 cm.

646 Bacon, Thomas, 1700 (*ca*.)-1768.
Four sermons, preached at the
parish church of St. Peter, in Talbot

county, in the province of Maryland,
by the Rev. Thomas Bacon ... Viz.
Two sermons to black slaves, and two
sermons for the benefit of a charity
working-school, in the above parish,
for the maintenance and education of
orphans and poor children, and negroes. London, Printed by J. Oliver,
1753. Reprinted at Bath, by R.
Cruttwell, 1783.
1 p. l., [v]-vi p., 1 l., 192 p.
16 1/2 cm.

647   Bacqueville de la Potherie, Claude
       Charles Le Roy, 1668-1738.
          Histoire de l'Amérique septen-
       trionale ... Par mr. de Bacque-
       ville de la Potherie ... Paris,
       J.-L. Nion et F. Didot, 1722.
          4 v. plates (part fold.) Maps
       (part fold., incl. music) 16 1/2
       cm.

648   Badger, George E[dmund] 1795-1866.
          American steam navigation; speech
       of Hon. George E. Badger ... for the
       Collins steamers. In Senate of the
       United States, May 6, 1852. Washing-
       ton, D.C., Buell & Blanchard, 1852.
          13 p.   23 cm.

649   Badger, William Whittlesey.
          Washington; or, A vision of liber-
       ty: a poem, delivered before the
       Genesee lyceum at Lima, N.Y., on the
       occasion of their annual celebration
       of Washington's birthday, February
       22, 1859. By William Whittlesey
       Badger ... New York, Thatcher &
       Hutchinson, 1859.
          24 p.   19 1/2 cm.

650   Badia, Marco Antonio.
          Compendio della guerra nata per
       confini in America tra la Francia e
       l'Inghilterra, poi accesa ed

intrapresa da molti principi in
Europa. Descritto dal principio
fin' al fine da Marc' Antonio Badia.
Amsterdam, 1763.
    xvi, 168 p. front. (port.) 19
cm.

651   [Badin, Stephen Theodore] 1768-1853.
       Origine et progrès de la mission
du Kentucky, (États-Unis d'Amerique);
par un témoin oculaire ... Paris,
A. Le Clère, 1821.
    1 p. l., 32 p.   20 cm.

652   Baers, Johannes, d. 1653.
       Olinda, ghelegen int landt van
Brasil, inde capitania van Phernam-
buco, met mannelijcke dapperheyt
ende groote couragie inghenomen,
ende geluckelijck verovert op den
16. Februarij a°. 1630. Onder
het beleydt vanden seer manhaften
ende cloeckmoedigen zee-helt, den
Heere Henrick Lonck, generael weg-
hen de geoctroyeerde West-Indische
compagnie, over een machtige vloote
schepen, door den vvel-edelen, seer
gestrengen ende grootmoedige Heere
Diederich van Weerdenburg, heere van
Lent, velt-overste ende colonel over
dry regimenten infanterie. Cost
ende claer bescheven, door Joannem
Baers. Amsterdam, H. Laurentsz.,
1630.
    3 p. l., 3-38 p.   19 cm.

654   Bagot, Lewis, bp. of St. Asaph, 1740-
1802.
       A sermon preached before the incor-
porated Society for the propagation
of the gospel in foreign parts; at
their anniversary meeting in the
parish church of St. Mary-le-Bow,
on Friday, February 19, 1790. By
the Right Reverend Lewis, lord bishop of Norwich. London, Printed by

S. Brooke, M DCC XC.
23 p.   21 1/2 x 16 cm.

655   Bailey, G[oldsmith] F   1823-1862.
            Intervention for freedom. Address
      of Hon. G.F. Bailey, at Fitchburg,
      Friday evening, Aug. 24th, 1860.
      [Reported by Mr. H.E. Rockwell]
      [Fitchburg? 1860]
            8 p.   22 cm.

656   Bailey, Isaac, d. 1824.
            American naval biography. Com-
      piled by Isaac Bailey ... Provi-
      dence (R.I.) Published by Isaac
      Bailey, near the Turk's head, H.
      Mann & co. printers,--1815.
            iv, [5]-257, [1] p.   18 1/2
      cm.

657   Bailey, John J   d. 1873.
            Waldimar. A tragedy, in five
      acts. By John J. Bailey ... [Not
      published] New-York [J. Van Norden,
      printer] 1834.
            124 p., 1 l.   24 cm.

658   Bailey, J[ohn]W.
            Knox college, by whom founded and
      endowed; also, a review of a pam-
      phlet, entitled "Rights of Congrega-
      tionalists in Knox college." By
      J.W. Bailey. Chicago, Press & Tri-
      bune printing office, 1860.
            131 p.   21 1/2 cm.

659   Bailey, Philip James, 1816-1902.
            The international policy of the
      great powers. By Philip James Bail-
      ey ... London, Saunders, Otley,
      and co., 1861.
            xv, 275 p.   16 cm.

660   Bailey, Robert, b. 1773.
            The life and adventures of Robert
      Bailey, from his infancy up to

December, 1821. Interspersed with
anecdotes, and religious and moral
admonitions. Written by himself.
Richmond, Printed for the author, by
J. & G. Cochran, 1822.
   2 p. l., [9]-348 p., 1 1.   front.
(port.) 3 pl.   21 1/2 cm.

661   Bailey, Silas, 1809-1874.
         The moral significance of war. A
      discourse delivered in the Baptist
      meeting house, in Franklin, Indiana,
      on the occasion of the national fast;
      September 26, 1861.   By Rev. Silas
      Bailey ...   Indianapolis, Dodd & co.,
      printers, 1861.
         cover-title, 20 p.   23 1/2 cm.

662   Bailey, William.
         Records of patriotism and love of
      country. By William Bailey ...   Wash-
      ington: Printed and published. And
      may be had of all booksellers in the
      U.S. [Stamford? Eng., Drakard and
      Wilson, printers] 1826.
         xiii, [2], 216 p.   22 cm.

663   Baillie, Hugh.
         A letter to Dr. Shebear: contain-
      ing a refutation of his arguments
      concerning the Boston and Quebec acts
      of Parliament: and his aspersions
      upon the memory of King William, and
      the Protestant dissenters. By Hugh
      Baillie ...   London, Printed for J.
      Donaldson, 1775.
         1 p. l., 54 p.   20 1/2 cm.

664   Baily, John, *fl.* 1811-1850.
         Central America; describing each of
      the states of Guatemala, Honduras,
      Salvador, Nicaragua, and Costa Rica;
      their natural features, products,
      population, and remarkable capacity
      for colonization ...   By John Baily
      ...   London, T. Saunders, 1850.

xii, 164 p.   3 pl. (incl. front.)
19 cm.

665   Baines, Edward, 1774-1848.
Baine's [!] history of the late war,
between the United States and Great
Britain: with a critical appendix,
&c., by Ebenezer Harlow Cummins, A.M.
Baltimore, Printed by B. Edes, 1820.
xii, [13]-167, xivii p.   18 1/2
cm.

666   Baird, Henry Carey, 1825-1912.
Protection of home labor and home
productions necessary to the prosperity of the American farmer. By Henry Carey Baird. [New York, New York
tribune office, 1860]
16 p.   23 1/2 cm.

667   Baird, Robert, 1798-1863.
The Christian retrospect and register; a summary of the scientific, moral and religious progress of the
first half of the XIXth century. By
Robert Baird. New York, M.W. Dodd,
1851.
xii, [13]-420 p.   19 1/2 cm.

668   Baird, Robert, 1798-1863.
Geschichte der Mässigkeits-
gesellschaft in den Vereinigten
Staaten Nord-Amerika's, von R. Baird.
Berlin, G. Eichler, 1837.
xii, [4], 340 p.   18 cm.

669   Baird, Robert, 1798-1863.
Impressons and experiences of the
West Indies and North America in 1819.
By Robert Baird ... Philadelphia,
Lea & Blanchard, 1850.
354 p.   18 cm.

670   Baird, Robert, 1798-1863.
Kerkelijke geschiedenis, kerkelijke
statistiek en godsdienstig leven der

Vereenigde Staten van Noord-Amerika.
Door Robert Baird. Naar de hoog-
duitsche uitgave van dr. R. Brandes,
bewerkt door A.W. van den Worm ...
met eene voorrede van d^r· N.C. Kist
... Schoonhoven, S.E. van Nooten,
1846-49.
2 v. fold. map. 23 cm.

671   Baird, Robert, 1798-1863.
... The progress and prospects of
Christianity in the United States of
America; with remarks on the subject
of slavery in America; and on the
intercourse between British and American churches, by R. Baird ... London, Partridge and Oakey; [etc., etc.,
1851]
iv, [5]-72 p.   21 cm.

672   Baird, Robert, 1798-1863.
Religion in the United States of
America. Or, An account of the origin, progress, relations to the
state, and present condition of the
evangelical churches in the United
States. With notices of unevangelical
denominations. By the Rev. Robert
Baird ... Glasgow and Edinburgh.
Blackie and son; [etc., etc.] 1844.
xix, 1 , 736 p. 2 maps (incl.
front.)   24 cm.

673   Baird, Robert, 1798-1863.
State and prospects of religion in
America; being a report made at the
conference of the Evangelical alliance, in Paris, August 25th, 1855.
By the Rev. Robert Baird ... London, E. Suter [etc.] 1855.
91 p. fold. map. 22 cm.

674   Baird, Samuel John, 1817-1893, *comp.*
A collection of the acts, deliverances, and testimonies of the supreme
judicatory of the Presbyterian church
from its origin in America to the

present time. With notes and documents, explanatory and historical:
constituting a complete illustration
of her polity, faith, and history.
Compiled for the Board of publication by the Rev. Samuel J. Baird.
Philadelphia, Presbyterian board of
publication, 1856.
   xxiii, [1], 856 p.   23 1/2 cm.

675   Baird, Spencer Fullerton, 1823-1887.
   The birds of North America; the
descriptions of species based chiefly on the collections in the Museum
of the Smithsonian institution. By
Spencer F. Baird ... with the coopera-
tion of John Cassin ... and George N.
Lawrence ... With an atlas of one
hundred plates ... Philadelphia, J.B.
Lippincott & co., 1860.
   3 p. l., iii -lvi, 1005 p. *and*
atlas of c col. pl.   30 cm.

676   Baird, Spencer Fullerton, 1823-1887.
   Catalogue of North American birds,
chiefly in the museum of the Smithsonian institution. By Spencer F.
Baird ... Washington, Smithsonian
institution, 1858.
   1 pl l., [xvii]-lvi p.   30 1/2
x 24 cm.

677   Baird, Spencer Fullerton, 1823-1887.
   Catalogue of North American rep-
tiles in the Museum of the Smithsonian institution. Part I.--Serpents.
By S.F. Baird and C. Girard. Washington, Smithsonian institution, 1853.
   xvi, 172 p.   23 1/2 cm.

678   Baird, Spencer Fullerton, 1823-1887.
   The mammals of North America; the
descriptions of species based chiefly
on the collections in the museum of
the Smithsonian institution. By
Spencer F. Baird ... With eighty-

seven plates of original figures,
illustrating the genera and species,
and including details of external
form and osteology. Philadelphia,
J.B. Lippincott & co. [1857]-59.
   4 p. 1., xi-xxxiv, 735, 55, [2],
[737]-764 p. illus., LXXXVII pl.
(partly col.) 30 x 24 1/2 cm.

679   Baird, Spencer Fullerton, 1823-1887.
         On the serpents of New-York; with
      a notice of a species not hitherto
      included in the fauna of the state.
      By Spencer F. Baird. Albany, C. Van
      Benthuysen, printer, 1854.
         1 p. 1., 28 p. 2 pl. 23 cm.

680   Bajon,   *fl.* 1763.
         Mémoires pour servir à l'histoire
      de Cayenne, et de la Guiane Fran-
      coise, dans lesquels on fait connoître
      la nature de climat de cette con-
      trée, les maladies qui attaquent les
      Européens nouvellement arrivés, &
      celles qui régnent sur les blancs
      & les noirs; des observations sur
      l'histoire naturelle du pays, & sur
      la culture des terres ... Par M.
      Bajon ... Paris, Grangé [etc.]
      1777-78.
         2 v. plates. 20 1/2 cm.

681   [Baker, Daniel] *fl.* 1650-1660.
         Yet one warning more, to thee O
      England: together, with a very tender
      lamentation with bowels of compassion
      & mourning, yet over thee O land. By
      one through whom the eternal, powerful,
      and heavenly Voice, is uttered and
      sounded forth as a trumpet, to awaken
      the nations and inhabitants of the
      earth; and directed to the eares of
      thee O England, and thine O lofty
      city London; which may eccho and ring
      again in the ears of New-England, and
      be heard throughout the whole earth
      ... A prisoner I am in Worcester city-

gaol, this 9th. month, the 16th.
day, and of the year accounted 1660.
D.B.   London, Printed for R. Wilson,
1660.
  1 p. 1., 37, [1] p.   18 x 14 cm.

682   Baker, Edward Dickinson, 1811-1861.
      Speech of Hon. E.D. Baker, of Ore-
gon, delivered in the Senate of the
United States, January 2d, and 3d,
1861, upon the secession question.
Washington, H. Polkinhorn, printer
[1861]
  3 p.   22 1/2 cm.

683   Baker, George E   ed.
      The life of William H. Seward with
selections from his works, ed. by
George E. Baker. New York, Redfield,
1855.
  410 p.   front. (port.)   18 1/2
cm.

684   Baker, George Melville, 1832-1890.
      Our twelve months' cruise: a vale-
dictory delivered before the Mercantile library association, members'
course, May, 1866. By George M.
Baker. Boston, For private distribution, 1866.
  16 p.   22 x 18 cm.

685   Baker, Henry Felt, 1797-1857.
      Banks and banking in the United
States. By Henry F. Baker ... Boston, Ticknor, Reed, and Fields,
1853.
  2 v.   23 1/2 cm.

686   Baker, James, d. 1854.
      The life of Sir Thomas Bernard,
baronet. By the Rev. James Baker
... London, J. Murray, 1819.
  xiii, 190 p., 1 l.   front. (port.)
22 cm.

687   Baker, James Loring.
        Exports and imports, as showing
        the relative advancement of every
        nation in wealth, strength, and inde-
        pendence. [In a series of articles
        contributed to the Boston transcript.]
        By James L. Baker ... Philadelphia,
        1859.
            30 p.   22 1/2 cm.

688   [Baker, James Loring]
        A review of the tariff of 1846 ...
        in a series of articles contributed
        to the Evening transcript, over the
        signature of "Profit and loss" ...
        3d ed. Boston, A.J. Wright, 1856.
            iv, [5]-48 p.   23 1/2 cm.

689   Baker, James Loring.
        Slavery; by J.L. Baker ...   Phila-
        delphia, J.A. Norton 1860.
            19 p.   23 cm.

690   Baker, John Freeman.
        Our martyr President. By John F.
        Baker. [New York, 1865]
            1 p. 1., 5 p.   23 1/2 cm.

691   Baker, John Martin.
        A view of the commerce between the
        United States and Rio de Janeiro, Bra-
        zil ... By John M. Baker ... Wash-
        ington, D.C., Printed at the office
        of the Democratic review, 1838.
            118 p.   front. (fold. map)   21 cm.

692   Baker, John Martin.
        A view of the commerce of the Unit-
        ed States and the Mediterranean sea-
        ports, including the Adriatic and
        Morea; with maps of the principal
        harbours in those seas ...   From the
        manuscript of the late John Martin
        Baker ... by his son, Louis Baker.
        Philadelphia, Barrington & Murphy,
        1847.

112 p.   13 maps.   22 1/2 cm.

693   Baker, La Fayette Charles, 1826-1868.
        History of the United States se-
        cret services, by General L.C. Baker
        ... Philadelphia, L.C. Baker, 1867.
        704 p.   front. (port.) plates.   24
        cm.

694   Baker, William Deal 1812-1876.
        The Saturniad; being a full and true
        account of the rise, progress, and
        downfall of the University of Quilsyl-
        vane. In three cantos. By Hyton
        Hosmot [*pseud*.] Philadelphia, Print-
        ed for the publisher, 1832.
        63 p.   15 cm.

695   The Balance, and State journal. v. 1-7,
        Jan. 5, 1802-Dec. 27, 1808; [new
        ser.] v. 1-2, Jan. 4, 1809-Dec. 1810;
        [ser. 3] v. 1, Jan. 1 -Dec. 24, 1811.
        Albany [etc.] Croswell & Frary [etc.]
        10 v.   32-55 cm.

696   Balbi, Adriano, 1782-1848.
        Essai statistique sur le royaume
        de Portugal et d'Algarve, comparé
        aux autres États de l'Europe, et
        suivi d'un coup d'oeil sur l'état
        actuel des sciences, des lettres et
        des beaux-arts parmi les Portugais
        des deux hémisphères ... par Adrien
        Balbi ... Paris, Rey et Gravier,
        1822.
        2 v.   tables (part fold.)   21 cm.

697   Balcarce, Mariano, b. 1808.
        Buenos-Ayres, sa situation présente,
        ses lois liberales, sa population
        immigrante, ses progrès commerciaux
        et industriels, par M. Balcarce. 2.
        éd.   Paris, Impr. de A. Blondeau,
        1857.
        2 p. l., 76 p.   23 cm.

698   Balch, Thomas, 1821-1877, *ed.*
        Papers relating chiefly to the
Maryland line during the revolution.
Ed. by Thomas Blach ... Philadelphia,
Printed for the Seventy-six society,
1857.
        2 p. 1., 218 p., 1 1. 23 1/2 cm.

699   Baldridge, Samuel Coulter, 1829-1898.
        The martyr prince. A sermon on the
occasion of the assassination of
President Lincoln, delivered in the
Prebyterian church, Friendsville,
Sabbath morning, April 23d, 1865. By
the pastor, Rev. S. C. Baldridge.
Cincinnati, O., Press of J.B. Boyd,
1865.
        21 p.   23 1/2 cm.

700   [Baldwin, Charles N   ]
        A universal biographical dictionary,
containing the lives of the most celebrated characters of every age and
nation ... to which is added, a dictionary of the principal divinities
and heroes of Grecian and Roman myth-
ology; and a biographical dictionary
of eminent living characters. Richmond, Vir., N. White, 1826.
        444 p. front. (port.)   21 cm.

701a Baldwin, Ebenezer, *d.* 1837.
        Annals of Yale college, from its
foundation, to the year 1831. By
Ebenezer Baldwin. To which is added,
an appendix, bringing it down to 1838.
2d ed. New Haven, B. & W. Noyes,
1838.
        viii, 343 p.   22 1/2 cm.

701b Baldwin, Ebenezer, *d.* 1837.
        Annals of Yale college, in New
Haven, Connecticut, from its foundation, to the year 1831. With an appendix, containing statistical tables,
and exhibiting the present condition

of the institution. By Ebenezer
Baldwin. New Haven, H. Howe, 1831.
    viii, 324 p.   24 cm.

702   [Baldwin, Ebenezer] 1745-1776.
        A funeral oration in memory of
    Mr. Jonathan Lyman, late tutor of
    Yale college, and since instructor
    of the academic school at Hatfield
    ... Pronounced in the meeting-house
    at Hatfield, June 18th, A.D. 1766
    ... New-Haven, Printed by S. Green,
    1767.
        19 p.   18 cm.

703   Baldwin, Ebenezer, *d*. 1837.
        Observations on the physical, in-
    tellectual, and moral qualities of
    our colored population: with remarks
    on the subject of emancipation and
    colonization. By Ebenezer Baldwin
    ... New Haven, L. H. Young, 1834.
        iv, [5]-52 p.   22 cm.

704   Baldwin, George Rumford, 1798-1888.
        Report on supplying the city of
    Charlestown with pure water: made
    for the City council by order of Hon.
    James Dana, mayor of Charlestown,
    by George R. Baldwin and Charles L.
    Stevenson, civil engineers. Boston,
    Little, Brown and company, 1860.
        77 p.   front. (fold. plan)   23
    1/2 cm.

705   Baldwin, Henry, 1780-1844.
        A general view of the origin and
    nature of the Constitution and gov-
    ernment of the United States, deduc-
    ed from the political history and
    condition of the colonies and states,
    from 1774 until 1788. And the deci-
    sions of the Supreme court of the
    United States. Together with opin-
    ions in the cases decided at Jan-
    uary term, 1837, arising on the
    restraints on the powers of the

155

states. By Henry Baldwin. ...
Philadelphia, Printed by J.C. Clark,
1837.
    v, [1], 197 p. illus.   23 cm.

706   Baldwin, John Denison, 1809-1883.
         State sovereignty and treason.
      Speech of Hon. John D. Baldwin, of
      Massachusetts, delivered in the
      House of representatives, Washing-
      ton, March 5, 1864, the House being
      in committee of the whole on the
      state of the Union. [Washington,
      H. Polkinhorn, printer, 1864]
         8 p.   23 1/2 cm.

707   Baldwin, Joseph Glover, 1815-1864.
         The flush times of Alabama and
      Mississippi. A series of sketches.
      By Joseph G. Baldwin. 2d ed. New-
      York, London, D. Appleton & co., 1854.
         x, 330 p. front., 3 pl.   19 1/2
      cm.

708   Baldwin, Joseph Glover, 1815-1864.
         Party leaders; sketches of Thomas
      Jefferson, Alex'r Hamilton, Andrew
      Jackson, Henry Clay, John Randolph,
      of Roanoke, including notices of
      many other distinguished American
      statesmen. By Jo. G. Baldwin ...
      New York, D. Appleton and company;
      [etc., etc.] 1855.
         2 p. 1., [7]-369 p.   19 cm.

709   Baldwin, Loammi, 1780-1838.
         Report on the Brunswick canal and
      rail road, Glynn County, Georgia.
      With an appendix containing the char-
      ter and commissioners' report. By
      Loammi Baldwin ... Boston, J.H.
      Eastburn, printer, 1837.
         48 p.   fold. map.   25 1/2 cm.

710   Baldwin, Loammi, 1780-1838.
         Report on the subject of

introducing pure water into the city
of Boston.   By Loammi Baldwin ...
Boston, J.H. Eastburn, city printer,
1834.
    78 p.   fold. map.   23 cm.

711   Baldwin, Samuel, 1731-1784.
        A sermon preached at Plymouth,
    December 22, 1775. Being the anni-
    versary thanksgiving, in commemora-
    tion of the first landing of the fath-
    ers of New-England, there; anno Domi-
    ni, 1620. By Samuel Baldwin ...
    America, Massachuseets-Bay: Boston,
    Printed by Powars and Willis, in
    Queen-street. 1776.
        39 p.   18 1/2 cm.

712   Baldwin, Thomas, 1753-1825.
        A sermon, delivered before His
    Excellency Caleb Strong, esq., gover-
    nor, the honorable the Council, Sen-
    ate, and House of representatives of
    the commonwealth of Massachusetts,
    May 26, 1802. Being the day of
    general election. By Thomas Bald-
    win, A.M., minister of the Second Bap-
    tist church in Boston. 2d ed. Bos-
    ton: Printed by Manning & Loring,
    no. 2, Cornhill, June, 1802.
        32 p.   23 cm.

713   Baldwin, Thomas, 1753-1825.
        A sermon, delivered to the Second
    Baptist society in Boston, on Lord's
    day, December 29, 1799. Occasioned
    by the death of General George Wash-
    ington ... By Thomas Baldwin ...
    Boston, Printed by Manning & Loring
    [1800]
        28 p.   21 cm.

714   Baldwin, Thomas, 1753-1826.
        A sermon, preached February 15,
    1802, before the honourable Senate
    and House of representatives of the

157

commonwealth of Massachusetts, on the
day of the interment of His Honor
Samuel Phillips, esq., lieutenant
governor, who died February 10,
1802, æ. 50. By Thomas Baldwin ...
Boston: Printed by Young and Minns,
state printers. 1802.
   21 p.   21 1/2 cm.

715   Baldwin, Thomas, *of Philadelphia*.
   A universal pronouncing gazetteer
... By Thomas Baldwin ... To which
is added an appendix ... With a supplement ... A new ed., carefully
rev., with the population inserted according to the census of 1850 ...
Philadelphia, Lippincott, Grambo
& co., 1852.
   xvi, [19]-692, iv, 55 p.   19 1/2
cm.

716   Balestier, Joseph Nerée.
   The annals of Chicago: a lecture
delivered before the Chicago lyceum,
January 21, 1840, by Joseph N.
Balestier. Republished from the original edition of 1840, with an introduction, written by the author in
1876, and also a review of the lecture, published in the Chicago tribune in 1872. Chicago, Fergus
printing company, 1876.
   48 p.   21 cm.

717   Balestier, Joseph Nerée.
   Historical sketches of Holland
lodge, with incidental remarks on
masonry in the state of New York.
An address ... by Joseph N. Balestier ... New York, The Lodge, 1862.
   3 p. 1.,[9]-101, [1] p., 1 1.
22 1/2 cm.

718   Ball, Benjamin Lincoln.
   Three days on the White Mountains;
being the perilous adventure of Dr.

B.L. Ball on Mount Washington, during
October 25, 26, and 27, 1855. Written by himself. Boston, N. Noyes,
1856.
72 p. 19 cm.

719   Ball, Charles.
Slavery in the United States. A
narrative of the life and adventures
of Charles Ball, a black man, who
lived forty years in Maryland, South
Carolina and Georgia, as a slave ...
Pittsburgh, J.T. Shryock, 1853.
1 p l., [v]-vi, [9]-446 p. 19
cm.

720   [Ballard, William] 1780-1827.
A sketch of the history of Framing-
ham, supposed to have been written
by Οὐδεῖσε, while in prison, aided
in the obtaining of documents, by his
brothers Nemo and Aucum; authors of A
residence in the South; and, A tour
through the West ... Boston, Printed for the publisher, 1827.
iv. [5]-70, [1] p. 21 cm.

721   Ballou, Adin, 1803-1890.
The voice of duty. An address delivered at the anti-slavery picnic
at Westminster, Mass., July 4, 1843.
By Adin Ballou ... Hopedale, Mil-
ford, Mass., Community press, 1843.
12 p. 24 cm.

722   Ballou, John.
The lady of the West; or, The
gold seekers ... by John Ballou.
Cincinnati, Author, 1855.
iv, 5-544 p. 19 cm.

723   Ballou, Maturin Murray, 1820-1895.
Biography of Rev. Hosea Ballou.
By his youngest son, Maturin M.
Ballou ... Boston, A. Tompkins, 1852.
viii, [9]-404 p. front. (port.)
20 cm.

724   Ballou, Maturin Murray, 1820-1895.
        History of Cuba; or, Notes of a
      traveller in the tropics. Being a
      political, historical, and statisti-
      cal account of the island, from its
      first discovery to the present time.
      By Maturin M. Ballou ... Boston,
      Phillips, Sampson and company; New
      York, J.C. Derby; [etc., etc.] 1854.
        viii, [9]-230 p.   front., plates.
      29 cm.

725   Balme, Joshua Rhodes.
        Synopsis of the American war.   By
      J.R. Balme ...   London, Hamilton,
      Adams & co.; [etc., etc.] 1865.
        2 p. l., p. 547-776.   17 1/2 cm.

726   Balmis, Francisco Xavier de.
        Demostración de las eficaces vir-
      tudes nuevamente descubiertas en las
      raices de dos plantas de Nueva-España,
      especies de ágave y de begónia, para
      la curación del vicio venéreo y
      escrofuloso ...   Por ...   Don Fran-
      cisco Xavier Bálmis ...   Madrid,
      En la impr. de la viuda de J. Ibarra,
      1794.
        4 p. l., 347 p.   2 fold. col. pl.
      21 1/2 cm.

727   Banchero, Giuseppe, *ed*.
        La tavola di bronzo, il Pallio di
      seta, ed il Codice colomboamericano,
      nuovamente illustrati per cura di
      Giuseppe Banchero ...   Genova, Fra-
      telli Ferrando, 1857.
        3 p. l., [ix]-lxxix, 588 p., 1
      l. fold. pl., port., fold. maps,
      fold. facsims.   28 cm.

728   Bancroft, Aaron, 1755-1839.
        An essay on the life of George
      Washington, commander in chief of
      the American army, through the revo-
      lutionary war; and the first

160

president of the United States. By
Aaron Bancroft, A.A.S., pastor of a
Congregational church in Worcester.
Worcester [Mass.] Printed by Thomas
& Sturtevant, sold by Thomas and
Andrews, I. Thomas and I. Thomas,
jun. October ... 1807.
    2 p. l., vii, 552 p. front. (port.)
22 1/2 cm.

729   Bancroft, Aaron, 1755-1839.
    An eulogy on the character of the
late Gen. George Washington. Delivered before the inhabitants of the
town of Worcester, commonwealth of
Massachusetts, on Saturday the 22d
of February 1800. By Aaron Bancroft. Printed according to a vote
of said town, requesting a copy for
the press, and directing that each
head of a family should be furnished with one. Worcester: Printed by
Isaiah Thomas, jun. March--1800.
    21 p.   23 cm.

730   Bancroft, Aaron, 1755-1839.
    The life of George Washington,
commander-in-chief of the American
Army through the revolutionary war,
and the first president of the United States. By Aaron Bancroft ...
Philadelphia, Porter & Coates [1808?]
    2 v. in 1. fronts. (ports.)   19
cm.

731   Bancroft, Aaron, 1755-1839.
    A sermon delivered in Worcester,
January 31, 1836, by Aaron Bancroft,
D.D., at the termination of fifty
years of his ministry ... Worcester, C. Harris, 1836.
    44 p.   23 cm.

732   Bancroft, Aaron, 1755-1839.
    A vindication of the result of the
late Mutual council convened in

Princeton. By Aaron Bancroft, D.D.
Worcester: Printed by William Manning, June, 1817.
   vi, [7]-63 p.   21 1/2 cm.

733   [Bancroft, Edward] 1744-1821.
      An essay on the natural history of
      Guiana, in South America. Contain-
      ing a description of many curious
      productions in the animal and vegeta-
      ble systems of that country. Togeth-
      er with an account of the religion,
      manners, and customs of several tribes
      of its Indian inhabitants. Inter-
      spersed with a variety of literary
      and medical observations. In sever-
      al letters from a gentleman of the
      medical faculty during his residence
      in that country ... London, T. Beck-
      et and P.A. DeHondt, 1769.
      2 p. l., iv. 402, [2] p. front.
      20 cm.

734   Bancroft, Edward, 1744-1821.
      Naturgeschichte von Guiana in Süd-
      Amerika. Worinn von der natürlichen
      beschaffenheit und den vornehmsten
      naturproducten des landes, ingleichen
      der religion, sitten und gebräuchen
      verschiedener stämme der wilden
      landeseinwohner, nachricht ertheilet
      wird. In vier briefen. Von Eduard
      Bancroft, esq. Aus dem englischen
      ... Frankfurt und Leipzig, J. Dods-
      ley und compagnie, 1769.
      x, [2], 248 p. front.   19 1/2
      cm.

735   Bancroft, Edward Nathaniel, 1772-1842.
      A sequel to an essay on the yellow
      fever; principally intended to prove,
      by incontestable facts and important
      documents, that the fever, called
      bulam, or pestilential, has no exis-
      tence as a distinct, or a contagious
      disease. By Edward Nathaniel

Bancroft ... London, Printed for
J. Callow, 1817.
1 p. l., [v]-xxii p., 1 l., 487
p. 22 cm.

736 Bancroft, George, 1800 1891.
Éloge funèbre du Président Abraham Lincoln, prononcé en séance
solennelle du Congrès des États-
Unis d'Amérique, par George Bancroft ... Traduction de l'anglais
par Gustave Jottrand. Bruxelle, A.
Lacroix, Verboeckhoven et cie, 1866.
43 p. 22 cm.

737 Bancroft, George, 1800-1891.
History of the colonization of
the United States. By George Bancroft. Abridged by the author ...
Boston, C.C. Little & J. Brown,
1841.
2 v. front., pl., map. 17 1/2
cm.

738 Bancroft, George, 1800-1891.
A history of the United States,
from the discovery of the American
continent ... By George Bancroft
... Boston, Little, Brown and company, 1834-75.
10 v. fronts. (ports.: v. 2-4,
8-9) 22 1/2 - 24 1/2 cm.

739 Bancroft, George, 1800-1891.
Joseph Reed; a historical essay.
By George Bancroft ... New York,
W.J. Widdleton, 1867.
64 p. 22 1/2 cm.

740 Bancroft, George, 1800-1891.
The league for the Union. Speech-
es of the Hon. George Bancroft, and
James Milliken, esq. Philadelphia,
W.S. & A. Martien, 1863.
20 p. 20 cm.

741   Bancroft, George, 1800-1891.
           Literary and historical miscel-
       lanies. By George Bancroft. New
       York, Harper & brothers, 1857.
       iv, 517 p.   25 cm.

742   Bancroft, George, 1800-1891.
           Memorial address on the life and
       character of Abraham Lincoln deliv-
       ered, at the request of both houses
       of the Congress of America, before
       them, in the House of representatives
       at Washington, on the 12th of Febru-
       ary, 1866. By George Bancroft. Wash-
       ington, Govt. print. off., 1866.
           80 p.   front. (port.)   31 x 25
       cm.

743   Bancroft, George, 1800-1891.
           An oration delivered on the fourth
       of July, 1826, at Northampton, Mass.
       By George Bancroft. Northampton, T.
       W. Shepard, printer, 1826.
           26 p.   21 cm.

744   Bancroft, George, 1800-1891.
           Poems. By George Bancroft. Cam-
       bridge [Mass.] The University
       press, 1823.
           2 p. 1., 77 p.   18 1/2 cm.

745   Bangor, *Me. Ordinances, etc.*
           The charter and ordinances of the
       city of Bangor, with acts of the
       Legislature relating to the city.
       Pub. by order of the City council.
       Bangor, Smith & Sayward, printers,
       1851.
           7, 208 p.   24 cm.

746   Bangs, Edward, 1756-1818.
           An oration, delivered at Worces-
       ter, on the Fourth of July, 1791.
       Being the anniversary of the indepen-
       dence of the United States.   By
       Edward Bangs, esq.   Printed at

Worcester, Massachusetts, By Isaiah
Thomas. Sold at his Bookstore in
Worcester, and by him and Company in
Boston. 1791.
16 p.   24 cm.

747   Bangs, Edward, 1756-1818.
An oration on the anniversary of
American independence, pronounced at
Worcester, July 4, 1800. By Edward
Bangs, esq. Worcester, Printed by
Isaiah Thomas, jun., July, 1800.
30 p.   23 cm.

748   Bangs, Edward Dillingham, 1790-1838.
An oration pronounced at Springfield, Mass., on the Fourth of July,
1823, being the forty seventh anniversary of the Declaration of American independence. By Edward D. Bangs,
esq. Pub. by request of the Committee of arrangements. Springfield,
A.G. Tannatt, printer, 1823.
16 p.   21 cm.

749   Bangs, Nathan, 1778-1862.
An authentic history of the missions under the care of the Missionary society of the Methodist Episcopal church. By Nathan Bangs ...
New-York, J. Emory and B. Waugh, for
the Methodist Episcopal church, 1832.
258 p.   front. (port.)   18 cm.

750   Bangs, Nathan, 1778-1862.
A history of the Methodist Episcopal church: by Nathan Bangs ...
3d ed., rev. and cor. ... New York,
Pub. by G. Lane & P.P. Sandford for
the Methodist Episcopal church, 1840-
53 [v. 1, '44]
4 v.   fronts. (v. 2, 3: ports.)
18 cm.

751   [Banister, Thomas] *fl.* 1715.
A letter to the Right Honourable

the Lords commissioners of trade &
plantations: or, A short essay on
the principal branches of the trade
of New-England. With the difficulties
they labour under; and some methods
of improvement. London: Printed
in the year 1715. [Boston, 1941]
  facsim.: 2 p. 1., 19 p. 22 cm.

752 [Banister, Thomas]
  Memoranda relating to the present
crisis as regards our colonies, our
trade, our circulating medium, and
railways. [By] Tomas Retsinab
[*pseud*] London, J. Ollivier, 1847.
  8 p. 21 1/2 cm.

753 Banister, William Bostwick, 1773-1853.
  An oration, delivered at Newburyport on the 34th anniversary of American independence; at the request of
the inhabitants of said town. By William B. Banister, esq. Newburyport:
From the press of E.W. Allen. 1809.
  20 p. 22 cm.

754 Bank bills or paper currency, and the
banking system of Massachusetts:
with remarks on present high prices.
By a conservative. Boston, Little,
Brown and company [etc.] 1856.
  16 p. 23 cm.

755 Banks, Henry, *fl.* 1781-1826.
  A memorial to the Congress of the
U. States, relating to revolutionary
events, by Henry Banks of Va.:
Frankfort, Ky., Printed by A.G.
Hodges, 1827.
  60 p. 17 1/2 cm.

756 Banks, Henry, *fl.* 1781-1826.
  Sketches & propositions, recommend-
ing the establishment of an independent system of banking; permanent
public roads, a new mode for the

recovery of interest on private
loans, changes at the penitentiary,
and a general system of defence, with
some observations necessary to illus-
trate these several topics. By Henry Banks ... Richmond, Manson, printer [1811?]
    65 p.   20 1/2 cm.

757   Banks, Thomas Christopher, 1765-1854.
        An analytical statement of the
      case of Alexander, earl of Stirling
      and Dovan &c. &c. &c. containing
      an explanation of his official digni-
      ties and peculiar territorial rights
      and privileges in the British colon-
      ies of Nova Scotia and Canada, &c.
      &c. and also shewing the descent of
      the Stirling peerage honours, sup-
      ported by legal evidence, and the
      law and usage of Scotland, appertain-
      ing thereto ... By Thomas C. Banks
      ... London, J. Cochrane and co.,
      1832.
        xliv, 123 p.   fold. map.   4 gen-
      eal. tab. (part fold.)   22 cm.

758   Banks, Thomas Christopher, 1765-1854.
        Baronia anglica concentrata; or,
      A concentrated account of all the
      baronies commonly called baronies
      in fee; deriving their origin from
      writ of summons, and not from any
      specific limited creation ... where-
      to is added The proofs of parliamen-
      tary sitting, from the reign of Edw.
      I to that of Queen Anne; also a
      glossary of dormants English, Scotch,
      and Irish peerage titles ... By
      Sir T.C. Banks ... Ripon [etc.]
      The author, 1844, '43.
        2 v.   28 cm.

759   Bannister, Saxe, 1790-1877.
        British colonization and coloured
      tribes. By S. Bannister ... London,

W. Ball, 1838.
xii, 323 p.   18 cm.

760   Bannister, Saxe, 1790-1877.
          Humane policy; or, Justice to the
       aborigines of new settlements essen-
       tial to a due expenditure of British
       money, and to the best interests of
       the settlers. With suggestions how
       to civilise the natives by an improv-
       ed administration of existing means.
       By S. Bannister ... London, T. & G.
       Underwood, 1830.
          2 p. l., [iii]-xii, 248, ccixxxii
       pp., 1 l.   fold. map.   22 cm.

761   Bannister, Saxe, 1790-1877.
          Records of British enterprise
       beyond sea, from the earliest orig-
       inal sources to the present times;
       with contemporary maps and illustra-
       tions. Vol. I.   By S. Bannister ...
       London, Longman, Brown, Green, and
       Longmans, 1849.
          5 p. l., [iii]-x, cxiv, 161 p.
       fold. map (facsim.)   22 1/2 cm.

762   Banvard, John, 1815-1891.
          Description of Banvard's panorama
       of the Mississippi river, painted on
       three miles of canvas: exhibiting a
       view of country 1200 miles in length,
       extending from the mouth of the Mis-
       souri river to the city of New Or-
       leans; being by far the largest pic-
       ture ever executed by man. Boston,
       J. Putnam, printer, 1847.
          48 p.   22 1/2 cm.

763   Banvard, Joseph, 1810-1887.
          The American statesman; or, Illus-
       trations of the life and character
       of Daniel Webster. Designed for
       American youth. By Rev. Joseph
       Banvard ... Boston, Gould and Lin-
       coln, 1853.

334 p. incl. front., illus. plates,
17 1/2 cm.

764   Banvard, Joseph, 1810-1887.
A guide to Providence River and
Narragansett Bay; from Providence
to Newport: in which all the towns,
villages, islands and important objects on both sides are named in order, with an account of the prominent
historic incidents connected with
them. By Joseph Banvard. Providence, Coggeshall & Stewart, 1858.
vi, [7]-66 p.   15 1/2 cm.

765   Banvard, Joseph, 1810-1887.
Novelties of the New world; or,
The adventures and discoveries of the
first explorers of North America. By
Joseph Banvard ...   Boston, Gould &
Lincoln, 1852.
324 p. incl. illus., pl. front.
17 cm.

766   Banvard, Joseph, 1810-1887.
Plymouth and the Pilgrims; or, Incidents of adventure in the history
of the first settlers.   By Joseph
Banvard. Boston, Gould and Lincoln, 1851.
2 p. l., [3]-288 p. incl. illus.,
map. front., 2 pl., port. 17 1/2
cm.

767   Banvard, Joseph, 1810 1887.
Priscilla; or, Trials for the truth.
An historic tale of the Puritans and
the Baptists. By Rev. Joseph Banvard ...   Boston, Heath and Graves,
1854.
11 p., 1 l., 13-405 p. incl.
plates. front.   18 1/2 cm.

768   Banvard, Joseph, 1810-1887.
Romance of American history, as
illustrated in the early events

connected with the French settlement at Fort Carolina; the Spanish colony at St. Augustine, and the English plantation at Jamestown. By Joseph Banvard ... Boston, Gould and Lincoln, 1852.
306 p. front., illus. 17 cm.

769 Banvard, Joseph, 1810-1887.
Tragic scenes in the history of Maryland and the old French war. With an account of various interesting contemporaneous events which occurred in the early settlement of America. By Joseph Banvard ... Boston, Gould & Lincoln; New York, Sheldon, Lamport & Blakeman, 1856.
xviii, [19]-239 p. incl. front., illus. 17 1/2 cm.

770 Baraga, Friedrich, *bp.*, 1797-1868.
A dictionary of the Otchipwe language, explained in English. This language is spoken by the Chippewa Indians, as also by the Otawas, Potawatamis and Algonquins, with little difference. For the use of missionaries, and other persons living among the above mentioned Indians. By the Rev. Frederic Baraga ... Cincinnati, Printed for J.A. Hemann, 1853.
vii, 662 p. 19 cm.

771 Baraga, Friedrich, *bp.*, 1797-1868.
A theoretical and practical grammar of the Otchipwe language, the language spoken by the Chippewa Indians; which is also spoken by the Algonquin, Otawa and Potawatami Indians, with little difference. For the use of missionaries and other persons living among the Indians of the above named tribes. By the Rev. Frederick Baraga ... Detroit, J. Fox, printer, 1850.
576 p. 17 cm.

772   Barait, Rafael Maria, 1810-1860.
       Resúmen de la historia de Vene-
zuela desde el año de 1797 hasta el
de 1830, par Rafael María Baralt y
Ramón Diaz. Tiene al fin un breve
bosquejo histórico que comprende los
años de 1831 hasta 1837. ... Paris,
Impr. de H. Fournier y comp^{ia}, 1841.
       2 v. ports. (incl. front.)   21
cm.

773   Barba, Alvaro Alonso, *b*. 1569.
       The first book of The art of
mettals, in which is declared the
manner of their generation and the
concomitants of them. Written in
Spanish in the year 1640. Translated into English in the year 1669.
London. S. Mearne, 1670.
       156 p.   16 cm.

774   The Barbadoes packet; containing several
original papers: giving an account of
the most material transactions that
have lately happened in a certain
part of the West-Indies. In a letter
from a gentleman of the said island
to his friend in London ... London,
Printed for S. Popping, 1720.
       6 p. l., 68 p.   20 cm.

775   Barbaroux, C[harles] O[gé] 1792-1867.
       Résumé de l'histoire des États-
Unis d'Amérique, par C.O. Barbaroux
... 2. ed. Paris, Lecointe et
Durey. 1824.
       3 p. l., 356 p.   13 1/2 cm.

776   Barbé-Marbois, François, *marquis* de,
       1745-1837.
       Histoire de la Louisiane et de la
cession de cette colonie par la
France aux États-Unis de l'Amérique
Septentrionale; précédée d'un
discours sur la constitution et le
gouvernement des États-Unis. Par

m. Barbé-Marbois, avec une carte
relative à l'étendu des pays cédés.
Paris, Impr. de Firmin Didot, 1829.
2 p. l., 485 p. fold. map. 21
cm.

777 [Barbé-Marbois, François, *marquis* de]
1745-1837.
Journal d'un déporté non jugé,
ou, Déportation en violation des lois,
décrétée le 18 fructidor an v (4
septembre 1797) ... Paris, Chatet
[etc.] 1835.
2 v. in 1. 21 cm.

778 [Barbé-Marbois, François, *marquis* de]
1745-1837.
Réflexions sur la colonie de
Saint-Domingue, ou, Examen approfondi,
des causes de sa ruine, et des
mesures adoptées pour la rétablir;
terminées par l'exposé rapide d'un
plan d'orgauisation propre à lui
rendre son ancienne splendeur;
adressées au commerce et aux amis
de la prospérité nationale ... Paris, Garnery, 1796.
2 v. 20 1/2 cm.

779 Barber, Daniel, 1756-1834.
The history of my own times. By
the Rev. Daniel Barber. ... Washington city, Printed for the author, by
S.C. Ustick, 1827-32.
3 v. 21 cm.

780 Barber, Edward Downing, 1806-1855.
"Popular excitements." An address
delivered before the Anti-masonic
convention holden at Middlebury, Vt.
Feb. 26th, 1830. By E.D. Barber.
Middlebury, Pub. at the request of
the Convention, 1830.
19 p. 21 cm.

781 Barber, John Warner, 1798-1885.

City guide to New Haven; being a
pocket directory for citizens and
strangers, to the prominent objects
of interest within and around the
city. By J.W. Barber and L.S. Punderson ... New Haven, J.W. Barber
& L.S. Punderson, 1860.
1 p. l., 36 p. map. 15 cm.

782   Barber, John Warner, 1798-1885.
... Elements of general history:
embracing all the leading events in
the world's history, from the earliest period to the end of the late
civil war in the United States. By
John W. Barber ... New Haven, Conn.,
H.C. Peck, 1866.
4, [7]-12, [2], [13]-296, [18] p.
front., illus. (incl. maps)   17 1/2
cm.

783   Barber, John Warner, 1798-1885.
Historical collections, being a
general collection of interesting
facts, traditions, biographical
sketches, anecdotes, &c., relating
to the history and antiquities of
every town in Massachusetts, with
geographical descriptions. Illustrated by 200 engravings. By John
Warner Barber ... Worcester, W.
Lazell, 1844.
viii, [9]-624 p.   front., illus.,
plates, fold. map.   22 1/2 cm.

784   Barber, John Warner, 1798-1885.
Historical collections of the
state of New Jersey; containing a
general collection of the most
interesting facts, traditions, biographical sketches, anecdotes, etc.
relating to its history and antiquities, with geographical descriptions of every township in the state.
Illustrated by 120 engravings. By
John W. Barber ... and Henry Howe

173

... New York, S. Tuttle, 1846.
512 p. col. front., illus. (incl.
plans) plates (1 col.) port. 23
cm.

785 Barber, John Warner, 1798-1885.
Historical collections of the
state of New York; containing a general collection of the most interesting facts, traditions, biographical
sketches, anecdotes, &c. relating
to its history and antiquities, with
geographical descriptions of every
township in the state. Illustrated
by 230 engravings. By John W. Barber ... and Henry Howe ... New York,
Pub. for the authors by S. Tuttle,
1841.
608 p. incl. pl front. (ports.)
illus., plates, fold, map. 24 cm.

786 Barber, John Warner, 1798-1885.
Historical, poetical and pictorial
American scenes; principally moral
and religious; being a selection of
interesting incidents in American history: to which is added a chronological table of important events in
the secession war. By John W. Barber
... and Elizabeth G. Barber. New
Haven, Conn., Pub. by J.W. & J. Barber for J.H. Bradley [1863]
190 p. col. front., illus., fold.
map. 19 1/2 cm.

787 Barber, John Warner, 1798-1885, *comp*.
History and antiquities of New
Haven, (Conn.) from its earliest
settlement to the present time.
Collected and comp. from the most
authentic sources. By J.W. Barber.
Illustrated with engravings. New
Haven, J.W. Barber, 1831-[32]
120 p. illus., col. plates, col.
plan. 19 cm.

788   Barber, John Warner, 1798-1885.
      History and antiquities of New
      Haven, Conn., from its earliest set-
      tlement to the present time. With
      biographical sketches and statisti-
      cal information of the public insti-
      tutions, &c., &c. By John W. Bar-
      ber ... and Lemuel S. Punderson.
      [2d ed.] New Haven, L.S. Punderson
      and J.W. Barber, 1856.
      4 , iv, [9]-180 p. front. (map)
      illus., plates (part col.)   20 cm.

789   Barber, John Warner, 1798-1885, *comp.*
      A history of the Amistad captives:
      being a circumstantial account of the
      capture of the Spanish schooner
      Amistad, by the Africans on board;
      their voyage, and capture near Long
      Island, New York; with biographical
      sketches of each of the surviving
      Africans; also, an account of the
      trials had on their case, before the
      district and circuit courts of the
      United States, for the district of
      Connecticut. Comp. from authentic
      sources, by John W. Barber ... New
      Haven, Ct., E.L. & J.W. Barber,
      1840.
      32 p. fold. front., illus. (incl.
      mpa)   22 1/2 cm.

790   Barber, John Warner, 1798-1885.
      Interesting events in the history
      of the United States: being a selec-
      tion of the most important and inter-
      esting events which have transpired
      since the discovery of this country
      to the present time. Carefully se-
      lected from the most approved author-
      ities. By J.W. Barber. New-Haven,
      J.W. Barber, 1828.
      iv,[9]-220, xxiv p. front. (fold.
      mpa) 15 pl.   17 1/2 cm.

791   Barber, John Warner, 1798-1885.

Our whole country; or, The past
and present of the United States,
historical and descriptive. In
two volumes, containing the general
and local histories and descriptions
of each of the states, territories,
cities, and towns of the Union; also
biographical sketches of distinguished persons ... Illustrated by
six hundred engravings ... almost
wholly from drawings taken on the
spot by the authors, the entire work
being on their part the result of
over 16,000 miles of travel and four
years of labor. By John Warner Barber ... and Henry Howe ... Cincinnati, H. Howe, 1861.
2 v. fronts. (ports.) illus., maps,
facsim. 24 cm.

792   Barber, John Warner, 1798-1885.
Views in New Haven and its vicinity:
with a particular description to each
view. Drawn and engraved by J.W.
Barber. New Haven, J.W. Barber [etc.]
1825.
11 p. 6 col. pl. 16 cm.

793   [Barbeu-Dubourg, Jacques] 1709-1779.
Calendrier de Philadelphie, ou
Constitutions de Sancho-Pança et du
Bon-homme Richard, en Pensylvanie.
[n.p.] 1778.
xxx, 6, 118 p. 16 cm.

794   Barco Centenera, Martin del, *b*. 1535.
La Argentina, o La conquista del
Rio de la Plata, poema histórico
por ... Martin del Barco Centenera.
[1601] Buenos-Aires, Imprenta del
estado, 1836.
1 p. l., ii, viii, 312, xxiv p.,
1 l. 33 cm.

795   Bard, William, 1777-1853.
Address, delivered before the

alumni of Columbia college, on the
third day of May, 1826, in the hall
of the college. By William Bard,
A.B. New-York, G. & C. Carvill,
1826.
36 p. 20 1/2 cm.

796　Barham, William.
Descriptions of Niagara; selected
from various travellers; with original additions by William Barham
... Gravesend [Eng.] The compiler
[1847]
180 p. illus. (map) 2 pl. (incl.
front.) 23 cm.

797　Barhydt, David Parish, *d.* 1908.
Industrial exchanges and social
remedies, with a consideration of
taxation. By Dav. Parish Barhydt
... New York, London, G.P. Putnam,
1849.
2 p. l., 238 p. 19 cm.

798　Baril, V　L　comte de la
Hure.
L'empire du Brésil: monographie
complète de l'empire sud-américain
... par V.L. Baril, comte de la
Hure. Paris, F. Sartorius, 1862.
xv, 576 p. front. (port.) 23
cm.

799　[Barinetti, Carlo]
A voyage to Mexico and Havanna;
including some general observations
on the United States. By an Italian.
New-York, Printed for the author by
C. Vinton, 1841.
x, 139 p. 20 x 11 1/2 cm.

800　Barker, David, 1797-1834.
An address in commemoration of the
independence of the United States,
delivered at Rochester, July 4, 1828
by David Barker, jr. ... Dover [N.

H.] G.W. Ela and co., printer, 1828.
28 p.   23 1/2 cm.

801   [Barker, Jacob] 1779-1871.
The ballot box, the palladium of
our liberties. New Orleans, July,
1863. [New Orleans] Printed for the
compiler, 1863.
65 p.   24 cm.

802   Barker, Jacob, 1779-1871.
Jacob Barker to the electors of
the First senatorial district of the
state of New-York. [New York? 1828]
20, [1] p.   23 1/2 cm.

803   Barker, Joseph, 1751-1815.
An address to a respectable number
of citizens, from several towns in
Plymouth County, convened in Halifax, July 4th, 1803, to celebrate
the anniversary of American independence. By Joseph Barker, A.M. Boston, Printed by Manning & Lorning,
no. 2, Cornhill [1803]
16 p.   21 cm.

804   Barker, Joseph, 1751-1815.
The stability of Christ's church.
A century sermon, preached at Middle-
boro', January 6, 1795. That day
completing one hundred years since a
church was first gathered in that
place. By Joseph Barker ... Boston:
Printed by J. Bumstead, Union-street,
1796.
31 p.   20 1/2 cm.

805   Barker, Robert, b. 1729.
... The unfortunate shipwright, or
Cruel captain, being a faithful narrative of the unparalleled sufferings
of Robert Barker ... London, Printed
for the benefit of the sufferer, 1795.
39 p. incl. front.   18 1/2 cm.

806   Barlow, Edward, 1639-1719.
          An exact survey of the tide. Expli-
       cating its production and propagation,
       variety and anomaly, in all parts of
       the world; especially near the coasts
       of Great Britain and Ireland. With
       a preliminary treatise concerning the
       origine of springs, generation of rain,
       and production of wind. With fifteen
       curious maps. The 2d ed. To which is
       added, A clear and succinct descrip-
       tion of an engine, which fetcheth wat-
       er out of the deep, and raiseth it to
       the height design'ed, progressively,
       by the same motion. By E. Barlow,
       gent. London, Printed for T. Wood-
       ward, 1722.
          7 p. 1., 122 p., 1 1., 240 p.   4
       fold. pl., 11 fold. maps.   20 cm.

807   Barlow, Joel, 1754-1812.
          Advice to the privileged orders,
       in the several states of Europe,
       resulting from the necessity and
       propriety of a general revolution
       in the principle of government. By
       Joel Barlow ... London--printed:
       New-York-Re-printed by Childs and
       Swaine, 1792-94.
          2 v.   18 1/2 cm.

808   Barlow, Joel, 1754-1812.
          Avis aux ordres privilégiés, dans
       les divers états de l'Europe, tiré
       de la nécessité, dans le sens propre
       ment dit, d'une revolution générale
       dans le principe du gouvernement.
       Par Joël Barlow ...   Paris, Barrois
       l'ainé, 1794-
          v.   22 1/2 cm.

809   Barlow, Joel, 1754-1812.
          The Columbiad. A poem. With the
       last corrections of the author. By
       Joel Barlow ...   Paris, Printed for
       F. Schoell, 1813.
          xi, [2], 448 p. 2 pl. (incl.

front.) 2 port.   27 cm.

810   Barlow, Joel, 1754-1812.
       The conspiracy of kings; a poem:
       addressed to the inhabitants of Eur-
       ope, from another quarter of the
       world ... By Joel Barlow ... Lon-
       don, J. Johnson, 1792.
       20 p.   27 1/2 x 22 cm.

811   [Barlow, Joel] 1754-1812.
       An elegy on the late Honorable
       Titus Hosmer, esq.; one of the coun-
       sellors of the state of Connecticut,
       a member of Congress, and a judge of
       the Maritime court of appeals for the
       United States of America. Hartford:
       Printed by Hudson & Goodwin [1780]
       15 p.   17 1/2 cm.

812   Barlow, Joel, 1754-1812.
       Letters from Paris, to the citi-
       zens of the United States of America,
       on the system of policy hitherto
       pursued by their government relative
       to their commercial intercourse with
       England and France, &c. By Joel Bar-
       low. London, Printed for J. Ridg-
       way, by A. Wilson, 1800.
       116 p.   22 1/2 cm.

813   Barlow, Joel, 1754-1812.
       Letter to Henry Gregoire ... in
       reply to his letter on The Columbiad.
       Washington, Printed by R.C. Weight-
       man, 1809.
       14 p.   21 1/2 cm.

814   Barlow, Joel, 1754-1812.
       An oration, delivered at the North
       church in Hartford, at the meeting
       of the Connecticut society of the
       Cincinnati, July 4th, 1787. In
       commemoration of the independence
       of the United States. By Joel Bar-
       low, esquire. Hartford. Printed

by Hudson and Goodwin [1787]
20 p.   20 1/2 cm.

815   Barlow, Joel, 1754-1812.
       Oration delivered at Washington,
       July fourth, 1809; at the request of
       the Democratic citizens of the Dis-
       trict of Columbia. By Joel Barlow.
       Washington city, Printed and publish-
       ed by R.C. Weightman, 1809.
       14 p.   22 cm.

816   [Barlow, Joel] 1754-1812.
       A poem, spoken at the public com-
       mencement at Yale college, in New-
       Haven; September 12, 1781. Hartford:
       Printed by Hudson & Goodwin [1781]
       16 p.   19 cm.

817   Barlow, Joel, 1754-1812.
       The prospect of peace. A poetical
       composition, delivered in Yale-
       college, at the public examination
       of the candidates for the degree of
       bachelor of arts; July 23, 1778.
       By Joel Barlow, A.B. New-Haven:
       Printed by Thomas and Samuel Green,
       1778.
       12 p.   20 1/2 cm.

818   Barlow, Joel, 1754-1812.
       Two letters to the citizens of the
       United States, and one to General
       Washington, written from Paris in
       the year 1799, on our political and
       commercial relations. By Joel Barlow,
       New-Haven: From Sidney's press,
       1806.
       v, [7]-119 p.   17 cm.

819   Barlow, Joel, 1754-1812.
       The vision of Columbus; a poem in
       nine books. By Joel Barlow, esquire.
       Hartford: Printed by Hudson and
       Goodwin, for the author. M.DCC.
       LXXXVII.

xii, [2], [25]-258, [12] p.   19
1/2 cm.

820   Barnard, Daniel Dewey, 1797-1861.
       A discourse on the life, character
       and public services of Ambrose Spencer,
       late chief justice of the Supreme
       court of New York: delivered by re-
       quest before the bar of the city of
       Albany, January 5, 1849. By Daniel
       D. Barnard ... Albany, W.C. Little
       & co., 1849.
       104 p.   23 1/2 cm.

821   Barnard, Daniel Dewey, 1797-1861.
       A discourse on the life, services
       and character of Stephen Van Ren-
       sselaer; delivered before the Albany
       institute, April 15, 1839. With an
       historical sketch of the colony and
       manor of Rensselaerwyck, in an appen-
       dix. By Daniel D. Barnard. Albany,
       Printed by Hoffman & White, 1839.
       144 p.   22 1/2 cm.

822   Barnard, Daniel Dewey, 1797-1861.
       Lecture on the character and ser-
       vices of James Madison, delivered be-
       fore the "Young men's association of
       mutual improvement in the city of
       Albany," February 28, 1837. By
       Daniel D. Barnard. Albany, Press of
       Hoffman and White, 1837.
       47 p.   23 1/2 cm.

823   Barnard, Daniel Dewey, 1797-1861.
       An oration, delivered before the
       honorable the corporation and the
       military and civic societies of the
       city of Albany, on the fourth of
       July, 1835. By Daniel D. Barnard.
       Published at the request of the com-
       mittee on the part of the corpora-
       tion. Albany, Printed by E.W. &
       C. Skinner, 1835.
       iv, [5]-51 p.   22 1/2 cm.

824   Barnard, Daniel Dewey, 1797-1861.
        Speeches and reports in the Assem-
        bly of New-York, at the annual ses-
        sion of 1838. By Daniel D. Barnard.
        Albany, (). Steele, 1838.
        xi, 228 p.   19 cm.

825   Barnard, Frederick Augustus Porter,
        1809-1889.
        Art culture: its relation to na-
        tional refinement and national moral-
        ity. An oration pronounced before
        the Alabama Alpha of the Society of
        the Phi beta kappa, at its anniver-
        sary. July 11th, 1854. By Freder-
        ick A. P. Barnard ... Tuscaloosa
        [Ala.] Printed by M.D.J. Slade,
        1854.
        25 p.   22 1/2 x 14 cm.

826   Barnard, Frederick Augustus Porter,
        1809-1889.
        Letters on college government, and
        the evils inseparable from the Amer-
        ican college system in its present
        form ... By Frederick A.P. Barnard
        ... New York, D. Appleton & co.,
        1855.
        104 p.   22 cm.

827   [Barnard, Frederick Augustus Porter]
        1809-1889.
        Letter to the President of the
        United States, by a refugee. Phila-
        delphia, J.B. Lippincott & co.,
        1863.
        32 p.   22 1/2 cm.

828   Barnard, George N.
        Photographic views of Sherman's
        campaign, from negatives taken in
        the field, by Geo. N. Barnard, offi-
        cial photographer of the military
        div. of the Mississippi ... New
        York, Press of Wynkoop & Hallenbeck,
        1866.

30 p.   23 cm.   *and* portfolio
of 61 pl.   42 1/2 x 52 1/2 cm.

829   Barnard, Henry, 1811-1900.
       Biographical sketch of Ezekiel
       Cheever, with notes on the free
       schools and early school-books of
       New England. By Henry Barnard ...
       Hartford, Conn., For sale by F.C.
       Brownell [1856?]
       2 p. l., 32 p.   illus.   22 cm.

830   Barnard, Henry, 1811-1900.
       Report on the condition and im-
       provement of the public schools of
       Rhode Island, submitted Nov. 1,
       1845. By Henry Barnard ... Pub. by
       order of the General assembly. Provi-
       dence, B. Cranston & co., 1846.
       255 p.   illus.   22 cm.

831   Barnard, Henry, 1811-1900.
       Tribute to Gallaudet. A discourse
       in commemoration of the life, charac-
       ter and services, of the Rev. Thomas
       H. Gallaudet, LL. D., delivered be-
       fore the citizens of Hartford, Jan.
       7th, 1852. With an appendix, contain-
       ing history of deaf-mute instruction
       and institutions, and other docu-
       ments. By Henry Barnard. Hartford,
       Brockett & Hutchinson, 1852.
       3 p. l., [5]-267, [1] p.   23 1/2
       cm.

832   Barnard, John, 1681-1770.
       The throne established by right-
       eousness. A sermon preach'd before
       His Excellency Jonathan Belcher, esq;
       His Majesty's council, and the repre-
       sentatives of the province of the
       Massachusetts-bay in New-England, May
       29, 1734, being the day for the elect-
       ing His Majesty's council there. By
       John Barnard, A.M. pastor of a
       church in Marblehead ... Boston:

Printed 1734.
2 p. 1., 60 p.   21 cm.

833   Barnard, John Gross, 1815-1882.
       The C.S.A. and the battle of Bull
Run. (A letter to an English friend.)
By J.G. Barnard ... New York, D. Van
Nostrand; [etc., etc.] 1862.
       2 p. 1., [3]-136 p. fold. maps,
fold. plans.   23 cm.

834   Barnard, John Gross, 1815-1882.
       The dangers and defences of New
York. Addressed to the Hon. J.B.
Floyd, secretary of war, by Major
J.G. Barnard ... Published by
order of the Chamber of commerce, by
permission of the secretary of war.
New York, D. Van Nostrand, 1859.
       62 p.   22 1/2 cm.

835   Barnard, John Gross, 1815-1882.
       Eulogy on the late Brevet Major-
General Joseph G. Totten, late chief
engineer, United States army. By
J.G. Barnard ... New York, D. Von
Nostrand, 1866.
       82 p.   18 1/2 cm.

836   Barnard, John Gross, 1815-1882.
       Letter to the editors of the Na-
tional intelligencer, in answer to
the charges against the United States
Military academy in the report of the
secretary of war, of July, 1861.
By Major J.G. Barnard ... New York,
D. Van Nostrand, 1862.
       18 p.   22 cm.

837   Barnard, John Gross, 1815-1882.
       Notes on sea-coast defence: con-
sisting of sea-coast fortification, the
fifteen-inch gun, and casemate em-
brasures. By Major J.G. Barnard
... New York, D. Van Nostrand, 1861.
       110 p., 1 1. fold. front., diagrs.

23 1/2 cm.

838   Barnard, John Gross, 1815-1882.
       The Peninsular campaign and its
       antecedents, as developed by the re-
       port of Maj.-Gen. Geo. B. McClellan,
       and other published documents. By
       J.G. Barnard ... New York, D. Van
       Nostrand, 1864.
       96 p.   18 1/2 cm.

839   Barnard, John Gross, 1815-1882.
       Report of the engineer and artillery
       operations of the Army of the Potomac,
       from its organization to the close of
       the Peninsular campaign. By Brig.-
       Gen. J.G. Barnard, chief engineer,
       and Brig.-Gen. W.F. Barry, chief of
       artillery ... New York D. Van Nos-
       trand, 1863.
       1 p. l.,   5 -230 p.   5 pl. (incl.
       front) 13 maps and plans (part fold.)
       24 cm.

840   Barnard, Thomas, 1748-1814.
       A discourse before the Society for
       propagating the gospel among the In-
       dians and others in North America,
       delivered November 6, 1806. By Thom-
       as Barnard ... Charlestown: Print-
       ed by Samuel Etheridge. 1806.
       39 p.   22 cm.

841   Barnard, Thomas, 1716-1776.
       A sermon preached before His Excel-
       lency Francis Barnard, esq; governor
       and commander in chief, the honour-
       able His Majesty's Council, and the
       honourable House of representatives, of
       the province of the Massachusetts-
       Bay in New-England, May 25th. 1763.
       Being the anniversary for the election
       of His Majesty's Council for said
       province. By Thomas Barnard, A.M.,
       pastor of the First church in Salem.
       Boston: Printed by Richard Draper,

186

printer to His Excellency the governor and the honorable His Majesty's Council. MDCCLXIII.
  45 p.   21 1/2 cm.

842   Barnard, Thomas, 1748-1814.
        A sermon, preached December 29,
      1799, in the North meeting house,
      Salem, the Lord's day after the melan-
      choly tidings were received of the
      death of General George Washington,
      who died Dec. 14, 1799. By Thomas
      Barnard ... Published by desire of
      the town. Salem, Printed by Thomas
      C. Cushing, at the Bible & heart
      [1800]
        27 p.   22 1/2 cm.

843   Barnard, Thomas, 1716-1776.
        A sermon preached to the Ancient
      and honourable artillery company
      in Boston, New-England, June 5,
      1758. Being the anniversary of
      their election of officers. By Thom-
      as Barnard, A.M. pastor of the First
      church in Salem. Boston: Printed
      and sold by Edes and Gill, at their
      printing-office, next to the prison
      in Queen street, 1758.
        32 p.   20 cm.

844   Barnes, Albert, 1798-1870.
        The conditions of peace. A thanks-
      giving discourse delivered in the
      First Presbyterian church. Phila-
      delphia, November 27, 1862. By
      Albert Barnes. Philadelphia, W.B.
      Evans, 1863.
        63 p.   21 1/2 cm.

845   Barnes, Albert, 1798-1870.
        Home missions. A sermon in be-
      half of the American home mission-
      ary society: preached in the cities
      of New York and Philadelphia. May,
      1849; by Albert Barnes. New York,

The American home missionary service, 1849.
48 p.   23 cm.

846   Barnes, Albert, 1798-1870.
        An inquiry into the Scriptural
        views of slavery ... Philadelphia,
        Perkins & Purves; Boston, B. Perkins
        & co., 1846.
        384 p.   20 cm.

847   Barnes, Albert, 1798-1870.
        The love of country. A sermon de-
        livered in the First Presbyterian
        church, Philadelphia. April 28,
        1861. By Albert Barnes. Philadel-
        phia, C. Sherman & son, printers,
        1861.
        48 p.   24 cm.

848   Barnes, Albert, 1798-1870.
        Our position. A sermon, preached
        before the General assembly of the
        Presbyterian church in the United
        States, in the Fourth Presbyterian
        church in the city of Washington,
        May 20, 1852. By Albert Barnes.
        New York, Newman & Ivison, 1852.
        39, [1] p.   20 1/2 cm.

849   Barnes, Albert, 1798-1870.
        The state of the country. A dis-
        course, delivered in the First Pres-
        byterian church, Philadelphia, June
        1, 1865. On the day appointed as a
        day of "humiliation and mourning"
        in view of the death of the President
        of the United States, by Albert
        Barnes. Philadelphia, H.B. Ashmead,
        printer, 1865.
        74 p.   23 cm.

850   Barnes, Albert, 1798-1870.
        Thanksgiving sermon. The virtues
        and public services of William
        Penn: a discourse delivered in the

First Presbyterian church, Philadelphia, November 27, 1845, by Albert Barnes ... Philadelphia, W.
Sloanaker: New York, W.H. Graham;
[etc., etc., 1845]
    24 p.   22 cm.

851   Barnes, David, 1731-1811.
        Discourse delivered at South Par-
      ish in Scituate, February 22, 1800.
      The day assigned by Congress, to
      mourn the decease and venerate the
      virtues of General George Washing-
      ton ... By David Barnes, D.D.   Pub-
      lished by desire. Boston: Manning
      & Loring, Printers, near the Old
      South Meeting-House. [1800]
        16 p.   21 1/2 cm.

852   Barnes, David M.
        The draft riots in New York.   July,
      1863.   The metropolitan police:
      their services during riot week.
      Their honorable record.   By David M.
      Barnes.   New York, Baker & Godwin,
      1863.
        117 p., 1 1.   23 1/2 cm.

853   Barnes, Isaac O.
        An address, delivered at Bedford,
      New Hampshire, on the one hundredth
      anniversary of the incorporation of
      the town, May 19, 1850.   By Isaac O.
      Barnes.   Boston, Printed by A. Mudge,
      1850.
        45 p.   22 1/2 cm.

854   Barnes, Joseph.
        Remarks on Mr. John Fitch's reply
      to Mr. James Rumsey's pamphlet, by
      Joseph Barnes ... Philadelphia,
      Printed by J. James, 1788.
        xvi, 16 p.   21 1/2 x 12 1/2 cm.

855   Barnes, Joseph.
        Treatise on the justice, policy,

and utility of establishing an effectual system for promoting the progress of useful arts, by assuring property in the products of genius. To
which are added, observations, on
the deficiency of, and exceptions to
the bill reported in March 1792. With
notes, tending to demonstrate, that
no property is secured in the products of genius, under the existing
patent system. Also, the principles
upon which a bill ought to be formed, to be effectual and equitable.
By Joseph Barnes. Philadelphia:
Printed by Francis Bailey, n° 116.
High-street. M DCC XCII.
34 p. 19 cm.

856   Barnes, Thomas, 1749-1816, *plaintiff*.
At the Supreme judicial court,
May term, 1810, in Cumberland ...
Thomas Barnes, *versus* the inhabitants of the First parish in Fal-
mouth. [n.p., 1810?]
16 p. 24 cm.

857   Barnes, William, 1824-1913.
The settlement and early history
of Albany; a prize essay, delivered
before the Young men's association,
December 26, 1850. By William
Barnes, esq. Albany, Gould, Banks &
Gould, 1851.
1 p. l., 25 p. fold. map. 23
cm.

858   Barnes, William, 1824-1913.
The settlement and early history
of Albany. By William Barnes.
Albany, N.Y., J. Munsell, 1864.
3 p. l., [5]-100 p. incl. pl.,
2 plans. front. 23 cm.

859   Barnes, William Horatio.
The body politic. By William
H. Barnes. Cincinnati, New York,

Moore, Wilstach & Baldwin, 1866.
xiii, 15-309 p.   19 1/2 cm.

860   Barnet, James, *ed*.
The martyrs and heroes of Illinois in the great rebellion. Biographical sketches. Ed. by James
Barnet ... Chicago, Press of J.
Barnet, 1865.
1 p. l., 8, xvi, 9 -263 p.
front., ports.   23 1/2 cm.

861   Barnett, Francis, *b*. 1785.
The hero of No fiction; or, Memoirs of Francis Barnett, the Lefevre
of "No fiction:" and a review of
that work. With letters and authentic documents ... Boston, C. Ewer
and T. Bedlington, 1823.
2 v.   15 cm.

862   Barnum, E   M.
... The gold and silver fields
of Oregon and Idaho. A statement
of the yield of precious metals from
the great basin of the Columbia, carefully prepared from the most authentic sources. By E.M. Barnum. [n.p.,
1867?]
12 p., 1 l.   23 cm.

863   Barnum, H   L.
The spy unmasked; or, Memoirs of
Enoch Crosby, alias Harvey Brich,
the hero of the "Spy, a tale of the
neutral ground," by Mr. Cooper ...
New York, J.&J. Harper; [etc., etc.]
1829.
2 v. in 1. fronts., 2 port.   18
cm.

864   Bannum, Phineas Taylor, 1810-1891.
The life of P.T. Barnum, written
by himself. New-York, Redfield,
1855.
viii, [9]-404 p.   front. (port.)

illus.   19 1/2 cm.

865   Barr, Thomas Hughes, 1807-1877.
        A discourse, delivered by the
        Rev. T.H. Barr, at Canaan Center,
        April 19, 1865, on the occasion of
        the funeral obsequies of our late
        President, Abraham Lincoln ...
        Wooster, O., Republican steam power
        press, 1865.
        11 p.   19 1/2 cm.

86.6   Barrande, Joachim, 1799-1883.
        ... Documents anciens et nou-
        veaux sur la faune primordiale et
        le système taconique en Amérique;
        par M.J. Barrande ...   [Paris,
        Impr. de L. Martinet, 1861]
        p. 203-321.   2 fold. pl.   23
        cm.

867   Barre academy, *Barre, Vt.*
        Annual catalogue.   Windsor [Vt.]
        v.   22 1/2 cm.

868   Barre, W.   L.
        The life and public services of
        Millard Fillmore.   By W.L. Barre
        ...   Buffalo, Wanzer, McKim & co.,
        1856.
        x, [11]-408 p.   front. (port.)
        18 cm.

869   Barre, W   L.
        Lives of illustrious men of
        America, distinguished in the annals
        of the republic as legislators, war-
        riors, and philosophers.   By W.L.
        Barre ...   Cincinnati, W.A. Clarke,
        1859.
        x, 11-906 p.   front., ports.   24
        cm.

870   Barrère, Pierre, 1690-1755.
        Nouvelle relation de la France
        équinoxiale, contenant la description

des côtes de la Guianne; de l'isle
de Cayenne; le commerce de cette
colonie; les divers changemens
arrivés dans ce pays; & les moeurs
& coûtumes des différens peuples
sauvages qui l'habitent ... Par
Pierre Barrere ...   Paris, Piget
[etc.] 1743.
   2 p. 1., iv, 250 p., 1 1.   17
fold. pl., 2 fold. maps.   16 1/2
cm.

871   Barrett, B[enjamin] F[iske] 1808-
    1892.
       Love towards enemies and the way
    to manifest it.   A sermon delivered
    in the New Church temple, Sunday,
    June 12th, 1864, by B.F. Barrett.
    Philadelphia, J.B. Lippincott and
    co., 1864.
       cover-title, 24 p.   18 cm.

872   Barrett, Joseph Hartwell, 1824-1910.
       Das leben und wirken Abraham Lin-
    coln's, des sechzehnten präsidenten
    der Vereinigten Staaten.   Nebst
    einer darstellung der kriegsereig-
    nisse, die während seiner administra
    tion stattfanden.   Von Joseph H.
    Barrett ...   Aus dem englischen
    frei übersetzt und mit zusätzen,
    erläuterungen und einer vorrede
    versehen von Johann L. C. Eggers.
    Cincinnati, Moore, Wilstach & Bald-
    win, 1866.
       xviii, [19]-786 p.   front. (port.)
    plates.   22 cm.

873   Barrett, Joseph Hartwell, 1824-1910.
       ... Life of Abraham Lincoln, (of
    Illinois.)   With a condensed view
    of his most important speeches;
    also a sketch of the life of Hanni-
    bal Hamlin (of Maine.)   By J.H.
    Barrett, Cincinnati, Moore, Wilstach,
    Keys & co., 1860.

viii, 9-216 p.   front., ports.
20 cm.

874   Barrett, Joseph Hartwell, 1824-1910.
       Life of Abraham Lincoln, present-
ing his early history, political career, and speeches in and out of
Congress; also a general view of
his policy as president of the United States; with his messages, proclamations, letters, etc., and a
concise history of the war. By Joseph H. Barrett. Cincinnati, Moore,
Wilstach & Baldwin, 1864.
       viii, 9-518 p. front. (port.)
20 cm.

875   Barrillon, François Guillaume.
       Politique de la France et de
l'humanité dans le conflit améri-
cain, par Barrillon ... Paris,
Guillaumin et cie, 1861.
       40 p.   25 cm.

876   Barringer, Daniel Moreau, 1806-
       1873.
       Speech of D.M. Barringer, of North
Carolina, on the tariff. Delivered
in the House of Representatives of
the U.S., July 1, 1846. [Washington]
J. & G.S. Gideon, printers [1846]
       15 p.   24 cm.

877   Barrington, Daines, 1727-1800.
       Miscellanies, by the Honourable
Daines Barrington ... London,
Printed by J. Nichols, sold by B.
White [etc.] 1781.
       573 p. 2 port., fold. map.
5 geneal. tab. (1 fold.) chart.
27 cm.

878   Barrington, Daines, 1727-1800.
       The possibility of approaching
the North pole asserted. By the Hon.
D. Barrington. A new ed. With an

194

appendix, containing papers on the same subject, and on a Northwest passage. By Colonel Beaufoy, F.R.S. Illustrated with a map of the North pole, according to the latest discoveries. New-York: Published by James Eastburn & co., at the Literary rooms, Broadway, corner of Pine-street. Abraham Paul, printer ... 1818.
   xiii, [15]-187 p. front. (fold. mpa) 23 cm.

879   Barrio, Paulino del.
      Noticia sobre el terreno carbonifero de Coronel i Lota, i sobre los trabajos de esplotación en el empremdidos [!] Por Don Paulino del Barrio ... Santiago [de Chile] Imprenta nacional, 1857.
      1 p. l., 107 p. 4 fold. pl., fold. mpa. 30 1/2 cm.

880   Barron, James, 1769-1851, *defendant*.
      Proceedings of the general court martial convened for the trial of Commodore James Barron, Captain Charles Gordon, Mr. William Hook, and Captain John Hall, of the United States' ship Chesapeake, in the month of January, 1808. Pub. by order of the Navy department. [Washington] Printed by J. Gideon, jr., 1822.
      496 p. 22 cm.

881   Barros, Andre' de.
      Vida do apostolica padre Antonio Vieyra da Companhia de Jesus, chamado por Antonomasia o Grande ... Lisboa, Nova Officina Sylviania, 1746.
      686 p. 20 cm.

882   Barros, João de, 1496-1570.
      Da Asia de João de Barros e de Diogo de Couto. Nova ed. ... Lisboa, Na Regia officina typografica,

1777-88.
        13 pt. in 24 v.   fronts. (ports.,
v. 1-3, 10) fold. maps.   18 1/2
cm.

883   Barrow, *Sir* John, *bart.*, 1764-1848.
        A chronological history of voy-
ages into the Arctic regions; undertaken chiefly for the purpose of discovering a north-east, north-west,
or polar passage between the Atlantic and Pacific ... By John Barrow,
F.R.S. London, J. Murray, 1818.
        3 p. l., 379, 48 p.   front. (fold.
map) illus.   21 1/2 cm.

884   [Barrow, *Sir* John, *bart.*] 1764-1848.
        ... A description of Pitcairn's
island and its inhabitants. With an
authentic account of the mutiny of
the ship Bounty, and of the subsequent fortunes of the mutineers. New
York, Harper & brothers, 1838.
        1 p. l., [ix]-xii, [13]-303 p.
front., pl.   16 cm.

885   Barrow, *Sir* John, *bart.*, 1764-1848.
        The life of George, lord Anson,
admiral of the fleet, vice-admiral
of Great Britain, and first lord
commissioner of the admiralty, previous to, and during, the seven-
years' war. By Sir John Barrow ...
London, J. Murray, 1839.
        xxxiv, 484 p.   front. (port.)
21 1/2 cm.

886   Barrow, *Sir* John, *bart.*, 1764-1848.
        The life of Richard, earl Howe,
K.G., admiral of the fleet, and
general of marines. By Sir John
Barrow ... London, J. Murray, 1838.
        xvi, 432 p.   front. (port.) 2
fold. facsim.   22 1/2 cm.

887   Barrow, Washington, 1817-1866.

Speech of Mr. Washington Barrow,
of Tennessee, on the reference of
the President's annual message, delivered in the House of representatives on Monday, January 24, 1848.
Washington, Printed by J. & G.S.
Gideon, 1848.
15 p.   23 1/2 cm.

888   Barrows, Elijah Porter, 1807-1888.
... A view of the American slavery
question. By E.P. Barrows, Jr. pastor of the First Free Presbyterian
church, New York. New York, J.S.
Taylor, 1836.
iv, [5]-114 p.   14 1/2 cm.

889   Barrows, William, 1815-1891.
The war and slavery and their relations to each other. A discourse,
delivered in the Old South church,
Reading, Mass., December 28, 1862.
Boston, J.M. Whittemore & co., 1863.
18 p.   23 1/2 cm.

890   [Barruel-Beauvert, Phillipe Auguste
de]
Bombardement et entière destruction de Grey-town. 2me lettre du
délégué de la population française
de Grey-town ... 2. éd. Paris
[Typ. A. Lebon] 1856.
41 p.   23 cm.

891   Barry, John Stetson, 1819-1872.
A genealogical and biographical
sketch of the name and family of
Stetson; from the year 1634, to
the year 1847. By John Stetson
Barry ... Boston, Printed for
the author, by W.A. Hall & co., 1847.
116 p.   22 1/2 cm.

892   Barry, John Stetson, 1819-1872.
A historical sketch of the town
of Hanover, Mass., with family

genealogies. By John S. Barry ...
Boston, Published for the author by
S.G. Drake, 1853.
    v, [6]-448 p. front., illus.
(incl. port., map, coats of arms)
plates, facsims. 22 1/2 cm.

893   Barry, Patrick.
         The theory and practice of the in-
      ternational trade of the United
      States and England, and of the trade
      of the United States and Canada ...
      by P. Barry ... Chicago, D.B. Cooke
      & co., 1858.
         161, [1] p. 22 cm.

894   Barry, William Taylor, 1785-1835.
         Letter of William T. Barry, post-
      master general, to the House of rep-
      resentatives of the United States;
      reviewing the report of the Select
      committee of that House, appointed
      to investigate the affairs of the
      Post office department. March 2,
      1835. Washington, Printed by Blair
      and Rives, 1835.
         30 p. 22 1/2 cm.

895   Barstow, Benjamin.
         A letter to the Hon. James Buch-
      anan, president elect of the United
      States. By Benjamin Barstow ...
      Concord, N.H., Printed at the office
      of the Democratic standard, 1857.
         16 p. 23 cm.

896   Barstow, Benjamin.
         Speech of Benjamin Barstow, of
      Salem, on the abolition propensities
      of Caleb Cushing. Delivered at the
      Massachusetts national Democratic
      convention, held at Boston, Sept. 22,
      1853 ... Boston, Office of the National
      tional Democrat, 1853.
         16 p. 23 1/2 cm.

897   Barstow, George, 1812-1883.
        The history of New Hampshire, from
        its discovery, in 1614, to the pas-
        sage of the Toleration act, in 1819.
        By George Barstow. Concord, N.H.,
        I.S. Boyd, 1842.
        iv, 456 p. front., ports.   23
        1/2 cm.

898   Barstow, George, 1812-1883.
        War the only means of preserving
        our nationality. An oration, deliv-
        ered at San Jose, Santa Clara Coun-
        ty, Cal., July 4, 1864, by George
        Barstow. San Francisco, Printed by
        Towne & Bacon, 1864.
        16 p.   23 cm.

899   Barthe, Joseph Guillaume, 1818--
        Le Canada reconquis par la France,
        par J.-G. Barthe ... suivi de
        pièces justificatives ... Paris,
        Ledoyen, 1855.
        1 p. l., a-p, xxxvi, 416 p., 1
        l. 4 pl. (1 fold.) 2 port. (incl.
        front.) fold. map.   21 1/2 cm.

900   Barthelmess, Richard.
        Bibliographie der freimaurerei in
        Amerika. (Nachtrag zu der Biblio-
        graphie des Br. Kloss). Zusammen-
        gestellt von R. Barthelmess, M.D.
        New York, G.B. Trübner, 1856.
        vi, 48 p.   23 cm.

901   Bartlett, David Vandewater Golden,
        1828-1912.
        Modern agitators: or, Pen portraits
        of living American reformers. By
        David W. [!] Bartlett ... New York,
        Auburn [N.Y.] Miller, Otron & Mulli-
        gan, 1855.
        iv, [5]-396 p. front., ports.
        20 cm.

902   Bartlett, David Vandewater Golden,

1828-1912.
Presidential candidates: containing sketches, biographical, personal
and political, of prominent candidates for the presidency in 1860.
By D.W. [!] Bartlett. New York, A.
B. Burdick, 1859.
vi, 7-360 p. 19 cm.

903   Bartlett, Elisha, 1804-1855.
The history, diagnosis, and treatment of the fevers of the United
States. By Elisha Bartlett ... [2d
ed.] Philadelphia, Lea and Blanchard,
1847.
xii p., 1 l., [33]-547 p. 23 1/2
cm.

904   Bartlett, Elisha, 1804-1855.
An oration delivered before the
municipal authorites and the citizens
of Lowell, July 4, 1848, by Elisha
Bartlett. Published by the Committee of arrangements. Lowell [Mass.]
J. Atkinson, printer, 1848.
38 p. 22 1/2 cm.

905   Bartlett, Elisha, 1804-1855.
A vindication of the character and
condition of the females employed in
the Lowell mills, against the charges contained in the Boston times,
and the Boston quarterly review. By
Elisha Bartlett, M.D. Lowell, L.
Huntress, printer, 1841.
24 p. 25 cm.

906   Bartlett, John Russell, 1805-1886.
Bibliography of Rhode Island. A
catalogue of books and other publications relating to the state of
Rhode Island, with notes, historical, biographical and critical. By
John Russell Bartlett. Printed by
order of the General assembly. Providence, A. Anthony, printer to the

state, 1864.
iv, [5]-287 p.   25 cm.

907   Bartlett, John Russell, 1805-1886.
Dictionary of Americanisms. A
glossary of words and phrases, us-
ually regarded as peculiar to the
United States. By John Russell Bartlett ... New York, Bartlett and Welford, 1848.
xxvii, 412 p.   23 cm.

908   Bartlett, John Russell, 1805-1886.
The literature of the rebellion. A
catalogue of books and pamphlets relating to the civil war in the United
States, and on subjects growing out
of that event, together with works on
American slavery, and essays from reviews and magazines on the same subjects. Comp. by John Russell Bartlett ... Boston, Draper and Halli-
day; Providence, S.S. Rider and bro.,
1866.
iv, [5]-477 p.   25 cm.

909   Bartlett, John Russell, 1805-1886.
Memoirs of Rhode Island officers
who were engaged in the service of
their country during the great rebellion of the South. Illustrated with
thirty-four portraits. By John Russell Bartlett ... Providence, S.S.
Rider & brother, 1867.
viii, [9]-452 p. pl., 34 port.
26 1/2 x 22 1/2 cm.

910   Bartlett, John Sherren, 1790-1863.
Maize, or Indian corn. Its advantages as a cheap and nutritious article of food. With directions for its
use. By John S. Bartlett ... London, Wiley & Putnam, 1846.
24 p.   18 cm.

911   Bartlett, Joseph, 1763-1827.

Physiognomy, a poem. By Joseph
Bartlett ... Portsmouth [N.H.]
Printed by W. Treadwell, 1810.
19 p.   18 cm.

912   Bartlett, Josiah, 1759-1820.
A discourse on the origin, prog-
ress, and design of free masonry.
Delivered at the meeting-house in
Charlestown, in the commonwealth of
Massachusetts, on the anniversary of
St. John the Baptist, June 24, A.D.
1793. By Josiah Bartlett, M.D. ...
Boston: Printed by Brother Thomas and
John Fleet. 1793.
31 p.   19 1/2 cm.

913   Bartlett, Josiah, 1759-1820.
A dissertation on the progress of
medical science, in the commonwealth
of Massachusetts. Read at the annual
meeting of the Massachusetts medical
society, June 6th, 1810. By Josiah
Bartlett. Boston, Printed by T.B.
Wait and co., 1810.
48 p.   22 cm.

914   Bartlett, Josiah, 1759-1820.
An historical sketch of Charlestown, in the county of Middlesex,
and commonwealth of Massachusetts,
read to an assembly of citizens at
the opening of Washington hall, Nov.
16, 1813. By Josiah Bartlett, M.D.
Boston: Printed by John Eliot, No.
5, Court-Street, 1814.
24 p.   22 cm.

915   Bartlett, Josiah, 1759-1820.
An oration occasioned by the death
of John Warren, M.D., past grand master. Delivered in the Grand lodge
of Massachusetts, at a quarterly meeting, in Boston, June 12, 1815. ...
By Josiah Bartlett ... Boston, Printed for C. Stelbins, for Russell,

Cutler & co., 1815.
24 p.   23 cm.

916   Bartlett, Josiah, 1759-1820.
An oration, on the death of General
George Washington, delivered at the
request of the selectmen and Parish
committee, before the inhabitants of
Charlestown, in the county of Middlesex, and commonwealth of Massachusetts, on Saturday, Feb. 22, 1800.
Being the day set apart by the Congress of the United States, to testi-
fy the grief of the citizens, on that
melancholy event. By Josiah Bartlett ... Charlestown, Printed by
Samuel Etheridge, 1800.
iv, [5]-15 p.   21 cm.

917   Bartlett, Josiah, 1803-1853.
A memoir of the Hon. Josiah Bart-
lett, of Stratham, N.H., who died
April 16, 1838, aged seventy years.
By Josiah Bartlett, M.D.   Gilmanton,
N.H., Printed by A. Prescott, 1839.
7 p.   22 1/2 cm.

918   Bartlett, Montgomery Robert.
A statistical and chronological
view of the United States of North
America, and the several states and
territories carefully compiled from
the latest authorities, for the proprietor, by M.R. Bartlett ... New
York, Printed by Sleight & Van Norden,
1833.
45, [3] p.   14 cm.

919   Bartlett, Richard, 1794-1837.
Remarks and documents relating to
the preservation and keeping of the
public archives. By Richard Bartlett
... Concord [N.H.] A. M'Farland,
1837.
72 p.   25 cm.

920   Bartlett, Samuel Ripley, 1837--
            Concord fight. By S. R. Bartlett.
        Boston, A. Williams and co., 1860.
            33, [1] p. front.   19 cm.

921   Bartlett, Washington Allen, 1820-1871.
            Reply of Washington A. Bartlett,
        to the testimony taken before the
        Naval committee of the Senate; a cer-
        tified copy whereof was furnished by
        consent of the said committee. With
        an appendix of official documents and
        testimonials referred to. May, 1856.
        Washington, H. Polkinhorn, printer,
        1856.
            71, [1] p.   23 cm.

922   Bartlett, William Henry, 1809-1854.
            The Pilgrim fathers; or, The found-
        ers of New England in the reign of
        James the First. By W.H. Bartlett
        ... London, A. Hall, Virtue & co.,
        1853.
            3 p. l., [v]-xii, [13]-240 p.
        front., illus., plates.   24 1/2
        cm.

923   Bartlett, William Stoodley, 1809-1883.
            The frontier missionary: a mem-
        oir of the life of the Rev. Jacob
        Bailey, A.M., missionary at Pownal-
        borough, Maine; Cornwallis and Annap-
        olis, N.S.; with illustrations, notes,
        and an appendix; by William S. Bart-
        lett ... With a preface by Right
        Rev. George Burgess ... Boston, Ide
        and Dutton, 1853.
            xi, 365, [1] p. front., illus.,
        ports., map, facsim.   22 1/2 cm.

924   Bartley, James Avis, 1830--
            Lays of ancient Virginia, and other
        poems: by James Avis Bartley ...
        Richmond, J.W. Randolph, 1855.
            204 p.   19 1/2 cm.

925   Bartol, Cyrus Augustus, 1813-1900.
        The hand of God in the great man:
        a sermon delivered in the West church,
        Boston, occasioned by the death of
        Daniel Webster. By C.A. Bartol ...
        2d ed. Boston, Crosby, Nichols, and
        company, 1852.
        22 p.   24 cm.

926   Barton, Andrew, *pseud.?*
        The disappointment; or, The force
        of credulity. A new American comic-
        opera, of two acts. By Andrew Bar-
        ton, esq. ... New York: Printed in
        the year 1767.
        v, [7]-58 p.   16 1/2 cm.

927   Barton, Benjamin Smith, 1766-1815.
        Additional facts, observations, and
        conjectures relative to the genera-
        tion of the opossum of North-Ameri-
        ca. In a letter from Professor Bar-
        ton to Professor J.A.H. Reimarus, of
        Hamburgh. Philadelphia: Printed
        by S. Merritt, Watkin's alley. 1813.
        24 p.   23 1/2 cm.

928   [Barton, Benjamin Smith] 1766-1815.
        Archaeologiae americanae telluris
        collectanea et specimina. Or, Col-
        lections, with specimens, for a se-
        ries of memoirs on certain extinct
        animals and vegetables of North-
        America. Together with facts and
        conjectures relative to the ancient
        condition of the lands and waters
        of the continent. Illustrated by en-
        gravings. Part first. Philadelphia:
        Printed for the author. 1814.
        vii, [9]-64 p.   23 1/2 cm.

929   Barton, Benjamin Smith, 1766-1815.
        Facts, observations, and conjec-
        tures relative to the generation of
        the opossum of North-America. In a
        letter from Professor Barton to Mons.

Roume, of Paris. Philadelphia:
Printed by Thomas and George Palmer,
116, High-street, 1806.
14 p.   23 1/2 cm.

930   Barton, Benjamin Smith, 1766-1815.
       Flora virginica: sive Plantarum,
praecipue indigenarum, Virginiae
historia inchoata.   Iconibus illustrata.   Studio et cura Benjamin Smith
Barton ...   Pars prima.   Philadel-
phiae: typis D. Heartt, 1812.
       xii p., 1 l., [iii]-iv, 74 p.
23 1/2 cm.

931   Barton, Benjamin Smith, 1766-1815.
       Fragments of the natural history
of Pennsylvania.   By Benjamin Smith
Barton ...   Philadelphia, Printed
for the author by Way & Groff, 1799.
       xviii, 24 p.   35 1/2 cm.

932   Barton, Benjamin Smith, 1766-1815.
       A memoir concerning an animal of
the class of *Reptilia*, or *Amphibia*,
which is known, in the United-States,
by the names of alligator and hell-
bender.   By Professor Barton.   Philadelphia: Printed for the author.
Griggs and Dickinson, printers.
1812.
       iv.   5-26 p.   pl.   23 1/2 cm.

933   Barton, Benjamin Smith, 1766-1815.
       Observations on some parts of na-
tural history: to which is prefixed
an account of several remarkable
vestiges of an ancient date, which
have been discovered in different
parts of North America.   Part I.   By
Benjamin Smith Barton ...   London,
Printed for the author, sold by C.
Dilly [1787?]
       2 p. l., v. 7-76 p.   fold. pl.
22 cm.

934   Barton, Charles Crillon, *d.* 1851.
           Manifest of the charges preferred
       to the Navy department and subse-
       quently to Congress, against Jesse
       Duncan Elliott, esq., a captain in
       the navy of the United States, for
       unlawful conduct while commodore of
       the late Mediterranean squadron;
       and a refutation of the recrimination
       raised by that officer.   By Charles
       Crillon Barton ...   [Philadelphia]
       1839.
           iv, 46, xxiv p.   22 1/2 cm.

935   Barton, Cyrus, *d.* 1855.
           An address, delivered before the
       Republicans of Newport, and vicinity,
       July 4, 1828.   By C. Barton ...   New-
       port [N.H.]   D. Aldrich, 1828.
           16 p.   22 cm.

935   Barton, Cyrus, *d.* 1855.
           ... Defence of Cyrus Barton,
       against the attacks of Hon. Isaac
       Hill upon the establishment of the
       New-Hampshire patriot and state ga-
       zette.   [Concord? 1840]
           16 p.   22 cm.

936   Barton, Cyrus, *d.* 1855.
           ... Defence of Cyrus Barton, against
       the attacks of Hon. Isaac Hill upon
       the establishment of the New-Hamp-
       shire patriot and state gazette.
       [Concord? 1840]
           16 p.   22 cm.

937   Barton, David, 1783-1837.
           ... Speech of Mr. Barton, of Mis-
       souri, upon the power of the Presi-
       dent to remove federal officers; and
       upon the restraining power and duty
       of the Senate over an abusive exer-
       cise of that power; and in reply to
       the arguments of several members of
       the majority.   St. Louis, Printed by

Charless & Paschall, 1830.
16 p.   22 1/2 cm.

938   Barton, Edward H   *d.* 1859.
Report to the Louisiana state medical society, on the meteorology, vit-
al statistics, and hygiene of the
state of Louisiana. By E.H. Barton
... To which is added an appendix,
showing the experience of life insurance companies in Louisiana, with
tables of mortality for the use of
such companies, and the laws of probability of life (English calculation);
also, the experience of the London
life insurance offices, etc., by H.G.
Heartt ... New Orleans, Davies,
son & co., 1851.
2 p. l., [iii]-vi, [7]-69 p. incl.
tables.   3 fold. charts.   23 1/2
cm.

939   Barton, James L   *d.* 1869.
Address on the early reminiscences
of western New York and the lake region of country. Delivered before
the Young men's association of Buffalo. February 16, 1848. By James L.
Barton. [2d ed.] Buffalo, Press of
Jewett, Thomas & co., 1848.
69 p.   23 1/2 cm.

940   Barton, James L.   *d.* 1869.
Lake commerce. Letter to the Hon.
Robert M'Clelland, chairman of the
Committee on commerce in the U.S.
House of representatives, in relation
to the value and importance of the
commerce on the great western lakes.
By James L. Barton. 2d ed.--with
additional notes. Buffalo, Press of
Jewett, Thomas & co., 1846.
32 p.   fold. tab.   23 1/2 cm.

941   Barton, William, 1754-1817.
A dissertation on the freedom of

208

navigation and maritime commerce,
and such rights of states, relative
thereto, as are founded on the law
of nations: adapted more particularly to the United States; and interspersed with moral and political reflections, and historical facts.
With an appendix, containing sundry
state papers.   Philadelphia, J. Conrad, 1802.
339, xiv p.   23 cm.

942   Barton, William Paul Crillon, 1786-1856.
A flora of North America.   Illustrated by coloured figures, drawn
from nature.   By William P.C. Barton
...   Philadelphia, M. Carey & sons,
1821-23.
3 v.   106 col. pl.   28 1/2 cm.

943   Barton, William Paul Crillon, 1786-1856.
Outlines of lectures on materia
medica and botany, delivered in Jefferson medical college, Philadelphia.
By William P.C. Barton ...   Philadelphia, J.G. Auner, 1827-28.
2 v.   18 cm.

944   Barton, William Paul Crillon, 1786-1856.
A treatise containing a plan for
the internal organization and government of marine hospitals in the United States: together with a scheme
for amending and systematizing the medical department of the Navy.   By Wil
liam P.C. Barton, and a surgeon in
the Navy of the United States ...
Philadelphia: Printed for the author.
Sold by Edward Parker, no. 178, Market-street, and Philip H. Nicklin, no.
151, Chestnut-street, 1814.
xxv, [1] p., 1 l., 244 p.   pl.
22 1/2 cm.

945   Barton, William Sumner, 1824-1899.
Epitaphs from the cemetery on
Worcester common, with occasional

notes, references, and an index. By
W.S. Barton. Worcester, Printed by
H.J. Howland [1848]
36 p. 23 x 14 1/2 cm.

946   Bartram, William, 1739-1823.
Voyage dans les parties sud de
l'Amérique septentrionale; savoir:
les Carolines septentrionale et
méridionale, la Georgie, les Florides
orientale et occidentale, le pays
des Cherokées, le vaste territoires
des Muscogulges ou de la confédéra-
tion Creek, et le pays des Chactaws
... par Williams [!] Bartram. Imprimé à Philadelphie, en 1791, et à
Londres, en 1792, et tr. de l'angl.
par P.V. Benoist ... Paris, Car-
teret et Brosson [etc.] an VII
[1799]
2 v. front. (port.) 3 fold. pl.,
fold. map. 20 1/2 cm.

947   Basalenque, Diego, 1577-1651.
Arte de la lengua tarasca, dis-
puesto con nuevo estilo y claridad
por el r. p. m. fr. Diego Basalenque ... Con licencia: en Mexico,
por Francisco Calderon. Año de 1714.
Reimpreso en 1886, bajo el cuidado
y corrección del dr. Antonio Peña-
fiel ... México, Oficina tip. de la
Secretaria de fomento, 1886.
1 p. l., xxxii, iii -v, 7 -86
p., 1 1. 30 1/2 cm.

948   Bascom, Henry Bidleman, bp., 1796-1850.
Methodism and slavery: with other
matters in controversy between the
North and the South; being a review
of the manifesto of the majority, in
reply to the protest of the minority, of the late General conference
of the Methodist E. church, in the
case of Bishop Andrew. By H.B. Bascom ... Frankfort, Ky., Hodges,

Todd & Pruett, printers, 1845.
165 p.   24 1/2 cm.

949   Bascom, Jonathan.
An oration, delivered February 22,
1800. The day of public mourning for
the death of General George Washington. By Rev. Jonathan Bascom, of Orleans, to the people of his charge
... Boston, Printed by Samuel Hall,
1800.
15 p.   21 cm.

950   Basterot, Florimond Jacques, *comte* de.
De Québec a Lima; journal d'un
voyage dans les deux Amériques en
1858 et en 1859, par le vicomte de
Basterot. Paris, L. Hachette et
cie, 1860.
2 p. l., vii, 338 p., 1 l.   18
1/2 cm.

951   Batalla de Yanacocha. Canto heroyco al
triunfo de las armas pacificadoras,
dedicado al Ecmo. Sr. capitan jeneral presidente de la Republica de
Bolivia, gran mariscal de la del
Peru y jeneral en jefe del ejercito
unido ... Impreso en el Cuzco, año
de 1835. Reimpreso en Lima, Impr.
de E. Aranda, 1836.
19 p.   22 cm.

952   Batbie, Anselme Polycarpe, 1828-1887.
Traité théorique et pratique de
droit public et administratif, contenant l'examen de la doctrine et
de la jurisprudence; la comparaison
de notre législation avec les lois
politiques et administratives de
l'Angleterre, des États-Unis, de la
Belgique, de la Hollande, des principaux États de l'Allemagne et de
l'Espagne; la comparaison de nos
institutions actuelles avec celles
de la France avant 1789; et des

notions sur les sciences auxiliaires
de l'administration, l'économie politique et la statistique; par A.
Batbie ... Paris, Cotillon, 1861-68.
7 v.   22 cm.

953   Batchelder, Eugene, 1822-1878.
        Border adventures: or, The romantic
      incidents of a New-England town; and
      other poems. With an appendix. By
      Eugene Batchelder ... Boston, Tick-
      nor, Reed & Fields, 1851.
      48 p.   18 1/2 cm.

954   [Batchelder, Eugene] 1822-1878.
        Brother Jonathan's welcome to Kos-
      suth. A poem. By the author of
      "Border adventures, and other poems,"
      &c. ... Boston, Redding & company
      [etc., c1852]
      27 p.   24 cm.

955   Batchelder, J[ohn] P[utnam] 1784-1868.
        Second edition of "An advertise-
      ment," by C.B. Coventry ... with "A
      candid exposition of facts," by J.P.
      Batchelder ... Utica [N.Y.] Dauby
      & Maynard, printers, 1829.
      16 p.   23 1/2 cm.

956   [Batchelder, Samuel] 1784-1879.
        Introduction and early progress
      of the cotton manufacture in the Unit-
      ed States ... Boston, Little, Brown
      and company, 1863.
      iv, 108 p.   19 1/2 cm.

957   Batchelder, Samuel, 1830-1888.
        The young men of America. A prize
      essay. By Samuel Batchelder, jr.
      ... New York, Sheldon & company;
      Boston, Gould & Lincoln, 1860.
      70 p.   19 cm.

958   Bateman, Edmund.
        A sermon preached before the

honourable Trustees for establishing
the colony of Georgia, in America, and
the associates of the late Rev. Dr.
Bray; at their anniversary meeting,
March 19, 1740-1, at the parish-church
of St. Bride, alias St. Bridget, in
Fleet-street, London. By Edmund Bateman, D.D., rector of St. Dunstan in
the East, and chaplain to His Grace
the Archbishop of Canterbury. Published at the request of the Trustees.
London, Printed for J. and H. Pember-
ton, 1741.
 21 p. 21 1/2 cm.

959 Bates, Barnabas, 1785-1853.
 A brief statement of the exertions
of the friends of cheap postage in
the city of New York ... By Barnabas
Bates ... Also, remarks and statistics on the subject of cheap postage
and postal reform in Great Britain and
the United States. By Joshua Leavitt
... New York, W.C. Bryant & co.,
1848.
 xxvi p., 1 l., 52 p. 23 cm.

960 Bates, Edward, 1793-1869.
 Opinion of Attorney General Bates
on citizenship. Washington, Govt.
print. off., 1863.
 22 p. 22 cm.

961 Bates, Henry Walter, 1825-1892.
 The naturalist on the river Amazons.
A record of adventures, habits of animals, sketches of Brazilian and Indian life, and aspects of nature under the equator, during eleven years
of travel. By Henry Walter Bates
... 2d ed. ... London, J. Murray,
1864.
 xii, 466 p. incl., front., illus.,
plates. fold. amp. 20 cm.

962 Bates, Isaac Chapman, 1780-1845.

213

An oration, pronounced before the
Washington benevolent society of
the county of Hampshire, on their first
anniversary, 1812. In commemoration
of the nativity of Washington. By
Isaac C. Bates, esq. ... Northampton,
Printed by William Butler [1812]
24 p. 23 1/2 cm.

963   Bates, Joshua, 1776-1854.
An anniversary discourse, delivered at Dudley, Massachusetts, March
20, 1853. With topographical and
historical notices of the town. By
Joshua Bates, D.D. Boston, Press of
T.R. Marvin, 1853.
58 p. 23 1/2 cm.

964   Bates, Joshua, 1776-1854.
A sermon delivered before the
Society for propagating the gospel
among the Indians and others in North
America, at their anniversary, Nov.
4, 1813. By Joshua Bates ... Boston:
Published by Cummings and Hilliard,
for the society. Cambridge ... Hilliard & Metcalf. 1813.
44 p. 21 cm.

965   Bates, Mary.
The private life of John C. Calhoun. A letter originally addressed
to a brother at the North, communicated to the "International magazine," and now reprinted at the request of many personal friends. By
Miss Mary Bates. Charleston [S.C.]
Walker, Richards and co., 1852.
1 p. 1., [7]-31 p. 21 cm.

966   The battle of Chancellorsville and the
Eleventh army corps. New York, G.B.
Teubner, printer, 1863.
48 p. 22 1/2 cm.

967   Battle of Lake Erie monument association.

214

An account of the organization &
proceedings of the Battle of Lake
Erie monument association. And celebration of the 45th anniversary of
the battle of Lake Erie, at Put-in-
Bay island, on September tenth, 1858.
Sandusky, Printed by H.D. Cooke &
co., 1858.
49 p.   21 cm.

968   Battle-fields of the South, from Bull
Run to Fredericksburg; with sketches
of Confederate commanders, and gos-
sip of the camps. By an English com-
batant, (lieutenant of artillery on
the field staff.) ... London,
Smith, Elder and co., 1863.
2 v.   fronts. (fold. maps)   19
1/2 cm.

969   Batwell, Daniel.
A sermon, preached at York-town,
before Captain Morgan's and Captain
Price's companies of rifle-men, on
Thursday, July 20, 1775. Being the
day recommended by the Honorable Continental Congress for a general fast
throughout the twelve united colonies
of North-America. By Daniel Batwell
... Philadelphia, Printed by John
Dunlap, 1775.
1 p. 1., 20 p.   22 cm.

970   Baudissin, Adelbert Heinrich, *graf* von,
1820-1871.
Der ansiedler im Missouri-staate.
Den deutschen auswanderern gewidmet,
von graf Adelbert Baudissin. Iser-
lohn, J. Bädeker, 1854.
2 p. 1., 181 p.   fold. map.   19
1/2 cm.

971   Baumann, Ludwig Adolph, 1734?-1802.
... Abriss der staatsverfassung
der vornehmsten länder in Amerika.
Nebst einem anhange von den nor-
dlichen polarländern. Brandenburg,

Bey den gebrudern Halle, 1776.
4 p. 1., 700 p.   18 cm.

972   Baxter, Joseph, 1676-1745.
        Journal of several visits to the
      Indians on the Kennebec River, by the
      Rev. Joseph Baxter ... 1717. With
      notes by the Rev. Elias Nason ...
      Boston, D. Clapp & son, printers,
      1867.
        18 p.   15 1/2 cm.

973   Bayard, James.
        A brief exposition of the Consti-
      tution of the United States: with
      an appendix, containing the Declara-
      tion of independence and the Articles
      of confederation. And a copious
      index. By James Bayard. Philadel-
      phia, Hogan & Thompson, 1833.
        1 p. 1., [5]-166 p.   19 cm.

974   Bayard, James Asheton, 1767-1815.
        Mr. Bayard's speech, upon his mo-
      tion to amend the resolution offered
      by Mr. Giles, by striking out that
      part which is in italics. Delivered
      in the Senate of the United States,
      Tuesday, February 14, 1809 ... "Re-
      solved, that the several laws laying
      an embargo on all ships and vessels
      in the ports and harbors of the Unit-
      ed States be repealed ..." [Port-
      land, Me., 1809]
        24 p.   21 1/2 cm.

975   Bayard, James Asheton, 1767-1815.
        Speech of the Hon. James A. Bayard,
      in the Senate of the U. States, upon
      his motion made on the 16th of June,
      to postpone the further considera-
      tion of the bill declaring war against
      Great Britain, to the 31st of October.
      [Exeter, N.H., C. Norris & co., print-
      ers, 1812]
        16 p.   22 cm.

216

976   Bayard, James Asheton, 1767-1815.
           Speech of the Honorable James A.
Bayard, of Delaware. February 19,
20, 1802. On the bill received from
the Senate, entitled "An act to re-
peal certain acts respecting the
organization of the courts of the
United States." Hartford, Printed
by Hudson & Goodwin, 1802.
        48 p.   23 cm.

977   Bayard, James Asheton, 1799-1880.
           Abolition, and the relation of
races. Speech of Hon. James A.
Bayard, of Delaware. Delivered in
the Senate of the United States,
April 8, 1862. [Washington, L. Towers & co., printers, 1862]
        15 p.   24 1/2 cm.

978   [Bayard, James Asheton] 1799-1880.
           Remarks in the Senate of the Unit-
ed States. January 31, 1855, vindi-
cating the late James A. Bayard, of
Delaware, and refuting the groundless
charges contained in the "Anas" of
Thomas Jefferson, aspersing his character. [Wilmington, Del., G.A.
Wolf, 1907]
        38 p.   25 cm.

979   Bayard, Lewis Pintard, 1791-1840.
           Memorial of the Rev. Lewis P.
Bayard, D.D. containing a memoir
of his life, extracts from his journals and correspondence, notices of
his tour through Europe and the Holy
Land, selections from his sermons,
and the discourse preached on the
occasion of his decease, by the Rt.
Rev. Dr. Onderdonk ... Edited by
J.W. Brown ... New-York, D. Appleton & company, 1841.
        272 p.   18 cm.

980   Bayard, Nicholas, 1644?-1707, *defen-
        dant*.
            An account of the commitment, ar-
        raignment, tryal and condemnation of
        Nicholas Bayard esq; for high treason
        in endeavouring to subvert the govern-
        ment of the province of New York in
        America, by his signing and procur-
        ing others to sign scandalous libels,
        call'd petitions or addresses to his
        late Majesty King William, the Par-
        liament of England, and the Lord Corn-
        bury now governour of that province.
        Before William Atwood esq; Abraham
        de Peyster esq; and Robert Walters
        esq; appointed by a special commis-
        sion justices of oyer and terminer
        at the city of New York, February 19,
        1701. Collected from several memor-
        ials taken by divers persons private-
        ly ... Together with a true copy of
        the libels or addresses themselves.
        Printed at New York by order of His
        Excellency the Lord Cornbury, and re-
        printed at London, 1703.
            31, [1] p.   32 1/2 cm.

981   Bayard, Nicholas, 1644?-1707.
            Journal of the late actions of
        the French at Canada, by Col. Nicho-
        las Beyard, and Lieut. Col. Charles
        Lodowick. New York, Reprinted for J.
        Sabin, 1868.
            2 p. l., 55, [1] p.   23 1/2 x
        18 1/2 cm.

982   Bayard, Samuel, 1767-1840.
            A funeral oration, occasioned by
        the death of Gen. George Washington;
        and delivered on the first of Jan-
        uary, 1800. In the Episcopal
        church, at New-Rochelle,in the state
        of New-York, by Samuel Bayard, esq.
        New-Brunswick [N.J.] Printed by
        Abraham Blauvelt, 1800.
            24 p.   21 1/2 cm.

983   Bayard, William, 1764?-1826.
       An exposition of the conduct of
the two houses of G.G. & S. Howland,
and Le Roy, Bayard, & company, in
relation to the frigates Liberator
and Hope, in answer to a narrative
on that subject, by Mr. Alexandre
Contostavlos. By William Bayard.
New York, Printed by Clayton & Van
Norden, 1826.
       47 p.   23 cm.

984   ... Bayfield, lake Superior. Early
history, situation, harbor, &c.,
ocean commerce, mineral & agricultural resources, rail roads, stage
roads, &c., lumber, fisheries, &c.,
climate of lake Superior, pre-emption
lands, invitation to settlers. An
account of a pleasure tour to Lake
Superior, its climate, scenery, pic-
tured rocks, sailing days of the
steamboats, fare, &c. ... Philadelphia, 1858.
       cover-title, 14 p.   23 cm.

985   Bayley, Daniel, d. 1792, comp.
       A new and compleat introduction
to the grounds and rules of musick,
in two books: Book I. Containing
The grounds and rules of musick; or,
An introduction to the art of singing
by note, taken from Thomas Walter,
M.A. Book II. Containing a new and
correct introduction to the grounds
of musick, rudimental and practical;
from William Tans'urs Royal melody:
the whole being a collection of a
variety of the choicest tunes from
the most approved masters ... Printed for and sold by Bulkley Emerson,
and Daniel Bayley of Newbury, 1764.
       3 p. l., 25 p., 49 numb. l., 2 l.
10 x 16 1/2 cm.

986   [Bayley, Frederic William Naylor]

219

1808-1853.
Four years' residence in the West
Indies. By F.W.N. Bayley ... London, W. Kidd, 1830.
xiii p., 1 l., 693 p. front.,
plates, fold. tab. 23 1/2 cm.

987   Bayley, James Roosevelt, *abp.*, 1814-
1877.
A brief sketch of the history of
the Catholic church on the island of
New-York. By the Rev. J.R. Bayley
... New-York, E. Dunigan & brother, 1853.
4, [2], [5]-156 p.   18 cm.

988   Bayley, Richard, 1745-1801, *comp.*
Letters from the Health-office,
submitted to the Common council, of
the city of New-York. By Richard
Bayley. [New York] Printed by John
Furman, no. 102, Pearl-street, third
door below the corner of Old-slip
[1799]
100 p.   22 cm.

989   Baylies, Francis, 1783-1852.
Eulogy on the Hon. Benjamin Russell, delivered before the Grand
lodge of Free and accepted masons
of the state of Massachusetts, March
10, 1845. By Brother Francis Baylies. Boston, Printed at the office
of the Freemansons' magazine, 1845.
66 p.   22 cm.

990   Baylies, Francis, 1783-1852.
An historical memoir of the colony
of New Plymouth ... By Francis
Baylies. Boston, Hilliard, Gray,
Little, and Wilkins, 1830.
4 pt. in 2 v.   22 1/2 cm.

991   Baylies, Francis, 1783-1852.
An historical memoir of the colony
of New Plymouth, from the flight of

the Pilgrims into Holland in the year 1608, to the union of that colony with Massachusetts in 1692. By Francis Baylies. With some corrections, additions, and a copious index, by Samuel G. Drake ... Boston, Wiggin & Lunt, 1866.
2 v. front., ports., fold. maps. fold. geneal. tab. 25 cm.

992   Baylies, Francis, 1783-1852.
A narrative of Major General Wool's campaign in Mexico, in the years 1846, 1847, & 1848. By Francis Baylies ... Albany, Little & company, 1851.
78 p. front. (port.) 23 cm.

993   Bayly, William, 1737-1810.
The original astronomical observations made in the course of a voyage to the Northern Pacific Ocean, for the discovery of a North East or North West passage: wherein the North West coast of America and North East coast of Asia were explored. In His Majesty's ships the Resolution and Discovery, in the years MDCCLXXVI, MDCCLXXVII, MDCCLXXVIII, MDCCLXXIX, and MDCCLXXX. By Captain James Cooke ... and Lieutenant James King; and Mr. William Bayly ... Published by order of the Commissioners of longitude, at the expense of whom the observations were made. London, Printed by W. Richardson, 1782.
vii, [1] p., 2 l., 351. [1] p. incl. tables. fold. pl. 27 x 23 cm.

994   [Bayman, *Mrs*. A   Phelps]
Notes and letters on the American war. By an English lady. London, W. Ridgway, 1864.
1 p. l., ii, [3]-82 p. 20 cm.

995   Bayne, Peter, 1830-1896.
       The Christian life, social and in-
       dividual. By Peter Bayne ... Bos-
       ton, Gould and Lincoln; New York,
       Sheldon, Lamport & Blakeman, 1855.
       viii p., 1 l., [11]-528 p.   21
       1/2 cm.

996   Bazancourt, César Lecat, *baron* de,
       1810-1865.
       Le Mexique coutemporain par le
       baron de Bazancourt ...   Paris,
       Amyot, 1862.
       2 p. l., 388 p.   fold. map.   18
       cm.

997   Bazile, L.
       Le conseil des colons de Saint-
       Domingue, de leurs créanciers et
       ayant-cause.   Ouvrage qui contient:
       1°.   La loi expliquée par ses
       motifs, par la discussion, par le
       rapport de la commission prépara-
       toire; 2°.   Un commentaire de cette
       loi, et la solution des questions
       qu'elle fait naître; 3°.   L'or-
       donnance d'exécution; 4°.   Un tab-
       leau chronologique des lois sur
       les successions; par m. L. Bazile
       ...   Paris, E. Renduel [etc.] 1826.
       2 p. l., iv, 279 p.   14 cm.

998   Beach, David.
       A statement of facts, concerning
       the death of Samuel Lee, and the
       prosecution of David Sanford, for
       murder.   By David Beach ... New
       Haven, Printed for the Author [1807]
       14 p.   20 cm.

999   Beach, Lewis, 1835-1886.
       A word or two about the war.   By
       Lewis Beach.   New York, J.F. Trow,
       1862.
       28 p.   22 1/2 cm.

1000 Beach, Samuel B.
        Escalala: An American tale ...
      Utica, W. Williams, 1824.
        ix, [11]-100 p.   18 1/2 cm.

1001 Beadle, Delos White.
        Der amerikanische sachwalter;
      oder, Rechtsformenbuch für Deutsche;
      mit anweisungen, rathschlägen und
      warnungen hinsichtlich des gebrauchs
      dieser rechtsformen im praktischen
      amerikanischen leben, und mit darstell-
      ung der verschiedenheiten der gesetze
      der verschiedenen staaten über exem-
      tion, landkauf-brief, anspruchsrecht
      der handwerker ... u.s.w., mit einem
      auszug der constitution, dem siegel
      und der charte jedes staates der
      Union, und mit der Constitution der
      Ver. Staaten. Von Delos W. Beadle ...
      New-York, Phelps, Fanning & co.;
      Cincinnati, A. Ranney, 1852.
        1 p. 1., [5]-359, [1] p.   illus.
      (incl. maps)   20 cm.

1002 Beall, John Yates, 1835-1865, *defen-
      dant.*
        Trial of John Y. Beall, as a spy
      and guerrillero, by Military commis-
      sion. New York, D. Appleton and com-
      pany, 1865.
        94 p.   23 cm.

1003 Beaman, Fernando C   1814-1882.
        Provisional governments over the
      districts of country now in rebel-
      lion against the lawful authority of
      the United States. Speech of Hon.
      F.C. Beaman ... in the House of repre-
      sentatives, April 4, 1862. [Washing-
      ton, Office of the Congressional
      globe, 1862]
        7 p.   23 1/2 cm.

1004 Beaman, Fernando C   1814-1882.
        Reconstruction. Speech of F.C.

Beaman, of Michigan, in the House of representatives, March 22, 1864, on the bill to guarantee to certain states, whose governments have been usurped or overthrown, a republican form of government. Washington, H. Polkinhorn, printer, 1864.
15 p.   25 cm.

1005   Beamish, North Ludlow, 1797-1872.
The discovery of America by the Northmen, in the tenth century, with notices of the early settlements of the Irish in the western hemisphere. By North Ludlow Beamish ...   London, T. and W. Boone, 1841.
8 p. l., xiii p., 1 l., [47]-239, [3] p.   fold. pl., 2 fold. maps (incl. front.) geneal. tables (1 fold.)   22 x 13 1/2 cm.

1006   Bearcroft, Philip, 1697-1761.
A sermon preached before the Honorable Trustees for establishing the colony of Georgia in America, and the Associates of the late Reverend Dr. Bray; at their anniversary meeting March 16, 1737-8.   In the parish-church of St. Bridget, alias St. Bride, in Fleet-street London.   By Philip Bearcroft ...   Pub. at the particular request of the Trustees, and Associates.   London, Printed by J. Willis, 1738.
1 p. l., 22 p.   21 1/2 x 17 cm.

1007   Bearcroft, Philip, 1697-1761.
A sermon preached before the incorporated Society for the propagation of the gospel in foreign parts; at their anniversary meeting in the parish church of St. Mary-le-Bow, on Friday February 15, 1744 [*i.e.* 1745] By Philip Bearcroft ...   London, Printed by E. Owen, and sold by J. Roberts [etc.] 1744 [*i.e.* 1745]

73 p.   22 1/2 cm.

1008   Beardslee, George W.
        Rejection of the application for a
reissue upon new and amended claims of
the letters patent originally issued
in 1838 to Barnabas Langdon, embracing the letters of rejection from Hon.
Thomas Ewbank ... together with other
documents ... Albany, June, 1852.
By George W. Beardslee. Albany, Weed,
Parsons and company, 1852.
        39 p.   23 cm.

1009   Beardsley, Eben Edwards, 1808-1891.
        An address delivered in St. Peter's
church, Cheshire, October 1, 1844,
on occasion of the fiftieth anniversary of the Episcopal academy of Connecticut. By Rev. E.E. Beardsley, M.
A. New Haven, Stanley & Chapin, printers, 1844.
        46 p.   22 cm.

1010   Beardsley, Eben Edwards, 1808-1891.
        A sketch of William Beardsley:
one of the original settlers of Strat-
ford, Conn.; and a record of his
descendants of the third generation;
and of some who bear his name to the
present time. By E. Edwards Beardsley ... New Haven, Bassett & Barnett, 1867.
        iv, [5]-32 p.   22 1/2 cm.

1011   Beardsley, Levi, 1785-1857.
        Reminiscences; personal and other
incidents; early settlement of Otse-
go country; notices and anecdotes of
public men; judicial, legal, and
legislative matters; field sports;
dissertations and discussions. By
Levi Beardsley ... New-York, Printed by C. Vinten, 1852.
        x, 575 p. front. (port.)   22 1/2
cm.

1012 Beatson, Robert, 1742-1818.
Naval and military memoirs of
Great Britain from 1727 to 1783. By
Robert Beatson ... London, Printed
for Longman, Hurst, Rees and Orme;
[etc., etc.] 1804.
6 v. 21 1/2 cm.

1013 Beatty, Charles, 1715?-1772.
Double honour due to the laborious
gospel minister. Represented in a
sermon, preached at Fairfield, in
New-Jersey, the 1st of December, 1756.
At the ordination of the Reverend
Mr. William Ramsey. Published at
the desire of the hearers, by Charles
Beatty, minister of the gospel at
Nishaminy ... Philadelphia, Printed
by William Bradford, at the corner
of Front- and Market-streets [1757]
1 p. l., 56 p. 16 1/2 cm.

1014 Beatty, Charles, 1715?-1772.
The journal of a two months tour:
with a view of promoting religion
among the frontier inhabitants of
Pensylvania, and of introducing Christianity among the Indians to the west-
ward of the Alegh-geny mountains. To
which are added, remarks on the language and customs of some particular
tribes among the Indians, with a brief
account of the various attempts that
have been made to civilize and convert
them, from the first settlement of New
England to this day; by Charles Beatty ... London, Printed for W. Daven-
hill [etc.] 1768.
viii, [9]-110 p. 21 cm.

1015 Beauchamp, Alphonse de, 1767-1832.
Histoire de la conquête et des
révolutions du Pérou, par Alphonse de
Beauchamp ... Paris, Lenormant
etc. 1808.
2 v. in 1. fronts. (ports.) 20 cm.

1016   Beauchamp, Alphonse de, 1767-1832.
       Histoire de Brésil, depuis sa
       découverte en 1500 jusqu'en 1810
       ... Par M. Alphonse de Beauchamp
       ... Orné d'une nouvelle carte de
       l'Amerique Portugaise et de deux
       belles gravures ...   Paris, A. Eymery,
       1815.
       3 v.   fronts. (v. 3, fold. map)
       21 cm.

1017   Beauchamp, Alphonse de, 1767-1832.
       L'indépendance de l'empire du
       Brésil, présentée aux monarques
       européens; par m. Alphonse de Beau-
       champ ...   Paris, Delaunay, 1824.
       1 p. 1., xv, 138 p. 1 1.   23
       cm.

1018   Beaufoy, Mark, 1764-1827.
       Mexican illustrations, founded upon
       facts; indicative of the present
       condition of society, manners, reli-
       gion, and morals, among the Spanish
       and native inhabitants of Mexico:
       with observations upon the government
       and resources of the republic of Mexi-
       co, as they appeared during part of
       the years 1825, 1826, and 1827. In-
       terspersed with occasional remarks
       upon the climate, produce, and anti-
       quities of the country, mode of work-
       ing the mines, &c. By Mark Bacufoy
       ... London, Carpenter and son, 1828.
       xii, 310, [2] p. incl. front.,
       illus. 5 pl., fold. map.   22 1/2
       cm.

1019   Beaujour, Louis Auguste Félix, *baron
       de,* 1763-1836.
       Aperçu des États-Unis, au com-
       mencement du XIXe siècle, depuis
       1800 jusqu'en 1810 avec des tables
       statistiques. Par le chevalier
       Félix de Beaujour ...   Paris, L.G.
       Michaud, imprimeur [etc.] 1814

1020 Beaujour, Louis Auguste Félix, *baron*
      de, 1763-1836.
        Sketch of the United States of
      North America, at the commencement
      of the nineteenth century, from 1800
      to 1810; with statistical tables, and
      a new map, by the author; containing
      all the late discoveries ... By le
      chevalier Felix de Beaujour ... Tr.
      from the French, with illustrative
      notes and appendix by William Walton,
      esq. London, J. Booth [etc.] 1814.
        xx, ii p., 1 l., [5]-363 p. front.
      (fold. map) XVII tab. (14 fold.) 21
      1/2 cm.

1021 Beaumont, Arthur J.
        An American's defence of his gov-
      ernment, in an appeal to the common
      sense of the nations of Europe. By
      Arthur J. Beaumont ... [London]
      Printed for the author, and pub.
      by J. Miller, 1831.
        36 p.   22 cm.

1022 Beaumont, Arthur J.
        De la Constitution américaine, et de
      quelques calomnies dont elle a été
      l'objet de nos jours. Par A.-J.
      Beaumont ... Au bénéfice des réfu-
      giés italiens. Paris, G.G. Bennis
      [etc.] 1831.
        2 p. l., 60 p.   22 1/2 cm.

1023 Beaumont, J   A   B.
        Travels in Buenos Ayres, and the
      adjacent provinces of the Rio de la
      Plata. With observations, intended
      for the use of persons who contem-
      plate emigrating to that country; or,
      embarking capital in its affairs.
      By J.A.B. Beaumont, esq. London, J.
      Ridgway, 1828.
        xii, 270 p.   front. (fold. map)
      22 1/2 cm.

1024   Beauvallet, Léon, 1829-1885.
        Rachel and the New world. A trip
        to the United States and Cuba. Tr.
        from the French of Léon Beauvallet.
        New York, Dix, Edwards & co., 1856.
        2 p. l., [iii]-xiv, 404 p.   18
        cm.

1025   Beaven, James.
        Recreations of a long vacation;
        or, A visit to Indian missions in
        Upper Canada. By James Beaven ...
        London, J. Burns; [etc., etc.]
        1846.
        3 p. l., 196 p. incl. illus.,
        plates.   18 cm.

1026   Beauvois, Eugène, 1835-
        Découvertes des Scandinaves en
        Amérique, du dixième au treizième
        siècle, fragments de sagas island-
        aises, traduits pour la première
        fois en français par E. Beauvois ...
        Paris, Challamel nîné, 1859.
        77 p.   21 1/2 cm.

1027   Bechtel, Johannes, 1690-1777, *ed*.
        Kurzer catechismus vor etliche
        gemeinen Jesu aus der reformirten
        religion in Pennsylvania, die sich
        zum alten Berner synodo halten:
        herausgegeben von Johannes Bechteln,
        diener des Worts Gottes. [*Ornamont*]
        Philadelphia, Gedruckt bey Benjamin
        Franklin, 1742.
        42 p.   13 cm.

1028   Beck-Bernard, *Mme*. Lina (Bernard)
        Le Rio Parana; cinq annees de
        séjour dans la République Argentine,
        par M*me* Lina Beck Bernard.   Paris,
        Grassart; [etc., etc.] 1864.
        2 p. l., 294 p., 1 l.   18 1/2
        cm.

1029   Beck, John Brodhead, 1794-1851.

An historical sketch of the state
of medicine in the American colonies,
from their first settlement to the
period of the revolution, by John
B. Beck ... 2d ed. Albany, C. Van
Benthuysen, printer, 1850.
63 p. 23 1/2 cm.

1030 Beck, Lewis Caleb, 1798-1853.
An account of the salt springs at
Salina, in Onondaga county, state
of New York; with a chemical examination of the water and of several varieties of salt manufactured at Salina
and Syracuse. By Lewis C. Beck ...
New-York, Printed by J. Seymour, 1826.
36 p. 21 1/2 cm.

1031 Beck, Lewis Caleb, 1798-1853.
Botany of the United States north
of Virginia; comprising descriptions
of the flowering and fern-like plants
hitherto found in those states ...
By Lewis C. Beck ... 2d ed., rev.
and enl. New York, Harper & brothers,
1848.
lxiii, 480 p. 21 cm.

1032 Beck, Lewis Caleb, 1798-1853.
Report on the breadstuffs of the
United States, made to the commission-
er of patents, by Lewis C. Beck, M.D.
Washington, Printed by Wendell and
Van Benthuysen, 1849.
31 p. 24 cm.

1033 [Beck, Paul] 1760?-1844.
A proposal for altering the eastern front of the city of Philadelphia, with a view to prevent the re-
currence of malignant disorders, on
a plan conformable to the original
design of William Penn. By a citizen of Philadelphia. Philadelphia:
Printed and published by William Fry,
no. 63, South Fifth-street ... 1820.

11 p.   front. (fold. plan)   21
1/2 cm.

1034   Beckett, Sylvester Breakmore, 1812-
       1882.
          Guide book of the Atlantic and St.
       Lawrence, and St. Lawrence and Atlan-
       tic rail roads, including a full de-
       scription of all the interesting fea-
       tures of the White Mountains, by S.
       B. Beckett; with illustrations from
       original sketches by C.E. Beckett,
       engraved on wood by Baker, Smith &
       Andrew. Portland, Sanborn & Carter
       [etc.] 1853.
          vi, [2], [7]-180 p. incl. illus.,
       plates. pl., fold. map.   19 1/2
       cm.

1035   Beckford, William, d. 1799.
          Vues pittoresques de la Jamaïque,
       avec une description détaillée de
       ses productions, sur-tout des cannes
       à sucre, des travaux, du traitement
       et des moeurs des nègres, etc. Tr.
       de l'anglais de M.W. Beckfort, par
       J.S.P. Nouv. ed. ... Lausanne,
       Durand l'ainó et compe., 1793.
          2 v. in 1.   19 cm.

1036   Beckley, Hosea
          The history of Vermont; with de-
       scriptions, physical and topographi-
       cal. By Rev. Hosea Beckley, A.M.
       Brattleboro, G.H. Salisbury, 1846.
          xiv, [17]-396 p.   19 1/2 cm.

1037   Beckwith, George Cone, 1800-1870.
          The peace manual; or, War and its
       remedies. By Geo. C. Beckwith. Bos-
       ton, American peace society, 1847.
          252 p.   15 cm.

1038   Bedford, Gunning S.
          An address, introductory to a
       course of lectures delivered in

Clinton hall, New York, November 8,
1834, by Gunning S. Bedford ... 2d
ed. New York, Printed by J.M. Elliott, 1835.
29 p. 21 1/2 cm.

1039 Bedford, Gunning S.
An address introductory to a course
of lectures delivered in Clinton
hall, New York, November 15, 1835, by
Gunning S. Bedford ... New York,
Printed by J.M. Elliott, 1836.
32 p. 21 cm.

1040 Bedford, John [Russell] *4th duke of*,
1710-1771.
Correspondence of John, fourth
duke of Bedford: selected from the
originals at Woburn abbey. With an
introduction, by Lord John Russell.
London, Longman, Brown, Green, and
Longmans, 1842-46.
3 v. 22 cm.

1041 Bedinger, Daniel.
A letter from Daniel Bedinger, late
navy agent at Norfolk, to Robert
Smith, esq., secretary of the navy:
with an appendix, containing sundry
official and other papers ... Norfolk, Printed by A.C. Jordan, & co.,
1808.
18, 34 p. 21 cm.

1042 [Beecher, Catherine Esther] 1800-1878.
The duty of American women to
their country. New-York, Harper &
brothers, 1845.
164 p. 16 cm.

1043 Beecher, Catherine Esther, 1800-1878.
An essay on slavery and abolition-
ism, with reference to the duty of
American females. By Catharine E.
Beecher. Philadelphia, H. Perkins:
Boston, Perkins & Marvin, 1837.

152 p.   15 1/2 cm.

1044   Beecher, Catherine Esther, 1800-1878.
         The evils suffered by American
       women and American children: the
       causes and the remedy.   Presented
       in an address by Miss C.E. Beecher,
       to meetings of ladies in ... New
       York, and other cities.   Also, An
       address to the Protestant clergy of
       the United States.   New York, Harper
       & brothers [c1846]
         36 p.   24 cm.

1045   Beecher, Catherine Esther, 1800-1878.
         Suggestions respecting improvements
       in education, presented to the trus-
       tees of the Hartford female seminary,
       and published at their request.   By
       Catharine E. Beecher.   Hartford, Pack-
       ard & Butler, 1829.
         84 p.   21 1/2 cm.

1046   Beecher, Catherine Esther, 1800-1878.
         The true remedy for the wrongs of
       woman; with a history of an enter-
       prise having that for its object.
       By Catharine E. Beecher.   Boston,
       Phillips, Sampson, & co., 1851.
         viii, 263 p.   front., plans.   19
       cm.

1047   Beecher, Catherine Esther, 1800-1878.
         Truth stranger than fiction; a nar-
       rative of recent transactions, in-
       volving inquiries in regard to the
       principles of honor, truth, and jus-
       tice, which obtain in a distinguish
       ed American university, by Catherine
       E. Beecher ...   Boston, Phillips
       Sampson & co., 1850.
         3 p. l., [3]-296 p.   19 cm.

1048   Beecher, Charles, 1815-1900.
         The duty of disobedience to wicked
       laws.   A sermon on the fugitive slave

233

law. By Charles Beecher ... New-
York, J.A. Gray, printer, 1851.
22 p. 22 1/2 cm.

1049 Beecher, Charles, 1815-1900.
... The God of the Bible against
slavery. By Rev. Charles Beecher.
[New York, American anti-slavery
society, 1855]
11 p. 19 cm.

1050 Beecher, Charles, 1815-1900.
Spiritual manifestations. By
Charles Beecher ... Boston, Lee
and Shepard; New York, C.T. Dillingham, 1879.
1 p. 1., 7-322 p. incl. map. 20
cm.

1051 Beecher, Edward, 1803-1895.
Narrative of riots at Alton: in
connection with the death of Rev.
Elijah P. Lovejoy. By Rev. Edward
Beecher ... Alton [Ill.] G. Holton,
1838.
159 p. 19 cm.

1052 Beecher, George, 1809-1843.
The biographical remains of Rev.
George Beecher, late pastor of a
church in Chillicothe, Ohio, and
former pastor of a church in Rochester, New-York. New York, Leavitt,
Trow and co.; Boston, Crocker and
Brewster; [etc., etc.] 1844.
345 p. 17 1/2 cm.

1053 Beecher, Henry Ward, 1813-1887.
American rebellion. Report of the
speeches of the Rev. Henry Ward
Beecher, delivered at public meetings
in Manchester, Glasgow, Edinburgh,
Liverpool, and London; and at the
farewell breakfasts in London, Manchester, and Liverpool. Manchester,
Union and emancipation society;

234

[etc., etc.] 1864.
2 p. 1., 175 p.   21 cm.

1054   Beecher, Henry Ward, 1813-1887.
Defence of Kansas. By Henry Ward
Beecher. [Washington, Buell &
Blanchard, printers, 1856]
8 p.   24 cm.

1055   Beecher, Henry Ward, 1813-1887.
England and America: speech of
Henry Ward Beecher at the Free-trade
hall, Manchester, October 9, 1863
... Boston, J. Redpath, 1863.
39 p.   18 cm.

1056   Beecher, Henry Ward, 1813-1887.
Eyes and ears. By Henry Ward
Beecher. Boston, Ticknor and Fields,
1864.
vii, 419 p.   19 cm.

1057   Beecher, Henry Ward, 1813-1887.
Freedom and war. Discourses on
topics suggested by the times. By
Henry Ward Beecher. Boston, Ticknor and Fields, 1863.
2 p. 1., [iii]-iv p., 1 1., 445
p.   19 cm.

1058   Beecher, Henry Ward, 1813-1887.
Life thoughts, gathered from the
extemporaneous discourses of Henry
Ward Beecher. By one of his congregation. 10th thousand. Boston,
Phillips, Sampson and company, 1858.
xviii, 299 p.   20 cm.

1059   Beecher, Lyman, 1775-1863.
Autobiography, correspondence, etc.,
of Lyman Beecher, D.D. Ed. by
Charles Beecher ... New York, Harper
& brothers, 1864.
2 v.   illus., ports. (incl. front)
19 cm.

1060 Beecher, Lyman, 1775-1863.
    The memory of our fathers. A sermon delivered at Plymouth, on the twenty-second of December, 1827. By Lyman Beecher, D.D. Boston, T.R. Marvin, printer, 1828.
    39 p. 23 1/2 cm.

1061 Beecher, Lyman, 1775-1863.
    The memory of our fathers. A sermon delivered at Plymouth, on the twenty-second of December, 1827. By Lyman Beecher, D.D. 2d ed. Boston, T.R. Marvin, printer, 1828.
    30 p. 21 cm.

1062 Beecher, Lyman, 1775-1863.
    A reformation of morals practicable and indispensable. A sermon, delivered at New-Haven, on the evening of October 27, 1812, by Lyman Beecher ... 2d ed. Utica: Printed by Merrell and Camp. 1813.
    32 p. 20 1/2 cm.

1063 Beecher, Lyman, 1775-1863.
    The remedy for duelling. A sermon, delivered before the presbytery of Long-Island, at the opening of their session, at Aquebogue, April 16, 1806. By Lyman Beecher ... First published by request of the presbytery. Re-published by subscription. To which is annexed, the resolutions and address of the Anti-duelling association of New-York. New-York: Sold at the theological and classical book-store of Williams and Whiting, no. 118, Pearl-street, J. Seymour printer ... 1809.
    1 p. 1., 48 p. 20 1/2 cm.

1064 Beecher, Lyman, 1775-1863.
    A sermon, containing a general history of the town of East-Hampton, (L.I.) from its first settlement to

the present time. Delivered at
East-Hampton, January 1, 1806. By
Lyman Beecher, pastor of the church
in that place. Sag-Harbor, N.Y.
Printed by Alden Spooner. 1806.
   40 p.   21 cm.

1065   Beecher, Lyman, 1775-1863.
       A sermon, occasioned by the la-
mented death of Mrs. Frances M. Sands,
of New-Shoreham. Formerly an inhabitant of East-Hampton, (L.I.) Composed and now made public at the request
of her afflicted partner, and delivered at East Hampton, October 12, 1806.
By Lyman Beecher, pastor of the church
in that place. Sag-Harbor, N.Y.,
Printed by Alden Spooner. 1806.
   20 p.   22 cm.

1066   Beechey, Frederick William, 1796-1856.
       Narrative of a voyage to the Pacif-
ic and Beering's strait, to co-oper-
ate with the polar expeditions: performed in His Majesty's ship Blossom,
under the command of Captain F.W.
Beechey ... in the years 1825, 26,
27, 28 ... London, H. Colburn and
R. Bentley, 1831.
       2 v. front., plates, port., maps
(part fold.)   28 1/2 cm.

1067   Beechey, Frederick William, 1796-1856.
       A voyage of discovery towards the
North pole, performed in His Majesty's
ships Dorothea and Trent, under the
command of Captain David Buchan,
R.N.; 1818; to which is added, a
summary of all the early attempts to
reach the Pacific by way of the Pole.
By Captain F.W. Beechey ... London,
R. Bently, 1843.
       ix, [1] p., 1 l., 351, [1] p.
front., plates (part fold.) fold.
map.   21 1/2 cm.

1068   Beers, Frederick W
      Atlas of Muskingum Co., Ohio;
from actual surveys by and under the
direction of F.W. Beers, assisted
by Beach Nichols and others. New
York, Beers, Soule & Co., 1866.
      37 (i.e. 68) p. illus., col. maps
(1 fold.)   36 cm.

1069   Beers, William Pitt, 1766-1810.
      An oration, on the death of Gener-
al Washington; pronounced before the
citizens of Albany, on Thursday, January 9th, 1800. By William P.
Beers, esquire. Albany: Printed by
Charles R. and George Webster [1800]
      17 p.   21 1/2 x 18 cm.

1070   Beeson, John, b. 1803.
      A plea for the Indians: with facts
and features of the late war in Oregon. By John Beeson ... New York,
J. Beeson, 1857.
      viii, [9]-143 p.   19 cm.

1071   Beknopte en zakelyle beschryving der
voornaamste engelsche volkplantingen,
in Noord-Amerika; neffens aanmer-
kingen over den oorsprong en voort-
gang der tegenwoordige geschillen,
en des oorlogs, tusschen Groot-Britt-
tannie en deszelfs kolonisten. Amsterdam, P. Conradi, 1776.
      2 v.   22 1/2 cm.

1072   Belcher, Joseph, 1669-1723.
      God giveth the increase. An ordin-
ation sermon, preached at Bristol,
N.E., Aug. 30, 1721. When Mr. Nathanael Cotton was ordained the pastor
of the church there. By Joseph Belcher, A.M., pastor of the church in
Dedham ... Boston in New England:
Printed and sold by B. Green, In
Newbury street. 1722.
      2 p. l., iv, 38 p.   16 1/2 cm.

1073 Belcher, Joseph, 1669-1723.
      The worst enemy conquered. A
brief discourse on the methods and
motives to pursue a victory over
those habits of sin, which war
against the soul. Delivered, on June
6th, 1698, the day for election of
officers, in the artilery-company,
at Boston. By Mr. Joseph Belcher,
pastor of the church in Dedham ...
Boston in New-England. Printed by
Bartholomew Green, and John Allen,
1698.
      38 p.   14 1/2 cm.

1074 Belcher, Joseph, 1794-1859, *comp.*
      George Whitefield: a biography,
with special reference to his labors in America. Comp. by Joseph
Belcher ... New York, American
tract society [pref. 1857]
      514 p.   front. (port.)   plates.
19 1/2 cm.

1075 Belcher, Joseph, 1794-1859.
      The religious denominations in the
United States: their history, doctrine, government and statistics.
With a preliminary sketch of Judaism,
paganism and Mohammedanism. By Joseph Belcher ... Embellished with
nearly two hundred engravings. Philadelphia, J.E. Potter, 1854.
      xii, 13-1024 p. incl. illus.,
plates, ports. front.   25 cm.

1076 [Belden, Ezekiel Porter] 1828-1911.
      New-York--as it is; being the
counterpart of the metropolis of
America ... New-York, Printed by
J.P. Prall, 1849.
      24 p.   pl.   19 1/2 cm.

1077 Belden, Ezekiel Porter, 1823-1911.
      New-York: past, present, and future;
comprising a history of the city of
New-York, a description of its

present condition, and an estimate
of its future increase. By E. Porter Belden ... New-York, G.P. Putnam; Boston, B.B. Mussey & co.;
[etc., etc.] 1849.
    4 p. 1., [vii]-viii p., 1 1., [11]
-125 p. front., illus., plates,
fold. plan. 19 1/2 cm.

1078 Beleña, Eusebio Buenaventura, 1736-
      1794.
    Recopilación sumaria de todos los
autos acordados de la Real audiencia
y sala del crimen de esta Nueva
España, y providencias de su superior
gobierno; de varias reales cédulas y
ordenes que despues de publicada la
Recopilación de Indias han podido
recogerse asi de las dirigidas á la
misma Audiencia ó gobierno, como de
algunas otras que por sus notables
decisiones convendrá no ignorar: por
el doctor Don Eusebio Bentura Beleña
... México, Impresa por Don F. de
Zúñiga y Ontiveros, 1787.
    6 v. in 2. illus. (ports.)   29
1/2 cm.

1079 Die belgische neutralität. [Berlin, G.
      Stilke, 1915]
    33 p. incl. facsims.   26 x 20 1/2
cm.

1080 Belgrove, William.
    A treatise upon husbandry or plant-
ing. By William Belgrove. A regu-
lar bred, and long experienc'd plant-
er, of the island of Barbados. And
may be of great use to the planters
of all the West-India islands. Boston: New-England, Printed by D.
Fowle in Ann-Street, near the Town-
Dock. 1755.
    1 p. 1., 86 p.   17 1/2 cm.

1081 Belknap, Jeremy, 1744-1798.

A discourse intended to commemo-
rate the discovery of America by
Christopher Columbus; delivered at
the request of the Historical society in Massachusetts, on the 23d day
of October, 1792, being the completion of the third century since that
memorable event. To which are added
four dissertations, connected with
various parts of the discourse ...
By Jeremy Belknap ... Printed at the
Apollo press, in Boston, by Belknap
and Hall, State street, 1792.
132 p.   20 1/2 cm.

1082   [Belknap, Jeremy] 1744-1798.
The foresters, an American tale:
being a sequel to the History of
John Bull, the clothier. In a series
of letters to a friend. Boston,
Printed by I. Thomas and E.T. Andrews, 1792.
216 p.   front.   17 cm.

1083   Belknap, Jeremy, 1744-1798.
The history of New-Hampshire. Vol.
I. Comprehending the events of one
complete century from the discovery
of the river Pascataqua. By Jeremy
Belknap ... Philadelphia, Printed
for the author by R. Aitken, 1784.
viii, 361, lxxxiv p.   21 1/2 cm.

1084   Belknap, Jeremy, 1744-1798.
The history of New-Hampshire. By
Jeremy Belknap, D.D. From a copy
of the original ed., having the auth-
or's last corrections. To which are
added notes, containing various corrections and illustrations of the
text, and additional facts and notices of persons and events therein
mentioned. By John Farmer ... Dover,
N.H., G. Wadleigh, 1862.
2 p. l., [iii]-xvi, 512 p.   front.
(port.)   26 cm.

1085 Bell, Agrippa Nelson, 1820--
        Malignant pustule in the United
      States. By A.N. Bell ... Albany,
      Steam press of C. Van Benthuysen,
      1862.
        25 p.   23 cm.

1086 [Bell, Andrew] *of Southampton, fl.*
        1838-1866.
        Men and things in America; being
      the experience of a year's residence
      in the United States, in a series of
      letters to a friend ... By A. Thoma-
      son [*pseud.*] London, W. Smith; [etc.,
      etc.] 1838.
        viii, 296 p.   18 cm.

1087 Bell, Hiram, 1808-1855.
        Speech of Hon. Hiram Bell, of
      Ohio, in reply to Hon. E.B. Olds on
      the presidency. Generals Scott and
      Pierce, their comparative qualifica-
      tions and merits. &c. Delivered in
      the House of representatives, July
      20, 1852. [Washington] Gideon &
      co., printers [1852]
        8 p.   24 cm.

1088 Bell, John, 1796-1872.
        The mineral and thermal springs
      of the United States and Canada. By
      John Bell ... Philadelphia, Perry
      and McMillan, 1855.
        xx, [13]-395 p.   17 cm.

1089 Bell, John, 1796-1872.
        On baths and mineral waters ... By
      John Bell ... Philadelphia, H.H.
      Porter, 1831.
        xviii p., 1 l., [17]-532 p.   20
      cm.

1090 Bell, John, 1797-1869.
        Mr. Bell's suppressed report in
      relation to difficulties between
      the eastern and western Cherokees.

[Washington? D.C., 1840?]
23 p.   23 1/2 cm.

1091   Bell, John, 1797-1869.
Speech of John Bell, of Tennessee,
on slavery in the United States, and
the causes of the present dissensions
between the North and the South. Delivered in the Senate of the United
States on the 5th and 6th of July,
1850. Washington, Gideon and co.,
printers, 1850.
30 p.   22 1/2 cm.

1092   Bell, Joshua Fry, 1811-1870.
Speech of Mr. J.F. Bell, of Kentucky, on the Oregon question, delivered in the House of representatives
of the United States, February 4, 1846.
Washington, J.&G.S. Gideon, printers,
1846.
14 p.   24 cm.

1093   Bell, Luther Vose, 1806-1862.
Eulogy of Gen. Zachary Taylor, late
president of the United States, delivered by the appointment of the
city authorities and citizens, con-
jointly, of the city of Cambridge,
August 13, 1850. By Luther V. Bell.
Cambridge [Mass.] Printed at the
Chronicle office, 1850.
43 p.   23 1/2 cm.

1094   Bell, Robert, *fl.* 1570.
Rerum hispaniscarvm scriptores
aliquot ... Ex bibliotheca clarissimi
viri dn. Roberti Beli Angli nvnc
accvrativs emendativsqve recusi, &
in duos tomos digesti, adiecto in
fine indice copiosissimo ... Franco-
fvrti, ex officina typographica A.
Wecheli, 1579--
v.   33 1/2 cm.

1095   Bell, *Rev.* William.

243

Hints to emigrants; in a series of letters from Upper Canada. By the Rev. William Bell ... Edinburgh, Printed for Waugh & Innes, 1824.
iv, 236 p. front. (fold. map) fold. plans. 18 1/2 cm.

1096 Bellamy, Joseph, 1719-1790.
The law, our school-master; a sermon preached at Litchfield June 8, 1756, before the Association of Litchfield County. By Joseph Bellamy ... Published with great enlargements ... New-Haven, Printed by J. Parker, and company [1762]
1 p. l., 77, [1] p. 19 cm.

1097 Bellamy, Joseph, 1719-1790.
A sermon delivered before the General assembly of the colony of Connecticut, at Hartford, on the day of the anniversary election, May 13th, 1762. By Joseph Bellamy, A.M., minister of the gospel at Bethlem ... New-London [Conn.]: Printed and sold by Timothy Green, printer to the colony of Connecticut. [1762]
43 p. 17 1/2 cm.

1098 Bellamy, Joseph, 1719-1790.
The works of Joseph Bellamy, D.D., first pastor of the church in Bethlem, Conn., with a memoir of his life and character ... Boston, Doctrinal tract and book society, 1853, '50.
2 v. 25 cm.

1099 Bellardi, Luigi, 1818-1889.
Saggio di ditterologia messicana di Luigi Bellardi ... Torino, Dalla Stamperia reale, 1859-61.
2 pt. in 1 v. 4 pl. 28 x 23 cm.

1100 Bellecombe, André Ursule Casse de, 1822-1897.

... Discours prononcé à la séance
d'ouverture du Comité d'archéologie
américaine le 23 juillet 1863, par
A. de Bellecombe, président. Paris,
Au local du Comité, 1863.
22 (*i.e.* 20) p.   20 1/2 cm.

1101   Bellegarde, [Jean Baptiste Morvan] de,
1648-1734.
Histoire universelle des voyages
faits par mer & par terre, dans
l'Ancien & dans le Nouveau monde.
Pour éclaircir la géographie ancienne
& moderne. Par Mr. l'abbé de Bellegarde. Amsterdam, P. Humbert, 1708.
7 p. l., 438 p.   7 pl. (incl.
front.) fold. map.   15 1/2 cm.

1102   Bellegarrigue, A.
Les femmes d'Amérique, par A.
Bellegarrigue. Paris, Blanchard,
1853.
96 p.   15 1/2 cm.

1103   [Bellemare, Louis *i.e.* Eugène Louis
Gabriel de] 1809-1852.
Der waldläufer, scenen aus dem
mexikanischen waldleben, von Gabriel
Ferry ⌊*pseud.*⌋ ... Aus dem französi-
schen von dr. G. Füllner. Durch-
gesehener neudruck ... Halle a.d.
S., O. Hendel [1897]
4 v. in 1.   18 cm.

1104   [Bellemare, Louis] 1809 1852.
... Les révolutions du Mexique;
préface par George Sand. Paris,
E. Dentu, 1864.
3 p. l., [ix]-xx, 255 p., 1 l.
18 1/2 cm.

1105   Bellemare, Louis, 1809-1852.
Scènes de la vie mexicaine, par
Gabriel Ferry (Louis de Bellemare)
... Paris, L. Hachette et cie, 1856.
2 p. l., 335, [1] p.   17 1/2
cm.

245

1106   Bellemare, Louis de, 1809-1852.
      Scènes de la vie militaire au
Mexique, par Gabriel Ferry (Louis
de Bellemare) Paris, L. Hachette
et cie., 1858.
     3 p. l., [3]-295 p., 2 l.   18
1/2 cm.

1107   Bellemare, Louis de, 1809 - 1852.
      Scènes de la vie sauvage au Mexi-
que, par Gabriel Ferry [*pseud*.] ...
3. éd. ...   Paris, Charpentier,
1856.
     3 p. l., 347 p., 1 l.   17 1/2
cm.

1108   Bellemare, Louis *i.e.* Eugene Louis
Gabriel de, 1809-1852.
      Les squatters, La clairière du
bois des Hogues; par Gabriel Ferry
(Louis de Bellemare) 2. éd.   Paris,
L. Hachette et c^{ie}, 1860.
     3 p. l., [3]-200 p., 2 l.   18
cm.

1109   [Bellin, Jacques Nicolas] 1703-1772.
      Description des débouquemens qui
sont au nord de l'isle de Saint-
Domingue ... [2d. éd.] Versailles,
Impr. du Département de la marine,
1773.
     5 p. l., 152 p. xxxiv charts
(part fold.)   25 1/2 cm.

1110   [Bellin, Jacques Nicolas] 1703-1772.
      Description géographique des
isles Antilles possédées par les
Anglois ... A Paris, De l'impr.
de Didot, 1758.
     xii, 171 p. illus., maps (part
fold.) Plans (part fold.)   25 1/2
x 19 1/2 cm.

1111   Bellin, Jacques Nicolas, 1703-1772.
      Le petit atlas maritime; recueil
de cartes et plans des quatre

parties du monde ... Par le S.
Bellin ... [Paris] 1764.
5 v. maps (part double) plans
(part double)   35 cm.

1112   Belloc, Hippolyte.
Histoires d'Amérique, et d'
Océanie, depuis les temps les plus
reculés jusqu'à nos jours, par M.
Belloc ... Ouvrage orné d'environ
31 belles planches gravées sur acier,
représentant les usages et cérémonies
des Américains au temps de la conquête, les principaux sites et les
monuments les plus remarquables, ainsi
que les costumes, armes et instruments
des sauvages de l'Océanie. Paris,
Impr. de Béthune et Plon, 1844.
2 p. l., 486, [2] p. plates
(partly col.)   22 cm.

1113   [Bellomont, Charles Coote, *earl of*]
1738?-1800.
A letter to Lord Viscount Beauchamp, upon the subject of his letter
to the First Belfast company of volunteers, in the province of Ulster ...
London, Printed for J. Debrett, 1783.
1 p. l., 48 p.   21 1/2 cm.

1114   [Bellon de Saint Quentin, J   ]
Dissertation sur la traite et
le commerce des Nègres. [Paris]
1764.
2 p. l., 174 p.   16 cm.

1115   Belloro, Tommaso, 1741-1821.
Notizie della famiglia di
Cristoforo Colombo raccolte da
Tommaso Belloro. Impressione
seconda con note dell'editore.
Genova, Presso A. Frugoni, 1821.
16 p.   21 cm.

1116   Bellot, Joseph René, 1826-1853.
Journal d'un voyage aux mers
polaires, exécuté à la recherche de

Sir John Franklin, en 1851 et 1852,
par J.R. Bellot ... précédé d'une
notice sur la vie et les travaux de
l'auteur, par m. Julien Lemer. Paris,
Perrotin, 1854.
lvi, 414 p., 1 l. front. (port.)
fold. map.   24 cm.

1117 Bellot, Joseph René, 1826-1853.
Memoirs of Lieutenant Joseph René
Bellot ... with his Journal of a
voyage in the polar seas, in search
of Sir John Franklin ... London,
Hurst and Blackett, 1855.
2 v.   front. (port.)   19 1/2 cm.

1118 Bellows, Henry Whitney, 1814-1882.
A discourse occasioned by the
death of William Ellery Channing,
D.D. pronounced before the Unitarian
societies of New-York and Brooklyn,
in the Church of the Messiah, October 13th, 1842. By Henry W. Bellows
... New-York, C.S. Francis & company, 1842.
iv, [5]-28 p.   23 cm.

1119 Bellows, Henry Whitney, 1814-1882.
Historical sketch of Col. Benjamin
Bellows, founder of Walpole: an
address, on occasion of the gathering
of his descendants to the consecration of his monument, at Walpole, N.H.,
Oct. 11, 1854. By Henry W. Bellows.
With an appendix, containing an account of the family meeting. New-
York, J.A. Gray, printer, 1855.
2 p. l., 125 p., 1 l. col. front.,
pl., fold. geneal. tab.   22 1/2 cm.

1120 Bellows, Henry Whitney, 1814-1882.
Public life in Washington: or, The
moral aspects of the national capital,
and the apparent tendencies of political thought and feeling in Congress
and Cabinet. An address read on Sunday
evening, May 7, 1866, to his own

congregation, by Henry W. Bellows ...
New York, J. Miller, 1866.
26 p.   23 cm.

1121   Bellows, Henry Whitney, 1814-1882.
        Unconditional loyalty. By Henry
        W. Bellows, D.D. New York, A.D.F.
        Randolph, 1863.
        16 p.   21 cm.

1122   Bellows, Henry Whitney, 1814-1882.
        ... The war to end only when the
        rebellion ceases. By Henry W. Bel-
        lows, D.D. New York, A.D.F. Randolph
        [1863]
        16 p.   21 1/2 cm.

1123   Belloy, Auguste, *marquis* de, 1815-1871.
        Christophe Colomb et la découverte
        du Nouveau monde, par M. le marquis
        de Belloy; compositions et gravures
        par Léopold Flameng. Paris, E.
        Ducrocq [1864]
        2 p. l., 204 p. front., illus.,
        plates, ports.   31 1/2 cm.

1124   Belly, Félix, 1816-1886.
        À travers l'Amérique Centrale. Le
        Nicaragua et le canal interocéanique.
        Par Félix Belly ... Paris, Librairie
        de la Suisse romande, 1867.
        2 v.   fold. maps.   24 cm.

1125   Belly, Félix, 1816-1886.
        Percement de l'isthme de Panama
        par le canal de Nicaragua. Exposé
        de la question. Par M. Félix Belly.
        Paris, Aux bureaux de la direction
        du canal, 1858.
        177 p., 1 l. 3 fold. maps.   24
        1/2 cm.

1126   Belmonte, Benjamin Elie Colaço.
        Neêrlands West-Indie in zijne
        belangen, en dr. W.R. van Hoëvell
        in zijn "Slaven en vrijen." Slavernij.

--Emancipatie.--Kolonisatie. Door
B.E.C. Belmonte ... Leiden, P.H.
van den Heuvell, 1855.
viii p., 1 l., 246 p. 23 cm.

1127 Belmonte, Benjamin Elie Colaço.
Over de hervorming van het
regeringsstelsel in Nederlandsch
West-Indië ... Leiden, P.H. van den
Heuvell, 1857.
4 p. l., xiv, 248 p. 21 1/2 cm.

1128 Belot, Charles.
La fièvre jaune à la Habane: sa
nature et son traitement. Par
Charles Belot ... Paris, J.B.
Baillière et fils; New York,
Baillière brothers; [etc., etc.]
1865.
3 p. l., 160 p. 22 1/2 cm.

1129 Belot, Gustave de.
La république de Salvador, par
Gustave de Belot ... Paris, Dentu,
1865.
3 p. l., [3]-90 p. 23 1/2 cm.

1130 [Belsham, Jacobus]
Canadia. Ode. Ἐπινίκιος. [Quo-
tation from Cicero] Londini, impensis auctoris, 1760.
2 p. l., 3-18 p. 26 x 20 cm.

1131 Belsham, W   J.
Chronology of the reigns of George
III & IV ... With a general chronology from the earliest records, by
W.J. Belsham, esq. London, Printed
for J. Cumberland, 1828.
[444] p. front. (port.) 11 1/2
x 7 cm.

1132 Belt, Edward W.
The reform conspiracy: a letter
addressed to Bradley T. Johnson, esq.,
of Frederick, [Md.] By E.W. Belt,

esq. ... Baltimore, Printed by
Sherwood & co., 1858.
  44 p.   23 cm.

1133 Beltrami, Giacomo Constantino, 1779-
      1855.
      La découverte des sources du
Mississippi et de la rivière Sanglante. Description du cours entier
du Mississippi, qui n'était connu,
que partiellement, et d'une grande
partie de celui de la rivière
Sanglante, presque entièrement in-
connue; ainsi que du cours entier
de l'Ohio. Aperçus historiques, des
endroits les plus intéressans, qu'on
y rencontre. Observations critico-
philosophiques, sur les moeurs, la
religion, les superstitions, les
costumes, les armes, les chasses, la
guerre, la paix, le dénombrement,
l'origine, &c. &c. de plusieurs nations indiennes. Parallele de ces
peuples avec ceux de l'antiquité,
du moyen âge, et du moderne. Coup
d'oeil, sur les compagnies nord-ouest,
et de la baie d'Hudson, ainsi que
sur la colonie Serlkirk. Preuves
evidentes, que le Mississippi est la
première rivière du monde. Par J.C.
Beltrami ... Nouvelle-Orléans, Impr.
par B. Levy, 1824.
      v p., 1 l., 327, [1] p.   21 1/2 cm.

1134 Beltrami, Giacomo Costantino, 1779-1855.
      A pilgrimage in Europe and America,
leading to the discovery of the
sources of the Mississippi and Bloody
River; with a description of the whole
course of the former, and of the Ohio.
By J.C. Beltrami ... London, Hunt
and Clarke, 1828.
      2 v. fronts. (v. 1, port.; v. 2,
fold, map) plates, fold, plans.   22
cm.

1135 [Beltrami, Giacomo Costantino]
To the public of New York, and
of the United States. The author
of "The discovery of the sources of
the Mississippi," &c. &c. New
York, J. Darke [1825]
36 p. 23 cm.

1136 Beltran, Pedro, *fl.* 1742.
Arte de el idioma maya reducido
a succintas reglas, y semilexicon
yucateco por ... Pedro Beltran de
Santa Rosa Maria ... hijo de esta
sta. recolección franciscana de
Merida. Formólo, y dictólo, siendo
maestro de lengua maya en el convento
capitular de n.s.p.s. Francisco, de
dicha ciudad. Año de 1742 ... En
Mexico, Por la viuda de d. J. Ber-
nardo de Hogal, 1746.
8 p. 1., 187, [1] p. 2 fold.
tab. 19 1/2 cm.

1137 Beman, Nathan Sidney Smith, 1785-1871.
Our civil war: the principles
involved, its causes and cure, being
a discourse delivered on Thanksgiving day, Nov. 27, 1862. [By] N.S.S.
Beman. Troy, N.Y., A.W. Scribner
& co., printers, 1863.
52 p. 22 1/2 cm.

1138 Beman, Nathan Sidney Smith, 1785-1871.
Thanksgiving in the times of civil
war: being a discourse delivered in
the First Presbyterian church, Troy,
New York, Nov. 28th, 1861. By N.S.S.
Beman. Troy, N.Y., A.W. Scribner &
co., printers, 1861.
46 p. 25 cm.

1139 Bembo, Pietro, *cardinal*, 1470-1547.
Della historia vinitiana di m.
Pietro Bembo card. volgarmente
scritta. Libri XII. Vinegia, 1552.

14 p. 1., 179 numb. 1., [3] p.
22 1/2 cm.

1140 Bembo, Pietro, *cardinal*, 1470-1547.
Della istoria viniziana di M.
Pietro Bembo, cardinale, da lui
volgarizzata, libri dodici, ora per
la prima volta secondo l'originale
pubblicati ... Vinegia, A. Zatta,
1790.
2 v. front. (port.) 31 1/2 cm.

1141 Bemis, George, 1816-1878.
American neutrality: its honorable
past, its expedient future ... By
George Bemis. Boston, Little, Brown,
and company, 1866.
vi p., 1 1., 211. [1] p. 23 1/2
cm.

1142 Bemis, George, 1816-1878.
Hasty recognition of rebel belliger-
ency, and our right to complain of it.
By George Bemis. Boston, A. Williams
& co. [1865]
viii p., 1 1., 57 p. 24 cm.

1143 Bemis, George, 1816-1878.
Precedents of American neutrality,
in reply to the speech of Sir Roundell
Palmer, attorney-general of England,
in the British House of commons,
May 13, 1864. By George Bemis. Boston, Little, Brown and company, 1864.
viii, 83 p. 21 cm.

1144 Benavente, Diego José, 1789-1867.
Memoria sobre las primeras campañas
en la guerra de la independencia de
Chile ... por D.J. Benavente ...
Santiago, Impr. de la Opinion, 1845.
viii, 200 p. 22 cm.

1145 Benavides, Alonso de, *fl.* 1630.
Memorial qve fray Ivan de Santander
de la orden de San Francisco, comissario general de Indias, presenta a la

Magestad catolica del rey Don Felipe
Qvarto nuestro señor. Hecho por el
padre fray Alonso de Benauides
comissario del Santo Oficio, y
custodio que ha sido de las prouincias,
y conuersiones del Nueuo-Mexico.
Tratase en el de los tesoros espiri-
tuales, y temporales, que la Diuina
Magestad ha manifestado en aquellas
conuersiones, y nueuos descubrimien-
tos, por medio de los padres desta
serafica religion. Con licencia. En
Madrid, en la Imprenta real. año
1630.
1 p. l., 109 [i. e. 103] p.   21 cm.

1146 Benedict, David, 1779-1874.
A general history of the Baptist
denomination in America, and other
parts of the world. By David Benedict ... Boston: Printed by Lincoln
& Edmands, no. 53, Cornhill, for the
author. 1813.
2 v.   23 cm.

1147 Benedict, David, 1779-1874.
A history of all religions, as
divided into paganism, Mahometanism,
Judaism and Christianity, with an account of literary and theological institutions, and missionary, Bible,
tract and Sunday school societies;
with a general list of religious
publications; accompanied with a
frontispiece of six heads. By David
Benedict, A.M. Providence, J. Miller, printer, 1824.
360, 96 p. front. (ports.) plates.
18 cm.

1148 Benedict, Erastus Cornelius, 1800-1880.
The beginning of America; a discourse delivered before the New-York
historical society on its fifty-ninth
anniversary, Tuesday, November 17,
1863, by Erastus C. Benedict ... New-

254

York, Printed by J.F. Trow, 1864.
64 p.   25 cm.

1149   Benedict, George Grenville, 1826-1907.
         The battle of Gettysburgh, and the
         part taken therein by Vermont troops.
         By G.G. Benedict ...   Burlington,
         Free press print, 1867.
         24 p.   22 1/2 cm.

1150   Benedict, Kirby, 1810-1874.
         Anniversary address delivered be-
         fore the Historical society of New
         Mexico at Santa Fé, December 31,
         1860, by Kirby Benedict.   Santa Fé,
         N.M., Manderfield & Tucker, print-
         ers [1860]
         20 p.   23 cm.

1151   Benezet, Anthony, 1713-1784.
         Kurzer bericht von den leuten, die
         man Quäker nennet; ihrem ursprung,
         ihren religionsgrunden, und von
         ihrer niederlassung in America.
         Meistentheils aus verschiedenen
         autores zusammen gezogen, zum
         unterricht aller aufrichtigen nach-
         forscher, und insonderheit für
         ausländer. Durch Anton Benezet.
         Aus dem englischen übersetzt.   Phila-
         delphia: Gedruckt bey Melchior
         Steiner, in der Rees-strasse.   1783.
         45 p.   16 1/2 cm.

1152   [Benezet, Anthony] 1713-1784.
         The mighty destroyer displayed, in
         some account of the dreadful havock
         made by the mistaken use as well as
         abuse of distilled spirituous liq-
         ours. By a lover of mankind ...
         Philadelphia: Printed by Joseph
         Crukshank, between Second and Third
         streets, in Market-street, 1774.
         48 p.   16 1/2 cm.

1153   [Benezet, Anthony] 1713-1784.

Notes on the slave trade, &c.
[Philadelphia? 178-]
8 p.   16 cm.

1154   Benezet, Anthony, 1713-1784.
Observations sur l'origine les
principes, et l'établisement en
Amérique, de la societé connue sous
la dénomination de Quakers ou
trembleurs: extrait de divers auteurs.
Redigés, principalement, en faveur
des etrangers.   Par Antoine Benezet.
À Philadelphie.   Chez Joseph Crukshank, dans la rue du Marché, entre
la seconde et la troisieme rue.
MDCCLXXX.
36 p.   19 cm.

1155   Benezet, Anthony, 1713-1784.
A short account of the people
called Quakers; their rise, religious principles and settlement in
America, mostly collected from different authors, for the information
of all serious inquirers, particularly foreigners.   By Anthony Benezet.   Philadelphia: Printed by Joseph Crukshank, in Market-street,
between Second and Third streets,
1780.
27 p.   20 cm.

1156   [Benezet, Anthony] 1713-1784.
Some observations on the situation, disposition, and character of
the Indian natives of this continent
...   Philadelphia: Printed and sold
by Joseph Crukshank, in Market-street.
1784.
v, [6]-50 p.   17 cm.

1157   [Benezet, Anthony] 1713-1784.
Thoughts on the nature of war, and
its repugnancy to the Christian life.
Extracted from a sermon, on the 29th
November, 1759; being the day of

public thanksgiving for the successes obtained in the late war.
With some extracts from the writings of Will, Law and Th. Harley
[!] both clergymen of the Church of
England, on the necessity of self-
denial, and bearing the daily cross,
in order to be true followers of
Christ ... Philadelphia, Printed by
Henry Miller, In Second-street,
1766.
    30 p.   16 cm.

1158   Benezet, Anthony, 1713-1784.
    Views of American slavery, taken a
century ago. Anthony Benezet, John
Wesley ... Philadelphia, Pub. by
the Association of Friends for the
diffusion of religious and useful
knowledge, 1858.
    1 p. 1., 138 p.   16 cm.

1159   Benham, Asahel.
    Federal harmony; containing, in a
familiar manner, the rudiments of
psalmody; together with a collection
of church music. (Most of which are
entirely new.) By Asahel Benham.
The 6th ed. Middletown [Conn.]
Printed by M.H. Woodward [1795?]
    58 (*i.e.* 64) p.   11 1/2 x 19
cm.

1160   Benjamin, Judah Philip, 1811-1884.
    Defonce of tho national Domocracy
against the attack of Judge Doug-
las--constitutional rights of the
states. Speech of Hon. J.P. Benjamin, of Louisiana. Delivered in the
United States Senate, May 22, 1860.
[Washington, 1860]
    32 p.   24 cm.

1161   Benjamin, Judah Philip, 1811-1884.
    Extracts from the speech of Hon.
Mr. Benjamin, of Louisiana, on the

Kansas question: showing the true meaning of the Kansas law, and his reasons for joining the Democratic party. Delivered in the Senate, May 2, 1856. Washington, Printed at the Union office, 1856.
8 p.   24 cm.

1162   Benjamin, Judah Philip, 1811-1884.
Kansas bill. Speech of Hon. J.P. Benjamin, of La., delivered in Senate of United States on Thursday, March 11, 1858. Slavery protected by the common law of the new world. Guarantied by Constitution. Vindication of the Supreme court of the U.S. Washington, G.S. Gideon, printer, 1858.
29 p.   25 cm.

1163   Benjamin, Judah Philip, 1811-1884.
Relations of states. Speech of the Hon. J.P. Benjamin, of Louisiana, delivered in the Senate of the U.S., May 8, 1860, on the resolutions submitted by the Hon. Jefferson Davis, of Miss. on the 1st of March, 1860. [Baltimore, Murphy & co., 1860]
8 p.   22 cm.

1164   Benjamin, Judah Philip, 1811-1884.
Speech of Hon. J.P. Benjamin, of La., on the acquisition of Cuba, delivered in Senate, U.S., Friday, February 11, 1859. [n.p., 1859]
16 p.   22 1/2 cm.

1165   Benjamin, Judah Philip, 1811-1884.
Speech of Hon. J.P. Benjamin, of Louisiana, on the right of secession. Delivered in the Senate of the United States, Dec. 31, 1860. [Washington, Printed by L. Towers, 1861?].
16 p.   23 cm.

1166   Benjamin, Judah Philip, 1811-1884.
             ... The United States, *vs.* Andres
       Castillero. On cross appeal. Claim
       for the mine and lands of New Alma-
       den. Argument of Hon. J.P. Benjamin
       delivered on the 24th, 25th and 26th
       October, and 5th November, 1860, in
       reply to the government's special coun-
       sel. Reported by Sumner & Cutter.
       San Francisco, Commercial steam book
       and job printing establishment,
       1860.
             247 p.   25 1/2 cm.

1167   Benjamin, L   N   *comp.*
             The St. Albans raid; or, Investiga-
       tion into the charges against Lieut.
       Bennett H. Young and command, for
       their acts at St. Albans, Vt., on the
       19th October, 1864. Being a complete
       and authentic report of all the pro-
       ceedings on the demand of the United
       States for their extradition, under
       the Ashburton treaty. Before Judge
       Coursol, J.S.P., and the Hon. Mr.
       Justice Smith, J.S.C. With the argu-
       ments of counsel and the opinions of
       the judges revised by themselves.
       Comp. by L.N. Benjamin, B.C.L. Mon-
       treal, Printed by J. Lovell, 1865.
             2 p. 1., 480 p.   22 cm.

1168   Benjamin, Samuel Greene Wheeler, 1837-
       1914.
             Ode on the death of Abraham Lin-
       coln. By S.G.W. Benjamin. Boston,
       W.V. Spencer, 1865.
             15 p.   19 cm.

1169   Bennett, Daniel K   1830-1897.
             Chronology of North Carolina, show-
       ing when the most remarkable events
       connected with her history took
       place, from the year 1584 to the
       present time, with explanatory notes.
       By D.K. Bennett ... New York, J.M.

Edney, 1858.
iv, [5]-143, [1] p.   18 cm.

1170   Bennett, Emerson, 1822-1905.
        Clara Moreland; or, Adventures in
        the far South-west. By Emerson
        Bennett ...   With ... illustrations.
        From original designs by Stephens,
        engraved by Beeler. Philadelphia,
        T.B. Peterson [C1853]
            334 p.   front., plates.   19 1/2
        cm.

1171   Bennett, Emily Thacher B.
        Song of the rivers. By Emily T.B.
        Bennett. ...   New York, Dexter &
        company; Cincinnati, R.W. Carroll &
        co., 1865.
            262 p.   19 cm.

1172   Bennett, Frederick Debell.
        Narrative of a whaling voyage round
        the globe, from the year 1833 to
        1836.   Comprising sketches of Poly-
        nesia, California, the Indian archi-
        pelago, etc. with an account of south-
        ern whales, the sperm whale fishery,
        and the natural history of the cli-
        mates visited. By Frederick Debell
        Bennett ...   London, R. Bentley,
        1840.
            2 v.   fronts., illus., map.   21
        1/2 cm.

1173   Benson, Alfred G.
        Memorial of Alfred G. Benson to
        the Senate and House of representa-
        tives of the United States. [New
        York, 1855]
            28 p.   23 1/2 cm.

1174   Benson, Egbert, 1746-1833.
        ... Memoir, read before the His-
        torical society of the state of New
        York, December 31, 1816. By Egbert
        Benson ...   [Re-printed from a copy,

with the author's last corrections.]
(*In* New York historical society.
Collections. New York, 1848.   22
1/2 cm.   2d ser., v. 2, p. [77]-148)

1175 [Benson, Egbert] 1746-1833.
      Vindication of the captors of Major
      André. New-York: Published by Kirk
      & Mercein, at the office of the Edin-
      burgh and Quarterly reviews, no. 22
      Wall-street, T. & W. Mercein, print-
      ers, no. 93 Gold-street, 1817.
      99 p.   19 cm.

1176 Benson, Egbert, 1746-1833.
      Vindication of the captors of Major
      André, by Egbert Benson, LL.D., with
      introduction and appendix. New York,
      Priv. print. [for F.S. Hoffman] 1865.
      ix, 134 p.   23 1/2 cm.

1177 Benson, Egbert, 1746-1833.
      Vindication of the captors of Major
      André. By Egbert Benson. New York,
      Reprinted for J. Sabin, 1865.
      84 p.   22 1/2 cm.

1178 Benson, Henry Clark, *b.* 1815.
      Life among the Choctaw Indians,
      and sketches of the South-west. By
      Henry C. Benson, A.M. ... With an in-
      troduction by Rev. T.A. Morris ...
      Cincinnati, Pub. by L. Swormstedt &
      A. Poe, for the Methodist Episcopal
      church, 1860.
      314 p.   19 1/2 cm.

1179 [Bentham, Edward] 1707-1776.
      De tumultibus americanis deque
      eorum concitatoribus meditatio
      senilis. Oxonii, J. Fletcher, and
      D. Prince; Londini, B. White, 1776.
      2 p. l., 36 p.   20 cm.

1180 Bentham, Jeremy, 1748-1832.
      Canada. Emancipate your colonies!

An unpublished argument, by Jeremy
Bentham. London, E. Wilson, 1838.
xvi, 18 p.   20 cm.

1181   [Bentham, Jeremy] 1748-1832.
A fragment on government; being an
examination of what is delivered, on
the subject of government in general,
in the introduction to Sir William
Blackstone's Commentaries: with a
preface in which is given a critique
on the work at large ... London, T.
Payne [etc.] 1776.
1 p. l., lvii p., 1 l., 208 p.
20 cm.

1182   Bentley, William, 1759-1819.
A sermon, before the governor, the
honorable Council, and both branches
of the legislature of the commonwealth
of Massachusetts, on the day of general election, May 27, 1807. By William
Bentley, A.M., minister of the Second
church in Salem. Boston: Printed by
Adams and Rhoades, printers to the
state. 1807.
25 p.   19 1/2 cm.

1183   Benton, Nathaniel Soley.
A history of Herkimer county, including the upper Mohawk valley, from
the earliest period to the present
time: with a brief notice of the
Iroquois Indians, the early German
tribes, the Palatine immigrations ...
also biographical notices of the most
prominent public men of the county:
with important statistical information.
By Nathaniel S. Benton. Albany, J.
Munsell, 1856.
v, [1], [5]-497 p. front., illus.,
plates, port., maps (part fold.)
22 cm.

1184   Benton, Thomas Hart, 1782-1858.
... Letter from Col. Benton to the
people of Missouri. Central national

262

highway from the Mississippi River
to the Pacific. [St. Louis, 1854]
14 p.   24 1/2 cm.

1185 [Benton, Thomas Hart] 1782-1858.
Thirty years' view; or, A history
of the working of the American government for thirty years, from 1820 to
1850. Chiefly taken from the Congress debates, the private papers of
General Jackson, and the speeches of
ex-Senator Benton, with his actual
view of the men and affairs: with
historical notes and illustrations,
and some notices of eminent deceased
contemporaries: by a senator of
thirty years ... New York, D. Appleton and company; Boston, F. Parker,
1854-56.
2 v. fronts. (v. 1: port.)   23
1/2 cm.

1186 Benzoni, Girolamo, b. 1519.
Der Newenn weldt vnd indianischen
königreichs, newe vnnd wahrhaffte
history, von allen geschichten, hand-
lungen, thaten, strengem vnnd ernst-
lichem regiment der Spanier gegen den
Indianern, vngläublichem grossem gut'
von goldt, sylber, edelgestein, peer-
lin, schmaragdt, vnnd andern reich-
tumb, so die Spanier darinn erobert:
sambt von den sorglichen schiffarthen,
kriegen, schlachten vnnd streit, ero-
herung vnd verhergung vieler prouintz,
landtschafften, vnd königreich, so sich
bey vnser gedächtnuss haben darinn
verloffen vnd zugetragen. Dessgleichen
von der Indianer wunderbarlichen
sitten, statuten, glauben, religion,
gottesdienst, ceremonien, gebräuch in
essen vnd trincken, kleidung, hand-
thierung vnnd gewerbschafft, &c.
Item von ihrer eygenschafft, natur,
seltzamen gewächss der früchten,
bäwmen, metallen, specerey vnd andere

263

vnbekandtliche ding mehr, so von ih-
nen in vnsere landtschafft geführt
werden. Erstlich, durch Hierony-
mum Benzon von Meyland in welscher
spraach waḥrhafftig beschrieben, vnnd
selbs persönlich in XIIII, jaren
durch wanderet. Vorhin nie in
teutscher spraach dessgleichen ges-
ehen: erst jetzt mit sonderm fleiss
allen regenten vnd oberherrn, sambt
liebhabern der historien zu nutz auss
dem latein in das teutsch gebracht.
Durch, Nicolaum Höniger ... Basel,
Getruckt durch S. Henricpetri [1579]
4 p. 1., ccix, [1] p. 31 1/2 cm.

1187 Benzoni, Girolamo, *b*. 1519.
Historia Indiae Occidentalis, tomis
duobus comprehensa. Prior, res ab
Hispanis in India Occidentali hactenus gestas, acerbum illovum in eas
gentes dominatum, insignéque in Gallos
ad Floridam insulam saeuitiae exemplum
describit. Alter verò, Brasilie (quae
& America dicitur) rerúmque in ea ob-
seruatione dignarum a nobis penitus
incognita descriptionem continet.
Hieronymo Benzone ... & Ioanne Lerio
... autoribus. Ex eorum autem idio-
mate in latinum sermonem Vrbani
Calvetonis & G.M. studio conuersi
... Addita est Totius Indiae Occidentalis ... descriptio ... [Geneva]
E. Vignon, 1586.
16 p. 1., 480 p., 8 1.; 32 p. 1.,
341 (*i.e.* 359), [17] p. illus., fold.
pl. 17 1/2 cm.

1188 Berard, Augusta Blanche, 1824-1901.
Berard's history of the United
States. Rev. by C.E. Bush ...
Philadelphia, Cowperthwait & co.,
1878.
352 p. illus., maps. 19 1/2 cm.

1189 [Berettari, Sebastiano] 1543-1622.

... The lives of Father Joseph
Anchieta, of the Society of Jesus;
the Ven. Alvera von Virmundt, religious of the Order of the Holy Supul-
chre; and the Ven. John Berchmans,
of the Society of Jesus ... London [etc.] T. Richardson and son,
1849.
     xiv, 412 p. incl. front. (port.)
20 cm.

1190   Berg, Joseph Frederick, 1812-1871.
        Loyalty a Christian obligation:
a sermon preached on Thanksgiving
day, November 24, 1859, by Joseph
F. Berg, D.D., in the Third Reformed
Dutch church, corner of Tenth and
Filbert streets. Philadelphia,
Hayes & Zell, 1859.
        22 p.   23 1/2 cm.

1191   Berger, Friedrich Ludwig von, 1701-1735.
        Gründliche erweisung dass Ihro
römisch-käyserl. Majestät in dero
oesterreichischen Niederlanden ...
commercia zu stabiliren, und zu
aufrichtung einer Ost- und West-
Indischen companie ... privilegia
zu ertheilen, berechtiget. Entworffen
von Friederich Ludewig edl. herrn von
Berger. Regenspurg und Leipzig,
J.C. Peetz, 1723,
        3 p. l., [3]-59 p.   21 cm.

1192   [Bergh, Henry] 1811-1888.
        "Married off," a satirical poem,
by H.B. With eight illustrations by
Florence Claxton. London, Ward and
Lock, 1860.
        75 p. incl. front., plates.   19
cm.

1193   Berkel, Adriaan van.
        Amerikaansche voyagien, behelzende
een reis na rio de Berbice, gelegen
op het vaste land van Guiana, aande

265

wilde-kust van America, mitsgaders
een andere na de colonie van Suriname, gelegen in het noorder deel
van het gemelde landschap Guiana.
Ondermengd met alle de byzonderheden
noopende de zeden, gewoonten, en
levenswijs der inboorlingen, boom-
en aardgewassen, waaren en koop-
manschappen, en andere aanmerkelijke
zaaken. Beschreven door Adriaan van
Berkel ... Amsterdam, J. ten Hoorn,
1695.
4 p. l., 139, [4] p. 2 pl. (1
fold.) 20 x 16 1/2 cm.

1194 Berkeley, George, *bp. of Cloyne*, 1685-
1753.
A miscellany, containing several
tracts on various subjects. By the
Bishop of Cloyne ... London, Printed
for J. and R. Tonson [etc.] 1752.
vi p., 1 l., 9-267, [1] p. 20 cm.

1195 [Berkeley, George] *bp. of Cloyne*, 1685-
1753.
A proposal for the better supplying of churches in our foreign plantations, and for converting the sav-
age Americans to Christianity ...
London, Printed by H. Woodfall, 1724.
22 p. 19 cm.

1196 Berkeley, George, *bp. of Cloyne*, 1685-
1753.
A sermon preached before the incorporated Society for the propagation of the gospel in foreign parts;
at their anniversary meeting in the
parish-church of St. Mary-le-Bow,
on Friday, February 18, 1731 [*i.e.*
1732] By George Berkeley, D.D., dean
of Londonderry. London, Printed by
J. Downing, 1732.
78, [1] p. 22 1/2 cm.

1197 Berkeley, George Charles Grantley
Fitzhardinge, 1800-1881.

The Englsih sportsman in the Western prairies. By the Hon. Grantley
F. Berkeley ... London, Hurst &
Blackett, 1861.
3 p. 1., [v]-xi p., 1 1., 431
p. front., plates, 25 cm.

1198 Berkeley, *Sir* William, 1608?-1677.
A discourse and view of Virginia.
By Sir William Berkeley (governor
of Virginia) London, 1663 [re-
printed, Norwalk, Conn., W.H. Smith,
jr., 1914]
8, 12 p. 23 1/2 cm.

1199 [Bermúdez, José Manuel] 1764-1830.
Fama postuma del excelentísimo é
ilustrísimo señor doctor Juan
Domingo Gonzalez de la Reguera ...
Por el mismo autor de la Oración
funebre. Lima, Impr. real de los
huérfanos, 1805.
1 p. 1., cxviii, 2 , 38 p. front.
(port.) 20 cm.

1200 Bernáldez, Andrés, *d*. 1513?
Historia de los reyes católicos,
D. Fernando y Dª Isabel. Crónica
inédita del siglo XV, escrita por
el bachiller Andrés Bernáldez ...
Granada, Impr. y libreria de D.J.
M. Zamora, 1856.
2 v. 21 1/2 cm.

1201 Bernard, Jean Frédéric, *d*. 1752, *od*.
Recueil d'arrests et autres
pièces pour l'établissement de la
Compagnie d'Occident. Relation de
la baie de Hudson. Les navigations
de Frobisher, au détroit qui porte
son nom. Amsterdam, J.F. Bernard,
1720.
100, 253 p. 3 pl., fold. map.
16 1/2 cm.

1202 Bernard, Louis, *b*. 1781.

Coup d'oeil sur la situation agri-
cole de la Guiane française, par M.
le général Louis Bernard. Paris,
Imprimerie d'A. Blondeau, 1842.
2 p. l., 63 p.   22 1/2 cm.

1203   Bernard, Louis, *b.* 1781.
Mémoire sur la culture du poivrier
à la Guiane française, depuis son
introduction dans cette colonie en
1787, jusqu'à la présente année 1843.
Par le général Louis Bernard ... Paris, Imprimerie d'A. Blondeau, 1843.
2 p. l., 63 p.   22 cm.

1204   Bernard, Mountague.
A lecture on alleged violations
of neutrality by England in the present war. By Mountague Bernard ...
June, MDCCCLXIII. London, W.
Ridgway, 1863.
45 p.   20 cm.

1205   Bernard, Mountague, 1820-1882.
On the principle of non-interven-
tion. A lecture delivered in the
hall of All souls' college, by
Mountague Bernard ... Oxford &
London, J.H. & J. Parker [1860]
1 p. l., 36 p.   23 cm.

1206   Berquin-Duvallon
Vue de la colonie espagnole du
Mississipi, ou des provinces de
Louisiane et Floride Occidentale;
en l'année 1802, par un observateur
résident sur les lieux ... B ......
-Duvallon, éditeur. Paris, Imprimerie expéditive, an XI, 1803.
xx, 318, 5, [4] p.   2 fold. maps.
21 1/2 cm.

1207   Berrian, Richard.
The American telegraph and signal
book. By Richard Berrian ... Intended as a universal register.
Arranged in the order of classes and

grades, for the purpose of communi-
cating any degree of information
from one vessel to another, either by
day or night, as far as the eye can
see, or the ear hear; and to any
part of the habitable globe if necessary. New-York, Printed by J.W.
Bell, 1823.
iv, [5]-44 p.   1 illus.   18 cm.

1208   Berrian, Samuel.
An oration, delivered before the
Tammany society, or, Columbian order, Tailor's, Cooper's, Hibernian
provident, Shipwright's, Columbian,
Manhattan, and Cordwainer's societies, in the city of New-York, on
the Fourth of July, 1811. By Samuel
Berrian ... New-York: Printed and
published by Joseph Harmer, no. 19
William-street, 1811.
22 p., 1 l.   20 cm.

1209   Berrian, William, 1787-1862.
Facts against fancy; or, A true
and just view of Trinity church. By
the Rev. William Berrian ... New
York, Pudney & Russell, printers,
1855.
74 p.   23 cm.

1210   Berrian, William, 1787-1862.
An historical sketch of Trinity
church, New-York. By the Rev. William Berrian ... New York, Stanford
and Swords, 1847.
2 p. l., [9]-386 p.   front.,
plates.   24 cm.

1211   Berrian, William, 1787-1862.
Semi-centennial sermon, by the
Rev. Wm. Berrian, D.D., rector of
Trinity church, New-York. Published
at the request and by order of the
vestry. New-York, Pudney & Russell,
printers, 1860.

31 p.   23 cm.

1212   Berry, Harrison, b. 1816.
        Slavery and abolitionism, as viewed
        by a Georgia slave. By Harrison
        Berry, the property of S.W. Price,
        Covington, Georgia. Atlanta, Frank-
        lin printing house, Wood, Hanleiter,
        Rice & co., 1861.
        viii, [9]-41 p., 1 l. port.
        21 cm.

1213   Berry, Henry.
        The speech of Henry Berry, (of
        Jefferson,) in the House of dele-
        gates of Virginia, on the abolition
        of slavery. [Richmond, 1832]
        8 p.   22 1/2 cm.

1214   Berry, Philip.
        A review of the Bishop of Oxford's
        counsel to the American clergy, with
        reference to the institution of sla-
        very. Also supplemental remarks on
        the relation of the Wilmot proviso to
        the interests of the colored class.
        By the Rev. Philip Berry ... Washing-
        ton, W.M. Morrison; New York, Stan-
        ford & Swords; [etc., etc.] 1848.
        26 p.   22 cm.

1215   Berry, Philip.
        A review of the Mexican war on
        Christian principles: and an essay
        on the means of preventing war. By
        the Rev. Philip Berry ... [Reprinted
        from the Southern Presbyterian re-
        view] Columbia, S.C., Printed by
        A.S. Johnston, 1849.
        ix, 87 p.   23 1/2 cm.

1216   Berry, Robert Taylor, 1812-1877.
        A national warning; a sermon preached
        March 3, 1844, in the Bridge street
        Presbyterian church, Georgetown, Dis-
        trict of Columbia. By the Rev. R.T.
        Berry ... Intended as an improvement

of the calamity that occurred on
board of the steam frigate Princeton, Capt. Stockton, February 28th,
1844. Published at the request of
the congregation. Philadelphia,
W.S. Martien, 1844.
   22 p.   16 cm.

1217   Berryer, Pierre Antoine, 1790-1868.
       Discours de m. Berryer sur les
emprunts mexicains, contractés en
France, prononcés le 22 et le 23
juillet dans la discussion du budget
de 1868 au Corps législatif. Paris,
Impr. de S. Raçon et c^{ie}, 1867.
   1 p. 1., [5]-62 p.   14 cm.

1218   Beschke, William.
       Memorial to the United States'
Congress and government, concerning
European navies and the American
navy; the breech-loading and steady
ship-gun, and the improved war-steam-
er with submerged propellers, invented
by William Beschke, and modelled by
him partly through the pecuniary aid
of Mr. E.N. Scherr. Philadelphia
[King & Baird, printers] 1852.
   64 p.   19 cm.

1219   Beschke, William, *of Washington, D.C.*
       Memorial to the Congress, govern-
ment and people of the United States:
concerning several great inventions
of national importance, and the in-
fringements of a U.S. patent in building ironclad vessels and iron tur-
rets. Most respectfully submitted
by William Beschke ... In January,
1865 ... [Philadelphia? 1865]
   38, [1], 15 p.   illus.   22 1/2
cm.

1220   Beste, John Richard Digby, 1806-1885.
       The Wabash: or, Adventures of an
English gentleman's family in the
interior of America ... By J.

271

Richard Beste ... London, Hurst
and Blackett, 1855.
2 v. fronts. 20 cm.

1221 Betagh, William.
A voyage round the world. Being
an account of a remarkable enterprize,
begun in the year 1719, chiefly to
cruise on the Spaniards in the great
South ocean. Relating the true historical facts of that whole affair:
testifyd by many imployd therein; and
confirmed by authorities from the
owners. By William Betagh, captain
of marines in that expedition. London, Printed for T. Combes [etc.]
1728.
8 p. 1., 342, [3] p. 20 cm.

1222 Bethune, George Washington, 1805-1862.
The claims of our country on its
literary men. An oration before the
Phi beta kappa society of Harvard
university, July 19, 1849. By George
W. Bethune. Cambridge, J. Bartlett,
1849.
52 p. 21 1/2 cm.

1223 Bethune, George Washington, 1805-1862.
A discourse on the death of Wil-
liam Henry Harrison, late president
of the United States of America. ...
April 11, 1841, by George W. Bethune
... Philadelphia, Printed by J.C.
Clark, 1841.
22 p. 24 cm.

1224 Bethune, George Washington, 1805-1862.
The duties of educated men; an oration before the literary societies
of Dickinson college, Carlisle,
Pa., July, 1843. By George W.
Bethune ... Philadelphia, Published
for the societies, 1843.
40 p. 23 cm.

1225 Bethune, George Washington, 1805-1862.

Memoirs of Mrs. Joanna Bethune, by
her son, the Rev. George W. Bethune,
D.D. With an appendix, containing
extracts from the writings of Mrs.
Bethune. New York, Harper and brothers, 1863.
xi, 1 1., ⌊15⌋-250 p. incl. plates.
20 cm.

1226 Bethune, George Washington, 1805-1862.
Orations and occasional discourses,
by George W. Bethune, D.D. New York,
London, G.P. Putnam, 1850.
vii, 428 p.   19 1/2 cm.

1227 Bethune, George Washington, 1805-1862.
The prospects of art in the United
States. An address before the Artists'
fund society of Philadelphia, at the
opening of their exhibition, May,
1840. By George W. Bethune ...   Philadelphia. Printed for the Artists'
fund society, by J.C. Clark, 1840.
45 p.   24 cm.

1228 Bettendorf, João Filippe, b. 1626?
Compendio da doutrina christãa na
lingua portugueza, e brasilica.
Composto pelo p. João Filippe
Betendorf, antigo missionario do
Brasil, e reimpresso de ordem de S.
Alteza Real o principe regente nosso
senhor por fr. José Mariano da Con-
ceição Vellozo. Lisboa, Na offic.
de Simão Thaddéo Ferreira, 1800.
viii, 131, [2] p.   14 1/2 cm.

1229 Bettridge, William Craddock, 1791-
1879.
A brief history of the church in
Upper Canada: containing the acts
of Parliament imperial and provin-
cial; royal instructions; proceedings of the deputation, correspondence with the government; clergy
reserves' question ... By William
Bettridge ...   London, W.E. Painter,

1838.
1 p. l., iv, [5]-143, [1] p.   20
1/2 cm.

1230 Beukma, K   Jz.
Brieven van K. Jz. Beukma;
bevorens landbouwer op de boerderij
Castor, in het kerspel Zuurdijk,
gemeente Leens, doch verhuisd naar
de Vereenigde Staaten van Noord-
Amerika, in den jare 1835, aan deszelfs
achtergelaten familie in de provincie
Groningen. Groningen, W. Zuidema,
1835-38.
3 v. in 1. fold. pl., fold. map.
23 cm.

1231 [Beverley, Robert] *ca.* 1673-*ca.* 1722.
The history and present state of
Virginia, in four parts. I. The
history of the first settlement of
Virginia, and the government thereof,
to the present time. II. The natural productions and conveniences of
the country, suited to trade and improvement. III. The native Indians,
their religion, laws, and customs,
in war and peace. IV. The present
state of the country, as to the policy of the government, and the improvements of the land. By a native
and inhabitant of the place. London, printed for R. Parker, MDCCV.
6 p. l., 16, [4], 104, 40, 64, 83
p. front., 14 pl., fold. tab.   19
1/2 cm.

1232 Beverley, Robert, *ca.* 1673 - *ca.* 1722.
The history of Virginia, in four
parts ... By Robert Beverley, a
native and inhabitant of the place.
Reprinted from the author's 2d rev.
ed., London, 1722. With an introduction by Charles Campbell ... Richmond, Va., J.W. Randolph, 1855.
xx, 264 p. front., plates.   22
cm.

1233   Beyer, Moritz, 1807-1854.
     Amerikanische reisen. Von M. Beyer
und L. Koch ... Leipzig, I. Müller,
1839-41.
     4 v.   18 cm.

1234   Beyer, Moritz, 1807-1854.
     Het boek der landverhuizers; of,
Gids en raadsman bij de verhuizing
naar Noord-Amerika, ten opzigte van
den overtogt, de aankomst en de
vestiging aldaar ... Amsterdam,
Hoogkamer & comp^e., 1846.
     viii, 120 p. front.   12 cm.

1235   Biart, Lucien, 1828-1897.
     ... Le bizco; une passion au
Mexique. Paris. J. Hetzel, 1867.
     3 p. l., 349 p.   17 1/2 cm.

1236   Biart, Lucien, 1828-1897.
     La terre tempérée: scènes de la
vie mexicaine, par Lucien Biart.
Paris, J. Hetzel, 1866.
     2 p. l., iv, 306 p., 1 l.   17
1/2 cm.

1237   Bibaud, Maximilien, 1824--
     Biographie des sagamos illustres
de l'Amérique Septentrionale.
Précédée d'un index de l'histoire
fabuleuse de ce continent. Par F.M.
Maximilien Bibaud ... Montréal, Impr.
de Lovell et Gibson, 1848.
     xxv, [27]-309 p.   21 cm.

1238   Bibaud, Maximilien, 1824--
     Dictionnaire historique des
hommes illustres du Canada
et de l'Amérique, par Bibaud, jeune
... Montréal, Bibaud et Richer,
1857.
     389 p., 1 l.   19 cm.

1239   Bibaud, Maximilien *i.e.* François Marie
Uncas Maximilien, 1824--
     Les machabées canadiens, lu au

Cabinet de lecture de Montréal, le
25 janvier 1859. Par Bibaud, jeune.
Montréal, Imprimé par Cérat et
Bourguignon, 1859.
28 p.   18 1/2 cm.

1240   Bibaud, Maximilien, 1824--
Tableau historique des progres
materiels et intellectuels du
Canada, par Bibaud, jeune ...
Cabinet de lecture de Montréal.   6
avril 1858. [Montréal] Imprimé par
Cérat et Bourguignon [1858]
50 p.   19 1/2 cm.

1241   Bibaud, Michel, 1782-1857.
Épîtres, satires, chansons,
épigrammes, et autres pièces de
vers. Par M. Bibaud.   Montréal,
Imprimées par L. Duvernay, 1830.
178 p.   17 1/2 cm.

1242   Bibaud, Michel, 1782-1857.
Histoire du Canada, et des Cana-
diens, sous la domination anglaise
... 1. éd.   Par M. Bibaud.   Mont-
Réal, Impr. de Lovell et Gibson,
1844.
418 p., 1 l.   18 1/2 cm.

1243   Bibb, Henry, b. 1815.
Narrative of the life and adventures of ... an American slave, written by himself.   With an introduction
by Lucius C. Matlack.   New York,
The author, 1849.
1 p. l., xii, [13]-204, [3] p.
illus.   19 cm.

1244   Bibliothèque américaine, contenant des
mémoires sur l'agriculture, le
commerce, les manufactures, les
moeurs et les usages de l'Amérique;
l'analyse des ouvrages scientifiques
de ce pays, ainsi que de ceux des
Européens qui y ont voyagé; et des
extraits des journaux publiés en

276

Amérique, sur tout ce qui peut in-
téresser le commerçant et l'homme
d'état; par une société de savans
et d'hommes de lettres ... Paris,
H. Caritat [etc.] 1807.
   9 pt. in 3 v. fold. tables (vol.
I)   20 1/2 cm.

1245 Bibra, Ernst, *freiherr* von, 1806-1878.
     Erinnerungen aus Süd-Amerika, von
Ernst, freiherrn von Bibra ...
Leipzig, H. Costenoble, 1861.
   3 v.   18 cm.

1246 Bickell, Richard.
     The West Indies as they are; or,
A real picture of slavery: but
more particularly as it exists in
the island of Jamaica. In three
parts. With notes. By the Rev. R.
Bickell ...   London, Printed for
J. Hatchard and son [etc.] 1825.
   xvi, 256 p.   21 1/2 cm.

1247 [Bickford, James]
     The authentic life of Mrs. Mary
Ann Bickford, who was murdered in
the city of Boston, on the 27th of
October, 1845. Comprising a large
number of her original letters and
correspondence never before published ... Boston, The compiler,
1846.
   48 p.   18 1/2 cm.

1248 Bickley, George W   L.
     Adalaska; or, The strange and
mysterious family of the cave of
Genreva. By Geo. W.L. Bickley ...
Cincinnati, H.M. Rulison, 1853.
   viii, 19-106 p. incl. front.,
plates.   22 1/2 cm.

1249 Bickley, George W   L.
     History of the settlement and
Indian wars of Tazewell county,

Virginia; with a map, statistical
tables ... By Geo. W.L. Bickley
... Cincinnati, Morgan & co., 1852.
xxii p., 1 1., 25-267 p. incl.
front., plates, map. 21 cm.

1250 Biddle, Charles.
      Comunicaciones, entre el señor
Carlos Biddle, coronel de los E.
Unidos del Norte, i la Sociedad
amigos del pais. Panama, J. Bous-
quet, 1836.
      1 p. 1., 20 p.   fold. diagr.
19 1/2 cm.

1251 Biddle, Charles John, 1819-1873.
      The alliance with the Negro.
Speech of Hon. Charles J. Biddle
of Pennsylvania; delivered in the
House of representatives of the
United States, March 6, 1862.
[Washington, L. Towers & co., print-
ers, 1862]
      8 p.   24 cm.

1252 Biddle, Charles John, 1819-1873.
      Eulogy upon the Hon. George Miff-
lin Dallas, delivered before the bar
of Philadelphia, February 11, 1865,
by Charles J. Biddle. [Philadelphia,
M'Laughlin brothers, printers, 1865]
      51 p.   23 cm.

1253 Biddle, Craig, 1823-1910.
      Address: delivered before the
Philadelphia society for promoting
agriculture, on its seventy-fifth
anniversary, February 11th, 1860.
By the president, Craig Biddle ...
Philadelphia, King & Baird, printers, 1860.
      28 p.   22 1/2 cm.

1254 Biddle, George Washington, 1818-1897.
      Contribution among terre-tenants.
A lecture read May 6th, 1863, before

the Law academy of Philadelphia, by
George W. Biddle ... Session 1862-
63. Philadelphia, Printed for the
Law academy only, by Crissy &
Markley, 1863.
  31 p.   22 1/2 cm.

1255 Biddle, James Cornell, 1795-1838.
        An address delivered before the
      Philomathean and Phrenakosmian socie-
      ties of Pennsylvania college. By
      James C. Biddle.   July 4, 1838.
      Gettsburg, 1838.
        31 p.   21 1/2 cm.

1256 Biddle, James Cornell, 1795-1838.
        A statement, by James C. Biddle
      and William M. Meredith ... Phil-
      adelphia, 1822.
        35 p.   23 1/2 cm.

1257 Biddle, Nicholas, 1786-1844.
        An address delivered before the
      alumni association of Nassau-hall,
      on the day of the annual commence-
      ment of the College of New-Jersey,
      September 30, 1835. By Nicholas
      Biddle, LL.D.   3d od.   Princeton,
      N.J., R.E. Hornor, 1835.
        20 p.   20 1/2 cm.

1258 Biddle, Nicholas, 1786-1844.
          An ode to Bogle. By Nicholas
      Biddle.   July 16, 1829 ... Phila-
      delphia, Priv. print. for F.J.
      Dreer, 1865.
        8 p. front. (port.)   31 cm.

1259 Biddle, Nicholas, 1786-1844.
        Oration delivered before the
      Pennsylvania state Society of Cin-
      cinnati, on the fourth of July,
      MDCCCXI. By Nichola Biddle, esq.
      Published at the request of the
      society. Philadelphia, C. and A.
      Conrad and co., 1811.

28 p.   23 1/2 cm.

1260   [Biddle, Richard] 1796-1847.
        Captain Hall in America. By an
        American. Philadelphia, Carey &
        Lea, 1830.
        120 p.   23 cm.

1261   [Biddle, Richard] 1796-1847.
        A memoir of Sebastian Cabot; with
        a review of the history of maritime
        discovery. Illustrated by documents
        from the rolls, now first published.
        Philadelphia, Carey and Lea, 1831.
        viii, v, [7]-327 p.   22 cm.

1262   [Biddle, Richard] 1796-1847.
        A review of Captain Basil Hall's
        Travels in North America, in the
        years 1827 and 1828. By an Ameri-
        can. London, R.J. Kennett, 1830.
        149 p.   21 cm.

1263   Bierce, Lucius Verus, 1801-1876.
        Historical reminiscences of Summit
        County [Ohio] By Gen. L.V. Bierce.
        Akron, O., T. & H.G. Canfield, 1854.
        157, [1] p.   1 illus.   16 1/2
        cm.

1264   Bigelow, Abijah.
        The voters' guide: or, The power,
        duty & privileges of the constitu-
        tional voters in the commonwealth
        of Massachusetts. To which are
        added, original remarks, with vari-
        ous extracts from historians, and
        the writings and public speeches of
        eminent political characters ... tend-
        ing to explain the causes of the
        rise and fall of republican govern-
        ments. By Abijah Bigelow ... Leomin-
        ster [Mas.] Printed by S. & J.
        Wilder, Feb. 4, 1807.
        viii, [9]-156 p.   17 1/2 cm.

1265   Bigelow, Erastus Brigham, 1814-1879.

Remarks on the depressed condition
of manufactures in Massachusetts,
with suggestions as to its causes and
its remedy. By E.B. Bigelow. Boston, Little, Brown and company, 1858.
28 p.   23 1/2 cm.

1266   Bigelow, Erastus Brigham, 1814-1879.
The tariff question; considered
in regard to the policy of England
and the interests of the United
States. With statistical and comparative tables. By Erastus B.
Bigelow ... Boston, Little, Brown
and company, 1862.
x p., 1 1., 242 p. incl. tables
35 1/2 cm.

1267   Bigelow, Jacob, 1787-1879.
American medical botany, being a
collection of the native medicinal
plants of the United States, containing their botanical history and chemical analysis, and properties and
uses in medicine, diet and the arts,
with coloured engravings. By Jacob
Bigelow, M.D. Rumford professor and
lecturer on materia medica and botany in Harvard university ... Boston: Published by Cummings and
Hilliard, at the Boston bookstore,
no. 1, Cornhill. University press
... Hilliard and Metcalf. 1817-
20.
3 v. LX col. pl.   27 cm.

1268   [Bigelow, Jacob] 1787-1879.
Eolopoesis. American rejected
addresses. Now first published
from the original manuscripts. New
York, J.C. Derby; Boston, Phillips,
Sampson, & co.; [etc., etc., c1855]
240 p.   18 1/2 cm.

1269   Bigelow, Jacob, 1787-1879.
A history of the cemetery of Mount

Auburn. By Jacob Bigelow ... Boston and Cambridge, J. Munroe and company, 1860.
xii p., 2 1., 263 p.   front., plates, 2 fold. plans.   18 cm.

1270   Bigelow, Jacob, 1787-1879.
Inaugural address, delivered in the chapel of the University at Cambridge, December 11, 1816. By Jacob Bigelow ... Rumford professor in Harvard university. Boston, Printed by Wells and Lilly, 1817.
vi, [7]-24, [2] p.   23 1/2 cm.

1271   Bigelow, Jacob, 1787-1879.
Some account of the White mountains of New Hampshire. By Jacob Bigelow ... [Boston, 1816]
18 p.   22 1/2 cm.

1272   Bigelow, John, 1817-1911.
Jamaica in 1850; or, The effects of sixteen years of freedom on a slave colony. By John Bigelow ... New York & London, G.P. Putnam, 1851.
1 p. 1., iii, iv,   214 p.   incl. tables.   17 1/2 cm.

1273   Bigelow, John, 1817-1911.
Memoir of the life and public services of John Charles Frémont ... By John Bigelow ... New York, Derby & Jackson; Cincinnati, H.W. Derby & Co., 1856.
x, [11]-480 p.   front. (port.) plates.   19 cm.

1274   Bigelow, John Reynolds.
The American's own book; or, The constitutions of the several states in the Union ... Embellished with the seals of the different states. By J.R. Bigelow. New-York, Gates, Stedman, & co. [etc.] 1849.

536 p.   front., illus., pl., fold.
map.   23 cm.

1275   Bigelow, Timothy, 1767-1821.
An address, delivered on the third
anniversary of the Washington benevolent society, April 30, 1814.   By
the Hon. Timothy Bigelow.   Boston,
Printed by C. Stebbins, 1814.
19 p.   21 cm.

1276   Bigelow, Timothy, 1767-1821.
An eulogy on the life, character
and services of Brother George
Washington, deceased.--Pronounced
before the fraternity of free and
accepted Masons, by request of the
Grand lodge, at the Old South meeting-house, Boston, on Tuesday, Feb.
11, 1800.   Being the day set apart
by them to pay funeral honors to
their deceased brother.   By Brother
Timothy Bigelow.   To which are added, two addresses to the deceased,
when President of the United States,
and his answers: together with--the
letter of condolence of the Grand
lodge to Mrs. Washington, and her
answer ...   Boston, Printed by I.
Thomas and E.T. Andrews [1800]
26 p.   21 cm.

1277   [Bigelow, Tyler]
Address, delivered at the eighth
anniversary of the Massachusetts
peace society, Dec. 25, 1823.   Boston, Printed by J.B. Russell, 1824.
24 p.   24 cm.

1278   Biggs, James.
The history of Don Francisco de
Miranda's attempt to effect a revolution in South America, in a series
of letters.   By James Biggs.   Rev.,
cor., and enlarged.   To which are
annexed, sketches of the life of
Miranda, and geographical notices of

Caraccas ... London, Printed for
the author by T. Gillet, 1809.
xv, [1], 312 p.   23 cm.

1279   [Biggs, James]
The history of Don Francisco de
Miranda's attempt to effect a revolution in South America, in a series of letters.   By a gentleman who
was an officer under that general.
... To which are annexed, sketches
of the life of Miranda, and geographical notices of Caraccas.   3d
ed.   Boston, E. Oliver, 1811.
xi, 312 p.   18 1/2 cm.

1280   Bigland, John, 1750-1832.
A geographical and historical
view of the world: exhibiting a
complete delineation of the natural
and artificial features of each
country; and a succinct narrative
of the origin of the different nations, their political revolutions,
and progress in arts, sciences, literature, commerce &c.   The whole
comprising all that is important
in the geography of the globe, and
the history of mankind.   By John
Bigland ...   With notes, correcting
and improving the part which relates
to the American continent and islands.
By Jedidiah Morse ...   Boston: Printed
by Thomas B. Wait and co.   Sold by
them, and by Mathew Carey, Philadelphia, and Samuel Pleasants, Richmond.   1811.
5 v.   22 1/2 cm.

1281   Bigler, William, 1814-1880.
Address of Hon. William Bigler,
delivered at New Hope, Bucks County,
September 17, 1863.   Harrisburg,
Pa., "Patriot and union" steam
print [1863]
13 p.   24 cm.

1282   Bigler, William, 1814-1880.
            State of the Union. Speech of
        Hon. Wm. Bigler, of Pennsylvania,
        delivered in the Senate of the Unit-
        ed States, January 21, 1861. [Wash-
        ingtom, D.C., H. Polkinhorn's steam
        job press, 1861]
            16 p.   24 cm.

1283   [Biglow, William] 1773-1844.
            Commencement, a poem: or rather,
        Commencement of a poem. Recited
        before the Phi beta kappa society,
        in their dining hall, in Cambridge,
        Aug. 29, 1811. By a brother ...
        Salem, Printed by T.C. Cushing, 1811.
            8 p.   23 1/2 cm.

1284   Biglow, William, 1773-1844.
            History of Sherburne, Mass. from
        its incorporation, MDCLXXIV, to the
        end of the year MDCCCXXX; including
        that of Framingham and Holliston, so
        far as they were constituent parts
        of that town. By William Biglow ...
        Milford, Mass., Printed and pub. by
        Ballou & Stacy, 1830.
            80 p.   22 1/2 cm.

1285   Biglow, William, 1773-1844.
            History of the town of Natick,
        Mass., from the days of the apostol-
        ic Eliot, MDCL, to the present time,
        MDCCCXXX. By William Biglow. Bos-
        ton, Marsh, Capen, & Lyon, 1830.
            87, [1] p.   23 1/2 cm.

1286   [Biglow, William] 1773-1844.
            Re-re-commencement: a kind of a
        poem: calculated to be recited be-
        fore an "Assemblage" of New-England
        divines, of all the various denomina-
        tions; but which never was so re-
        cited, and in all human probability
        never will be. By a friend of every-
        body and every soul ... Salem,
        Printed by Thomas C. Cushing, 1812.

8 p.   23 1/2 cm.

1287   Bigney, Mark Frederick, 1817-1886.
       The forest pilgrims, and other
       poems. By M.F. Bigney. New Orleans,
       J.A. Gresham; New York, M. Doolady,
       1867.
       xii, [13]-258 p.   19 cm.

1288   Bigot, Jacques, 1644-1711.
       Copie d'vne || lettre || escrite
       par || le père Jacques Bigot de la
       Com- || pagnie de Jésus, || l'an
       1684, || pour accompagner un collier
       de pource- || laine envoiée par les
       Abnaquis de la || Mission de Sainct
       François de Sales || dans la Nouvelle
       France au tombeau || de leur sainct
       patron à Annecy. || Manate, || De la
       Presse Cramoisy de Jean-Marie Shea.
       || 1858.
       9, [1] p.   19 cm.

1289   Bigot, Jacques, 1644-1711.
       Relation de ce qvi | s'est passé
       | de plvs remarqvable | dans la Mis-
       sion Abnaquise de | Sainct Joseph de
       Sillery, Et dans l'Establissement
       de la Nouuelle Mission | De Sainct
       François de Sales, | l'année 1684. |
       Par le R.P. Jacques Bigot, de la |
       Compagnie de Jésus. | A Manate: |
       De la Presse Cramoisy de Jean-Marie
       Shea. | M.DCCC.LVII.
       61 (*i.e.* 63), [1] p.   19 1/2 cm.

1290   Bigot, Jacques, 1644-1711.
       Relation || de la || Mission Abna-
       quise || de || St. François de Sales
       || L'Annee 1702. || Par le Père Jacques
       Bigot, || De la Compagnie de Jésus.
       || Nouvelle-York: || Presse Cramoisy
       de Jean Marie Shea. || M.DCCC.LXV.
       26 p.   21 1/2 cm.

1291   Bigsby, John Jeremiah.
       The shoe and canoe, or Pictures of

travel in the Canadas ... With facts
and opinions on emigration, state policy, and other points of public interest ... By John J. Bigsby ... London, Chapman and Hall, 1850.
2 v. front., pl., maps (part
fold.) plan. 19 1/2 cm.

1292 Bill, Ledyard, 1836-1907, *ed.*
History of the Bill family. Ed.
by Ledyard Bill. New York, 1867.
vii, 8 -367, 1 p. front.
(port.) 24 1/2 cm.

1293 Billardon de Sauvigny, Edmé Louis.
Vashington; ou, La liberté du
nouveau monde, tragédie en quatre
actes; par m. de Sauvigny ... Paris,
Maillard d'Orivelle, 1791.
56 p. 21 1/2 cm.

1294 Billaud-Varenne, Jacques Nicolas, 1756-
1819.
Mémoires de Billaud-Varennes, ex-
conventionnel, écrits au Port-au-
Prince en 1818, contenant la relation de ses voyages et aventures
dans le Mexique, depuis 1805 jusqu'en
1817; avec des notes historiques et
un précis de l'insurrection américaine, depuis son origine jusqu'en
1820; par M******* ... Paris, Plan-
cher [etc.] 1821.
2 v. 20 1/2 cm.

1295 Billings, *Mrs.* Eliza (Allen) *b.* 1826.
The female volunteer; or, The life,
and wonderful adventures of Miss
Eliza Allen, a young lady of East-
port, Maine ... [n.p., 1851]
1 p. 1., 7-68 p. incl. illus.,
plates. 21 cm.

1296 Bingham, Hiram, 1789-1869.
A residence of twenty-one years
in the Sandwich islands; or, The
civil, religious, and political

history of those islands: comprising
a particular view of the missionary
operations connected with the introduction and progress of Christianity
and civilization among the Hawaiian
people. By Hiram Bingham ... Hartford [Conn.] H. Huntington; New York,
S. Converse, 1847.
  xvi, [17]-616 p. front. (port.)
plates, fold. map.   24 cm.

1297 Bingham, Hiram, 1789-1869.
      A residence of twenty-one years in
the Sandwich islands; or the civil,
religious, and political history of
those islands: comprising a particular view of the missionary operations
connected with the introduction and
progress of Christianity and civilization among the Hawaiian people. By
Hiram Bingham ... 3d ed., rev. and
cor. To which is added a table of
missionaries of the American board
to the Sandwich islands. Canandai-
gua, N.Y., H.D. Goodwin, 1855.
  xvi, 17 616, 4 p. front.
(port.) illus., 6 pl., fold. map.
22 1/2 cm.

1298 Bingham, J[oel] F[oote] 1827-
      Bright republic. A song and
chorus, written for the National
jubilee, July 45h, 1865. By Rev.
J.F. Bingham. Music by William
Krauskopf. [Buffalo? 1865]
  [4] p.   21 1/2 cm.

1299 Bingham, Joel Foote, 1827-1914.
      Great providences toward the
loyal part of this nation. A discourse delivered at a united service
of the seven Presbyterian congregations of Buffalo, November 24, 1864,
on occasion of the annual thanksgiving, both of the state and of the nation. By Joel F. Bingham ... Buffalo, Breed, Butler and company, 1864.

59 p.   22 1/2 cm.

1300   Bingham, Joel Foote, 1827-1914.
       The hour of patriotism. A dis-
course delivered at the united service of the First, Lafayette street,
North, and Westminster Presbyterian
churches, Buffalo, November 27, 1862,
the day of the annual Thanksgiving
in the state of New York. By Joel
F. Bingham, pastor of Westminster
congregation. Buffalo, Franklin
steam printing house, 1862.
       39 p.   21 cm.

1301   Bingham, Joel Foote, 1827-1914.
       National disappointment. A dis-
course occasioned by the assassination
of President Lincoln. Delivered in
Westminster church, Buffalo, Sunday
evening, May 7th, 1865. By Joel F.
Bingham ... Buffalo, Breed, Butler
and company, 1865.
       36 p.   23 1/2 cm.

1302   Bingham, John Armor, 1815-1900.
       The power and duty of Congress to
provide for the common defence and
the suppression of the rebellion.
Speech of Hon. Jno. A. Bingham, of
Ohio, in the House of representatives,
January 15, 1862. [Washington,
Scammell & co., printers, 1862]
       8 p.   24 1/2 cm.

1303   Bingham, John Armor, 1815-1900.
       Self-preservation the right and
duty of the general government, the
Rebel states but organized conspira-
cies--not constitutional states, nor
entitled to state rights. Speech
of Hon. John A. Bingham, of Ohio,
in the House of representatives,
March 12, 1862. [Washington, 1862]
       8 p.   24 cm.

1304   Bingham, John Armor, 1815-1900.

Speech of Hon. John A. Bingham, of Ohio, on the civil rights bill; delivered in the House of representatives, March 9, 1866. Washington, Printed at the Congressional globe office, 1866.
8 p.   23 cm.

1305 Bingham, John Armor, 1815-1900.
Trial of the conspirators, for the assassination of President Lincoln, &c. Argument of John A. Bingham, special judge advocate, in reply to the arguments of the several counsel for Mary E. Surratt, David E. Herold, Lewis Payne, George A. Atzerodt, Michael O'Laughlin, Samuel A. Mudd, Edward Spangler, and Samuel Arnold, charged with conspiracy and the murder of Abraham Lincoln, late president of the United States. Delivered June 27 and 28, 1865, before the Military commission. Washington, D.C. Washington, Govt. print. off., 1865.
122 p.   22 1/2 cm.

1306 Bingham, J   C.
The spoiler spoiled. A sermon, preached in the free Presbyterian churches of Neshanock and Hopewell, Thursday, June 1st, 1865. By Rev. J.C. Bingham ... Mercer, Printed at the office of the Whig and dispatch [1865]
13 p.   19 1/2 cm.

1307 Bingham, Kinsley Scott, 1808-1861.
The rise and fall of the Democratic party. Speech of Hon. Kinsley S. Bingham, of Michigan. Delivered in the United States Senate, May 24, 1860. [n.p., The Republican congressional committee, 1860]
16 p.   24 1/2 cm.

1308 [Binney, Horace] 1780-1875.

The alienigenae of the United States
under the present naturalization laws.
2d ed. Philadelphia, C. Sherman,
printer, 1853.
32 p.   23 cm.

1309 Binney, Horace, 1780-1875.
Correspondence and remarks in regard to Bishop Doane's signature of
the name of Horace Binney, as a sub-
scriber to the new church edifice in
Burlington. Philadelphia, C. Sherman, printer, 1849.
87, [1] p.   24 cm.

1310 Binney, Horace, 1780-1875.
An eulogium upon the Hon. William
Tilghman, late chief justice of
Pennsylvania. By Horace Binney.
Philadelphia, Mifflin and Parry,
printers, 1827.
46 p.   21 1/2 cm.

1311 Binney, Horace, 1780-1875.
An eulogy on the life and character of John Marshall, chief justice
of the Supreme court of the United
States. Delivered at the request
of the councils of Philadelphia, on
the 24th September, 1835. By Horace
Binney. Philadelphia, Printed by
J. Crissy and G. Goodman, 1835.
70 p.   23 1/2 cm.

1312 [Binney, Horace] 1780-1875.
The leaders of the old bar of Philadelphia ... Philadelphia [H.B.
Ashmead, printer] 1866.
v, [7]-120 p.   24 1/2 cm.

1313 Binney, Horace, 1780-1875.
Letter from Horace Binney ... To
the general committee of invitation
and correspondence of the Union
league of Philadelphia ... [Phila-
delphia, 1863]
4 p.   23 cm.

1314   Binney, Horace, 1780-1875.
             Remarks to the bar of Philadel-
        phia, on the occasion of the deaths
        of Charles Chauncey and John Ser-
        geant. By Horace Binney. Phila-
        delphia, C. Sherman, printer, 1853.
             39 p.   23 1/2 cm.

1315   Binney, Horace, 1780-1875.
             Speech of the Hon. Horace Binney,
        on the question of the removal of
        the deposites. Delivered in the
        House of representatives, January,
        1834. Washington, Printed by Gales
        and Seaton, 1834.
             56 p.   23 cm.

1316   Binney, William.
             Oration on the death of Abraham
        Lincoln, by William Binney, esq.
        Providence, R.I. [Knowles, Anthony
        & co., printers] 1865.
             3 p. l., [5]-57 p. front, mounted
        photos. (ports.)   30 cm.

1317   Binney, William Greene, 1833-
             ... Bibliography of North American
        conchology previous to the year 1860.
        Prepared for the Smithsonian insti-
        tution by W.G. Binney ... Washing-
        ton, Smithsonian institution, 1863-
        64.
             2 v.   23 1/2 cm.

1318   Binney, William Greene, 1833-
             ... Land and fresh water shells
        of North America ... Washington,
        Smithsonian institution, 1865-73.
             4 v. illus. 23 1/2 - 24 cm.

1319   Binns, John, 1772-1860.
             An oration commemorative of the
        birthday of American independence,
        delivered before the Democratic
        societies of the city and county of
        Philadelphia, on the 4th of July,

1810.
11 p.   21 1/2 cm.

1320   Binns, John, 1772-1860.
Recollections of the life of John
Binns ... written by himself, with
anecdotes, political, historical,
and miscellaneous. With a portrait
... Philadelphia, Printed and for
sale by the author and by Parry and
M'Millan, 1854.
xi, [13]-349 p.   front. (port.)
19 cm.

1321   Binns, William.
A sermon on the death of Presi-
dent Lincoln, preached by the Rev.
W. Binns, in the Unitarian chapel,
Birkenhead, on Sunday evening, April
23rd, 1865. Reprinted from the
"Birkenhead & Cheshire advertiser."
Birkenhead [Eng.] J. Oliver, print-
er, 1865.
13 p.   16 cm.

1322   [Biondelli, Bernardino] 1804-1886.
Scoperta dell'America fatta nel
secolo x da alcuni Scandinavi.
Milano [Tip. Bernardoni] 1839.
1 p. l., 20 p.   23 cm.

1323   Bionne, Henri, *d.* 1881.
La question du percement de
l'isthme de Panama devant un congrès international, par M. Henry
Bionne ... Paris, E. Lacroix,
1864.
16 p.   fold. map.   24 1/2 cm.

1324   Biot, Jean Baptiste, 1774-1862.
Mélanges scientifiques et
littéraires par J.-B. Biot ...
Paris, Michel Lévy frères, 1858.
3 v. 2 maps (1 fold.) diagrs.
22 cm.

1325   Birch, Edmund Pendleton, 1824-1883.

The refined poetry of the South.
[From the "Southern confederacy."]
The devil's visit to "Old Abe."
By Rev. E.P. Birch ... [New York,
1862]
4 p.   25 cm.

1326   Birch, Thomas Ledlie, *d.* 1808.
Seemingly experimental religion,
instructors unexperienced--converters
unconverted--revivals killing reli-
gion--missionaries in need of teach-
ing--or, War against the gospel by
its friends.   Being the examination
and rejection of Thomas Ledlie Birch
... by the rev. Presbytery of Ohio
... the trial of the Rev. John Mc-
Millan, before the rev. Presbytery
of Ohio, for defaming Birch; the
trial and acquittal of the rev.
Presbytery of Ohio, before the very
rev. General assembly of the Presbyterian church of America, for the rejection of Birch; and injustice in
permitting the Rev. John McMillan to
escape church censure.   With remarks
thereon ...   By the Rev. Thomas Ledlie
Birch ...   Washington--Printed for
the author--MDCCCVI.
144 p.   22 cm.

1327   Bird, Francis William, 1809-1894.
The Hoosac tunnel: its condition
and prospects, by F.W. Bird ...
Boston, Wright & Potter, printer,
1865.
28 p.   23 1/2 cm.

1328   Bird, Francis William, 1809-1894.
Review of Gov. Banks' veto of
the revised code, on account of its
authorizing the enrolment of colored
citizens in the militia ...   By F.W.
Bird.   Boston, J.P. Jewett & company,
1860.
58, iv p.   23 1/2 cm.

1329 [Bird, Henry Merttins]
      A view of the relative situation
      of Great Britain and the United
      States of North America: by a mer-
      chant. London, Printed by H.L.
      Galabin and sold by J. Debrett
      [etc.] 1794
      2 p. l., 43 p.   21 cm.

1330 [Bird, Isaac] 1793-1876.
      Genealogical sketch of the Bird
      family, having its origin in Hart-
      ford, Conn. Hartford, E. Geer,
      steam printer and stationer, 1855.
      24 p.   22 cm.

1331 Bird, James, 1788-1839.
      Francis Abbott, the recluse of
      Niagara: and Metropolitan sketches;
      2d series. By James Bird. London,
      Baldwin and Cradock, 1837.
      vi, 192 p.   23 1/2 cm.

1332 [Bird, Robert Montgomery] 1806-1854.
      Calavar; or, The knight of the
      conquest: a romance of Mexico ...
      Philadelphia, Carey, Lea & Blanchard,
      1834.
      2 v.   19 x 11 1/2 cm.

1333 [Bird, Robert Montgomery] 1806-1854.
      The Hawks of Hawk-Hollow. A tradi-
      tion of Pennsylvania. By the author
      of "Calavar" ... Philadelphia, Carey,
      Lea & Blanchard, 1835.
      2 v.   19 x 12 cm.

1334 Bird, William A   1796-1878.
      The boundary line between the
      British provinces and the United
      States. A paper read before the
      Buffalo historical society February
      1st, 1864. By William A. Bird, esq.
      Buffalo, Printing house of Wheeler,
      Matthews & Warren, 1864.
      8 p.   22 cm.

1335   Birkbeck, Morris, 1764-1825.
          Letters from Illinois. By Morris
       Birkbeck ...   2d ed.   London, Printed
       for Taylor and Hessey, 1818.
          xv, 114 p.   23 cm.

1336   Birkbeck, Morris, 1762?-1825.
          Lettres sur les nouveaux établisse-
       mens qui se forment dans les parties
       occidentales des États-Unis d'Amér-
       ique.   Par Morris Birkbecks [!]   Tr.
       sur l'édition originale de Phila-
       delphie ...   Paris, L'Huillier
       [etc.] 1819.
          2 p. l., xvi, 156 p.   fold. map.
       21 cm.

1337   Birkbeck, Morris, 1764-1825.
          Notes on a journey in America, from
       the coast of Virginia to the territory
       of Illinois: with proposals for the
       establishment of a colony of English;
       accompanied by a map, illustrating
       the route.   By Morris Birkbeck ...
       Printed from the last ed. pub. in
       Philadelphia.   Dublin, Reprinted for
       Thomas Larkin, 1818.
          viii, 9 -158 p.   fold. map.   23
       cm.

1338   Birkinshaw, Maria Louisa.
          The chevaliers; a tale, with a
       true account of an American revival,
       by Maria Louisa Birkinshaw.   London,
       Simpkin, Marshall and co., 1860.
          2 p. l., 416 p.   22 1/2 cm.

1339   Birney, James Gillespie, 1792-1857.
          ... Correspondence, between the
       Hon. F.H. Elmore, one of the South
       Carolina delegation in Congress,
       and James G. Birney, one of the secre-
       taries of the American anti-slavery
       society.   New York, American anti-
       slavery society, 1838.
          68 p.   23 cm.

1340   Birney, James Gillespie, 1792-1857.
           Letter on colonization, addressed
       to the Rev. Thornton J. Mills,
       corresponding secretary of the Ken-
       tucky colonization society. By James
       G. Birney, esq., late vice-president
       of the Kentucky colonization society.
       New York, Office of the Anti-slavery
       reporter, 1834.
       46 p.   18 1/2 cm.

1341   Birney, James Gillespie, 1792-1857.
           Mr. Birney's second letter. To
       the ministers and elders of the Pres-
       byterian church in Kentucky. [n.p.,
       1834]
       16 p.   18 cm.

1342   Birney, James Gillespie, 1792-1857.
           The sinfulness of slaveholding
       in all circumstances; tested by rea-
       son and Scripture. By James G.
       Birney. Detroit, Printed by C.
       Willcox, 1846.
       iv, [5]-60 p.   21 cm.

1343   [Bisble, D   T   ]
           An appeal for the speedy comple-
       tion of the water line of Virginia,
       and through that of the great cen-
       tral water line of the union, which
       will reach from the wharves of Nor-
       folk, far into Kansas, and eventually
       to the very bases of the Rocky moun-
       tains ... Norfolk, C.H. Wynne, print-
       er, Richmond, 1857.
           cover-title, ii, [3]-24 p.   fold.
       map.   24 1/2 cm.

1344   Bishop, Abraham, 1763-1844.
           Connecticut republicanism; an ora-
       tion on the extent and power of polit-
       ical delusion, delivered in New-
       Haven on the evening preceding the
       public commencement, September 1800.

Philadelphia, Printed for M. Carey,
1800.
   80 p.   22 cm.

1345 Bishop, Abraham, 1763-1844.
      Connecticut Republicanism. An
      oration on the extent and power of
      political delusion. Delivered in
      New-Haven, on the evening preceding
      the public commencement, September,
      1800.   By Abraham Bishop ... [New
      Haven?] 1800.
      2 p. l., 64, xi p.   21 cm.

1346 Bishop, Abraham, 1763-1844.
      Georgia speculation unveiled ...
      By Abraham Bishop. Hartford, Print-
      ed by Elisha Babcock, 1797-98.
      2 v.   20 cm.

1347 Bishop, Abraham, 1763-1844.
      Oration delivered in Wallingford,
      on the 11th of March, 1801, before
      the Republicans of the state of Con-
      necticut, at their general thanksgiv-
      ing, for the election of Thomas
      Jefferson to the presidency and of
      Aaron Burr to the vice presidency
      of the United States of America.
      By Abraham Bishop ... New Haven:
      Printed by William W. Morse, 1801.
      vi, [7]-111, [1] p.   21 1/2 cm.

1348 Bishop, Abraham, 1763-1844.
      Oration, in honor of the election
      of President Jefferson, and the
      peaceable acquisition of Louisiana,
      delivered at the National festival, in
      Hartford, on the 11th of May, 1804.
      By Abraham Bishop. [New Haven] Print-
      ed for the general committee of Re-
      publicans. From Sidney's press, 1894.
      24 p.   20 1/2 cm.

1349 Bishop, Abraham, 1763-1844.
      Proofs of a conspiracy, against
      Christianity, and the government of

the United States; exhibited in
several views of the union of church
and state in New-England. By Abraham
Bishop. Hartford, J. Babcock, printer, 1802.
   iv, [5]-166 p.   21 1/2 cm.

1350   Bishop, Albert Webb, 1832-1901.
   Loyalty on the frontier, or Sketches
of Union men of the South-west; with
incidents and adventures in rebellion
on the border. By A.W. Bishop ...
St. Louis, R.P. Studley and co.,
printers, 1863.
   228 p.   20 cm.

1351   Bishop, Albert Webb.
   An oration delivered at Fayette-
ville, Arkansas, by Brig.-Gen. Albert W. Bishop ... July 4, 1865.
New York, Baker & Godwin, printers, 1865.
   27 p.   23 cm.

1352   Bishop, *Mrs*. Harriet E   1817-1883.
   Floral home; or, First years of
Minnesota. Early sketches, later
settlements, and further develop-
ments, by Harriet E. Bishop. New
York, Sheldon, Blakeman and company, 1857.
   342 p.   front., illus. plates,
ports.   20 cm.

1353   Bishop, Joel Prentiss, 1814-1901.
   Commentaries on the criminal law.
By Joel Prentiss Bishop ...   4th
ed., rev. and enl. ...   Boston,
Little, Brown, and company, 1868.
   2 v.   24 1/2 cm.

1354   Bishop, Joel Prentiss, 1814-1901.
   Secession and slavery: or, The
effect of secession on the relation
of the United States to the seceded
states and to slavery therein; considered as a question of constitutional

law ... By Joel Prentiss Bishop
... Boston, A. Williams & co., 1864.
iv, 5-112 p.   23 1/2 cm.

1355   Bishop, Joel Prentiss, 1814-1901.
        Thoughts for the times.   By Joel
Prentiss Bishop.   Boston, Little,
Brown and company, 1863.
        36 p.   22 cm.

1356   Bishop, John Leander, 1820-1868.
        A history of American manufactures,
from 1608-1860 ... comprising annals
of the industry of the United States
in machinery, manufactures, and
useful arts, with a notice of the
important inventions, tariffs, and
the results of each decennial census.
By J. Leander Bishop, M.D.   To which
is added, notes on the principal
manufacturing centres, and remarkable
manufactories at the present time
... Philadelphia, E. Young & co.,
1861-
        v.   23 cm.

1357   Bishop, Matthew, *fl.* 1701-1744.
        The life and adventures of Matthew
Bishop of Deddington in Oxfordshire.
Containing an account of several actions by sea, battles and sieges by
land, in which he was present from
1701 to 1711, interspersed with many
curious incidents, entertaining con-
versations and judicious reflections.
Written by himself.   London, Printed
for J. Brindley [etc.] 1744.
        viii, [4], 283, [1] p.   20 1/2
cm.

1358   Bishop, Putnam P.
        Liberty's ordeal.   By Putnam P.
Bishop.   New York, Sheldon & company, 1864.
        128 p.   17 cm.

1359   Bishop, Robert Hamilton, 1777-1855.

An outline of the history of the
church in the state of Kentucky, during a period of forty years: containing the memoirs of Rev. David
Rice, and sketches of the origin and
present state of particular churches,
and of the lives and labours of a
number of men who were eminent and
useful in their day. Collected and
arranged by Robert H. Bishop ... Lexington, T.T. Skillman, 1824.
xii, [13]-420 p. 18 cm.

1360 Bissett, George, d. 1788.
A sermon preached in Trinity-
church, Newport, Rhode Island, on
Monday, June 3, 1771; at the funeral
of Mrs. Abigail Wanton, late consort
of the Hon. Joseph Wanton, jun. esq;
who departed this life on Friday,
May 31, 1771, in the 36th year of her
age. By George Bisset, M.A. Published at the request of the relatives
of the deceased. Newport: Printed
by S. Southwick, in Queen-street,
1771.
20 p. 22 cm.

1361 Bisset, Robert, 1759-1805.
The history of the negro slave
trade, in its connection with the
commerce and prosperity of the West
Indies, and the wealth and power of
the British empire. By Robert Bisset ... London, S. Highley [etc.]
1805.
2 v. 22 cm.

1362 Bisset, Robert, 1759-1805.
The history of the reign of George
III. to the termination of the late
war. To which is prefixed, A view
of the progressive improvement of
England, in prosperity and strength,
to the accession of His Majesty ...
By Robert Bisset ... London, T.N.
Longman and O. Rees; [etc., etc.]

1803.
6 v.   21 1/2 cm.

1363   Bisset, Robert, 1759-1805.
The life of Edmund Burke. Comprehending an impartial account of his
literary and political efforts, and
a sketch of the conduct and character of his most eminent associates,
coadjutors, and opponents. The 2d
ed. ... By Robert Bisset, LL.D.
London, Printed and pub. by G. Car-
thorn; [etc., etc.] 1800.
2 v. front. (port.)   21 1/2 cm.

1364   Björck, Tobias Er.
Dissertatio gradualis,
de plantatione ecclesiae svecanae
in America, quam ... in Regio Upsal.
athenaeo, praeside ... Andrew Brön-
wall ... in audit. Gust. maj. d. 14
jun. an. MDCCXXXI. examinandam modeste
sistit Tobias E. Biörck, americano-
dalekarlus. Upsaliae, literis Wer-
nerianis [1731]
4 p. l., 34 p.   illus., fold. map.
19 x 15 1/2 cm.

1365   Black Hawk, *Sauk chief*, 1767-1838.
Life of Ma-ka-tai-me-she-kia-
kiak or Black Hawk, embracing the
tradition of his nation--Indian
wars in which he has been engaged--
cause of joining the British in their
late war with America, and its his-
tory--description of the Rock river vil
lage--manners and customs--encroach-
ments by the whites, contrary to
treaty--removal from his village in
1831. With an account of the cause
and general history of the late war,
his surrender and confinement at
Jefferson barracks, and travels
through the United States. Dictated
by himself. J.B. Patterson, of Rock
Island, Ill., editor and proprietor.
Boston, Russell, Odiorne & Metcalf:

New York, M. Bancroft: [etc., etc.]
1834.
   155 p. front. (port.)   19 cm.

1367 Black, Jeremiah Sullivan, 1810-1883.
     The doctrines of the Democratic
and Abolition parties contrasted.--
Negro equality.--The conflict between
"higher law" and the law of the land.
Speech of Hon. Jeremiah S. Black, at
the hall of the Keystone club, in
Philadelphia, October 24, 1864. [Phil-
adelphia, Printed at the "Age" office,
1864]
   8 p.   21 1/2 cm.

1368 [Black, Jeremiah Sullivan] 1810-1883.
     Observations on Senator Douglas's
views of popular sovereignty, as ex-
pressed in Harpers' magazine, for
September, 1859. Washington, T.
McGill, printer, 1859.
   16 p.   24 1/2 cm.

1369 Black, Jeremiah Sullivan, 1810-1883.
     Speech of Hon. Jeremiah S. Black,
at the Democratic mass convention,
in Lancaster city, September 17, 1863.
Harrisburg, Pa., "Patriot and union"
steam print [1863]
   7 p.   22 1/2 cm.

1370 Black list. A list of those Tories who
took part with Great-Britain, in the
revolutionary war, and were attainted
of high treason, commonly called the
Black list! To which is prefixed
the legal opinions of Attorney Generals Mc.Kean & Dallas, &c. Philadelphia, Printed for the proprietor, 1802.
   16 p.   21 1/2 cm.

1371 Black Republican imposture exposed!
Fraud upon the people! The accounts
of Fremont examined; showing an
astounding disregard of the public
interest, only to be accounted for by

extravagance, recklessness, or an ut-
ter want of judgment! Washington,
1856.
    14 p.   24 1/2 cm.

1372 Blackburn, William Maxwell, 1828-1898.
        The crime against the Presidency.
      A sermon, delivered Sunday, April
      16, 1865, in the Fourth Presbyterian
      church, Trenton, N.J., by the pastor,
      Rev. William M. Blackburn. Trenton,
      N.J., Murphy & Bechtel, printers, 1865.
        24 p.   22 cm.

1373 Blackford, Dominique de.
        Précis de l'état actuel des colonies
      angloises dans l'Amérique Septentrio-
      nale, par M. Dominique de Blackford.
      Milan, Chez les frères Reycends,
      1771.
        99 p.   16 1/2 cm.

1374 Blackie, Walter Graham, 1816-1906.
        The imperial gazetteer; a general
      dictionary of geography, physical,
      political, statistical and descrip-
      tive ... Edited by W.G. Blackie ...
      With seven hundred illustrations,
      views, costumes, maps, plans, &c. ...
      Glasgow [etc.] Blackie and son,
      1855.
        2 v.   fronts., illus. (incl. maps,
      plans)   27 1/2 cm.

1375 Blackley, Frederick Rogers.
        The Greenland minstrel, a poem
      in six cantos: with an introductory
      narrative: illustrated from drawings
      taken on the spot, during a voyage
      to Greenland, in the year 1826. By
      the Rev. Frederick R. Blackley ...
      London, Simpkin and Marshall, 1839.
        xxx p., 1 1., 148 p. front.,
      illus., plates.   16 1/2 cm.

1376 Blackmore, Richard Doddridge, 1825-1900.

The fate of Franklin. By Richard
Doddridge Blackmore ... London, R.
Hardwicke, 1860.
42 p.   22 cm.

1377 Blackwell, Robert S   1823-1863.
      A practical treatise on the power
to sell land for the nonpayment of
taxes assessed thereon, embracing
the decisions of the federal courts,
and of the supreme judicial tribunals
of the several states. By Robert S.
Blackwell ... Chicago, D.B. Cooke
& co., 1855.
      xxxi, [1] p., 1 1., 776 p.   23
1/2 cm.

1378 Blackwell, Robert S   1823-1863.
      A practical treatise on the power
to sell land for the nonpayment of
taxes, embracing the decisions of
the federal courts, and of the supreme judicial tribunals of the several states. By Robert S. Blackwell
... 2d ed., rev. and enl.   Boston,
Little, Brown and company, 1864.
      xxxii, 668 p.   24 1/2 cm.

1379 The Bladensburg races. Written shortly
      after the capture of Washington city,
      August 24, 1814. [Probably it is
      not generally known, that the flight
      of Mahomet, the flight of John Gil-
      pin, and the flight of Bladensburg,
      all occurred on the twenty-fourth of
      August.] [Washington?] Printed
      for the purchaser .... 1816.
      12 p.   14 1/2 cm.

1380 Bladh, Carl Edvard, 1790-1851.
      Resa till Montevideo och Buenos
Ayres, jemte beskrifning öfver Plata-
floden och de förenta provinserna
af samma namn, Paraguay, Misiones och
republiken Oriental del Uruguay,
eller Cisplatina, af C.E. Bladh ...
Stockholm, Tryckt hos L.J. Hjerta,

1839.
    7 p 1., 400, [2] p.   2 fold. tab.
19 1/2 x 11 1/2 cm.

1381   Blagden, George Washington, 1802-1884.
        Remarks, and a discourse on sla-
very, by G.W. Blagden. Boston,
Ticknor, Reed, and Fields, 1854.
        30 p.   24 cm.

1382   [Blaine, James Gillespie] 1830-1893.
        Memoir of Luther Severance ...
Augusta, Me., Printed at the office
of the Kennebec journal, 1856.
        33 p.   23 1/2 cm.

1383   Blair, Francis Preston, 1821-1875.
        The destiny of the races of this
continent. An address delivered before the Mercantile library association of Boston, Massachusetts. On
the 26th of January, 1859. By Frank
P. Blair, jr., of Missouri. Washington, D.C., Buell & Blanchard,
printers, 1859.
        88 p.   22 1/2 cm.

1384   Blair, James, 1656-1743.
        Our Saviour's divine Sermon on the
Mount, contain'd in the vth, vith,
and viith chapters of St. Matthew's
gospel, explained: and the practice
of it recommended in divers sermons
and discourses ... To which is prefix'd, a paraphrase on the whole Sermon on the Mount: and two copious indexes annex'd; one of the Scriptures
explain'd, the other of the particular heads treated of in the work. By
James Blair, M.A., commissary of
Virginia, president of William and
Mary ... The 2d ed. With a recommendatory preface by the Reverend Dr.
Waterland. London. Printed for J.
Brotherton [etc.] MDCCXL.
        4 v.   20 1/2 cm.

1385   Blair, John Durbarrow, 1759-1823.
       A sermon on the death of Lieutenant
       General George Washington, delivered
       in the capitol in Richmond, by John
       D. Blair, chaplain to the House of
       delegates. Printed by Meriwether
       Jones, Printer to the Commonwealth,
       January--1800.
       18 p.   17 1/2 cm.

1386   Blair, Montgomery, 1813-1883.
       Comments on the policy inaugurated
       by the President, in a letter and
       two speeches. By Montgomery Blair
       ... New York, Hall, Clayton &
       Medole, printers, 1863.
       20 p.   23 1/2 cm.

1387   Blair, Samuel, 1741-1818.
       A discourse delivered in the First
       Presbyterian church of Philadelphia,
       on Wednesday, May 9th, 1798, recom-
       mended by the President of the United
       States to be observed as a day of
       fasting, humiliation, and prayer,
       throughout the United States of North
       America. By Samuel Blair ... Phil-
       adelphia: Published by James Wat
       ters, & co. To be had also of the
       principal booksellers. 1798.
       31 p.   22 cm.

1388   Blair, Samuel, 1741-1818.
       An oration pronounced at Nassau-
       hall, January 14, 1761; on occasion
       of the death of His late Majesty
       King George II. By Samuel Blair ...
       Woodbridge, in New Jersey: Printed
       by James Parker, M.DCC.LXI.
       8 p.   19 1/2 cm.

1389   Blake, Dominick T   d. 1839.
       An historical treatise on the
       practice of the Court of chancery
       of the state of New-York; containing
       all the proceedings of a suit, as

in the Court for the trial of impeach-
ments and correction of errors. By
D.T. Blake ... New-York, Printed
by J.T. Murden for David Banks, law
bookseller, New-York, and William
Gould, law bookseller, Albany, 1818.
xxxix, 483, 167 p. 24 1/2 cm.

1390 Blake, Francis, 1774-1817.
An oration, pronounced at Worcester, (Mass.) on the thirty-sixth
anniversary of American independence,
July 4, 1812. By Francis Blake. Pub.
at the request of a numerous assembly of citizens from various parts
of the county and the members of the
Washington benevolent society, who
joined in the celebration. Worcester, Printed by Isaac Sturtevant
[1812]
36 p.   22 cm.

1391 Blake, George, 1768?-1841.
A masonic eulogy, on the life of
the illustrious Brother George Washington, pronounced before the breth-
ren of St. John's lodge, on the evening of the 4th Feb. 5800. At their
particular request. By Brother George
Blake ... Boston, Printed by Brother
John Russell, 5800 [1800]
23 p.   21 1/2 cm.

1392 Blake, George, 1768?-1841.
An oration, pronounced July 4th,
1795, at the request of the inhabitants of the town of Boston, in
commemoration of the anniversary of
American independence. By George
Blake ... Boston, Printed and sold
by Benjamin Edes, 1795.
28 p.   21 1/2 cm.

1393 Blake, Harrison Gray, 1818-1876.
Slavery in the District. Speech
of Hon. H.G. Blake, of Ohio,

delivered in the House of representatives, April 11, 1862, on the bill
for the release of certain persons
held to service or labor in the District of Columbia. [Washington,
Scammell & co., printers, 1862]
   8, 4 p.   24 cm.

1394 Blake, Henry Nichols, 1838-
     Three years in the Army of the Poto-
mac. By Henry N. Blake, late captain
in the Eleventh regiment Massachusetts
volunteers ... Boston, Lee and
Shepard, 1865.
    vi, 7-319 p.   18 1/2 cm.

1395 Blake, James
     ... Annals of the town of Dorches-
ter. By James Blake. 1750. Boston,
D. Clapp, jr., 1846.
    vi, [7]-95 p. front. (facsim.)
18 1/2 cm.

1396 Blake, John Lauris, 1788-1857.
     American universal geography, for
schools and academies ... By Rev.
J.L. Blake ... Boston, Russell,
Odiorne & co., 1833.
    2 p. 1., 144 p. illus., maps.
25 1/2 cm.

1397 Blake, John Lauris, 1788-1857.
     ... A biographical dictionary:
comprising a summary account of the
lives of the most distinguished persons of all ages, nations, and pro-
fessions; including more than two
thousand articles of American biography. By the Rev. John L. Blake,
... 13th ed. Philadelphia, H. Cowperthwait & co., 1856.
    viii, 9-1366 p.   28 cm.

1398 Blake, John Lauris, 1788-1857.
     A history of the American revolu-
tion. First published in London

under the superintendence of the
Society for the diffusion of useful
knowledge. Improved with maps and
other illustrations. Also rev. and
enl., by Rev. J.L. Blake ... New
York, A.V. Blake, 1844.
vi, [7]-252 p. illus., 3 maps
(incl. front.) 16 cm.

1399 Blake, Joseph M., 1809-1879.
Libel suit of Chief Justice Ames
against Thomas R. Hazard. Hon. Joseph M. Blake's argument for defendant upon plaintiff's demurrer.
Providence, A.C. Greene, printer,
1862.
38 p. 22 cm.

1400 Blake, Mortimer, 1813-1884.
A centurial history of the Mendon
association of Congregational ministers, with the Centennial address,
delivered at Franklin, Mass., Nov.
19, 1851, and biographical sketches
of the members and licentiates. By
Rev. Mortimer Blake. Boston, Published for the Association, by S.
Harding, 1853.
vi, [7]-348 p. 19 1/2 cm.

1401 Blake, Samuel, 1797-1867.
Blake family. A genealogical
history of William Blake, of Dorchester, and his descendants, comprising all the descendants of Samuel and
Patience (White) Blake. With an appendix, containing wills, &c. of members of the family ... By Samuel
Blake ... Boston, E. Clapp, jr.,
1857.
140 p. illus. 25 1/2 cm.

1402 Blake, William J.
The history of Putnam County,
N.Y.; with an enumeration of its
towns, villages, rivers, creeks,

lakes, ponds, mountains, hills, and
geological features; local traditions; and short biographical sketches
of early settlers, etc. By William
J. Blake ... New York, Baker &
Scribner, 1849.
iv, [13]-368 p.   18 1/2 cm.

1403 Blake, William O
The history of slavery and the
slave trade, ancient and modern.
The forms of slavery that prevailed
in ancient nations, particularly in
Greece and Rome. The African slave
trade and the political history of
slavery in the United States. Comp.
from authentic materials by W.O. Blake.
Columbus, O., H. Miller, 1861.
xvi, [17]-866 p.   front., plates.
25 cm.

1404 Blake, William P[hipps] 1826-
Description of the fossils and
shells collected in California by
William P. Blake, geologist of the
United States Pacific railroad survey in California, under the command
of Lieut. R.S. Williamson, in 1853-
54. Washington, 1855.
cover-title, 34 p.   22 1/2 cm.

1405 Blakslee, Solomon, 1762-1835.
An oration, delivered at East-
Haddam, Feb. 22, 1800, agreeable to
the proclamation of the President of
the United States; on the death of
the late General George Washington.
By Solomon Blakslee ... Hartford:
Printed by Hudson and Goodwin, 1800.
15 p.   24 cm.

1406 Blanc, Hippolyte, b. 1820.
Le merveilleux dans le Jansénisme,
le magnétisme, le Méthodisme et le
Baptisme americains, l'épidémie de

Morzine, le spiritisme; recherches
nouvelles par Hippolyte Blanc. Paris,
H. Plon, 1865.
x p., 1 l., 445 p.   21 1/2 cm.

1407 [Blanchard, Amos] *of Cincinnati.*
The American biography; containing
biographical sketches of the officers
of the Revolution and of the principal statesmen of that period. To which
are added the life and character of
Benedict Arnold and the narrative of
Major André. Comp. from authentic
sources. Wheeling, F. Kenyon, 1833.
616 p.   22 cm.

1408 [Blanchard, Amos] *of Cincinnati.*
American military biography; containing the lives, characters, and
anecdotes of the officers of the
Revolution who were most distinguished
in achieving our national independence.
Also the life of Gilbert Motier La
Fayette .. [Cincinnati?] Printed for
subscribers, 1825.
431 p.   plates (part fold.)   18
1/2 cm.

1409 [Blanchard, Calvin]
A crisis chapter on government.
[New York, 1865?]
4 p.   24 cm.

1410 Blanchard, Charles.
Chief Justice Caton's Seymour letter. Remarks by Charles Blanchard,
of Ottawa, Illinois, published in the
Ottawa republican, April 4 & 11,
1863. [Ottawa, Ill., 1863]
12 p.   25 cm.

1411 Blanchard, Ira Henry Thomas, *d.* 1845.
A discourse delivered by Rev. I.H.T.
Blanchard, in South Natick, December
9, 1834. Occasioned by the death of
John Atkins, esq. Boston, J. Dowe,

1835.
29 p.   24 cm.

1412   Blanchard, Joshua Pollard, 1782-1868.
        Principles of the revolution: show-
ing the perversion of them and the
consequent failure of their accomplish-
ment. By J.P. Blanchard. Boston,
Press of Damrell and Moore, 1855.
        24 p.   23 cm.

1413   Blatchford, Richard M.
        Extract from a report to the trus-
tees of the Apalachicola land company,
by Richard M. Blatchford, esq., president of the Board of directors, and
special agent of said company, appointed to examine and report upon
the situation of the property of the
company. Made May 17, 1837. [New
York? 1837]
        16 p.   22 1/2 cm.

1414   Blatchford, Samuel, 1767-1828.
        An address, delivered to the
Oneida Indians, September 24, 1810,
by Samuel Blatchford, D.D., together with the reply, by Christian, a
chief of said nation. Pub. by request of the Board of directors of
the Northern missionary society, and
the proceeds of the sale, devoted by
the author, to the benefit of the
Society. Albany: Printed by Websters and Skinner, at their book-
store, corner of State and Pearl-
streets. [1810.]
        11 p.   23 1/2 cm.

1415   Blatchford, Thomas Windeatt, 1794-1866.
        Eulogy on Samuel McClellan, M.D.,
prepared by order of the Medical
society of the state of New-York,
and read at the annual meeting in
Albany, February 3, 1857, by Thomas
W. Blatchford, M.D. Albany, C. Van

Benthuysen, printer, 1857.
23 p. front. (port.) 23 1/2 cm.

1416 [Blauvelt,   ]
Fashion's analysis; or, The winter
in town. A satirical poem. By Sir
Anthony Avalanche [*pseud.*] With
notes, illustrations, etc., by
Gregory Glacier, gent. [*pseud.*] Part
I. New York, Printed for J. Osborn,
1807.
84 p. 16 1/2 cm.

1417 Bleeker, Leonard.
The order book of Capt. Leonard
Bleeker, major of brigade in the
early part of the expedition under
Gen. James Clinton, against the
Indian settlements of western New
York, in the campaign of 1779. New
York, J. Sabin, 1865.
138 p. 22 x 17 1/2 cm.

1418 Bliss, George, 1764-1830.
An address, delivered at the opening of the town-hall in Springfield,
March 24, 1828. Containing sketches
of the early history of that town,
and those in its vicinity. With an
appendix. By George Bliss ...
Springfield, Tannatt & co., 1828.
68 p. 23 cm.

1419 Bliss, George, 1793-1873.
Historical memoir of the Springfield cemetery, read to the proprietors at their meeting, May 23, 1857.
By George Bliss ... Accompanied by
an address delivered at the consecration of the cemetery, September 5,

1841, by Rev. Wm. B.O. Peabody.
Springfield, Mass., S. Bowles and
company, printers, 1857.
23 p.   23 cm.

1420   Bliss, George, 1793-1873.
Historical memoir of the Western
railroad. By George Bliss. Springfield, Mass., S. Bowles & company,
printers, 1863.
190 p., 1 1.   22 1/2 cm.

1421   [Bliss, Henry] 1797?-1873.
Consideration of the claims and
conduct of the United States respecting their north eastern boundary, and
of the value of the British colonies in
North America. London, J. Hatchard
and son, 1826.
2 p. 1., 112 p. map, fold. tab.
21 1/2 cm.

1422   Bliss, Philemon, 1814-1889.
Success of the absolutists. Their
idealism; what and whence is it?
Speech of Hon. Philemon Bliss, of
Ohio, in the House of representatives,
May 24, 1858. Washington, Buell &
Blanchard, printers, 1858.
15, [1] p.   25 cm.

1423   The blockheads: or, The affrighted officers. A farce. Boston: Printed
in Queen-street, M,DCC,LXXVI.
19, [2] p.   21 cm.

1424   Blodget, Lorin, 1823-1901.
The commercial and financial strength
of the United States, as shown in
the balances of foreign trade and the

increased production of staple articles. By Lorin Blodget. Philadelphia,
King & Baird, printers, 1864.
39 p.   22 1/2 cm.

1425   Blome, Richard, d. 1705.
A description of the island of
Jamaica; with the other isles and
territories in America, to which the
English are related, viz. Barbadoes,
St. Christophers, Nievis, or Mevis,
Antego, St. Vincent, Dominica, Mont-
serrat, Anguilla. Barbada, Bermudes,
Carolina, Virginia, Maryland, New-
York, New-England, New-Found-Land.
Published by Richard Blome. Together
with The present state of Algiers.
London, Printed by J.B. for D. New-
man, 1678.
3 p. 1., 88 p., 1 1., 17 p., 2
1. port., 4 fold. maps.   18 cm.

1426   Boutelle, John Alonzo.
The Burke and Alvord memorial. A
genealogical account of the descendants of Richard Burke of Sudbury,
Mass. Comp. by John Alonzo Boutelle
of Woburn, Mass., for William A.
Burke of Lowell, Mass. ... Boston,
Printed by H.W. Dutton and son, 1864.
239 p.   24 cm.

1427   Bradford, Samuel Fisher, 1776-1837.
The imposter detected, or, A review of some of the writings of "Peter
Porcupine." By Timothy Tickletoby
[*pseud.*] ... To which is annexed A
refreshment for the memory of William Cobbett, by Samuel F. Bradford,
2d ed. Philadelphia: From the free

and independent political & literary
Press of Thomas Bradford, printer,
bookseller & stationer, No. 8, South
Front Street. 1796.
    xvii, [19]-51, 23 p.   23 cm.

1428 Branagan, Thomas, b. 1774.
    The penitential tyrant; or, Slave
trader reformed: a pathetic poem,
in four cantos. By Thomas Branagan.
2d ed., enl. ... New-York: Printed
and sold by Samuel Wood, no. 362,
Pearl-street. 1807.
    xii, 290, [9] p. front., illus.
14 1/2 cm.

1429 Branagan, Thomas.
    Serious remonstrances, addressed
to the citizens of the southern
states, and their representatives:
being an approach to their natural
feelings & common sense: consisting
of speculations and animadversions,
on the recent report of the slave
trade, in the American republic:
with an investigation relative to the
consequent evils resulting in the
citizens of the northern states from
that event. Interspersed with a sim-
plified plan for colonizing the free
negroes of the northern, in conjunc-
tion with those who have, or may emigrate from the southern states, in a
distant part of the national territory:
considered as the only possible means
of avoiding the deleterious evils at-
tendant on slavery in a republic. By
Thomas Branagan ... Philadelphia:
Printed and published by Thomas T.
Stiles, No. 251, North Front-street,

1805.
xiv, [15]-133 p.   18 cm.

1430 Branch, William, jr.
Life, a poem in three books: descriptive of the various characters in
life; the different passions, with
their moral influence; the good and
evil resulting from their sway; and
of the perfect man. Dedicated to the
social and political welfare of the
people of the United States. By William Branch, junior ... Richmond:
From the Franklin Press. W.W. Gray,
Printer, 1819.
xii, 218 p., 1 1.   17 cm.

1431 Brand, Charles.
Journal of a voyage to Peru: a
passage across the cordillera of the
Andes, in the winter of 1827, performed
on foot in the snow; and a journey
across the pampas. By Lieut. Chas.
Brand, R.N. London, H. Colburn, 1828.
xvii, [2],   346 p.   front., plates.
21 cm.

1432 Brandegee, Augustus, 1828-
Speech of Hon. Augustus Brandegee,
of Connecticut, delivered in the House
of representatives, December 12, 1864,
on the bill reported by the Committee
on naval affairs, locating the naval
station for iron clads at New London,
Conn. Washington, D.C., McGill &
Witherow, printers, 1864.
16 p.   24 cm.

1433 Brandes, Karl.
Sir John Franklin; die unterneh-
mungen für seine rettung, und die

nordwestliche durchfahrt, von dr.
Karl Brandes ... Nebst einer tabelle
der arktischen temperaturne vom prof.
dr. H.W. Dove, und einer karte von
Henry Lange. Berlin, Nicolai, 1854.
    viii, 312 p. fold. map. 2 fold.
tab. 23 cm.

1434 Brandin, Abel Victorino.
    De la influencia de los diferentes
climas del universo sobre el hombre,
y en particular, de la influencia de
los climas de la America meridional.
Por Don Abel Victorino Brandin ...
Lima, J.M. Masias, 1826.
    8 p. 1. 114 p., 1 l. 20 1/2 cm.

1435 Brandt, Geeraert, 1626-1685.
    La vie de Michel de Ruiter ... Où
est comprise l'histoire maritime des
Provinces Unies, depuis l'an 1652.
jusques à 1676. Tr. du hollandois de
Gerard Brandt ... Amsterdam, Waes-
berge, Boom, à Someren & Goethals, 1698.
    4 p. 1., 717, 17 p. front. (port.)
8 pl. (part fold.) 37 cm.

1436 Brannan, Jon, *comp*.
    Official letters of the military
and naval officers of the United
States, during the war with Great
Britain in the years 1812, 13, 14,
& 15. With some additional letters
and documents elucidating the history
of that period. Collected and arranged by John Brannan. Washington
city, Printed by Way & Gideon, for
the editor, 1823.
    516 p. 22 cm.

1437 Brannan, William Penn, 1825-1866.

Vagaries of Vandyke Browne. An
autobiography in verse. By William
P. Brannan ... Cincinnati, R.W.
Carroll & co., 1865.
230 p.   17 cm.

1438   Brantly, William Theophilus, 1787-1845.
Our national troubles. A thanksgiving sermon. Delivered in the
First Baptist church, before the First
and the Tabernacle Baptist congregations of Philadelphia, on Thursday
morning, Nov. 29, 1860. By William
T. Brantly ... Philadelphia, T.B.
Peterson & brothers, 1860.
32 p.   23 cm.

1439   Brashears, Noah.
Columbia's wreath; or, Miscellaneous
poems, composed between the years 1814,
and 1830, by N. Brashears. 2d ed.,
with corrections and additions ... City
of Washington, Pub. for the author
by S.A. Elliot, printer, 1830.
xi, [13]-120 p.   19 cm.

1440   Brasseur de Bourbourg, Charles Étienne,
1814-1874.
Histoire de nations civilisées du
Mexique et de l'Amérique-Centrale,
durant les siècles antérieurs à
Christophe Colomb, écrite sur des
documents originaux et entièrement
inédits, puisés aux anciennes archives
des indigènes par M. l'abbé Brasseur
de Bourbourg ... Paris, A. Bertrand,
1857-59.
4 v. fold. map.   24 cm.

1441   Brasseur de Bourbourg, Charles Étienne,

1814-1874.

Histoire du Canada, de son église
et de ses missions, depuis la découverte de l'Amérique jusqu'à nos jours,
écrite sur des documents inédits com-
pulsés dans les archives de l'arche-
vêché et de la ville de Québec, etc.
Par M. l'abbé Brasseur de Bourbourg
... Plancy [etc.] Société de Saint
Victor; Paris, Sagnier et Bray, 1852.
2 v.   21 1/2 cm.

1442   Brasseur de Bourbourg, Charles Etienne,
       1814-1874.
       Lettres pour servir d'introduction
à l'histoire primitive des nations
civilisées de l'Amérique Septentrionale, adressées à Monsieur le duc
de Valmy. Par M. l'abbé E. Charles
Brasseur de Bourbourg ... Cartas
para servir de introducción à la
historia primitiva de las naciones
civilizadas de la América Setentrion-
al. Mexico, Impr. de M. Murguía,
1851.
       75 p.   30 1/2 cm.

1443   Brasseur de Bourbourg, Charles Étienne,
       1814-1874.
       S'il existe des sources de l'his-
toire primitive du Mexique dans les
monuments égyptiens et de l'histoire
primitive de l'Ancien monde dans les
monuments américains? Par m. Brasseur de Bourbourg ... Extrait du
volume intitulé Relation des choses
de Yucatan [de Diego de Landa] Paris,
Maisonneuve et cie; [etc., etc.]
1864.
       2 p. l., 146 p.   21 1/2 cm.

1444 Brasseur ("de Bourbourg"), Charles
Étienne, 1814-1874.
Voyage sur l'isthme de Tehuantepee,
dans l'état de Chiapas et la république de Guatémala, exécuté dans
les annees 1859 et 1860. Par M.
l'abbé Brasseur de Bourbourg ... [1.
ptic.] Paris, A. Bertrand, 1861.
209 p., 1 1. 22 1/2 cm.

1445 Brauns, Frederic William, 1830-1895.
Joy in tribulation. A sermon,
preached in the Franklin St. Presbyterian church, Baltimore, on Nov. 28,
1861, Thanksgiving day, by Rev. F.W.
Brauns. Baltimore, Printed by J.D.
Toy, 1861.
15 p. 22 cm.

1446 [Braxton, Carter M   ]
Map of the battle field of Fredericksburg, explained by extracts
from official reports; also, Gen. R.E.
Lee's report of the battle. Lynchburg, Virginian power-press book and
job office, 1866.
44 p. fold. map. 21 cm.

1447 Bray, John, 1782-1822.
The Indian princess; or, La belle
sauvage. An operatic melo-drame in
three acts. By J.N. Barker. Philadelphia, Printed by T. & G. Palmer,
for G.E. Blake, no. 1, South Third-
Street. 1808.
iv, 74 p. 15 cm.

1448 Bray, Thomas, 1656-1730.
The acts of Dr. Bray's visitation.
Held at Annopolis [!] in Mary-land,
May 23, 24, 25. Anno 1700. London,

Printed by W. Downing, 1700.
2 p. l., 3-17 p.   30 cm.

1449 Bray, Thomas, 1656-1730.
A memorial representing the present state of religion on the contin
ent of North America. By Thomas Bray,
D.D. London, Printed by William Downing 1700 ... reprinted for the Thomas
Bray club. [n.p., 1916]
2 p. l., 7-30 p.   24 1/2 cm.

1450 Brayman, James O   1815-1887, ed.
Thrilling adventures by land and
sea. Being remarkable historical
facts, gathered from authentic
sources. Edited by James O. Brayman.
... Buffalo, G.H. Derby and co.,
1852.
xi, [13]-504 p. incl. plates.   20
cm.

1451 Brazer, John, 1787-1846.
A discourse on the life and character of the late Hon. Leverett Saltonstall, delivered in the North church,
Salem, Mass., Sunday, May 18, 1845.
By John Brazer ... Printed by request--
not published. Salem, Printed at the
Gazette office, 1845.
52 p.   23 cm.

1452 Brazer, Samuel, 1785-1823.
Address, pronounced at Worcester,
on May 12th, 1804, in commemoration
of the cession of Louisiana to the
United States. By Samuel Brazer,
junior ... Printed at Worcester,
by Sewall Goodridge, May 19th, 1804.
15, [1] p.   23 cm.

1453 Brazer, Samuel, jr.
Oration, pronounced at Lancaster,
July 4, 1806, in commemoration of
the anniversary of American independence. By Samuel Brazer, junior ...
Published at the unanimous request of
the company, engaged in the celebration. Worcester [Mass.] Printed at
the press of the National aegio, by
Samuel Cotting. July 1806.
24 p.   22 1/2 cm.

1454 Breck, Robert L.
The habeas corpus, and martial law.
By Robert L. Breck. Prepared for
the Danville quarterly review for December, 1861. Cincinnati, R.H. Collins, printer, 1862.
39 p.   21 1/2 cm.

1455 Breck, Samuel, 1771-1862.
Address delivered before the Block-
ley and Merion agricultural society,
on Saturday, September 29th, 1828,
on the on [!] their late president,
the Hon. Richard Peters. By Samuel
Breck ... Philadelphia, Printed by
Lydia R. Bailey, 1828.
27 p.   21 1/2 cm.

1456 Breck, Samuel, 1771-1862.
Discourse before the Society of
the sons of New England of the city
and county of Philadelphia, on the
history of the early settlement of
their country; being their first anniversary. Delivered December 21, 1844,
by their president, Samuel Breck. Philadelphia, J.C. Clark, printer, 1845.
44 p.   23 cm.

1457   Breck, Samuel, 1771-1862.
         Historical sketch of continental
       paper money. By Samuel Breck. Phil-
       adelphia. Printed by J.C. Clark;
       reprinted by A.C. Kline, 1863.
         cover-title, 33, [1] p.   23 cm.

1458   Breck, Samuel, 1771-1862.
         Sketch of the internal improve-
       ments already made by Pennsylvania;
       with observations upon her physical
       and fiscal means for their extension;
       particularly as they have reference
       to the future growth and prosperity
       of Philadelphia. Illustrated by a
       map of the state of Pennsylvania:
       2d ed., rev. and enl. By Samuel
       Breck ... Philadelphia, M. Thomas,
       1818.
         2 p., 1., [3]-81, [1] p.   map.
       23 1/2 cm.

1459   Breckinridge, Robert Jefferson, 1880-
       1871.
         An address delivered before the
       Colonization society of Kentucky,
       at Frankfort, on the 6th day of
       January, 1831. By Robert J. Breckin-
       ridge ... Frankfort, K., A.G.
       Hodges, printer, 1831.
         24 p.   22 cm.

1460   Breckinridge, Robert J[efferson] 1800-
       1871.
         ... The civil war: its nature and
       end, by the Rev. Robert J. Breckin-
       ridge ... Reprinted from the Dan-
       ville quarterly review, for Dec., 1861.
       Cincinnati, Office of the Danville
       review, 1861.
         cover-title, 639-672 p.   23 1/2 cm.

1461 Breckinridge, Robert Jefferson, 1800-
1871.
A discourse on the formation and
development of the American mind.
Delivered before the literary socie-
ties of Lafayette college, at Easton,
Pa., on the 20th September 1837.
And now published at their request
... By Robert J. Breckinridge ...
Baltimore, R.J. Matchett, printer,
1837.
40 p.   20 1/2 cm.

1462 [Breckinridge, Robert Jefferson] 1801-
1871
The nation's success and gratitude.
[The substance of a discourse delivered in Danville, Ky., on the 26th
of November, 1863, the day of national thanksgiving and prayer] Philadelphia, H.B. Ashmead, printer, 1864.
cover-title, 22 p.   21 1/2 cm.

1463 Breckinridge, Robert Jefferson, 1800-
1871.
Our country: its peril and its
deliverance. From advance sheets of
the Danville quarterly review, for
March, 1861. By the Rev. Robert J.
Breckinridge ... Cincinnati, At the
office of the Danville review, 1861.
cover-title, 43 p.   23 cm.

1464 Breckinridge, Robert Jefferson, 1800-
1871.
Speech of Robert J. Breckinbridge,
delivered in the courthouse yard at
Lexington, Ky., on the 12th day of
October, 1840, in reply to the "speech
of Robert Wickliffe, delivered in the

court-house in Lexington, on the 10th
day of August, 1840, upon the occasion
of resigning his seat as senator from
the county of Fayette"; and in defence of his personal character, his
political principles and his religious connexions. More particularly
in regard to the questions of the power of the legislature on the subject
of slavery, of the importation of
slaves, of abolitionism, of British
influence, of religious liberty, etc.
Lexington, Ky., N.L. & J.W. Finnell,
printers, 1840.
    iv, [5]-32 p.   20 1/2 cm.

1466 Breckinridge, Robert Jefferson, 1800-
     1871.
     ... "State of the country." By
     the Rev. Robert J. Breckinridge
     ... Cincinnati, Office of the Dan-
     ville review, 1861.
     [i], 292-348 p.   23 1/2 cm.

1467 Breckinridge, Robert Jefferson, 1801-
     1871.
     The third defence of Robert J.
     Breckinridge against the calumnies
     of Robert Wickliffe ... Baltimore,
     Printed by R.J. Matchett, 1843.
     cover-title, [3]-90, p.   23 cm.

1468 Breed, William Pratt, 1816-1889.
     Faith and patience. A sermon for
     the times, by Rev. William P. Breed.
     Preached in the West Spruce street
     Presbyterian church, Philadelphia,
     Thanksgiving morning, November 27,
     1862. Repeated, by request, Febru-
     ary 8, 1863. Philadelphia, J.
     Alexander, printer, 1863.

2 p. 1., [3]-25 p.   22 1/2 cm.

1469 Breed, William Pratt, 1816-1889.
    The lights which God hath shewed
us. A Thanksgiving discourse, delivered Nov. 28, 1861, in the West Spruce
street Presbyterian church, Philadelphia, by Rev. W.P. Breed ... Philadelphia, J. Alexander, printer, 1861.
    26 p.   22 cm.

1470 Breed, William Pratt, 1816-1889.
    The national nest-stirring. A dis-
course on the times, delivered in the
West Spruce St. Presbyterian church
... May 5, 1861, by Rev. William P.
Breed ... Philadelphia, H.B. Ashmead,
printer, 1861.
    15 p.   22 cm.

1471 Breese, Sidney, 1800-1878.
    Speech of Hon. S. Breese, of Illi-
nois, on the Oregon question. Delivered in the Senate of the United
States, Monday, March 2, 1846. Washington, Printed at the office of Blair
and Rives, 1846.
    22 p.   21 1/2 cm.

1472 Breese, Sidney, 1800-1878.
    Speech of Mr. Breese, of Illinois,
on the Mexican question, and the ten
regiment bill. Delivered in the
Senate of the United States, Monday,
February 14, 1848. Washington, Printed at the Congressional globe office,
1848.
    14 p.   25 cm.

1473 Bremer, Fredrika, 1801-1865.

The homes of the New world; impressions of America. By Fredrika Bremer. Tr. by Mary Howitt ... New York, Harper & brothers, 1853.
2 v. 19 1/2 cm.

1474 [Brent, Henry Johnson] 1811-1880.
Was it a ghost? The murders in Bussey's wood. An extraordinary narrative. Boston, Loring [^{C}1868]
vi p., 1 l., 9-143 p. front. map. 20 1/2 cm.

1475 Brent, John Carroll.
Letters on the National institute, Smithsonian legacy, the fine arts, and other matters connected with the interests of the District of Columbia. By John Carroll Brent. Washington, J. & G.S. Gideon, 1844.
90 p. 22 1/2 cm.

1476 Brenton, Edward Pelham, 1774-1839.
Life and correspondence of John, earl of St. Vincent ... by Edward Pelham Brenton ... London, H. Colburn, 1838.
2 v. fronts. (v. 1: port.; v. 2; map) 21 1/2 cm.

1477 Brenton, Edward Pelham, 1774-1839.
The naval history of Great Britain, from the year MDCCLXXXIII. to MDCCCXXXVI. By Edward Pelham Brenton ... A new and greatly improved ed., illustrated with portraits, plans, etc. ... London, H. Colburn, 1837.
2 v. fronts., plates (1 fold.) fold. map, fold. plans. 23 1/2 cm.

1478   Brents, John A.
        The patriots and guerillas of East
Tennessee and Kentucky. The sufferings of the patriots. Also the experience of the author as an officer in
the Union army. Including sketches
of noted guerillas and distinguished
patriots. By Major J.A. Brents. New
York, J.A. Brents, 1863.
        171 p. plates. 19 cm.

1479   Brereton, John, fl. 1603.
        A briefe and true relation of the
discouerie of the north part of Virginia; being a most pleasant, fruit-
full and commodious soile: made this
present yeere 1602, by Captaine Bartholomew Gosnold, Captaine Bartholow-
mew Gilbert, and diuers other gentlemen their associate ... Written by
M. Iohn Brereton ... Whereunto is annexed a treatise, conteining important inducements for the planting in
those parts, and finding a passage
that way to the South Sea, and China.
Written by M. Edward Hayes ... Londini, impensis Geor. Bishop, 1602.
        24 p.   24 1/2 cm.

1480   Brereton, John A.
        Florae columbianae prodromus,
exhibens enumerationem plantarum
quae hactenus exploratae sunt; or A
prodromus of the Flora columbiana,
exhibiting a list of all the plants
which have as yet been collected.
Comp. by John A. Brereton ... Washington, Printed by J. Elliot, 1830.
        86 p.   17 cm.

1481   Bressani, Francesco Giuseppe, 1612-1672.

Breve relations d'alevne missioni
de' PP, della Compagnia di Giesù
nella Nuona Francia, del P. Francesco
Gioseppe Bressani ... Macerata,
Heredi d'A. Grisei, 1653.
2 p. l., 127, [1] p.   20 1/2 cm.

1482   Bressani, Francesco Giuseppe, 1612-1672.
Relation abrégée, de quelques missions des pères de la Compagnie de
Jésus dans la Nouvelle-France, par le
R.P.F.-J. Bressany, de la même compagnie. Tr. de l'italien et augmenté
d'un avant-propos, de la biographie
de l'auteur, et d'un grand nombre
de notes et de gravures, par le R.P.F.
Martin, de la même compagnie. Montréal, Des presses à vapeur de J.
Lovell, 1852.
336 p. illus., plates, fold.
maps, fold. diagr.   22 1/2 cm.

1483   Brett, William Henry, 1818-1886.
The Indian tribes of Guiana; their
condition and habits. With researches
into their past history, superstitions,
legends, antiquities, languages, &c.
By the Rev. W.H. Brett ... London,
Bell and Daldy, 1868.
xiii p., 2 l., [3]-500 p. illus.,
19 pl. (8 col., incl. front.) fold.
map.   23 cm.

1484   [Breugel, Gaspard Philippe Charles van]
1789-1888.
Dagverhaal van eene reis naar
Paramaribo en verdere omstreken in
de kolonie Suriname. Amsterdam,
C.G. Sulpke, 1842.
vi, 121, [1] p.   22 cm.

1485 Brevoort, James Carson, 1818-1887.
        History and its sources: an ad-
dress read before the Long Island historical society at the annual meeting
May 7th, 1868, by James Carson Brevoort ... Brooklyn [Union steam
presses] 1868.
        23 p.   28 1/2 cm.

1486 Brewer, Thomas Mayo, 1814-1880.
        ... North American oölogy. By
Thomas M. Brewer ...   Part I.--
Raptores and Fissirostres ... [Wash-
ington, Smithsonian institution, 1857]
        viii, 132 p. v pl.   32 1/2 cm.

1487 Brewer, William A
        Remarks of Mr. Brewer, of Cambridge,
before the joint special committee of
the legislature, on the subject of the
liquor law, at the public hearing in
the hall of the House of Representatives, Tuesday, p.m. March 15, 1853.
Boston, C.C.P. Moody, printer [1853]
        12 p.   18 1/2 cm.

1488 Brewster, Charles Warren, 1802-1868.
        Rambles about Portsmouth. Sketches
of persons, localities, and incidents
of two centuries: principally from
tradition and unpublished documents.
By Charles W. Brewster ... Portsmouth, N.H., C.W. Brewster & son,
1859-69.
        2 v.   23 cm.

1489 Brewster, Francis E.
        The philosophy of human nature.
By Francis E. Brewster ... Philadelphia, Getz & Buck, 1851.

viii p., 1 1., [25]-471 p.   20 cm.

1490   Brewster, Francis E.
       Slavery and the Constitution. Both
       sides of the question. By Francis
       E. Brewster. Philadelphia, 1850.
       24 p.   22 cm.

1491   Brewster, Jarvis.
       An exposition of the treatment of
       slaves in the southern states, partic-
       ularly in the states of Maryland, Vir-
       ginia, North Carolina, South Carolina
       and Georgia; together with a system
       of reformation recommended. By Jar-
       vis Brewster ...   Printed by D. & J.
       Fitz Randolph, N. Brunswick [N.J.]
       1815.
       24 p.   21 cm.

1492   Brewster, Mrs. Martha, fl. 1757.
       Poems on divers subjects ...   By
       Martha Brewster, of Lebanon. New-
       London printed: Boston re-printed:
       and sold by Edes & Gill, at their
       printing-office next to the prison
       in Queen-street [1757]
       35 p.   20 1/2 cm.

1493   Briano, Giorgio.
       Cristoforo Colombo; trilogia, di
       Giorgio Briano; parte prima, rappre-
       sentata per la prima volta in Torina
       dalla Drammatica compagnia reale, le
       sere del 24, 25 e 26 gennaio 1842
       ...   Torino, Tip. Fratelli Castellaz-
       zo, 1842.
       viii, [2], [11]-120 p.   22 cm.

1494   Brice, John, ed.

333

A supplement to the Selection of
all the laws of the United States, now
in force, relative to commercial subjects, with marginal notes & references to the same, classed under separate heads, including in continuation,
all the laws passed during the third
session of the Thirteenth, and the
first session of the Fourteenth Congress of the United States. By John
Brice ... Baltimore: Published by
the editor. For sale by Neal, Wills
& Cole, J.J. Harrod, E.J. Coale, &
F. Lucas. R.J. Matchett, printer,
1816.
80 p.   23 cm.

1495   Bridel, Jean Louis, 1759-1821.
Le pour et le contre; ou, Avis à
ceux qui se proposent de passer dans
les États-Unis d'Amérique. Suivi
d'une description de Kentucky et du
Genesy, deux des nouveaux établisse-
mens les plus considérables de cette
partie du nouveau monde ... Par L.
Bridel ...   Paris, Levrault, Schoell
& comp., 1803.
2 p. l., 162 p. fold. map.   18
1/2 cm.

1496   Bridge, Thomas, 1657-1715.
Jethro's advice recommended to the
inhabitants of Boston, in New-England,
viz. to chuse well-qualified men, and
haters of covetousness, for town
officers. In a lecture on Exodus 18.
21. 9th 1st month 1709.'10. By
Thomas Bridge, pastor of a church in
Boston ... Boston: Printed by John
Allen, for and Sold by Nicholas Boone,
at the Sign of the Bible in Cornhill.

1710.
32 p.   15 1/2 cm.

1497 Bridge, Thomas, 1657-1715.
       What faith can do. A brief essay,
on the nature & power of a true faith.
In some notes of a sermon, taken in
shorthand, when it was preached unto
a few Christians in a neighbourhood,
meeting in their usual course, at the
house of one of their neighbours; in
Boston. 15th. d. 6th m. 1712. By
Thomas Bridge, M.A. Pastor to one of
the churches in Boston. Published by
some of the hearers. Boston, Printed
& Sold by Timothy Green, at the Lower-
end of Middle-Street, 1713.
       1 p. 1., ii, 28 p.   15 1/2 cm.

1498 Bridgeport, Conn., Library association.
       Catalogue of the library of the
Bridgeport library association, Jan-
uary 1860. Bridgeport, Pomeroy &
Morse, printers, 1860.
       88 p.   23 cm.

1499 Bridges, George Wilson.
       The annals of Jamaica. By the Rev.
George Wilson Bridges ...   London,
J. Murray, 1827-28.
       2 v.   22 cm.

1500 Bridgewater, Mass.
       Celebration of the two-hundredth
anniversary of the incorporation of
Bridgewater, Massachusetts, at West
Bridgewater, June 3, 1856; including
the address by Hon. Emory Washburn,
of Worcester; poem by James Reed ...
and other exercises of the occasion.

With an appendix ... Boston, Printed
by J. Wilson and son, 1856.
viii, [9]-167 p. front., port.
24 1/2 cm.

1501 Bridgham, Samuel Willard, 1774-1840.
An oration, delivered in the Benevolent Congregational meeting-house in
Providence, on the Fourth of July,
A.D. 1798, in commemoration of American independence. By Samuel W. Bridgham ... Published by request. Providence: Printed by Carter and Wilkinson, and sold at their book-store.
1798.
12 p. 19 1/2 cm.

1502 Bridgham, Samuel Willard, 1774-1840.
An oration, on the propriety of
introducing the science of jurisprudence into a course of classical education. Pronounced in the Baptist meeting-house, in Providence, at the anniversary commencement of Rhode-Island
college, September 6th, A.D. 1797.
By Samuel W. Bridgham ... Published
at the request of the students. Providence, Printed by Carter and Wilkinson,
1797.
7 p. 19 1/2 cm.

1503 Bridgman, Thomas, b. 1795.
Epitaphs from Copp's hill burial
ground, Boston. With notes. By
Thomas Bridgman ... Boston and Cambridge, J. Munroe and company, 1851.
xxiii, [1] 252, 8 p. front., illus.
20 cm.

1504 Bridgman, Thomas, b. 1795, comp.

Inscriptions on the grave stones in
the grave yards of Northampton, and of
other towns in the valley of the Connecticut, as Springfield, Amherst,
Hadley, Hatfield, Deerfield, &c., with
brief annals of Northampton ... Trans
cribed by Thomas Bridgman. Northampton,
Mass., Hopkins, Bridgman & co., 1850.
    xii, [13]-227 p. front., port.
18 1/2 cm.

1505 Bridgman, Thomas, b. 1795.
    Memorials of the dead in Boston;
containing exact transcripts of inscriptions on the sepulchral monuments in
the King's Chapel burial ground, in
the city of Boston. With copious historical and biographical notices of the
early settlers of the metropolis of
New England. By Thomas Bridgman. Boston, B.B. Mussey & co., 1853.
    3 p. 1., [5]-339, [4], 17 p. front.
(double plan) illus.   20 cm.

1506 Bridgman, Thomas, b. 1795.
    The Pilgrims of Boston and their
descendants: with an introduction
by Hon. Edward Everett, LL.D.; also,
inscriptions from the monuments in
the Granary burial ground, Tremont
street. By Thomas Bridgman ... New
York [etc.] D. Appleton and company;
Boston, Phillips, Sampson & company,
1856.
    xvi, 406 p. front., illus., plates,
ports., fold. geneal. tab.   23 cm.

1507 A brief and perfect journal of the late
    proceedings and success of the English
    army in the West-Indies, continued

337

until June thc [!] 24th. 1655. Together with some quaeres inserted and
answered. Published for satisfaction
of all such who desire truly to be
informed in these particulars. By
I.S., an eye-witnesse ... London,
Printed, 1655.
27 (i.e. 29) p.   18 1/2 x 14 1/2
cm.

1508 A brief examination of the expediency
of repealing the naturalization laws.
Originally published in the Native
American newspaper, New Orleans.
New Orleans, 1840.
19 p.   25 1/2 cm.

1509 A brief extract, or summary of important arguments advanced by some late
distinguished writers, in support of
the supremacy of the British legislature, and their right to tax the Americans, addressed to the freemen and
liverymen of London, and recommended
to the serious perusal of every candid and dispassionate man. By a liv-
eryman. London, Printed for J. Wilkie, 1775.
8 p. 1., [13]-48 p.   21 cm.

1510 A brief outline of the rise, progress,
and failure of the revolutionary
scheme of the nineteen Van Buren
electors of the Senate of Maryland,
in the months of September, October,
and November, 1836 ... Baltimore,
Printed by Sands & Neilson, 1837.
90 p.   23 cm.

1511 ... A brief popular account of all the

338

financial panics and commercial re-
vulsions in the United States, from
1690 to 1857: with a more particular history of the two great revul-
sions of 1837 and 1857. By members
of the New-York press ... New York,
J.C. Hancy, 1857.
   cover-title, 59 p.   19 cm.

1512   Brief remarks on the slave registry
       bill; and upon a special report of
       the African institution, recommending
       that measure.
          (In The Pamphleteer. London, 1816.
       22 1/2 cm.   v. 7, p. [545]-595)

1513   A brief review of the rise and progress,
       services and sufferings, of New Eng-
       land, especially the province of
       Massachuset's-Bay.   Humbly submitted
       to the consideration of both Houses
       of Parliament.   London, Printed for
       J. Buckland, 1774.
          32 p.   21 cm.

1514   A brief sketch of the political impor-
       tance of the British colonies ...
       Edinburgh, Bell & Bradfute, 1826.
          1 p. l., 87 p.   22 cm.

1515   Briet, Philippe, 1601-1668.
          Parallela geographiae veteris et
       novae.   Auctore Philippo Brietio
       ...   Parisiis, sumptibus Sebastiani
       Cramoisy et Gabrielis Cramoisy, 1648-
       49.
          3 v.   maps (partly fold.) diagrs.
       25 cm.

1516   Brieven over het bestuur der colonien
       Essequebo en Demerary, gewisseld

tusschen de Heeren Aristodemus en
Sincerus. Nevens bylagen, tot deeze
briefwisseling, en eene voorreden van
den Nederlandschen uitgeever. Amsterdam, W. Holtrop, 1785-88.
12 v. fold. tables. 21 1/2 cm.

1517 Briggs, George Ware, 1810-1895.
An address delivered at the funeral
of Deacon William P. Ripley, in the
First church at Plymouth, Sunday
afternoon, Nov. 13, 1842. By George
W. Briggs. Plymouth, Printed by J.
Thurber, 1842.
16 p. 25 1/2 cm.

1518 Briggs, George Ware, 1810-1895.
Eulogy on Abraham Lincoln, by George
W. Briggs, D.D. June 1, 1865. With
the proceedings of the City council on
the death of the President. Salem,
Mass. [G.W. Pease, printer] 1865.
48 p. 23 cm.

1519 Briggs, John.
The history of Jim Crow. By John
Briggs. London, Smallfield and
son, 1839.
3 p. l., 321, [1] p. 20 1/2 cm.

1520 Brigham, William, 1806-1869.
An address delivered before the inhabitants of Grafton, on the first
centennial anniversary of that town,
April 29, 1835. By William Brigham.
Boston, Light & Horton, 1835.
49 p. 22 1/2 cm.

1521 Bright, Jesse David, 1812-1875.
Speech of Hon. Jesse D. Bright,

of Indiana, on the bill for the admission of Kansas as a state. Delivered in the United States Senate,
March 20, 1858. Washington, D. [C.]
Indianians' Democratic club, 1858.
15 p. 25 cm.

1522 Bright, John, 1811-1889.
A liberal voice from England. Mr.
John Bright's speech at Rochdale,
December 4, 1861, on the American
crisis ... New York, G.P. Putnam,
1862.
cover-title, 13 p. 24 cm.

1523 Bright, Jonathan Brown, 1800-1879.
The Brights of Suffolk, England;
represented in America by the descendants of Henry Bright, jun., who
came to New England in 1630, and settled in Watertown, Mass. By J.B.
Bright ... Boston, Printed by J.
Wilson & son, 1858.
xvi p., 2 l., 345 p. front.,
illus., plates, ports., map, plans,
cost of arms. 23 1/2 cm.

1524 Brighton, John George.
Admiral Sir P.B.V. Broke ... a
memoir. Comp. by Rev. J.G. Brighton
... chiefly from journals and letters
in the possession of Rear-Admiral Sir
George Broke-Middleton ... London,
S. Low, son, and Marston, 1866.
xvi, 488 p. front., plates (1
fold.) ports. 23 cm.

1525 Brightwell, Cecilia Lucy, 1811-1875.
Byepaths of biography by C.L.
Brightwell. London, New York [etc.]

T. Nelson and sons [1863]
2 p. 1., [9]-278 p. front., plates.
18 cm.

1526   Bril-gesicht voor de verblinde eyghen
baetsuchtige handelaers op Brasil.
By forme van advijs door een lief-
hebber van't vaderlandt geschreven
aen synen vriendt ... Gedrvckt ...
op het jaer, 1638.
7 p.   19 1/2 cm.

1527   Brimblecomb, Nicholas, *pseud.*
Uncle Tom's cabin in ruins! Triumphant defence of slavery! In a series of letters to Harriet Beecher
Stowe, by Nicholas Brimblecomb, esq.
...   Boston, C. Waite, 1853.
2 p. 1., 162 p.   18 cm.

1528   [Brinsley, John] *fl.* 1633.
A consolation for ovr grammar
schooles: or, A faithfull and most
comfortable incouragement, for laying
of a sure foundation of all good learn-
ing in our schooles, and for prosper-
ous building thereupon. More spe-
cially for all those of the inferiour
sort, and all ruder countries and
places; namely, for Ireland, Wales,
Virginia, with the Sommer Ilands,
and for their more speedie attaining
of our English tongue by the same
labour, that all may speake one and
the same language. And withall, for
the helping of all such as are desir-
ous speedilie to recouer that which
they had formerlie got in the grammar
schooles; and to proceed aright therein, for the perpetuall benefit of
these our nations, and of the churches

342

of Christ. [2d ed.] London, Printed
by R. Field for T. Man, 1622.
   8 p. l., 84, [2] p.   19 x 14 1/2
cm.

1529 Brinton, Daniel Garrison, 1837-1899.
     Notes on the Floridian peninsula,
its literary history, Indian tribes
and antiquities. By Daniel G. Brinton, A.B. Philadelphia. J. Sabin,
1859.
    viii, [13]-202 p.   17 1/2 cm.

1530 Brisbane, Albert, 1809-1890.
     Social destiny of man; or, Asso-
ciation and reorganization of industry ... By Albert Brisbane. Philadelphia, C.F. Stollmeyer, 1840.
    xiv, [2], 480 p. pl.   19 cm.

1531 Brisbin, James Sanks, 1837-1892.
     The campaign lives of Ulysses S.
Grant, and Schuyler Colfax. By Gen.
James S. Brisbin. Cincinnati, C.F.
Vent & co.; Chicago, J.S. Goodman
& co., 1868.
    1 p. l., vii-x, 11-411, [4] p.
front., ports., illus., maps, plans,
18 1/2 cm.

1532 Brissot do Warvillo, Jacquos Piorro,
    1754-1793.
     The life of J.P. Brissot, deputy
from Eure and Loire, to the National convention. Written by himself.
Tr. from the French. 2d ed. London,
Printed for J. Debrett, 1794.
    2 p. l., 92 p. front. (port.)
21 cm.

1533 [Bristed, Charles Astor] 1820-1874.

... The cowards' convention. New
York, Loyal publication society, 1864.
cover-title, 16 p.   22 1/2 cm.

1534   Bristed, Charles Astor, 1820-1874.
       The interference theory of govern-
       ment. By Charles Astor Bristed ...
       New York, Leypoldt & Holt, 1867.
       109 p.   17 1/2 cm.

1535   Bristed, Charles Astor, 1820-1874.
       Now is the time to settle it. Sug-
       gestions on the present crisis. By
       Charles Astor Bristed. New York, M.B.
       Brown, printer, 1862.
       24 p.   18 1/2 cm.

1536   Bristed, John, 1778-1855.
       Les États-Unis d'Amérique; ou,
       Tableau de l'agriculture, du com-
       merce, des manufactures, des finances,
       de la politique, de la littérature,
       des arts, et du caractère moral et
       religieux du peuple anglo-américain;
       tr. de l'anglais de John Bristed ...
       Paris, A. Eymery, 1826.
       2 v.   20 1/2 cm.

1537   Bristed, John, 1778-1855.
       Hints on the national bankruptcy
       of Britain, and on her resources to
       maintain the present contest with
       France. By John Bristed. New York,
       E. Sargeant, 1809.
       1 p. l., [viii]-ix, [v]-xii, 688
       p.   22 cm.

1538   Bristol County (Mass.) agricultural
       society.
       Transactions. Boston, 18
       v.   23 1/2 cm.

1539 Britannia major: the new scheme, or es-
      say, for discharging the debts, improv-
      ing the lands, and enlarging the trade,
      of the British dominions in Europe and
      America ... London, J. Noon, 1732.
         viii, 70 p.   20 1/2 cm.

1540 Britannia triumphant: or, An account of
      the sea-fights and victories of the
      English nation, from the earliest
      times, down to the conclusion of the
      late war ... To which is prefixed a
      large introduction, containing the
      history of navigation, from the earli-
      est accounts to the present time; with
      the lives of the most celebrated ad-
      mirals. By a society of naval gentle-
      men ... A new ed. London, Sold by
      R. James [etc.] 1777.
         276 p. front., port.   22 cm.

1541 British North America: comprising Cana-
      da, British central North America,
      British Columbia, Vancouver's is-
      land, Nova Scotia and Cape Breton,
      New Brunswick, Prince Edward's island,
      Newfoundland and Labrador ...   Lon-
      don, The Religious tract society
      [186-?]
         viii, 370 p. 2 fold. maps (incl.
      front.)   17 1/2 cm.

1542 Brito Freire, Francisco de.
         Nova Lusitania, historia da guerra
      brasilica, a purissima alma e sav-
      dosa memoria do serenissimo principe
      dom Theodosio, principe de Portvgal,
      e principe do Brasil. Por Francisco
      de Brito Freyre. Decada primeira.
      Lisboa, J. Gabram, 1675.

9 p. 1., 460 p., 4 1., 64, [39] p.
35 cm.

1543 Brito Freire, Francisco de.
Viage da armada da companhia do
commercio, e frotas do estado do
Brasil. A cargo do general Francisco
de Brito Freyre. Impressa por man-
dado de el rey, nosso senhor. Anno
1655. [Lisboa, J. Galram, 1675]
4 p. 1., 64 p. 35 cm.

1544 [Britton, John] 1771-1857.
Sheridan and Kotzebue. The enter-
prising adventures of Pizarro, preceded by a brief sketch of the voyages
and discoveries of Columbus and Cor-
tez: to which are subjoined the histories of Alonzo and Cora, on which
Kotzebue founded his two celebrated
plays of The virgin of the sun and
The death of Rolla. Also varieties
and oppositions of criticisms on the
play of Pizarro: with biographical
sketches of Sheridan and Kotzebue. The
whole forming a comprehensive account
of those plays and the grand ballads
of Cora,--and Rolla and Cora, at the
Royal Circus, and Royal Amphitheatre.
... London, J. Fairburn [etc.] 1799.
viii, 144 p., 2 1. front. 20 1/2
cm.

1545 Brockett, Linus Pierpont, 1820-1893.
The life and times of Abraham Lincoln, sixteenth president of the
United States. Including his speeches,
messages, inaugurals, proclamations,
etc., etc. By L.P. Brockett ... Philadelphia, Bradley & co.; Rochester, N.
Y., R.H. Curran; [etc., etc.] 1865.

1 p. 1., 9-750 p. front. (port.)
plates.   22 1/2 cm.

1546 Brockett, Linus Pierpont, 1820-1893.
      Men of our day; or, Biographical
sketches of patriots, orators, statesmen, generals, reformers, financiers
and merchants, now on the stage of
action: including those who in military, political, business and social
life, are the prominent leaders of
the time in this country. By L. P.
Brockett ... Elegantly illustrated
with forty-two portraits from life.
Philadelphia, Penn'a, Cincinnati, O.
[etc.] Zeigler, McCurdy & co., 1868.
      xxiv, 17-653 p. front., ports.
22 1/2 cm.

1547 Brockett, Linus Pierpont, 1820-1893.
      Our great captains. Grant, Sher-
man, Thomas, Sheridan, and Farragut.
By L.P. Brockett ... New York, C.B.
Richardson, 1866.
      1 p. 1., [5]-292 p. illus. (maps)
5 port. (incl. front.)   19 1/2 cm.

1548 [Brockett, Linus Pierpont] 1820-1893.
      The philanthropic results of the
war in America. Collected from official and other authentic sources, by
an American citizen. Dedicated by
permission to the United States sani-
tary commission. New York, Sheldon
& co.; [etc., etc.] 1864.
      160 p.   15 1/2 cm.

1549 Brockway, Diodate, 1776-1849.
      A sermon, preached at Hartford,
before the honorable General assembly, of the state of Connecticut, on

the anniversary election, May 11,
1815. By Diodate Brockway, A.M.,
pastor of the church in Ellington.
Hartford: Printed by Hudson and Goodwin, 1815.
29 p. 23 1/2 cm.

1550 Brockway, Thomas, 1745-1807.
America saved: or, Divine glory
displayed, in the late war with Great-
Britain. A Thanksgiving sermon,
preached in Lebanon, Second society,
and now offered to the public, at
the desire of a number of the hearers.
By Thomas Brockway, A.M., pastor of
the church in said society ... Hartford, Printed by Hudson and Goodwin
[1784]
24 p. 19 cm.

1551 Brockwell, Charles.
The natural and political history
of Portugal. From ... 1090 down to
the present time ... To which is added, the history of Brazil, and all
other dominions subject to the crown
of Portugal in Asia, Africa, and
America. By Cha. Brockwell ... London, Printed for the author, 1726.
15 p. 1., 398, [22] p. pl., 2
fold. maps. 19 1/2 cm.

1552 Brodhead, John Romeyn, 1814-1873.
The final report of John Brodhead,
agent of the state of New-York, to
procure and transcribe documents in
Europe, relative to the colonial history of said state. Made to the
governor, 12th February, 1845.
Albany, E. Mack, printer, 1845.
1 p. 1., 374 p., 1 1. 24 1/2 cm.

1553   Brodhead, John Romeyn, 1814-1873.
        The government of Sir Edmund An-
dros over New England, in 1688 and
1689. Read before the New York
historical society, on Tuesday evening, 4th December, 1866, by John
Romeyn Brodhead. Morrisania, N.Y.
[Bradstreet press] 1867.
        2 p. l., 40 p.   23 1/2 cm.

1554   Brodie, Walter.
        Pitcairn's Island, and the island-
ers, in 1850. By Walter Brodie ...
Together with extracts from his
private journal, and a few hints
upon California; also, the reports
of all the commanders of H. M. ships
that have touched at the above island
since 1800. 2d ed. London, Whittaker
& co., 1851.
        iv, [5]-260 p. illus., pl., 2
port. (incl. front.)   19 1/2 cm.

1555   Brodigan, Thomas.
        A botanical, historical, and prac-
tical treatise on the tobacco plant,
in which the art of growing and cur-
ing tobacco in the British Isles is
made familiar to every capacity, as
deduced from the observation of the
author in the United States of America, and his practice in field cultivation in Ireland. By Thomas Brodigan, esq. London, Longman, Rees,
Orme, Brown & Greene [etc.] 1830.
        xv, 236 p.   22 cm.

1556   Brokesby, Francis, 1637-1714.
        Some proposals towards propagating
of the gospel in our American plantations. Humbly offerr'd in a letter

to Mr. Nelson, a worthy member of the
Society for propagating the gospel in
foreign parts. By Francis Brokesby,
B.D. To which is prefix'd, Mr. Morgan Goodwin's Brief account of religion in the plantations: with the
causes of the neglect and decay thereof in those parts. The 2d ed. To
which is added, a postscript and con-
tents. London, G. Sawbridge, 1708.
3 p. l., 30 (*i.e.* 28) p. 23 cm.

1557 Bromley, Clara Fitzroy (Kelly)
A woman's wanderings in the western
world; a series of letters addressed
to Sir Fitzroy Kelly, M.P., by his
daughter Mrs. Bromley. London,
Saunders, Otley, and co., 1861.
2 p. l., 299, [1] p. front.,
plates. 19 cm.

1558 Bromley, Walter.
An address delivered at the Free-
mason's hall, Halifax, August 3d,
1813. By Walter Bromley, late pay-
master of the 23d regiment Welsh
fusiliers. On the deplorable state of
the Indians. Halifax, A.H. Holland,
printer, 1813.
16 p. 21 cm.

1559 Bromley, Walter.
Mr. Bromley's second address, on
the deplorable state of the Indians,
delivered in the "Royal Acadian
school," at Halifax, in Nova-Scotia,
March 8, 1814 ... [Halifax] Printed
at the Recorder office, 1814.
55 p. 16 1/2 cm.

1560 Bromme, Traugott, 1802-1866.

Gemälde von Nord-Amerika in allen
beziehungen von der entdeckung an
bis auf die neueste zeit. Eine
pittoreske geographic für alle,
welche unterhaltende belehrung
suchen und ein umfassendes reise-
handbuch für jene, welche in diesem
lande wandern wollen. Von Traugott
Bromme ... Stuttgart, J. Scheible,
1842.
2 v. front. (port.) 87 pl. 22
1/2 cm.

1561 [Bromme, Traugott] 1802-1866.
Louisiana. Ein taschenbuch für
auswanderer und freunde der länder-
und völkerkunde. Baltimore, Md.,
C. Scheld und co., 1837.
4 p. 1., 54 p. 20 cm.

1562 Bromme, Traugott, 1802-1866.
Rathgeber für auswanderungslustige.
Wie und wohin sollen wir auswandern:
nach den Vereinigten Staaten oder
Britisch Nord-Amerika--nach dem land
jenseits der Felsengebirge oder dem
freistaat Texas ... oder ist es
besser, unsere kräfte den weniger
kultivirten theilen des deutschen
vaterlandes zu widmen? Eine
umfassende beleuchtung der bisherigen
deutschen auswanderung und aller
deutschen ansiedelungspläne, beschrei-
bung der in vorschlag gebrachten
auswanderungsgebiete und gewissen-
hafte schilderung derer vortheile
und nachtheile. Von Traugott Bromme.
Mit 17 karten und plänen. Stuttgart,
Hoffmann, 1846.
iv, 346, [1] p. fold. maps. (incl.
front.) 21 cm.

1563 [Bromwell, William]
      Locomotive sketches, with pen and
pencil, or, Hints and suggestions to
the tourist over the great central
route from Philadelphia to Pittsburg
... Philadelphia, J.W. Moore, 1854.
    192 p. incl. illus., plates. map.
18 1/2 cm.

1564 Brooke, Henry, 1703?-1783.
      Gustavus Vasa, the deliverer of his
country. Inscrib'd to His Excellency
General Washington, commander in
chief of the forces of the thirteen
United States of America ... Written by Henry Brooke ... Philadelphia,
R. Bell, 1778.
    3 p 1., [9]-88, [6] p.   20 cm.

1565 Brookes, Richard, *fl.* 1750.
      Brookes's Universal gazetteer, re-
modelled and brought down to the present time. By John Marshall, with numerous additions by the American editor,
and the population of every town, county, territory and state, according to
the census of 1840. Philadelphia,
E.H. Butler, 1843.
    2 p. 1., [9]-56, [4], [5]-816 p.
illus.   25 cm.

1566 ... Brookline directory ... v. 1- 1868-
19 Boston, Mass., W.A. Greenough &
Co., 1868-ᶜ19
    v. fold. maps.   24-26 1/2 cm.

1567 Brooklyn, *Charters.*
      An act to consolidate the cities
of Brooklyn and Williamsburgh and
the town of Bushwick into one municipal government, and to incorporate the

same. Passed April 17, 1854 ...
Brooklyn, I. Van Anden's steam presses, 1854.
   113 p.   23 cm.

1568   Brooklyn, *N. Y. Charters*.
     The charter of the city of Brooklyn,
and the special laws relating thereto; together with the ordinances for
the government of the city. Pub. by
order of the Common council. Brooklyn, G.C. Bennett, 1857.
   xv, 9 -312, iv p.   23 1/2 cm.

1569   Brooklyn. *Ordinances, etc.*
     Acts relating to the city of Brook-
lyn, and the ordinances thereof, together with an appendix, containing
the old charters, statistical information, *&c. &c.* Brooklyn, A. Spooner
& son, printers, 1840.
   283 p. incl. tables   22 cm.

1570   Brooklyn. *Ordinances, etc.*
     Ordinances of the village of Brook-
lyn.   [Brooklyn, G.L. Birch, printer, 1828?]
   40 p.   21 1/2 cm.

1571   Brooklyn. *Water works*.
     A report on the extent and charac-
ter of the district supplying water
to the city of Brooklyn, by Theodore
Weston, C.E. with a communication in
relation to the same, from James P.
Kirkwood, esq. engineer of the works.
And an analysis of the water of the
Jamaica reservoir, by Prof. A.K.
Eaton, chemist. Brooklyn, N.Y. [D.
Van Nostrand] 1861.

1 p. 1.,   5 -66 p. incl. illus.,
tables.   fold. map, fold. diagr..
24 cm.

1572   Brooks, Charles, 1795-1872.
       Address delivered in Oak-Grove
cemetery, Medford, Mass., September
6, 1866, at the consecration of the
monument erected in honor of the Medford volunteers, by Charles Brooks.
Boston, Press of J. Wilson & son,
1866.
       14 p.   23 cm.

1573   Brooks, Charles, 1795-1872.
       History of the town of Medford,
Middlesex County, Massachusetts,
from its first settlement, in 1630,
to the present time, 1855.   By
Charles Brooks ...   Boston, J.M.
Usher, 1855.
       viii, 576 p.   front., illus.,
plates, ports.   23 1/2 cm.

1574   Brooks, Charles, 1795-1872.
       The tornado of 1851, in Medford,
West Cambridge and Waltham, Middle-
sex County, Mass.   Being a report by
Rev. Charles Brooks, and reports by
other committees.   Boston, J.M.
Usher, 1852.
       72 p.   front.   15 1/2 cm.

1575   Brooks, Charles Timothy, 1813-1883.
       Aquidneck; a poem, pronounced on
the hundredth anniversary of the incorporation of the Redwood library
company, Newport, R.I.   August XXIV.
MDCCCXLVII.   With other commemorative
pieces.   By Charles T. Brooks.   Providence, C. Burnett, jr., 1848.

354

iv p., 1 l., [7]-63 p.   17 1/2 cm.

1576   Brooks, David, 1744-1802.
The religion of the revolution. A
discourse, delivered at Derby, Conn.,
1774; by David Brooks, A.M., upon the
causes that led to the separation of
the American colonies from Great Britain, and the establishment of a free
government. Rochester, N.Y., Press of
Curtis & Butts, 1854.
iv, [5]-13 p.   22 cm.

1577   Brooks, Edward, 1784-1859.
A correspondence between Edward
Brooks and John A. Lowell, with remarks by Edward Brooks, referring to
documents annexed. Boston, Printed
by S.N. Dickinson, 1847.
177, 72 p.   24 cm.

1578   Brooks, John, 1752-1825.
An eulogy, on General Washington;
delivered before the inhabitants of
the town of Medford, agreeably to
their vote and at the request of
their committee, on the 13th of January, 1800. By John Brooks ... Boston, Printed by Samuel Hall, no. 53,
Cornhill, 1800.
15 p.   21 cm.

1579   Brooks, Nathan Covington, 1809-1898.
A complete history of the Mexican
war: its causes, conduct, and consequences: comprising an account of the
various military and naval operations,
from its commencement to the treaty of
peace ... By N.C. Brooks ... Philadelphia, Grigg, Elliot & co.;

355

Baltimore, Hutchinson & Seebold, 1849.
xvi, [5]-558 p. incl. front. 11 pl., 22 port., 2 maps, 11 plans. 22 1/2 cm.

1580 Brooks, Nathan Covington, 1809-1898.
The history of the church, a poem: by N. C. Brooks, A.M. ... Baltimore, Pub. by the society, Woods and Crane, printers, 1841.
60 p. 18 1/2 cm.

1581 Brooks, Phillips, *bp.*, 1835-1893.
The life and death of Abraham Lincoln. A sermon preached at the Church of the Holy Trinity, Philadelphia, Sunday morning, April 23, 1865, by the Rev. Phillips Brooks ... Philadelphia, H.B. Ashmead, printer, 1865.
24 p. 23 cm.

1582 Brooks, Phillips, *bp.*, 1835-1893.
Our mercies of re-occupation. A thanksgiving sermon, preached at the church of the Holy Trinity, Philadelphia, November 26, 1863. By Phillips Brooks. Philadelphia, W.S. & A. Martien 1863.
32 p. 22 cm.

1583 Broom, Jacob, 1808-1864.
An address delivered at Castle Garden, Feb. 22, 1854, before the Order of united Americans, on the occasion of their celebration of the one hundred & twenty-second anniversary of the birthday of Washington, by Jacob Broom, esq. ... Pub. by the chancery O.U.A., state of New York. New York,

W.B. Weiss, printer, 1854.
19 p.   23 cm.

1584   Broom, Walter William.
An Englishman's thoughts on the
crimes of the South, and the recom-
pence of the North.   By W.W. Broom
...   New York, C.S. Westcott & co.,
printers, 1865.
24 p.   22 1/2 cm.

1585   Broomall, John Martin, 1816-1894.
Reconstruction.   Speech of Hon.
J.M. Broomall, of Pa., delivered in
the House of representatives, Jan. 8,
1867.   [Washington, McGill & Witherow,
printers, 1867]
8 p.   24 1/2 cm.

1586   Bross, William, 1813-1890.
Address of the Hon. William Bross
... on the resources of the far West,
and the Pacific railway, before the
Chamber of commerce of the state of
New York, at a special meeting, Tuesday, January 25, 1866.   New-York, J.W.
Amerman, printer, 1866.
30 p.   23 cm.

1587   Bross, William, 1813-1890.
America as a field for the exertions
of the Christian scholar.   An address
delivered before the alumni of Williams
college, by Hon. William Bross ... at
the commencement, Tuesday afternoon,
July 31, 1866.   Song of the old church
at Williamstown.   A poem, delivered
on the same occasion, by Rev. J. Clement French ...   Chicago, Printed at
the Tribune company's book and job
office, 1866.

55 p.   22 1/2 cm.

1588   Brossard, Alfred de.
        Considérations historiques et poli-
        tiques sur les républiques de La
        Plata dans leurs rapports avec la
        France et l'Angleterre, par m. Al-
        fred de Brossard ...   Paris, Guillau-
        min et cie., 1850.
        2 p. l., 471, [1] p.   21 1/2 cm.

1589   Brosses, Charles de, 1709-1777.
        Vollständige geschichte der schiff-
        arthen nach den noch gröstentheils
        unbekanten südländern, aus dem fran-
        zosischen des Herrn präsidenten de
        Brosse übersetzt, mit anmerkungen
        begleitet und mit verschiedenen zusä-
        tzen versehen von Johann Christoph
        Adelung ...   Halle, J.J. Gebauer,
        1767.
        xii, 668 p.   VI fold. maps.   25
        x 20 1/2 cm.

1590   Brotherhead, William, *ed*.
        The book of the signers: contain-
        ing fac-simile letters of the signers
        of the Declaration of independence.
        Illustrated also with sixty-one en-
        gravings from original photographs and
        drawings, of their residences, por-
        traits, &c., from the collections of
        an association of American antiquar-
        ies.   Ed. by William Brotherhead.
        Philadelphia, W. Brotherhead, 1861.
        viii, 114 p.   illus. (incl. fac-
        sims., ports.)   40 1/2 x 32 1/2 cm.

1591   Brotherhead, William.
        General Fremont, and the injustice
        done him by politicians and envious

military men. By W. Brotherhead ...
Philadelphia, W. Brotherhead, 1862.
10 p. 22 cm.

1592 Brothers, Thomas.
The United States of North America
as they are; not as they are generally described: being a cure for
radicalism ... By Thomas Brothers
... London, Longman, Orme, Brown,
Green & Longmans, 1840.
viii, 517 p. 22 1/2 cm.

1593 Brough, John, 1811-1865.
The defenders of the country and its
enemies. The Chicago platform dissected. Speech of Governor Brough,
delivered at Circleville, Ohio, Sept.
3 ... Cincinnati, Gazette co. printing house, 1864.
16 p. 23 cm.

1594 Brougham and Vaux, Henry Peter Brougham,
1st baron, 1778-1868.
Historical and political dissertations. By Henry, lord Brougham ...
London and Glasgow, R. Griffin and
company, 1857.
5 p. 1., 424 p. 19 cm.

1595 Brougham and Vaux, Henry Peter Brougham,
baron, 1778-1868.
Lord Brougham's speech upon the
Ashburton treaty, delivered in the
House of lords on Friday, 7th April,
1843. London, J. Ridgway, 1843.
1 p. 1., 70 p. 21 1/2 cm.

1596 Brougham and Vaux, Henry Peter Brougham,
1st baron, 1778-1868.

Speeches of Henry lord Brougham,
upon questions relating to public
rights, duties, and interests; with
historical introductions, and a critical dissertation upon the eloquence
of the ancients. Edinburgh, A. and
C. Black; [etc., etc.] 1838.
4 v.   22 1/2 cm.

1597   Brougham and Vaux, Henry Peter Brougham,
1st baron, 1778-1868.
Speeches on social and political subjects with historical introductions.
By Henry, lord Brougham ...   London
and Glasgow, R. Griffin and company,
1857.
2 v.   19 cm.

1598   Brownell, Henry Howard, 1820-1872.
The people's book of American history: comprising the New world.   By
Henry Howard Brownell ...   Hartford,
L. Stebbins [^c1854]
2 v. in 1.   col. plates, ports.
(part col.)   24 cm.

1599   Brownell, Henry Howard, 1820-1872.
The people's book of ancient and
modern history; comprising the Old
world: namely, the Jews, Assyria,
Egypt, Greece, Rome, Persia, India,
China, the Mahometans, Spain, Germany, France, England, Sweden and
Norway, the Netherlands, Denmark,
Portugal, Italy, Switzerland, etc.
By Henry Howard Brownell, A.M.   With
numerous coloured illustrations, by
eminent artists.   Hartford, L. Stebbins, 1851.
736 p.   pl., port.   25 cm.

1600   Brownell, Henry Howard, 1820-1872.
        War-lyrics and other poems. By
    Henry Howard Brownell. Boston, Tick-
    nor and Fields, 1866.
        viii, 243 p.   19 cm.

1601   Brownell, Thomas, *d.* 1872.
        Documents in the case of Thomas
    Brownell. [New York? 1855]
        cover-title, 14 p., 1 1.   22 1/2
    cm.

1602   Brownell, Thomas Church, *bp.*, 1779-
    1865.
        A sermon, addressed to the legis-
    lature of the state of Connecticut,
    at the annual election in New-Haven,
    May 1st, 1822. By Thomas Church
    Brownell ... New-Haven, Published
    by order of the legislature, J.
    Barber, printer, 1822.
        16 p.   24 cm.

1603   Browning, Charles, *b.* 1765.
        An appeal to the citizens of Mary-
    land, one of the United States of
    America. From the legitimate descen-
    dents of the Baltimore family. By
    Charles Browning ... Baltimore,
    Printed by T.R. Lusby, 1821.
        88 p.   22 cm.

1604   Browning, Samuel.
        Poems by Samuel Browning. Vol. 1.
    London, Printed by W.H. Green, 1846.
        xi, [3], [17]-320 p.   front.
    (port.) illus.   19 cm.

1605   Brownlow, William Gannaway, 1805-1877.
        A political register, setting forth

the principles of the Whig and Loco-
foco parties in the United States,
with the life and public services of
Henry Clay. Also an appendix personal to the author; and a general
index. By William G. Brownlow ...
Jonesborough, Tenn., Pub. at the
office of the "Jonesborough Whig,"
1844.
1 p. l., [v]-vii, [1], [9]-349 p.
illus.   21 1/2 cm.

1606   Brownson, Orestes Augustus, 1803-1876.
The American republic: its consti-
tution, tendencies, and destiny. By
O.A. Brownson, LL. D. New York, P.
O'Shea, 1866.
xvi, 439 p.   23 1/2 cm.

1607   Brownson, Orestes Augustus, 1803-1876.
The spirit-rapper; an autobiography.
By O.A. Brownson ... Boston, Little,
Brown and company; [etc., etc.] 1854.
xi, 402 p.   20 cm.

1608   Bruce, Hamilton, *comp.*
The warehouse manual, and general
custom house guide, with forms of entries, oaths, bonds, etc. ... Sched-
ule of the rates of storage, adopted
by the chamber of commerce of the
city of New York, provisions relative
to drawback, extracts from treasury
regulations, etc. Comp. and arranged
by Hamilton Bruce ... New York,
The author, 1862.
xvi, 17-216 p. incl. tables.   24
cm.

1609   Bruce, James C.
An address delivered before the

alumni and graduating class of the
University of North Carolina, at
Chapel Hill, on the afternoon of June
third, 1841, by James C. Bruce, esq.,
of Halifax, Virginia. Raleigh, Printed at the office of the North Carolina standard, 1841.
   26 p.   22 cm.

1610   Bruce, Lewis.
   The happiness of man the glory of
God. A sermon preached before the
Honourable Trustees for establishing
the colony of Georgia in America, and
the Associates of the late Rev. Dr.
Bray; at their anniversary meeting,
March 15, 1743, in the parish church
of St. Margaret, Westminster. By
Lewis Bruce ... London, Printed by
D. Browne, 1744.
   1 p. 1., 53 p.   22 1/2 x 17 1/2
cm.

1611   Bruce, Peter Henry, 1692-1757.
   Memoirs of Peter Henry Bruce, esq.,
a military officer, in the services
of Prussia, Russia, and Great Britain.
Containing an account of his travels
in Germany, Russia, Tartary, Turkey,
the West Indies, &c., as also several
very interesting private anecdotes
of the Czar, Peter I, of Russia. London, Printed for the author's widow,
and sold by T. Payne and son, 1782.
   6 p. 1., 446 p.   26 1/2 cm.

1612   Bruce, Peter Henry, 1692-1757.
   Memoirs of Peter Henry Bruce, esq.,
a military officer, in the services
of Prussia, Russia, and Great Britain.
Containing an account of his travels

in Germany, Russia, Tartary, Turkey,
the West Indies, &c., as also, several very interesting private anecdotes
of the Czar, Peter I. of Russia.
Dublin, Printed by J. and R. Byrn,
1783.
   xv, 527 p.   21 cm.

1613 Brunson, Alfred, 1793-1882.
      Prairie du Chien. Its present posi-
      tion and future prospects. Milwau-
      kee, Daily sentinel press, 1857.
      12 p.   12 cm.

1614 Brunt, Jonathan, *b*. 1760.
      Extracts, from Locke's Essay on the
      human understanding; and other writ-
      ers; containing a defence of natural,
      judicial, and constitutional rights,
      on the principles of morality, reli-
      gion, & equal justice, against the
      private and public intrigues of arti-
      ficial society. Together with a
      short account of the publisher's diffi-
      culties, intermixed with some political
      remarks. To which is added, an uni-
      versal prayer, for the conversion, to
      genuine Christianity, of the great fam-
      ily of mankind. Frankfort, Kentucky,
      Printed and sold by J. Brunt. Novem-
      ber, 1804.
      36 p.   18 1/2 cm.

1615 Brush, John C.
      A small tract entitled A candid
      and impartial exposition of the vari-
      ous opinions on the subject of the
      comparative quality of the wheat and
      flour in the northern and southern
      sections of the United States, with
      a view to develope the true cause of

the difference. To which are added
instructions showing how to improve
the character of the northern flour
to an equality with that of the
South; and preserve the latter from
that depreciation which, in some
places, it is of late so evidently
undergoing; in a letter from John C.
Brush ... to Samuel Latham Mitchill
... Washington, Printed by J. Gideon,
junior, 1820.
      52 p.   23 cm.

1616   Brush, Samuel.
         An address delivered at Canandai-
       gua, Ontario county, N.Y., February
       2, 1866. Before a public meeting of
       citizens. By Samuel Brush ... Canan-
       daigua, N.Y., Printed at the Ontario
       repository & messenger office, 1866.
         27 p.   21 cm.

1617   Bryan, Daniel, 1795-1866.
         The appeal for suffering genius: a
       poetical address for the benefit of
       the Boston Bard; and the triumph of
       truth, a poem. By Daniel Bryan. Wash-
       ington city, Printed for the author by
       Way & Gideon, 1826.
         2, xiii p., 1 l., [17]-80 p.   22
       1/2 cm.

1618   Bryan, Daniel, 1795-1866.
         Thoughts on education in its con-
       nexion with morals, a poem recited
       before the literary and philosophical
       society of Hampden Sidney college,
       Va. At the fifth anniversary meeting
       of the institution, held in Septem-
       ber, 1828. By Daniel Bryan. Richmond,

365

T.W. White, 1830.
iii, [4]-40 p.   21 cm.

1619   Bryan, Daniel, 1795-1866.
        A tribute to the memory of the
Rev. George G. Cookman: consisting
of a brief discourse; and The lost
ship, a poem on the fate of the steamer President: delivered in the Alexandria lyceum, June 15, 1841, by Daniel Bryan. Alexandria [Va.] Bell &
Entwisle, 1841.
        16 p.   23 1/2 cm.

1620   Bryan, George J
        Life of George P. Barker, with
sketches of some of his celebrated
speeches: the proceedings of the
Bar of Erie County on the occasion of
his death; and the funeral sermon of
John C. Lord, D.D. By George J. Bryan. Buffalo, O.G. Steele, 1849.
        viii, [9]-215, [1] p. incl. front.
(port.)   18 1/2 cm.

1621   Bryan, Hugh, 1699-1753.
        Living Christianity delineated, in
the diaries and letters of two eminent-
ly pious persons lately deceased; viz.
Mr. Hugh Bryan, and Mrs. Mary Hutson,
both of South-Carolina. With a preface by the Reverend Mr. John Conder,
and the Reverend Mr. Thomas Gibbons
... London, Printed for J. Buckland,
MDCCLX.
        xi, 171 p.   17 1/2 cm.

1622   Bryan, James.
        A plea for the establishment of
veterinary colleges in the United
States, being a lecture delivered

October, 1854, before the State agricultural society of Pennsylvania, at
Powelton, Philadelphia. By James
Bryan ... Philadelphia, J.M. Wilson,
1855.
16 p. 21 cm.

1623 Bryan, James, 1810-1881.
Progress of medicine during the
first half of the nineteenth century. Being an introductory lecture
to the spring session in the Philadelphia college of medicine. Delivered
March 17, 1851. By James Bryan ...
Published by the class. Philadelphia,
Grattan & M'Lean, 1851.
28 p. 23 1/2 cm.

1624 Bryant, Charles S.
A history of the great massacre by
the Sioux Indians, in Minnesota, including the personal narratives of
many who escaped. By Charles S. Bryant, A.M., and Abel B. Murch ... Cincinnati, R.W. Carroll & co., 1868.
xii, 13-504 p. 6 port. (incl.
front.) pl. 20 1/2 cm.

1625 Bryant, James Ray M'Corkle, 1802-1866.
Eulogium on Chief Justice Marshall,
delivered in the Unitarian church,
Washington city, on the 24th of September, 1835, by James R.M. Bryant,
at the request of the Union literary
society ... Washington, Printed by
J. Gideon, jr., 1835.
16 p. 24 1/2 cm.

1626 Bryant, William Cullen, 1794-1878.
The embargo; or, Sketches of the
times. A satire. The second edition,

corrected and enlarged. Together with
the Spanish revolution, and other
poems. Boston, Printed for the auth-
or by E.G. House, no. 5, Court street,
1809.
 35, [1] p.   19 cm.

1627 Bryant, William Cullen, 1794-1878.
       A funeral oration, occasioned by
the death of Thomas Cole, delivered
before the National academy of design, New-York, May 4, 1848. By William Cullen Bryant. Pub. by order of
the Council of the academy. New York,
D. Appleton & company; Philadelphia,
G.S. Appleton, 1848.
 42 p.   24 1/2 cm.

1628 Bryant, William Cullen, 1794-1878.
       Letters of a traveller; or, Notes
of things seen in Europe and America.
By William Cullen Bryant. New York,
G.P. Putnam; [etc., etc.] 1850.
 442 p.   20 1/2 cm.

1629 Bryant, William Cullen, 1794-1878.
       Voices of nature. By William Cullen
Bryant ... New York, D. Appleton and
company, 1865.
 91 p.   illus.   16 cm.

1630 Bryce, James Bryce, *viscount*, 1838-1922.
       The American commonwealth, by James
Bryce ... New ed., completely rev.
throughout, with additional chapters.
New York, The Macmillan company, 1910.
 2 v.   21 cm.

1631 Brydges, *Sir* Samuel Egerton, *bart.*,
       1762-1837.

Restituta; or, Titles, extracts,
and characters of old books in English literature, revived. By Sir
Egerton Bridges ... London, Printed
by T. Bensley for Longman, Hurst,
Rees, Orme, and Brown, 1814-16.
4 v. 22 cm.

1632 Buchan, David Stewart Erskine, *11th earl
of*, 1742-1829.
An account of the life, writings,
and inventions of John Napier, of
Merchiston; by David Stewart, earl of
Buchan, and Walter Minto, L.L.D. Illustrated with copperplates ... Perth,
Printed by R. Morison, junr. for R.
Morison and son and sold by G.G.J.
and J. Robinson, London, 1787.
vii, [9]-134 p. front. (port.) v
pl. 27 1/2 cm.

1633 Buchanan, Isaac, 1810-1883.
The relations of the industry of
Canada, with the mother country and
the United States, being a speech by
Isaac Buchanan ... together with a
series of articles in defence of the
national sentiments contained therein,
which originally appeared in the columns of the "Hamilton spectator" ...
To which is added a speech delivered
by him at ... London, Canada West
... besides an extended introductory
explanation, and an appendix containing various valuable documents. Ed.
by Henry J. Morgan ... Montreal,
Printed by J. Lovell, 1864.
551 p. front. (port.) illus. 21
1/2 cm.

1634 Buchanan, James, *pres. U.S.*, 1791-1868.

Mr. Buchanan's administration on the
eve of the rebellion. New York, D.
Appleton and company, 1866.
x, [9]-296 p.   24 cm.

1635 Buck, Edward.
Massachusetts ecclesiastical law.
By Edward Buck ...   Boston, Gould
and Lincoln; New York, Sheldon and
company; [etc., etc.] 1866.
viii p., 1 l., 15-310 p.   20 cm.

1636 Buck, William Joseph, 1825-
History of Buck's county, Pennsylvania. By William J. Buck. With an
appendix, containing a history of the
early settlement of the township of
Wrightstown. By Charles W. Smith,
M.D. Willow Grove, Pa., 1855.
118, 24 p. front., pl., ports.
22 1/2 cm.

1637 Buck, William Joseph, 1825-
History of Montgomery county within the Schuylkill valley: containing
sketches of all the townships, bor-
oughs and villages, in said limits,
from the earliest period to the present time; with an account of the Indians, the Swedes, and other early
settlers, and the local events of
the revolution; besides notices of the
progress in population, improvements,
and manufactures; prepared chiefly
from original materials: by William
J. Buck ... Norristown [Pa.] Printed by E.L. Acker, 1859.
v, [7]-124, iii, [1] p.   24 cm.

1638 Buckholtz, L   von.
Tactics for officers of infantry,

cavalry and artillery. Arranged and
comp. by L. v. Buckholtz ... Richmond, Va., J.W. Randolph, 1861.
121 p.   15 1/2 cm.

1639 Buckingham, Henry A.
Harry Burnham, the young Continental; or, Memoirs of an American
officer during the campaigns of the
revolution, and sometime a member
of Washington's staff. By Henry A.
Buckingham. New York, Burgess &
Garrett [1852]
256 p.   23 1/2 cm.

1640 Buckingham, Joseph Tinker, 1779-1861.
Specimens of newspaper literature:
with personal memoirs, anecdotes, and
reminiscences. By Joseph T. Buckingham ... Boston, C.C. Little and J.
Brown, 1850.
2 v. fronts. (ports.) illus.   20
cm.

1641 Buckingham, Samuel Giles.
A memorial of the Pilgrim fathers.
By S.G. Buckingham ... Springfield,
S. Bowles & company, printers, 1867.
52 p.   21 cm.

1642 Buckler, Thomas Hepburn, 1812-1901.
A history of epidemic cholera, as
it appeared at the Baltimore city and
county alms-house, in the summer of
1849, with some remarks on the medical topography and diseases of this
region. By Th. H. Buckler ... Baltimore, Printed by J. Lucas, 1851.
45, [1] p.   fold. front., fold.
maps, fold, plan, fold. tables.   22
1/2 cm.

1643 Buckminster, Joseph, 1751-1812.
Religion and righteousness the bas-
is of national honor and prosperity.
A sermon, preached to the North and
South parishes in Portsmouth, frater-
nally united in observance of the 22d
February, 1800: the day appointed by
Congress to pay tributary respect to
the memory of Gen. Washington. By
Joseph Buckminster, A.M. Portsmouth,
New-Hampshire, Printed at the United
States' oracle-office, by Charles
Peirce. 1800.
28 p.   23 x 13 1/2 cm.

1644 Buckminster, Joseph Stevens, 1784-1812.
Extract from a discourse by the
Rev. J.S. Buckminster, preached in
the church in Brattle square, Boston,
October, 1811, the Sabbath after the
interment of Hon. James Bowdoin. Albany, Printed by J. Munsell, 1848.
8 p.   25 cm.

1645 Buckminster, Joseph Stevens, 1784-1812.
A sermon, delivered at the interment of the Reverend William Emerson,
pastor of the First Church of Christ
in Boston, who died May 12, 1811, in
the forty-third year of his age. By
Joseph Stevens Buckminster ... Boston: Printed by Joseph T. Buckingham, Winter-street, 1811.
24 p.   22 cm.

1646 Buckminster, Joseph Stevens, 1784-1812.
A sermon preached at the church in
Brattle street, Boston, December 18th,
1808. The Lord's day after the pub-
lick funeral of His Excellency James
Sullivan, governour of the commonwealth

of Massachusetts. By Joseph S. Buckminster ... Boston, J. Belcher, printer, State Street. 1809.
    41 p. 23 cm.

1647 Buckner, Aylett, 1828-1864.
    Speech of Aylett Buckner, of Ken-
tucky, on the propriety of organizing governments for the territories.
Delivered in the House of representatives, Feb. 17, 1849. [Washington,
Towers, printer, 1849]
    16 p. 24 cm.

1648 Buckner, Henry F 1818-1882, *ed.*
    Mäskōke hymns. Original, collect-
ed, and revised. By H. F. Buckner
... and G. Herrod ... Marion, Ala.,
Domestic and Indian mission board of
the Southern Baptist convention, 1860.
    140 p. 12 1/2 cm.

1649 Budan, A.
    La Guadeloupe pittoresque; texte
et dessins par A. Budan. Paris,
Noblet et Baudry, 1863.
    3 p. 1., [3]-44 p., 1 1. 11 pl.
(1 fold.) 55 x 40 cm.

1650 [Budd, Thomas] *d.* 1698.
    A brief answer to two papers pro-
cured from friends in Maryland, the
one concerning Thomas Budds favouring
John Lynam, &c. the other concerning
his owning George Keith's principles
and doctrines. [Philadelphia, W.
Bradford, 1692]
    4 p. 18 1/2 x 14 1/2 cm.

1651 Budd, Thomas, *d.* 1698.
    Good order established in

373

Pennsylvania and New-Jersey, in America, being a true account of the country; with its produce and commodities there made in the year 1685. By Thomas Budd. A new ed., with an introduction and ... notes. By Edward Armstrong ... New York, W. Gowans, 1865. 111 p. 25 cm.

1652 [Budd, Thomas] *d.* 1698.
A true copy of three judgments given forth by a party of men, called Quakers at Philadelphia, against George Keith and his friends. With two answers to the said judgments. [Philadelphia, W. Bradford, 1692] 9, 2-7, [1] p. 18 x 14 1/2 cm.

1653 Budington, William Ives, 1815-1879.
The history of the First church, Charlestown, in nine lectures, with notes. By William I. Budington ... Boston, C. Tappan, 1845. 258 p., 1 l. front. (port.) 23 1/2 cm.

1654 Budington, William Ives, 1815-1879.
Our Puritan fathers, our glory: a sermon preached in commemoration of the 220th anniversary of the founding of the First church in Charlestown, Mass., Sunday, November 14, 1852. By William I. Budington ... Charlestown, McKim & Cutter, 1852. 32 p. 23 cm.

1655 Buel, Alexander,Woodruff, 1813-1868.
Speech of Hon. Alex. W. Buel, in defence of the Constitution and the union. Delivered at a public dinner given to him by his fellow-citizens,

at Detroit, November 19, 1850 ...
Washington, T. Ritchie, printer, 1851.
31 p.   23 cm.

1656   Buel, David, 1784-1860.
Troy for fifty years: a lecture,
delivered before the Young men's association of the city of Troy, on the
21st December, 1840. By David Buel,
jun. ... Troy, N.Y., N. Tuttle, printer, 1841.
35, [1] p.   21 cm.

1657   Buel, Jesse, 1778-1839.
The farmer's companion; or, Essays
on the principles and practice of American husbandry. With the address, prepared to be delivered before the agricultural and horticultural societies
of New Haven County, Connecticut, and
an appendix, containing tables and other matter useful to the farmer. By
the late Hon. Jesse Buel ... Boston,
Marsh, Capen, Lyon, and Webb, 1839.
303 p.   illus.   19 1/2 cm.

1658   Buell, Don Carlos, 1818-1898.
Statement of Major General Buell,
in review of the evidence before the
military commission, appointed by the
War department in November, 1862.
Campaign in Kentucky, Tennessee, northern Mississippi and north Alabama in
1861 and 1862. [n.p. 1863]
cover-title, 71, [1] p.   23 cm.

1659   Buell, P   L.
The poet soldier. A memoir of the
worth, talent and patriotism of
Joseph Kent Gibbons, who fell in the
service of his country during the

great rebellion. By P.L. Buell. With
an introduction by Nelson Sizer. New
York, S.R. Wells, 1868.
   48 p.   front. (port.)   19 1/2 cm.

1660   Buell, Samuel, 1716-1798.
   A faithful narrative of the remarkable revival of religion, in the congregation of Easthampton, on Long-
Island, in the year of Our Lord, 1764;
with some reflections. By Samuel
Buell, D.D. late minister of the gospel in that place. To which are added,
sketches of the author's life--memoirs
of his daughter, Mrs. Conklin [!], and
his son, Samuel Buell, which were annexed to the sermons published on the
occasion of their death. And, also,
An account of the revival of religion in Bridgehampton & Easthampton,
in the year 1800. Sag-Harbor: Printed by Alden Spooner. 1808.
   144 p.   front. (port.)   17 1/2 cm.

1661   Buell, Samuel, 1716-1798.
   A sermon, delivered at the ordina-
tion of the Reverend Aaron Woolworth,
A.M., to the pastoral charge of the
church in Bridge-Hampton, on Long-
Island, August 30, 1787. By Samuel
Buell, A.M., pastor of the church at
East-Hampton, Long-Island. Eliza-
beth-town, (New-Jersey) Printed by
Shepard Kollock, on Golden-Hill, 1788.
   46 p.   19 cm.

1662   Buenos Aires.
   Actas capitulares desde el 21 has-
ta el 25 de mayo de 1810, en Buenos-
Aires. 1. ed. Buenos-Aires,

Imprenta del estado, 1836.
1 p. l., iv, [3]-55 p.   33 cm.

1663 Buffalo. Chamber of commerce.
Annual report ... including statistics of the trade and commerce of
Buffalo. Buffalo, 1884.
v.   23 cm.

1664 Buffalo. *Charters*.
Revised charter, by-laws, and ordinances of the city of Buffalo. Buffalo, Clapp, Matthews and co.'s steam
press, 1855.
1 p. l., 70, 77, xi p.   23 1/2 cm.

1665 Buhle, M.
Reisen durch die Vereinigten Staaten von Amerika. Hrsg. von M. Buhle
... Nürnberg, Raspe, 1808.
3 pts. in 2 v.   16 cm.

1666 Buhoup, Jonathan W.
Narrative of the central division,
or army of Chihuahua, commanded by
Brigadier General Wool: embracing
all the occurrences ... from the time
of its rendezvous at San Antonio de
Bexar till its juncture with Gen'l
Taylor, and its final disbandment at
Camargo--with an account of its suffer-
ings while passing through a barren
and hostile country--together with a
description of the battle of Buena
Vista, &c. and an interesting appendix.
By Jonathan W. Buhoup ... Pittsburgh,
M.P. Morse, 1847.
xii, [13]-168 p.   18 1/2 cm.

1667 Buist, George, 1770-1808.

A discourse occasioned by the death
of Brigadier-General John M'Pherson,
who was lost in the ship Rose in
bloom, shipwrecked on her passage
from Charleston to New-York, August
24th, 1806; delivered by desire, in
the Presbyterian church of Charleston,
S.C., November 30th, 1806, by the Rev.
George Buist, D.D. Charleston, Printed by W.P. Young, 1807.
42 p. 28 cm.

1668 Bulfinch, Benjamin S.
Georgia, a poem. To which are add-
ed, other metrical compositions, by
Benj. S. Bulfinch ... [Mount Zion,
Ga.] The author, 1820.
16 p. 22 cm.

1669 [Bulfinch, Thomas] 1796-1867.
The boy inventor; a memoir of
Matthew Edwards, mathematical-in-
strument maker ... Boston, Walker,
Wise & co., 1860.
viii, [9]-109 p. front. (port.)
pl. 17 cm.

1670 Bulfinch, Thomas, 1796-1867.
Oregon and Eldorado: or, Romance
of the rivers [Columbia and Amazon]
By Thomas Bulfinch ... Boston, J.E.
Tilton and company, 1866.
2 p. l., ix-xiv p., 1 l., 464 p.
20 cm.

1671 Bulkeley, Peter, 1583-1659.
The gospel-covenant; or, The covenant of grace opened. Wherein are
explained; 1. The difference betwixt
the covenant of grace and covenant
of workes. 2. The different

administration of the covenant before
and since Christ. 3. The benefits
and blessings of it. 4. The condition. 5. The properties of it.
Preached in Concord in New-England, by
Peter Bulkeley ... The 2d ed., much
enlarged, and corrected by the author
... London, Printed by M. Simmons,
and are to be sold by T. Kembe and A.
Kembe, 1651.
7 p. l., 432, [9] p. 18 x 14 1/2
cm.

1672 Bulkley, Charles Henry Augustus, 1819-
1893.
Niagara. A poem. By Rev. C.H.A.
Bulkley. New-York, Leavitt, Trow &
co., 1848.
vi p., 1 l., [9]-191, [1] p. 19
1/2 cm.

1673 Bulkley, Charles Henry Augustus, 1819-
1893.
Removal of ancient landmarks: or,
The causes and consequences of slavery extension. A discourse preached
to the Second Congregational church
of West Winsted, Ct., March 5th, 1854.
By C.H.A. Bulkley ... Hartford, Press
of Case, Tiffany and company, 1854.
23 p. 23 cm.

1674 Bulkley, Edwin Adolphus, 1826-1905.
The uncrowned nation. A discourse
commemorative of the death of Abraham
Lincoln, sixteenth president of the
United States: preached in the First
Presbyterian church of Plattsburgh,
N.Y., April 19, 1865, by the pastor,
Rev. Edwin A. Bulkley. Plattsburgh,
N.Y., J.W. Tuttle, printer, 1865.

16 p.   23 1/2 cm.

1675   Bullard, Henry Adams, 1788-1851.
        A discourse delivered before the
        Historical society of Louisiana, Jan-
        uary 13, 1836, by Henry A. Bullard
        ... New-Orleans, Printed by B. Levy,
        1836.
        30 p.   23 cm.

1676   Bullitt, John Christian, 1824-1902.
        A review of Mr. Binney's pamphlet
        on "The privilege of the writ of
        habeas corpus under the Constitution."
        By J.C. Bullitt. Philadelphia, J.
        Campbell, 1862.
        56 p.   23 cm.

1677   Bungay, George Washington, 1826-1892.
        The bobolink minstrel: or, Republi-
        can songster for 1860. Ed. by George
        W. Bungay ... New York, O. Hutchin-
        son, 1860.
        iv, [5]-72 p.   15 cm.

1678   Bungay, George Washington, 1818-1892.
        Crayon sketches and off-hand takings,
        of distinguished American statesmen,
        orators, divines, essayists, editors,
        poets, and philanthropists. By George
        W. Bungay ... Boston, Stacy and
        Richardson, 1852.
        viii, [9]-156 p.   19 1/2 cm.

1679   Bungay, George Washington, 1818-1892.
        Pen and ink portraits of the sena-
        tors, assemblymen, and state officers,
        of the state of New York. By G.W.
        Bungay ... Albany, J. Munsell, print-
        er, 1857.
        83, [1] p.   22 1/2 cm.

380

1680   Bunker Hill declaration. September 10,
            1840. [n.p., 1840]
            8 p.   22 1/2 cm.

1681   Bunn, Alfred, 1796?-1860.
            Old England and New England, in a
        series of views taken on the spot.
        By Alfred Bunn ... London, R. Bent-
        ley, 1853.
            2 v. col. front., fold. tab.   19
        cm.

1682   Bunnell, David C   b. 1793.
            The travels and adventures of David
        C. Bunnell, during twenty-three years
        of a sea-faring life; containing an
        accurate account of the battle on Lake
        Erie, under the command of Com. Oli-
        ver H. Perry; together with ten years'
        service in the navy of the United
        States. Also service among the Greeks,
        imprisonment among the Turks, &c. &c.
        Written by himself ... Palmyra, N.Y.,
        J.H. Bortles, 1831.
            199, [1] p.   fold. front., 2 pl.
        17 cm.

1683   Bunner, E.
            History of Louisiana, from its
        first discovery and settlement to the
        present time. By E. Bunner. New
        York, Harper & brothers, 1861.
            1 p. 1., [ix]-xi, [13]-267 p.
        16 cm.

1684   Burbank, Caleb, 1761-1849, *defendant*.
            Defence of Maj. Gen. Caleb Bur-
        bank, and the argument of the com-
        plainants, before the general court-
        martial, whereof Maj. Gen. Nathaniel
        Goodwin was president, held at

Worcester, on the 8th day of Sept.
1818, against charges preferred
against him, by Col. Prentice Cushing and others. Worcester [Mass.]
Printed by William Manning. Jan.
1819.
     iv, [5]-60 p., 1 1.   23 cm.

1685   Burbank, Caleb.
     Speech of Judge Burbank, in the
Senate of California, February 7th,
1861, on the union resolutions. Sacramento, J. Anthony & co., printers,
1861.
     19 p.   22 cm.

1686   Burch, Samuel.
     A digest of the laws of the corpor-
ation of the city of Washington, to
the first of June, 1823; with an appendix, containing the acts of cession from Maryland & Virginia, the
laws of the United States, relating
to the District of Columbia, the building regulations of the said city, &c.
Comp. by direction of the Council, by
Samuel Burch. City of Washington,
Printed by J. Wilson, 1823.
     363, [1], vii p.   3 fold. tab.
23 cm.

1687   Burchard, Jedediah.
     Sermons, addresses & exhortations,
by Rev. Jedediah Burchard: with an
appendix, containing some account of
proceedings during protracted meetings, held under his direction, in
Burlington, Williston, and Hines-
burgh, Vt., December, 1835 and January, 1836. By C.G. Eastman. Burlington [Vt.] C. Goodrich, 1836.

vi, [1], 119, [1] p.   17 1/2 cm.

1688   Burchard, Samuel Dickinson, 1812-1891.
          Causes of national solicitude. A
       sermon preached in the Thirteenth
       street Presbyterian church, New York,
       on Thanksgiving day, Nov. 25, 1847.
       By Rev. Samuel D. Burchard. New York,
       S.W. Benedict, 1848.
          23 p.   21 1/2 cm.

1689   Burchell, William Fitzer.
          Memoir of Thomas Burchell, twenty-
       two years a missionary in Jamaica.
       By his brother, William Fitz-er Bur-
       chell. London, B.L. Green, 1849.
          xii, 416 p. front. (port.)   20
       cm.

1690   Burchett, Josiah, 1666?-1746.
          A complete history of the most re-
       markable transactions at sea, from the
       earliest accounts of time to the con-
       clusion of the last war with France
       ... And in a more particular manner
       of Great Britain, from the time of the
       revolution, in the year 1688, to the
       aforesaid period ... By Josiah Bur-
       chett, esq. ... London, Printed by
       W.B. for J. Walthoe and J. Walthoe,
       junior, MDCCXX.
          28 p. 1., 800, [33] p. front.,
       9 fold. maps.   32 cm.

1691   Burchett, Josiah, 1666?-1746.
          Memoirs of transactions at sea dur-
       ing the war with France; beginning in
       1688, and ending in 1697 ... by Jos-
       iah Burchett ... London, J. Nutt,
       1703.
          22 p. 1., 408 p.   20 cm.

1692 Burder, George, 1752-1832.
          The Welch Indians; or, A collection
      of papers respecting a people whose
      ancestors emigrated from Wales to
      America, in the year 1170, with Prince
      Madoc, (three hundred years before
      the first voyage of Columbus), and
      who are said now to inhabit a beauti-
      ful country on the west side of the
      Mississippi [!] Dedicated to the Mis-
      sionary society by George Burder. Lon-
      don, Printed for T. Chapman [1797]
          35 p.   21 cm.

1693 Burdick, William.
          An oration on the nature and effects
      of the art of printing. Delivered in
      Franklin-Hall, July 5, 1802, before
      the Boston Franklin association. By
      William Burdick, vice-president of
      the society ... Printed by Munroe &
      Francis, Boston ... 1802.
          31 p.   21 cm.

1694 Burford, Robert, 1791-1861.
          Description of a view of the falls
      of Niagara, now exhibiting at the
      Panorama, Leicester square. Painted
      by the proprietor Robert Burford,
      from drawings taken by him in the
      autumn of 1832. London, Printed by
      T. Brettell, 1833.
          12 p.   fold. front. (plan)   21
      cm.

1695 Burge, William, 1787-1849.
          Jamaica. The speech of W. Burge,
      esq. Q.C., agent for Jamaica, at the
      bar of the House of commons, against
      the bill entituled "An act to provide

384

for the enactment of certain laws in
the island of Jamaica." Friday, 7th
June, 1839 ... [London, T.C. Han-
sard] 1839.
    40 p.   23 cm.

1696 Burges, Bartholomew.
    A short account of the solar sys-
tem, and of comets in general: together with a particular account of the
comet that will appear in 1789. By
Bartholomew Burges. Boston: Printed
and sold by B. Edes & son, no. 7,
State-street.--1789.
    16 p., 2 1. fold. map. 16 1/2
x 10 cm.

1697 Burges, Tristam, 1770-1853.
    Battle of Lake Erie, with notices
of Commodore Elliot's conduct in
that engagement. By Hon. Tristam
Burges. Philadelphia, W. Marshall
& co., 1839.
    xv, [17]-132 p. diagr. 18 cm.

1698 Burgess, Chalon, 1817-1903.
    The life and character of Abraham
Lincoln, with some lessons from his
death. A discourse delivered in the
M.E. church at a union meeting of
the Baptist, Methodist and Presbyterian congregations of Panama, April
30, 1865. By Rev. C. Burgess ...
Jamestown, N.Y., Bishop brothers,
printers, 1865.
    20 p. 21 1/2 cm.

1699 [Burgess, Ebenezer] 1790-1870.
    Address to the American society
for colonizing the free people of

colour of the United States ... November 21st, 1818. Washington: Printed by Davis and Force, Pennsylvania avenue. 1818.
    56 p.   21 cm.

1700   [Burgess, Ebenezer] 1790-1870, *comp*.
    Burgess genealogy. Memorial of the family of Thomas and Dorothy Burgess, who were settled at Sandwich, in the Plymouth colony, in 1637. Boston, Press of T.R. Marvin & son, 1865.
    2 p. l., [3]-196 p. front., plates (ports.)   23 1/2 cm.

1701   Burgess, George, *bp.*, 1809-1866.
    Poems of the Rt. Rev. George Burgess ... with an introduction by the Bishop of western New York. Hartford, Brown & Gross, 1868.
    viii, [2], 276 p.   20 1/2 cm.

1702   Burgoa, Francisco de, 1605-1681.
    Palestra historial de virtvdes, y exemplares apostólicos. Fundada del zelo de insignes heroes de la sagrada orden de Predicadores en este nvevo mvndo de la America en las Indias Occidentales. Consagrala alistada en orden regvlar a la emperatris de los cielos, y madre de misercordia Maria Señora Ntra. El M.R.P. mtro fr. Francisco de Bvrgoa, hijo de la mesma prouincia ... Con licencia de los svperiores. Impresso en Mexico. En la imprenta de Iuan Ruyz, Año de 1670. [México, Impr. del Museo nacional, 1903-04]
    xxii, 78 p. front.   33 1/2 cm.

1703   Burgoyne, John, 1722-1792.
          A letter from Lieut. Gen. Burgoyne
        to his constituents, upon his late
        resignation; with the correspondences
        between the secretaries of war and
        him, relative to his return to Amer-
        ica. London, Printed for J. Almon,
        1779.
          1 p. 1., 37 p.   21 1/2 cm.

1704   Burgoyne, John, 1722-1792.
          Orderly book of Lieut. Gen. John
        Burgoyne, from his entry into the
        state of New York until his surrender
        at Saratoga, 16th Oct. 1777. From
        the original manuscript deposited
        at Washington's head quarters, New-
        burgh, N.Y. Ed. by E.B. O'Callaghan,
        M.D. Albany, N.Y., J. Munsell, 1860.
          xxxiv, 221 p. front. (fold. map)
        pl., port.   21 1/ x 17 1/2 cm.

1705   Burgoyne, John, 1722-1792.
          A state of the expedition from
        Canada, as laid before the House of
        commons, by Lieutenant-General Bur-
        goyne, and verified by evidence; with
        a collection of authentic documents,
        and an addition of many circumstances
        which were prevented from appearing be-
        fore the House by the propagation of
        Parliament. Written and collected
        by himself ... London, Printed for
        J. Almon, 1780.
          viii, 140, lxii p., 1 l. front.
        (fold. map) fold. plans.   28 1/2
        cm.

1706   Burgoyne, Sir John Fox, bart., 1782-
        1871.

The military opinions of General Sir John Fox Burgoyne ... Collected and ed. by Captain the Honble George Wrottesley ... London, R. Bentley, 1859.
vii, 479 p. 22 1/2 cm.

1707 Burk, John Daly, *d.* 1808.
Bunker-Hill; or The death of General Warren; an historic tragedy. In five acts. By John Burk ... As played at the theatres in America, for fourteen nights, with unbounded applause ... New York: Printed by T. Greenleaf. M,DCC,XCVII.
55 p. 19 1/2 cm.

1708 Burke, Edmund, 1729?-1797.
A letter from Edmund Burke, esq; one of the representatives in Parliament for the city of Bristol, to John Farr, and John Harris, esqrs. sheriffs of that city, on the affairs of America. Bristol, Printed by W. Pine, 1777.
79 p. 20 1/2 cm.

1709 Burke, Edmund, 1729?-1797.
The speech of Edmund Burke, esq; on moving his resolutions for conciliation with the colonies, March 22, 1775, London, Printed for J. Dodsley, 1775.
2 p. 1., 65 p. 25 1/2 x 21 1/2 cm.

1710 [Burke, John] d. 1873.
The burden of the South, in verse; or, Poems on slavery, grave, humorous, didactic, and satirical. By

388

Sennoia Rubek [*pseud.*] New York, E.
Warner [1864]
96 p.   front.   23 1/2 cm.

1711   [Burke, John] *d.* 1873.
Stanzas to Queen Victoria, and
other poems. By Sennoia Rubek
[*pseud.*] New York, F.A. Brady, 1866.
206 p.   front.   23 1/2 cm.

1712   Burke, William, 1752-1836.
Memoir of William Burke, a soldier
of the revolution. Reformed from in-
temperance, and for many years a
consistent and devoted Christian.
Carefully prepared from a journal
kept by himself. To which is added
an extract from a sermon preached at
his funeral, by Rev. N. Miner. Hartford, Case, Tiffany, and co., 1837.
vi, 7-126 p.   16 1/2 cm.

1713   Burke, William, *fl.* 1805-1810.
Additional reasons, for our immediately emancipating Spanish America:
deduced, from the new and extraordinary circumstances, of the present
crisis: and containing valuable information, respecting the late important
events, both at Buenos Ayres, and in
the Caracas: as well as with respect
to the present disposition and views
of the Spanish Americans: being intended as a supplement to "South
American independence." By William
Burke ... 2d ed., enl. London, J.
Ridgway, 1808.
2 p. l., [vii]-xxxvi, 132 p.   20
cm.

1714   Burke, William, *M.D.*

The mineral springs of western Virginia; with remarks on their use, and the diseases to which they are applicable. The 2d ed., rev., cor. and enl. To which are added a notice of the Fauquier White Sulphur Spring, and a chapter on taverns, also a review of a pamphlet published by Dr. J.J. Moorman. By William Burke ... New York, Wiley and Putnam, 1846.

394 p. front. (fold. map) 16 1/2 cm.

1715 Burleigh, Joseph Bartlett.
The American manual; containing a brief outline of the origin and progress of political power, and the laws of nations; a commentary on the Constitution of the United States ... and a lucid exposition of the duties and responsibilities of voters, jurors, and civil magistrates; with questions, definitions, and marginal exercises ... Adapted to the use of schools, academies, and the public: by Joseph Bartlett Burleigh ... Philadelphia, Grigg, Elliot & co., 1848.

viii, 9-318, 55 p. 18 1/2 cm.

1716 Burleigh, Walter Atwood, 1820-1896.
Indian affairs. Speech of Hon. Walter A. Burleigh ... delivered in the House of representatives, February 9, 1869. Washington, F. & J. Rives & G.A. Bailey, 1869.

cover-title, [3]-14 p. 24 cm.

1717 Burleigh, William Henry, 1812-1871, *ed.*
The Republican pocket pistol, a collection of facts, opinions and arguments for freedom. Edited by

William H. Burleigh. no. 1-2, June-
July, 1860. New-York, H. Dayton,
1860.
  2 v. 15 cm.

1718 Burlingame, Anson, 1820-1870.
  An appeal to patriots against
fraud and disunion. Speech of Hon.
Anson Burlingame, of Massachusetts.
Delivered in the U.S. House of representatives, March 31, 1858. Washington, D.C., Buell & Blanchard, printers, 1858.
  8 p. 23 cm.

1719 Burmeister, Hermann, 1807-1892.
  Reise durch die La Plata-staaten,
mit besonderer rücksicht auf die
physische beschaffenheit und den
culturzustrand der Argentinischen
republik. Ausgeführt in den jahren
1857, 1858, 1859 und 1860 von dr.
Hermann Burmeister ... Halle, H.W.
Schmidt, 1861.
  2 v. front, 2 fold. maps. 22
cm.

1720 Burmeister, Hermann, 1807-1892.
  Reise nach Brasilien, durch die
provinzen von Rio de Janeiro und
Minas Geraës. Mit besonderer
rücksicht auf die naturgeschichte
der gold- und diamantendistriete,
von dr. Hermann Burmeister ... Berlin, Druck und verlag von G. Reimer,
1853.
  vii, 1 , 608 p. fold. map. 22
1/2 cm.

1721 Burn, Andrew, 1742-1814.
  Memoirs of the life of the late

Major-General Andrew Burn, of the
Royal marines; collected from his
journals: with copious extracts from
his principal works on religious subjects ... London, W. Winchester and
son, 1815.
2 v. front. (port.) 20 1/2 cm.

1722 Burnap, Uzziah Cicero, 1794-1854.
Bible servitude. A sermon, deliv-
ered in the Appleton-St. church,
Lowell, on the day of annual thanks-
giving, November 30, 1843. By U.C.
Burnap ... Lowell, A.E. Newton and
A.O. Ordway, 1843.
20 p. 22 1/2 cm.

1723 [Burnet, Jacob] 1770-1853.
Notes on the early settlement of
the North-western Territory. Cincinnati, Derby, Bradley & co., 1847.
2 p. l., [vii]-xvi, [17]-501 p.
port. 23 1/2 cm.

1724 Burnet, Matthias, 1749-1806.
An election sermon, preached at
Hartford, on the day of the anniver-
sary election, May 12, 1803. By
Matthias Burnet, D.D., pastor of the
First church in Norwalk. Hartford:
Printed by Hudson & Goodwin. 1803.
29 p. 21 1/2 cm.

1725 Burnet, Matthias, 1749-1806.
A sermon, preached the second Lord's
day after the death of his amiable
and excellent wife, Mrs. Ann Burnet,
who died in child-bed, July 7th,
1789. in the XXXVth year of her age.
By Matthias Burnet, A.M., pastor of
the First church in Norwalk,

Connecticut ... New-Haven: Printed
by Thomas and Samuel Green. MDCCXC.
24 p. 19 cm.

1726 Burnett, Alfred, b. 1823 or 4.
Incidents of the war: humorous,
pathetic, and descriptive. By Alfred
Burnett ... Cincinnati, Ricky &
Carroll, 1863.
x p., 1 l., 13-310 p. front.
(port.) plates. 18 1/2 cm.

1727 Burnett, Henry Clay, 1825-1866.
Force bill. Speech of Hon. Henry
C. Burnett, of Kentucky, in the House
of representatives, February 26, 1861.
[Washington, 1861]
8 p. 25 cm.

1728 Burnett, Peter Hardeman, 1807-1895.
The American theory of government
considered with reference to the
present crisis. By Peter H. Burnett ... New York, D. Appleton,
& co., 1861.
93 p. 23 cm.

1729 Burnett, Ward B.
Synopsis of a report made to the
president and directors of the Long
Island water works company, January,
1853. By Ward B. Burnett ... Williamsburgh [N.Y.] Printed at the
office of the Independent press, 1853.
16 p. fold. map. 22 cm.

1730 Burney, James, 1750-1821.
History of the buccaneers of America. By James Burney, F.R.S. captain in the royal navy. London,

Printed by L. Hansard & sons, for Payne and Foss, 1816.
xii, 326 p. 3 maps. 31 cm.

1731 Burnham, George Pickering, 1814-1902.
The history of the hen fever. A humorous record. By Geo. P. Burnham ... Boston, James French and company; New York, J.C. Derby: [etc., etc., 1855]
viii, 36, [9] 326 p. front. (port.) illus. 19 cm.

1732 Burnham, Richard, 1711-1752.
Pious memorials; or, The power of religion upon the mind, in sickness, and at death: exemplified in the experience of many divines and other eminent persons at those important seasons. Interspersed with what was most remarkable in their lives. By the late Mr. Richard Burnham ... With a recommendatory preface, by the Reverend Mr. James Hervey ... New ed. To which is now added, a large appendix, containing many valuable lives of ministers of the gospel, and other eminent Christians ... London, Printed for A. Millar, W. Law, and R. Cater, MDCCLXXXIX.
xvi, [17]-556 p. 21 cm.

1733 Burns, Robert, 1759-1796.
Poems, chiefly in the Scottish dialect. By Robert Burns, Philadelphia: Printed for, and sold by Peter Stewart and George Hyde, the west side of Second-street, the ninth door above Chestnut-street, M,DCC, LXXXVIII.
viii, [9]-304 p. 16 1/2 cm.

1734 Burnside, Samuel McGregore, 1783-1850.
      Oration, delivered at Worcester,
      on the thirtieth of April, A.D. 1813;
      before the Washington benevolent
      society of the county of Worcester,
      in commemoration of the first inaugu-
      ration of General Washington as pres-
      ident of the United States. By Sam-
      uel M. Burnside ... Worcester, Print-
      ed by Isaac Sturtevant, 1813.
        20 p.   23 cm.

1735 Burnyeat, John, 1631-1690.
      The truth exalted in the writings
      of that eminent and faithful servant
      of Christ, John Burnyeat, collected
      into this ensuing volume as a memor-
      ial to his faithful labours in and
      for the truth ... London, T. North-
      cott, 1691.
        4 p. 1., 20, 264 (*i.e.* 260) p.
      19 1/2 x 16 1/2 cm.

1736 Burr, Charles Chauncey, 1817 1883.
      The history of the Union, and of
      the Constitution. Being the sub-
      stance of three lectures on the col-
      onial, revolutionary, and constitu-
      tional periods of American history,
      with an appendix containing the Con-
      stitution of the United States, and
      the Virginia and Kentucky resolu-
      tions of '98. By C. Chauncey Burr
      ... 3d ed. New York, Van Evrie,
      Horton & co., 1863.
        iv, [4]-92, 4 p.   20 1/2 cm.

1737 Burr, Charles Chauncey, 1817-1883.
      Notes on the Constitution of the
      United States, with expositions of

the most eminent statesmen and jur-
ists. Historical and explanatory
notes on every article. By C. Chauncey Burr ... New York, J.F. Feeks
[1864]
   1 p. l., ii, [5]-95, [1], viii p.
19 1/2 cm.

1738   Burr, [William]
   Descriptive and historical view of
Burr's moving mirror of the lakes,
the Niagara, St. Lawrence and Saguer-
nay [!] rivers ... New York, Printed
by G.F. Bunce, 1850.
   iv, [5]-18 pp.   8 cm.

1739   Burrill, George Rawson, 1770-1818.
   An oration, pronounced at the Baptist meeting-house in Providence, on
Tuesday the seventh of January, 1800,
at the funeral ceremony on the death
of Gen. George Washington. By Col.
George R. Burrill. Providence: Printed by John Carter. [1800]
   15 p.   23 cm.

1740   Burroughs, Charles, 1787-1868.
   Memoirs and select papers of Horace
B. Morse, A.B. of Haverhill, N.H.,
who was drowned near Portsmouth har-
bour, June 22, 1825. By Charles Burroughs ... Portsmouth, N.H., Printed
by Miller and Brewster, 1829.
   vi, [7]-203 p.   17 1/2 cm.

1741   Burrows, E   J.
   The great rebellion of 1861. Twelve
months' history of the United States.
Showing what a republic can do. Skirmishes and battles. What the rebels
have done to destroy the Union.

The lessons of the year, etc., etc.
Collected and arranged by E.J. Burrows. Philadelphia, C. Sherman & son,
printers, 1862.
   60 p.   18 1/2 cm.

1742   Burrows, John Lansing, 1814-1893.
          ... A Christian merchant. A mem-
       oir of James C. Crane. By J. L.
       Burrows ... Charleston, S.C.,
       Southern Baptist publication society,
       1858.
          90 p.   front. (port.)   18 1/2
       cm.

1743   Burrows, John Lansing, 1814-1893.
          Palliative and prejudiced judg-
       ments condemned. A discourse deliv-
       ered in the First Baptist church, Rich-
       mond, Va., June 1, 1865, the day ap-
       pointed by the President of the Unit-
       ed States for humiliation and mourn-
       ing on account of the assassination
       of President Lincoln, together with
       an extract from a sermon, preached
       on Sunday, April 23rd, 1865, upon the
       assassination of President Lincoln.
       By J. Lansing Burrows, D.D. Rich-
       mond, Va., Office Commercial bulle-
       tin, 1865.
          12 p.   23 1/2 cm.

1744   Burton, *Sir* Richard Francis, 1821-1890.
          The City of the saints, and across
       the Rocky Mountains to California, by
       Richard F. Burton ... London, Long-
       man, Green, Longman, and Roberts,
       1861.
          x, [2], 707, [1] p.   front. illus.,
       plates, fold. map, fold plan.   22
       cm.

1745 Burton, Warren, 1800-1866.
        The scenery-shower, with word-paint-
      ings of the beautiful, the pictur-
      esque, and the grand in nature ... by
      Warren Burton ... Boston, W.D. Tick-
      nor & co., 1844.
        3 p. 1., 119 p.   15 1/2 cm.

1746 [Burton, Warren] 1800-1866.
        White slavery: a new emancipation
      cause, presented to the people of
      the United States. By the author of
      "The district school as it was."
      Worcester, M.D. Phillips; Boston, C.C.
      Little & co., [etc.] 1839.
        xi, [13]-199 p.   15 cm.

1747 Burton, William Evans, 1802-1860.
        Waggeries and vagaries. A series
      of sketches, humorous and descriptive.
      By W.E. Burton ... With eight origin-
      al illustrations by Darley. Phila-
      delphia, Carey & Hart, 1848.
        2 p. 1., 3-192 p. front., plates.
      18 cm.

1748 Burwell, William MacCreary, 1809-1888.
        Memoir explanatory of the Trans-
      union and Tehuantepec route between
      Europe and Asia. Prepared for the
      [Tehuantepec railroad] company by
      Wm. M. Burwell ... Washington,
      Printed by Gideon & co., 1851.
        36 p. fold. map.   22 1/2 cm.

1749 [Burwell, William MacCreary] 1809-1888.
        White acre vs. Black acre. A case
      at law, reported by J.G., esq., a
      retired barrister, of Lincolnshire,
      England. Richmond, Va., J.W.

Randolph, 1856.
251 p.   17 1/2 cm.

1750   Bushnell, Charles Ira, 1826-1883.
        An arrangement of tradesmen's cards,
political tokens, also, election med-
als, medalets, &c. current in the United States of America for the last sixty years, described from the originals,
chiefly in the collection of the auth-
or. With engravings. By Charles I.
Bushnell ... New York, Printed for
the author, 1858.
        4 p. 1., [vii]-x p., 1 1., [13]-118
p., 1 1.   4 pl.   23 cm.

1751   Bushnell, Charles Ira, 1826-1883.
        Crumbs for antiquarians, by Charles
I. Bushnell ... New-York, Priv.
print., 1864-66.
        2 v.   fronts., illus. (incl. fac-
sims.)   plates, ports.   25 1/2 cm.

1752   Bushnell, Charles Ira, 1826-1883.
        An historical account of the first
three business tokens issued in the
city of New York. By Charles I.
Bushnell. New York, Priv. print.,
1859.
        17 p.   front.   19 cm.

1753   [Bushnell, Charles Ira] 1826-1883.
        A memoir of Eli Bickford, a pa-
triot of the revolution. New York,
Priv. print., 1865.
        15 p.   front. (port.) pl.   23 1/2
cm.

1754   Bushnell, Charles Ira, 1826-1883.
        A narrative of the life and adven-
tures of Levi Hanford, a soldier

of the revolution. By Charles I.
Bushnell. New York, Priv. print.,
1863.
   iv, [5]-80 p., 1 1. 2 port.
(incl. front.)   25 1/2 cm.

1755   Bushnell, Horace, 1802-1876.
         The fathers of New England. An ora-
      tion delivered before the New England
      society of New-York, December 21,
      1849 and pub. at their request. By
      Horace Bushnell. New-York, G.P. Put-
      nam, 1850.
         44 p.   18 cm.

1756   Business directory of the principal
      southern cities. With a business
      register of northern firms who either
      have already, or desire to have, busi-
      ness relations with the Southern states.
      1866 and 1867. New York, Dunkley &
      Woodman; New Orleans, Blelock & co.;
      [etc., etc. C1866]
         453 p.   24 cm.

1757   Busk, Hans, 1815-1882.
         The navies of the world; their pres-
      ent state, and future capabilities.
      By Hans Busk ... London, New York,
      Routledge, Warnes, and Routledge,
      1859.
         xv, [1], 312, 127, [1] p. front.,
      illus., plates, plans.   18 cm.

1758   [Bustamante, Carlos María de] 1774-1848.
         Apuntes para la historia del
      gobierno del general D. Antonio
      López de Santa-Anna, desde princi-
      pios de octubre de 1841 hasta 6 de
      diciembre de 1844, en que fué depuesto

del mando por uniforme voluntad de
la nación. Escrita por el autor del
Cuadro histórico de la revolución
mexicana ... Mexico, Impr. de J.M.
Lara, 1845.
   1 p. l., iii, [2],460 p.   21 1/2
cm.

1759   Bustamante, Carlos María de, 1774-1848.
   Campañas del general d. Felix
María Calleja, comandante en gefe
del ejército real de operaciones,
llamado del centro. Su autor Carlos
Maria de Bustamante. Mexico, Impr.
del Aguila, dirigida por J. Ximeno,
1828.
   4 p. l., 200, 18, 6 p.   20 1/2
cm.

1760   Bustamante, Carlos María de, 1774-1848.
   El gabinete mexicano durante el
segundo período de la administración
del exmo. señor presidente d. Anas-
tasio Bustamante, hasta la entrega
del mando al exmo. señor presidente
interino d. Antonio Lopez de Santa-
Anna, y continuación del Cuadro histórico de la revolución mexicana,
escrito por ... don Carlos María
Bustamante ... México, J.M. Lara,
1842.
   2 v. in 1.   21 cm.

1761   Bustamante, Carlos María de, 1774-1848.
   ... Historia del emperador d.
Augustin de Iturbide hasta su muerte,
y sus consecuencias; y estableci-
miento de la república popular feder-
al. Su autor el lic. d. Carlos María
Bustamante ... México, Impr. de I.
Cumplido, 1846.

293, vii p.   22 1/2 cm.

1762   Bustamante, Carlos Maria de, 1774-1848.
        Martirologio de algunos de los
        primeros insurgentes por la libertad
        é independencia de la America mexicana,
        ó sea Prontuario é indice alfabetico
        de varios individuos ecclesiásticos y
        seculares de quienes se habla en las
        causas de las conspiraciones de abril
        y agosto de 1811, ó que resultan mas
        ó ménos indiciados de adhesion al par-
        tido de los rebeldes en otros espedi-
        entes de infidencia, ó por la opinion
        comun y general. Sacóse este precioso
        documento de los originales de la Jun-
        ta de seguridad ... Publícalo para
        honor de las primeras víctimas de la
        independencia mexicana ... Carlos
        María de Bustamante ... Mexico,
        Impr. por J.M. Lara, 1841.
        51 p.   fold.   tab.   22 cm.

1763   Bustamante, Carlos María de, 1774-1848.
        El nuevo Bernal Díaz del Castillo,
        ó sea, Historia de la invasión de los
        Anglo-Americanos en México. Escrita
        por el licenciado Carlos María de
        Bustamante ... México, Impr. de V.
        García Torres, 1847.
        2 v.   24 cm.

1764   Bustamante, José Luis, 1799-1857.
        Los cinco errores capitales de la
        intervención anglo-francesa en el
        Plata. Por José Luis Bustamante.
        Montevideo, 1849.
        viii, [9]-382, [2] p.   21 1/2 cm.

1765   [Butler, Benjamin Franklin] 1818-1893,
        ed.

Official documents relating to a
"Chaplain's campaign (not) with General Butler," but in New York ...
Lowell [Mass.] C. Hunt, printer, 1865.
   48 p.   22 1/2 cm.

1766 Butler, Caleb, 1776-1854.
      History of the town of Groton, in-
cluding Pepperell and Shirley, from
the first grant of Groton plantation
in 1655. With appendices, containing
family registers, town and state officers, population, and other statistics.
By Caleb Butler ... Boston, Press of
T.R. Marvin, 1848.
   xx, [9]-499 p. front., pl., 2 maps
(1 fold.) fold. plan, facsim.   22 1/2
cm.

1767 Butler, Caleb, 1776-1854.
      Some account of Deacon John Butler
of Pelham, N.H., and of his descendants. By Caleb Butler of Groton.
[Boston, 1848-49]
   p. 355-360, 73-76, 353-358.   22 1/2
cm.

1768 Butler, Clement Moore, 1810-1890.
      Address delivered by Rev. Clement
M. Butler, at the President's mansion,
on the occasion of the funeral of
Abel P. Upshur, T.W. Gilmer, and
others, who lost their lives by the
explosion on board the Princeton,
February 28, 1844 ... Washington,
Printed by J. and G.S. Gideon, 1844.
   8 p.   23 cm.

1769 Butler, Clement Moore, 1810-1890.
      Our country and our Washington.
A discourse, delivered on Sunday

morning, February 22, 1852, the birth-
day of Washington, in the hall of the
House of representatives, by the Rev.
C.M. Butler, D.D., chaplain of the
Senate of the United States. Washington, Printed by J.T. Towers, 1852.
   23 p.   22 cm.

1770   Butler, James Davie, 1815-1905.
       Deficiencies in our history. An ad-
dress delivered before the Vermont
historical and antiquarian society,
at Montpelier, October 16, 1846. By
James Davie Butler ... Montpelier,
Eastman & Danforth, 1846.
   36 p.   21 cm.

1771   Butler, John, *bp.*, 1717-1802.
       A sermon preached before the honour-
able House of commons, at the church
of St. Margaret's, Westminster, on Friday, December 13, 1776; being the day
appointed by His Majesty's royal
proclamation, to be observed as a day
of solemn fasting and humiliation. By
John Butler ... chaplain in ordinary
to His Majesty. London, Printed for
T. Cadell, 1777.
   16 p.   25 1/2 x 20 1/2 cm.

1772   Butler, Mann, 1784-1852.
       An oration on national independence,
(delivered by public request) on the
Fourth July, 1837, at Port Gibson,
Mississippi, consisting, principally,
of a sketch of the rise of the state
of Mississippi, from the exploration
of De Soto, in 1539, to the present
time. By Mann Butler. Frankfort,
Ky., Printed by A.G. Hodges, 1837.
   23 p.   23 1/2 cm.

1773 [Butler, William Allen] 1825-1902.
      Barnum's Parnassus; being confiden-
      tial disclosures of the prize commit-
      tee on the Jenny Lind song. With speci-
      mens of the leading American poets in
      the happiest effulgence of their gen-
      ius. Respectfully dedicated to the
      American eagle. New York, D. Apple-
      ton & company; Philadelphia, G.S. Ap-
      pleton, 1850.
         52 p.   18 1/2 cm.

1774 [Butler, William Allen] 1825-1902.
      Memorial of Charles H. Marshall.
      New York, D. Appleton and company,
      1867.
         96 p.   incl. front. (port.)   22
      1/2 cm.

1775 [Butler, William Allen] 1825-1902.
      Nothing to wear: an episode of
      city life. (From Harper's weekly.)
      Illustrated by Hoppin. New York,
      Rudd & Carleton, 1857.
         68 p. incl. front., plates.   16
      1/2 cm.

1776 [Butterfield, Horatio Quincy] 1822-1894.
      U.S. Christian commission. A dele-
      gate's story. [Philadelphia? 1863]
      cover-title, 8 p.   17 1/2 cm.

1777 Buttrick, Tilly, b. 1783.
      Buttrick's Voyages, travels, and
      discoveries, 1812-1819; reprint of
      the original edition: Boston, 1831.
      (In Thwaites, Reuben G., ed. Ear-
      ly western travels, 1748-1846. Cleve-
      land, 1904.   24 1/2 cm. v. 8, p.
      [15]-89)

1778 Byles, Mather, 1707-1788.
      The glories of the Lord of Hosts,
and the fortitude of the religious
hero. A sermon preached to the Ancient and honorable artillery company, June 2, 1740. Being the anniversary of their election of officers.
By Mather Byles ... The 3d ed. Boston, New-England: Re-printed by Thomas and John Fleet, at the Heart and
crown in Cornhill, 1769.
      26 p. 1 illus.   21 cm.

1779 Byles, Mather, 1707-1788.
      A poem on the death of His late
Majesty King George, of glorious
memory. And the accession of our
present sovereign King George II. to
the British throne. By Mr. Byles ...
[Boston, 1727]
      1 p. 1., v. p.   17 1/2 cm.

1780 Byles, Mather, 1707-1788.
      To His Excellency Governour Bel-
cher, on the death of his lady. An
epistle. By the Reverend Mr. Byles
... [Boston, 1736]
      1 p. 1., ii, 6 p.   23 cm.

1781 Byrdsall, Fitzwilliam.
      The history of the Loco-foco, or
Equal Rights Party, its movements,
conventions and proceedings. New
York, Clement & Packard, 1842.
      192 p.   18 cm.

1782 Byrne, Bernard M.
      Proceedings of a court martial for
the trial of Surgeon B.M. Byrne, held
at Ford Moultrie, S.C. on March 24th,
1859. Charleston, Walker, Evans &

406

co., 1859.
1 p. 1., 130 p.   23 cm.

C

1783 Cabell, *Mrs*. Julia (Mayo)
        An odd volume of facts and fic-
      tions, in prose and verse, by Julia
      Mayo Cabell. [2d ed.] Richmond,
      Nash and Woodhouse, 1852.
        276 p.   19 cm.

1784 The Cabinet, or A collection of choice
      things; comprising the beauties of
      American miscellanies for the last
      thirty years. By a citizen of New
      York. New-York: Printed by Fan-
      shaw & Clayton, no. 10 Cliff-street.
      1815.
        448 p.   22 cm.

1785 [Cabot, James Elliot] 1821-1903.
        Letter to the governor of Massa-
      chusetts, on occasion of his late
      proclamation, of August 20, 1861.
      Boston, A.K. Loring, 1861.
        12 p.   22 cm.

1786 Cabrera, Miguel, 1695-1768.
        Maravilla americana, y conjunto de
      raras maravillas, observadas con la
      direccion de las reglas de el arte
      de la pintura en la prodigiosa ima-
      gen de Nuestra Sra. de Guadalupe de
      Mexico, por don Miguel Cabrera, pin-
      tor ... Mexico, Impr. del Colegio
      de San Ildefonso, 1756.
        9 p. 1., 30 p., 3 1.   20 1/2 cm.

1787 Cabrera y Quintero, Cayetano, *d*. 1775.

Escudo de armas de Mexico: celestial protección de esta nobilissima ciudad, de la Nueva-España, y de casi todo el nuevo mundo, Maria Santissima, en su portentosa imagen del mexicano Guadalupe, milagrosamente apparecida en el palacio arzobispal el año de 1531. Y jurada su principal patrona el passado de 1737. En la angustia que ocasionò la pestilencia ... Describiala de orden ... del ilustríssimo, y excelentíssimo señor dr. d. Juan Antonio de Vizarron, y Eguiarreta ... d. Cayetano de Cabrera, y Quintero ... a expensas, y solicitud de esta nobilíssima ciudad ... Mexico, Impresso por la viuda de d. J.B. de Hogal, 1746.

17 p. l., 522, [24] p. front., illus. (coat of arms) 30 cm.

1788 Caccia, Antonio.
Europa ed America; scene della vita dal 1848 al 1850 del D^r. Antonio Caccia. Monaco, G. Franz, 1850.

2 p. l., 500 p. 17 1/2 cm.

1789 Caddell, Cecilia Mary, *d.* 1877.
... Historia de las misiones en el Japon y Paraguay, escrita en ingles por C.M. Cadell, tr. directamente por d. Casimiro Pedregal ... 2. ed. Madrid, S. Sanchez Rubio, 1857.

4 p. l., xi, [9]-390, 6 p. 6 pl. 18 cm.

1790 [Cadwalader, John] 1742-1786.
A reply to General Joseph Reed's Remarks, on a late publication in the Independent gazetteer, with some observations on his Address to the

people of Pennsylvania. Philadelphia,
Printed and sold by T. Bradford, 1783.
    54 p.   21 1/2 cm.

1791 Cady, Daniel Reed, 1813-1879.
        Memorial of Lieut. Joseph P. Bur-
    rage; a funeral sermon, preached De-
    cember 25, 1863, by Rev. Daniel R.
    Cady ... Boston, Gould and Lincoln,
    1864.
        43 p.   19 cm.

1792 [Cahoone, Sarah S   ]
        Sketches of Newport and its vicin-
    ity; with notices respecting the his-
    tory, settlement and geography of
    Rhode Island.   Illustrated with en-
    gravings.   New-York, J.S. Taylor &
    co., 1842.
        213 p. front., plates.   19 1/2
    cm.

1793 [Caines, George] 1771-1825.
        An enquiry into the law merchant
    of the United States; or, Lex merca-
    toria americana, on several heads of
    commercial importance ...   In two
    volumes. Vol. I.   New-York: Printed
    By Isaac Collins & son, for Abraham
    and Arthur Stansbury.   1802.
        viii, 648, cixvii, [1], [ix]-xxxviii,
    [2] p.   22 cm.

1794 Cairnes, John Elliott, 1823-1875.
        The Southern Confederacy and the
    African slave trade.   The correspon-
    dence between Professor Cairnes ...
    and George M'Henry, esq. ...   With an
    introduction and notes, by the Rev.
    George B. Wheeler ...   Dublin,
    McGlashan & Gill, 1863.

409

xxviii, 61 p.   21 1/2 cm.

1795 Cairo city property, *Cairo, Ill.*
        Circular. Engineers' reports and
other documents relating to the Cairo
city property at the confluence of
the Ohio and Mississippi rivers, Illinois. Trustees: Thomas S. Taylor,
Philadelphia. Charles Davis, New-
York. New-York, H. Cogswell, printer, 1847.
        2 p. 1., 40 p., 1 1. 2 fold. maps.
22 cm.

1796 Calamy, Edmund, 1671-1732.
        An historical account of my own
life, with some reflections on the
times I have lived in. (1671-1731.)
By Edmund Calamy, D.D. Now first
printed. Edited and illustrated with
notes, historical and biographical,
by John Towill Rutt ... London, H.
Colburn and R. Bentley, 1829.
        2 v. front. (port.)   22 1/2 cm.

1797 Calatayud y Borda, Cipriano Gerónimo,
        1735-1814.
        Oracion funebre que en las solemnes
exequias de la r.m. Maria Antonia
de San Joseph, Larrea, Arispe, de
Los Reyes: quatro veces ministra en
el monasterio de trinitarias descal-
zas de esta ciudad de Lima: dixo en
la iglesia del referido monasterio
en XXX. de octubre de M.DCC.LXXXII.
el r. p. pr. fr. Cypriano Gerónimo
de Calatayud y Borda ... En Lima,
En la Imprenta de los huérfanos,
M.DCC.LXXXIII.
        58 p. 1., 144 p.   20 cm.

1798   Calderón de la Barca, Frances Erskine
          (Inglis) 1804-1882.
            Life in Mexico, during a residence
        of two years in that country. By
        Madame C——— de la B——— ... With
        a preface, by W.H. Prescott ... Lon=
        don, Chapman and Hall, 1843.
            xii, 436 p.   22 1 2 cm.

1799   Caldwell, Charles, 1772-1853.
            An elegiac poem on the death of Gen-
        eral Washington. By Charles Caldwell
        ... Philadelphia: Printed at the
        office of "The True American." 1800.
            2 p. l., 12 p.   22 cm.

1800   Caldwell, Charles, 1772-1853.
            An oration commemorative of Ameri-
        can independence, delivered before the
        American Republican society of Phila-
        delphia, on the Fourth of July, 1810.
        By Charles Caldwell, M.D. Pub. by or-
        der of the society. Philadelphia:
        Printed for Bradford and Inskeep, No.
        4, S. Third street. Fry and Kammerer,
        printers. 1810.
            34 p.   23 cm.

1801   Caldwell, Joseph Blake, d. 1811.
            An oration, pronounced on the
        thirtysecond anniversary of American
        independence, at Barre, in the county
        of Worcester, July 4, 1808: by Joseph
        B. Caldwell, A.M. To which is added
        an appendix, containing fourteen
        spirited resolutions, adopted on the
        occasion. Worcester, Isaiah Thomas,
        jun.; Isaac Sturtevant, printer, July
        1808.
            31 p.   22 cm.

1802   Caldwell, Samuel Lunt, 1820-1887.
       A sermon preached in the First Bap-
tist meeting-house, Providence, Sunday morning, June 9, 1861, before the
Second regiment of Rhode Island volunteers: by Samuel L. Caldwell ...
Providence, Knowles, Anthony & co.,
printers, 1861.
       32 p.   23 1/2 cm.

1803   [Calef, John] 1725-1812.
       ... The siege of Penobscot by the
rebels: containing a Journal of the
proceedings of His Majesty's forces
detached from the 74th and 82d regi-
ments, consisting of about 700 rank
and file, under the command of Captain
Brigadier-General Francis M'Lean,
and of three of His Majesty's sloops
of war, of 16 guns each, under the command of Captain Henry Mowat, senior
officer; when besieged by three thous-
and three hundred (rebel) land forces,
under the command of Brigadier-General
Solomon Lovell, and seventeen rebel
ships and vessels of war, under the
command of G. Saltonstall, commodore.
To which is annexed a Proclamation
issued June 15, 1779, by General M'Lean
and Captain Barclay to the inhabitants;
also Brigadier-General Lovell's Proclamation to the inhabitants; and his
letter to Commodore Saltonstall, found
on board the rebel ship Hunter; together with the names, force, and commanders, of the rebel ships destroyed
in Penobscot Bay and River, August 14
and 15, 1779. With a chart of the
Peninsula of Majabigwaduce, and of
Penobscot River. To which is subjoined
a Postscript, wherein a short account

of the country of Penobscot is given.
By J.C. esq., a volunteer. London,
Printed for G. Kearsley [etc.] 1781.
New York, Reprinted, W. Abbatt, 1910.
        55 p. front. (map)   26 1/2 cm.

1804   California. *Constitution*.
        Constitution of the state of Calif-
        ornia. San Francisco, Printed at the
        office of the Alta California, 1849.
        19 p.   24 cm.

1805   Callan, John F.   *comp*.
        The military laws of the United
        States, relating to the army, Marine
        corps, volunteers, militia, and to
        bounty lands and pensions, from the
        foundation of the government to the
        year 1858. By John F. Callan ...
        Baltimore, J. Murphy & co., 1858.
        xxxii, [33]-484 p.   23 1/2 cm.

1806   [Callender, James Thomson] 1758-1803.
        The history of the United States
        for 1796; including a variety of in-
        teresting particulars relative to the
        Federal government previous to that
        period. Philadelphia: From the press
        of Snowden & M'Corkle, No. 47, North
        Fourth Street.   1797.
        viii, 312 p.   21 cm.

1807   Callender, James Thomson, 1758-1803,
        supposed author.
        Letters to Alexander Hamilton,
        king of the Feds. Ci-devant secre-
        tary of the Treasury of the United
        States of America, inspector-general
        of the standing armies thereof,
        counsellor at law. &c. &c. &c. Be-
        ing intended as a reply to a

scandalous pamphlet lately published under the sanction, as it is presumed, of Mr. Hamilton, and signed with the signature of Junius Philaenus. By Tom Callender ... New-York:--Printed by Richard Reynolds, no. 27, Dey-street. 1802.
  64 p. 22 1/2 cm.

1808 Callender, James Thomson, 1758-1803.
  The prospect before us. Richmond, 1800-1801.
  3 v. in 1. 21 cm.

1809 Callender, James Thomson, 1758-1803.
  Sedgwick & co.; or, A key to the Six per cent cabinet. By James Thomson Callender. Philadelphia, Printed for the author, 1798.
  1 p. 1., 2-88 p. 22 1/2 cm.

1810 [Callender, James Thomson] 1758-1803.
  A short history of the nature and consequences of excise laws: including some account of the recent interruption to the manufactories of snuff and refined sugar ... Philadelphia: Printed for the booksellers. Dec. 7, 1795.
  116 p. 20 1/2 cm.

1811 Callender, James Thomson, 1758-1803.
  Sketches of the history of America. By James Thomson Callender ... Philadelphia: From the press of Snowden & M'Corkle, no. 47, North Fourth-street, 1798. [Price one dollar.]
  viii, [9]-263 p. 21 cm.

1812 Callender, John, 1706-1748.

414

An historical discourse on the civil
and religious affairs of the colony
of Rhode-Island and Providence plantations in New-England in America. From
the first settlement 1638, to the end
of the first century. By John Callender ... Boston: Printed and Sold by
S. Kneeland and T. Green in Queen-
street. 1739.
   1 p. l., 14, 120 p., 1 l.   19 cm.

1813 Callender, John, 1772-1833.
    An oration, pronounced July 4, 1797,
at the request of the inhabitants of
the town of Boston, in commemoration
of the anniversary of American independence. By John Callender ... Boston: Printed and Sold by Benjamin
Edes, Kilby-Street.--1797.
   19 p.   22 1/2 cm.

1814 Callicot, Theophilus Carey, b. 1826.
    Speech of Hon. Theophilus C. Calli-
cot of Kings, against the Personal
liberty bill. In Assembly, March 14,
1860. Albany, Comstock & Cassidy,
printers, 1860.
   13 p.   22 1/2 cm.

1815 The Calumet. New series of the Harbin-
ger of peace. Pub. under the direction of the American peace society
... v. 1, v. 2, no. 1-6; May/June
1831 - March./Apr. 1835. New-York,
L.D. Dewey [1831-35]
   2 v. in 1.   22 1/2 cm.

1816 Calvert, George Henry, 1803-1889.
    Oration, on the occasion of cele-
brating the fortieth anniversary of

the battle of Lake Erie; delivered
on the tenth of September, 1853, in
Newport, R.I., by George H. Calvert.
Cambridge [Mass.] Metcalf and company, printers, 1853.
40 p.   23 cm.

1817   Cambreleng, Churchill Caldom, 1786-1862.
Speech of Mr. Cambreleng, (in reply
to Mr. McDuffie and Mr. Storrs,) on
the proposition to amend the Constitution of the United States, respecting
the election of president and vice
president. Delivered in the House of
representatives, March 7, 1826. [Wash-
ington, 1826]
15 p.   18 cm.

1818   [Cameron, Allan]
The cultivation of flax, and prepara-
tion of flax cotton by the Chevalier
Claussen process. New York, 1852.
New York, Printed by J.A. Gray, 1852.
8 p.   22 1/2 cm.

1819   Campanella, Tommaso, 1568-1639.
A discourse touching the Spanish
monarchy. Laying down directions and
practices whereby the king of Spain
may attain to an universal monarchy.
Wherein also we have a political
glasse, representing each particular
country, province, kingdom, and empire of the world, with wayes of government by which they may be kept in
obedience. As also the causes of
the rise and fall of each kingdom and
empire. Written by Tho. Campanella.
Newly translated into English, according to the third edition of this book
in Latine. London, Printed for P.

Stephens, 1654.
4 p. 1., 232 p.   19 cm.

1820   Campbell, Charles, 1807-1876.
Genealogy of the Spotswood fam-
ily in Scotland and Virginia. By
Charles Campbell ... Albany, J.
Munsell, 1868.
2 p. 1., [3]-44 p.   24 1/2 cm.

1821   Campbell, George, 1719-1796.
The nature, extent, and importance,
of the duty of allegiance: a sermon
preached at Aberdeen, December 12,
1776, being the fast day appointed
by the King, on account of the rebellion in America. By George Campbell ... Aberdeen, Printed by J.
Chalmers and co., sold by Cadell,
Strand, London; [etc., etc.] 1777.
vi, 41 p.   21 x 16 1/2 cm.

1822   Campbell, James.
An oration, in commemoration of
the independence of the United States
of North-America, delivered July 4,
1787, at the Reformed Calvinist
church in Philadelphia, by James Campbell, esquire. To which is prefixed,
an introductory prayer delivered on
the same occasion, by the Rev. William Rogers, A.M. Pub. at the request of the Pennsylvania Society
of the Cincinnati. Philadelphia:
Printed and sold by Prichard and
Hall, in Market street, between Front
and Second streets. 1787.
24 p.   20 cm.

1823   Campbell, John, *bookseller, Philadelphia*.
Negro-mania: being an examination

417

of the falsely assumed equality of
the various races of men; demonstrated by the investigations of Champol-
lion, Wilkinson, Rosellini, Van-
Amringe, Gliddon, Young, Morton, Knox,
Lawrence, Gen. J.H. Hammond, Murray,
Smith, W. Gilmore Simms, English,
Conrad, Elder, Prichard, Blumenbach,
Cuvier, Brown, Le Vaillant, Carlyle,
Cardinal Wiseman, Burckhart, and Jefferson. Together with a concluding
chapter, presenting a comparative
statement of the condition of the negroes in the West Indies before and
since emancipation. By John Campbell ... Philadelphia, Campbell &
Power, 1851.
   549 p.   20 1/2 cm.

1824   Campbell, Thomas, 1777-1844.
      Gertrude of Wyoming; or, The Penn-
sylvanian cottage. By Thomas Campbell. With thirty-five illustrations,
engraved by the brothers Dalziel. New
York, D. Appleton & co., 1858.
   viii, 94, [2] p. illus. 19 1/2
cm.

1825   [Cañedo, Estanislao]
      La vérité sur la révolution actuelle
au Méxique. Paris, Impr. de A. Guyot
et Scribe, 1860.
   47 p.   24 cm.

1826   Carlier, Auguste, 1803-1890.
      Histoire du peuple américain, États-
Unis, et de ses rapports avec les
Indiens, depuis la fondation des
colonies anglaises jusqu'à la révolu-
tion de 1776, par Auguste Carlier ...
Paris, Michel Lévy frères, 1864.

2 v.   22 cm.

1827 Cartier, Jacques.
      Discovrs dv voyage fait par le
capitaine Jaques Cartier aux terres-
neufues de Canadas, Norembergue,
Hochelage, Labrador, et pays adjacens,
dites Nouuelle France, auec particu-
lieres moeurs, langage, et ceremonies
des habitants d'icelle. À Rouen, De
l'imprimerie de R. du Petit-Val, 1598.
      (*In* Ternaux-Compans, H[enri] Ar-
chives des voyages.   Paris [1840]
21 1/2 cm.   t. I, p. 117-153)

1828 Catesby, Mark, 1683-1749.
      Hortus Britanno-Americanus: or, A
curious collection of trees and shrubs,
the produce of the British Colonies
in North America; adapted to the soil
and climate of England ... London,
Printed by W. Richardson and S. Clark
for J. Ryall, 1763.
      vi, 41 p.   17 plates.   39 cm.

1829 Cathcart, John.
      A letter to the Honourable Edward
Vernon esq; vice-admiral of the Red,
&c., from John Cathcart, director of
the hospital in the late expedition
to the West-Indies, under the command
of the Honourable General Wentworth:
concerning some gross misrepresentations in a pamphlet, lately published,
and intitled, Original papers relating to the expedition to the island
of Cuba ... London, Printed for M.
Cooper, 1744.
      55 p.   18 1/2 cm.

1830 Catherwood, Frederick.

419

Views of ancient monvments in Central America, Chiapas and Yveatan, by
F. Catherwood ... New York, Barlett
[!] and Welford, 1844.
2 p. 1., 24 p.   25 pl., map.   54
1/2 cm.

1831   [Catineau-Laroche, Pierre Marie Sébas-
tien] 1772-1828.
De la Guyane Française, de son état
physique, de son agriculture, de son
régime intérieur, et du projet de la
peupler avec des laboureurs européens;
ou Examen d'un écrit de M. le marquis
de Barbé-Marbois, sur le même sujet.
Suivi de considérations sur le commerce colonial de la France et sur
l'administration spéciale de ses
colonies.   Paris, Impr. de C.J. Trou-
vé, 1822.
xj,   15 -230 p., 1 1.   21 1/2 cm.

1832   Catlin, George, 1796-1872.
Adventures of the Ojibbeway and
Ioway Indians in England, France, and
Belgium; being notes of eight years'
travels and residence in Europe with
his North American Indian collection,
by Geo. Catlin ...   3d ed.   London,
The author, 1852.
2 v. in 1.   front, plates, ports.
22 cm.

1833   Catlin, [George] 1796-1872.
Catalogue of Catlin's Indian gal-
lery of portraits, landscapes, manners and customs, costumes, &c. &c.,
collected during seven years' travel
amongst thirty-eight different tribes,
speaking different languages.   New-
York, Piercy & Reed, printers, 1838.

420

40 p.   17 cm.

1834   Catlin, George, 1796-1872.
       Catlin's notes of eight years' tra-
vels and residence in Europe, with
his North American Indian collection.
With anecdotes and incidents of the
travels and adventures of three different parties of American Indians
whom he introduced to the courts of
England, France, and Belgium ... 2d
ed. London, The author, 1848.
       2 v. front., pl., port.   21 1/2
cm.

1835   Catlin, George, 1796-1872.
       A descriptive catalogue of Catlin's
Indian collection, containing portraits, landscapes, costumes, &c.,
and representations of the manners
and customs of the North American Indians. Collected and painted entirely
by Mr. Catlin, during eight years' travel amongst forty-eight trives, mostly speaking different languages ...
London, The author, 1848.
       50, 50*-53*, 51-92 p.   21 1/2 cm.

1836   Catlin, George, 1796-1872.
       Die Indianer Nord-Amerikas und
die während eines achtjährigen
aufenthalts unter den wildesten
ihrer stamme erlebten abenteuer und
schicksale von G. Catlin. Nach der
fünften englischen ausgabe deutsch
herausgegeben von dr. Heinrich
Berghaus ... Mit 24 vom verfasser
nach der natur entworfenen gemälden.
2 ausg. Brussels [etc.] C. Muquardt,
1851.
       x p., 1 1., 382 p. incl. pl.   23

pl. (1 col.)   26 1/2 cm.

1837   Catlin, George, 1796-1872.
       Letters and notes on the manners,
customs, and condition of the North
American Indians. By Geo. Catlin.
Written during eight years' travel
amongst the wildest tribes of Indians
in North America. In 1832, 33, 34,
35, 36, 37, 38, and 39 ... London,
Pub. by the author; printed by Toss-
will and Myers, 1841.
       2 v. front. (v. 1) plates, ports.,
2 maps (1 fold.)   25 1/2 cm.

1838   Catlin, George, 1796-1872.
       Life amongst the Indians. A book
for youth. By George Catlin ...
London, Sampson Low, son, & Marston, 1867.
       xii, 339 p. front., illus., plates.
18 cm.

1839   Catskill association.
       Catskill association, formed for
the purpose of improving the town of
Catskill ... New York, December 28,
1836. New York, Mitchell & Turner,
1837.
       47 p.   map.   16 cm.

1840   Catto, William T.
       A semi-centenary discourse, deliv-
ered in the First African Presbyterian church, Philadelphia, on the
fourth Sabbath of May, 1857: with a
history of the church from its first
organization: including a brief notice of Rev. John Gloucester, its first
pastor. By Rev. William T. Catto,
pastor. Also, an appendix, containing

sketches of all the colored churches in Philadelphia. Philadelphia, J.M. Wilson, 1857.
111 p.   23 cm.

1841   Cauchon, Joseph.
L'union des provinces de l'Amérique britannique du Nord, par l'hon. Joseph Cauchon ... (Extrait du "Journal de Québec") Québec, Impr. de A. Coté et c^{ie}, 1865.
152 p.   21 1/2 cm.

1842   Caulkins, Frances Manwaring, 1795-1869.
History of New London, Connecticut. From the first survey of the coast in 1612, to 1852. By Frances Manwaring Caulkins ... New London, The author [Hartford, Ct., Press of Case, Tiffany and company] 1852.
xi, [13]-679, [1] p.   illus.   23 1/2 cm.

1843   Caulkins, Frances Manwaring, 1795-1869.
History of Norwich, Connecticut: from its possession by the Indians, to the year 1866. By Frances Manwaring Caulkins. [Hartford] The author, 1866.
xi, [17]-704 p.   front., illus., ports.   23 1/2 cm.

1844   [Causten, James H   ]
Review of the veto message of President Pierce of Feb. 17, 1855, on the bill relating to French spoliations. [Washington? 1855]
cover-title, 46 p.   22 1/2 cm.

1845   Cavada, Frederic Fernandez, 1832-1871.
Libby life: experiences of a

prisoner of war in Richmond, Va.,
1863-64, by Lieut. Colonel F.F.
Cavada, U.S.V. Philadelphia, King &
Baird, 1864.
   221 p. illus., plates. 19 cm.

1846 Cavelier, Jean.
      Relation || du voyage || Entrepris
par feu M. Robert Cave- || lier, Sieur
de la Salle, pour dé- || couvrir dans
le golfe du Mexique || l'embouchure
du Fleuve de || Missisipy. || Par son
Frère M. Cavelier, prêtre || de St.
Sulpice, l'un des compagnons de || ce
voyage. || À Manate: || De la Presse
Cramoisy de Jean-Marie Shea. ||
M.DCCC.LVIII. ||
      iv, 5-54 p., 1 l.   19 1/2 cm.

1847 [Cavender, Curtis H   ]
      Catalogue of works in refutation of
Methodism, from its origin in 1729,
to the present time ... Comp. by
H.C. Decanver [pseud.] Philadelphia,
J. Penington, 1846.
      54 p.   25 cm.

1848 Cheshire library association, *Cheshire,
Mass.*
      Catalogue of books belonging to
the Cheshire library association, of
Cheshire, Mass. Boston, Wright &
Potter, printers, 1868.
      24 p.   19 1/2 cm.

1849 Chesney, Charles Cornwallis, 1826-1876.
      Campaigns in Virginia, Maryland,
etc., etc., by Capt. C.C. Chesney,
R.E. ... 2d ed. rev. and enl.
London, Smith, Elder and co., 1864-65.

2 v. fold. front., maps (part
fold.)   20 1/2 cm.

1850 Chesney, Charles Cornwallis, 1826-1876.
A military view of recent cam-
paigns in Virginia and Maryland. By
Capt. C.C. Chesney ... London, Smith,
Elder and co., 1863-65.
2 v. front., maps (partly fold.)
19 1/2 cm.

1851 Chessman, Daniel, 1787-1839.
Memoir of Rev. Thomas Baldwin, D.D.,
late pastor of the Second Baptist
church in Boston, who died at Water-
ville, Me., August 29, 1825. Together with a funeral sermon, occasioned
by his death, delivered on the succeed-
ing Sabbath, in the Baptist meeting
house, in Hallowell, Me. By Rev.
Daniel Chessman ... With an appendix,
containing letters and hymns. Boston, Printed by True & Greene, 1826.
72, 12 p.   23 cm.

1852 Chester, Greville John, 1830-1892.
Translantic sketches in the West
Indies, South America, Canada, and
the United States. By Greville John
Chester ... London, Smith, Elder &
co., 1869.
xvi, 495, [1] p.   19 1/2 cm.

1853 Chester, John, 1785-1829.
A sermon, in commemoration of the
landing of the New-England Pilgrims.
Delivered in the 2d. Presbyterian
church, Albany, December 22d, 1820:
on the completion of the second century, since that event. By John
Chester ... Albany, Printed by E.

and E. Hosford, 1820.
31, [1] p.   24 cm.

1854   Chester, John, 1832-1910.
The lesson of the hour. Justice as
well as mercy. A discourse preached
on the Sabbath following the assassination of the President, in the Capitol
Hill Presbyterian Church, Washington,
D.C., by the pastor, Rev. John Chester.
[Washington] Washington chronicle
print, 1865.
16 p.   22 1/2 cm.

1855   Chester, Joseph Lemuel, 1821-1882.
Greenwood cenetery, and other poems,
by Joseph L. Chester. New York, Saxton and Miles; Boston, Saxton, Peirce
& co., 1843.
xi, [13]-132 p.   19 cm.

1856   Chester, Joseph Lemuel, 1821-1882.
Notes upon the ancestry of William
Hutchinson and Anne Marbury. From re-
searches recently made in England. By
Joseph Lemuel Chester ... Boston,
Printed by D. Clapp & son, 1866.
24 p.   26 x 21 cm.

1857   Chester, Joseph Lemuel, 1821-1882.
A preliminary investigation of the
alleged ancestry of George Washington;
first president of the United States
of America; exposing a serious error
in the existing pedigree. By Joseph
Lemuel Chester ... [Reprinted from
the Herald and genealogist, London,
and the Heraldie journal, Boston.]
Boston, H.W. Dutton & son, printers,
1866.
23 p.   25 cm.

1858   Chevalier, Henri Émile, 1828-1879.
        Adventures by sea and land of the
        Count De Ganay; or, The devotion and
        fidelity of woman. An episode of the
        colonization of Canada. Tr. from the
        French of H. Émile Chevalier. New
        York, J. Bradburn, 1863.
        v, [3], 310, [2] p.   19 cm.

1859   Chevalier, Henri Émile, 1828-1879.
        Legends of the sea. 39 men for
        one woman: an episode of the coloniza-
        tion of Canada. Tr. from the French
        of H. Émile Chevalier, by E.I. Sears
        ... New York, J. Bradburn, 1862.
        x, 310, [2] p.   19 cm.

1860   Chevalier, Michel, 1806-1879.
        Histoire et description des voies
        de communication aux États Unis et
        des travaux d'art qui en dépendent;
        par Michel Chevalier ... Paris, C.
        Gosselin; [etc., etc.] 1840-41.
        2 v.   30 cm.

1861   Chevalier, Michel, 1806-1879.
        L'isthme de Panama: examen his-
        torique et géographique des différ-
        entes directions suivant lesquelles
        on pourrait le percer et des moyens
        a y employer; suivi d'un aperçu sur
        l'isthme de Suez. Par Michel Cheva-
        lier ... Paris, C. Gosselin, 1844.
        2 p. 1., 182 p., 1 1. fold. map.
        21 1/2 cm.

1862   Chevalier, Michel, 1806-1879.
        La liberté aux États-Unis, par
        Michel Chevalier. Paris, Capelle,
        1849.
        55, [1] p.   22 1/2 cm.

1863 Chevalier, Michel, 1806-1879.
         Il Messico, per Michele Chevalier
      ... Milano, Corona e Caimi, 1864.
      2 p. l., 396 p.   19 cm.

1864 Chevalier, Michel, 1806-1879.
         Mexico: before and after the con-
      quest. By Michel Chevalier ... Tr.
      from the French, by Fay Robinson ...
      Philadelphia, Carey and Hart, 1846.
      2 p. l., [9]-91 p.   24 cm.

1865 Chevalier, Michel, 1806-1879.
         On the probable fall in the value of
      gold: the commercial and social conse-
      quences which may ensue, and the meas-
      ures which it invites. By Michael
      Chevalier ... Tr. from the French,
      with preface, by Richard Cobden, esq.
      New York, D. Appleton and company,
      1859.
         211 p.   24 cm.

1866 Chevalier, Michel, 1806-1879.
         Remarks on the production of the
      precious metals, and on the deprecia-
      tion of gold. By Monsr. Michel
      Chevalier ... Tr. by D. Forbes Camp-
      bell, esq. London, Smith, Elder, &
      co., 1853.
         xi, [17]-117 p.   22 1/2 cm.

1867 Chevalier, Michel, 1806-1879.
         Society, manners and politics in the
      United States; being a series of let-
      ters on North America. By Michael
      Chevalier. Tr. from the 3d Paris ed.
      Boston, Weeks, Jordan and company,
      1839.
         iv, 467 p.   22 cm.

1868   Chevallie, P   J.
       Claim of Beaumarchais' heir
       against the United States, by P.J.
       Chevallie, her attorney. January,
       1817. Washington, Printed by J.
       Elliot [1817]
          42 p.   23 cm.

1869   Cheves, *Mrs.* Elizabeth Washington (Foote)
          Sketches in prose and verse; by
       Mrs. E.W. Foote Cheves. Baltimore,
       Printed at the Publication rooms, 1849.
          xv, [1], [17]-264 p.   front. (port.)
       19 cm.

1870   Cheves, Langdon, 1776-1857.
          An oration, delivered in St. Phil-
       ip's church, before an assemblage of
       the inhabitants of Charleston, on the
       Fourth of July, 1810, in commeoration
       of American independence; by appoint-
       ment of the Seventy-six association,
       and published at the request of that
       society. By Langdom Cheves ... Charles-
       ton: Printed by E.S. Thomas, no. 115,
       East-Bay [1810]
          18 p.   21 cm.

1871   Chevrolat, Auguste.
          Coléoptères du Mexique, par A.
       Chevrolat ... Strasbourg, Impr.
       de G. Silbermann, 1834.
          vii p., 211 l.   17 1/2 cm.

1872   Chew, John H.
          God's judgments teaching righteous-
       ness. A sermon delivered on the na-
       tional fast day, January 4, 1861, in
       St. Matthew's parish, Prince George's
       County, Md., by the Rev. John H.
       Chew ... Washington, R.A. Waters,

printer, 1861.
13 p.   23 cm.

1873 Chiabrera, Gabriello, 1552-1638.
      Rime di Gabriello Chiabrera; in
      questa nuova edizione unite, ac-
      cresciute, e corrette ... Roma,
      Presso il Salvioni, 1718.
      3 v.   port.   19 cm.

1874 Chicago.
      Celebration of the eighty-sixth
      anniversary of the independence of
      the United States, in Chicago, July
      4th, 1862. Printed by authority.
      Chicago, 1862.
      31 p.   21 1/2 cm.

1875 Chicago. *Board of education.*
      Rules of the Board of education
      of the city of Chicago, codified by
      George C. Preston ... Under the
      direction of Graham H. Harris, presi-
      dent of the Board of education. [Chi-
      cago] 1904.
      xv, [3]-80 p.   26 cm.

1876 The Chicago almanac and advertiser, for
      the year 1855-- Chicago, Chicago
      printing company [1855]--
      v.   25 1/2 cm.

1877 Chicago illustrated.   [Chicago, R.F.
      Griffis, C1892]
         cover-title, [48] p.   illus.
      21 1/2 x 20 cm.

1878 Chicago magazine. The West as it is.
      v. 1, no. 1-5; Mar.-Aug. 1857.
      [Chicago, J. Gager & co. for Chi-
      cago Mechanics' institute, 1857]

[9]-451 p. illus., plates, ports.
23 cm.

1879 Chickering, Jesse, 1797-1855.
A statistical view of the population of Massachusetts, from 1765 to
1840. By Jesse Chickering. Boston,
C.C. Little and J. Brown, 1846.
160 p. 23 cm.

1880 Chidlaw, Benjamin Williams, 1811-1892.
A Thanksgiving sermon, preached before the Thirty-ninth O.V., U.S.A.,
at Camp Todd, Macon, Missouri. Nov.
28, 1861, and a sketch of the regiment. By Rev. B.W. Chidlaw ... Cincinnati, G. Crosby, 1861.
24 p. 19 cm.

1881 Child, David Lee
... The despotism of freedom; or,
The tyranny and cruelty of American
republican slave-masters, shown to
be the worst in the world; in a
speech, delivered at the first anniversary of the New England anti-
slavery society, 1832 ... Boston,
Boston young men's anti-slavery association, 1833.
iv, [5]-72 p. 18 cm.

1882 [Child, David Lee] 1794-1874.
An enquiry into the conduct of General Putnam, in relation to the battle of Bunker, or Breed's hill: and
remarks upon Mr. S. Swett's sketch
of that battle. Boston, Printed by
T.G. Bangs, 1819.
58 p. 22 cm.

1883 Child, David Lee, 1794-1874.

431

Report of the case of alleged con-
tempt, and breach of the privileges
of the House of representatives of
Massachusetts, tried before said
House, on complaint of William B.
Calhoun, speaker, against David L.
Child, a member. With notes by the
latter. Boston, Carter and Hendee,
1832.
151, [1] p.   24 cm.

1884   Child, David Lee, 1794-1874.
Review of a report to the House of
representatives of the commonwealth
of Massachusetts, on the case of
William Vans. With observations upon
the dispensing power of the legislature, and upon a decision of the Supreme judicial court, "nullifying" the
said power. By David L. Child ...
Boston, The Publisher, 1833.
iv, 98 p., 1 l., 15 p.   24 cm.

1885   Child, David Lee, 1794-1874.
Rights and duties of the United
States relative to slavery under the
laws of war. No military power to
return any slave. "Contraband of war"
inapplicable between the United States
and their insurgent enemies. By David
Lee Child. [Republished, with notes,
from "The Liberator."] ... Boston,
R.F. Wallcut, 1861.
48 p.   18 1/2 cm.

1886   Child, John.
New-England's Jonas cast up at Lon-
don. 1647. By Major John Child.
With an introduction and notes, by
W.T.R. Marvin. Boston, W.P. Lunt,
1869.

lii p., 1 l., 40 p.   20 1/2 x 16
1/2 cm.

1887 Child, Mrs. Lydia Maria (Francis) 1802-
         1880.
         Anti-slavery catechism ... Newbury-
      port, C. Whipple, 1836.
      36 p.   18 1/2 cm.

1888 Child, Lydia Maria (Francis) 1802-1880.
         An appeal in favor of that class of
      Americans called Africans. By Mrs.
      Child ... Boston, Allen and Ticknor,
      1833.
         3 p. l., 232 p. front., illus.
      20 cm.

1889 Child, Mrs. Lydia Maria (Francis) 1802-
         1880.
         Fact and fiction: a collection of
      stories. By L. Maria Child ... New
      York, C.S. Francis & co.: Boston,
      J.H. Francis, 1847.
      282 p.   18 cm.

1890 Child, Lydia Maria (Francis) 1802-1880.
         The freedmen's book. By L. Maria
      Child. ... Boston, Ticknor and Fields,
      1865.
         3 p. l., [v]-vi, 277 p.   18 cm.

1891 Child, Lydia Maria (Francis) 1802-1880.
         Good wives. By Mrs. D.L. Child
      ... Boston, Carter, Hendee and co.,
      1833.
         xiv p., 1 l., 316 p. front.   18
      1/2 cm.

1892 Child, Mrs. Lydia Maria (Francis), 1802-
         1880.
         Isaac T. Hopper: a true life. By

433

L. Maria Child ... Boston, J.P.
Jewett & co.; Cleveland, O., Jewett,
Proctor & Worthington; [etc., etc.]
1853.
   xvi, 493 p. 2 port. (incl. front.)
19 1/2 cm.

1893   Child, Lydia Maria (Francis) 1802-1880.
      Letters from New York. By L. Maria
      Child ... New York, C.S. Francis and
      company: Boston, J. Munroe & co.,
      1843.
         ix p., 1 l., 276 p.   19 1/2 cm.

1894   Child, *Mrs*. Lydia Maria (Francis) 1802-
      1880, *ed*.
         The oasis. Ed. by Mrs. Child. ...
      Boston, B.C. Bacon, 1834.
         xvi, 276 p. front., illus., plates,
      ports., facsim.   16 cm.

1895   Child, Mrs. Lydia Maria (Francis) 1802-
      1880.
         The right way the safe way, proved
      by emancipation in the British West
      Indies, and elsewhere. By L. Maria
      Child ... New York, 1860.
         96 p.   19 cm.

1896   Childs, Henry Halsey, 1783-1868.
         Eulogy on the death of John Doane
      Wells, M.D., late professor in the
      Berkshire medical institution, deliv-
      ered before the faculty and medical
      class. September, 1830. By Henry H.
      Childs ... [Published by request.]
      Pittsfield, Printed by P. Allen and
      son [1830]
         14 p.   22 cm.

1897   Childs, Orville Whitmore, 1803-1870.

Report of the survey and estimates
of the cost of constructing the inter-
oceanic ship canal, from the harbor
of San Juan del Norte, on the Atlantic,
to the harbor of Brito, on the Pacific,
in the State of Nicaragua, Central America, made for the American, Atlantic
and Pacific Ship Canal Co., in the
years 1850-51. J.D. Fay, principal
assistant. New York, W.C. Bryant,
printers, 1852.
ii, 153 p. fold. col. maps, col.
profile. 26 cm.

1898 Chydenius, Anders.
Americanska nafwerbätar ... under
Pehr Kalms inseende ... til almänt
ompröfwande öfwerlämnade i Åbo
Academies öfre sal f.m. den 26 maij
1753 ... Åbo, Jacob Merckell [1753]
[4], 7 p. illus. 21 cm.

1899 Claude d'Abbeville, father, d. 1632.
L'arrivée des pères capucins et la
conversion des sauvages a nostre
saincte foy, déclarée par le r.p.
Claude d'Abbeville, prédicateur
capucin. À Paris, Chez Jean Nigaut,
rue S. Jean de Latran a l'Alde,
1623. Avec permission. [Lyon, Imprim.
L. Perrin, 1876]
20 p., 2 1. 23 1/2 cm.

1900 Clibborn, Edward.
American prosperity. An outline of
the American debit or banking system
... By Edward Clibborn ... London,
R. Groombridge; [etc., etc.] 1837.
1 p. 1., 44 p. 21 1/2 cm.

1901 [Cliffton, William] 1772-1799.

The group: or, An elegant representa-
tion illustrated. Embellished with a
beautiful head of S. Verges, C.S.
Philadelphia: Printed for Thomas
Stephens, by Lang and Ustick. M.DCC.
XCVI.
    35, [1] p.   front. (port.)   20 x
15 1/2 cm.

1902 Clinch, Joseph Hart, *d*. 1884.
    The captivity in Babylon, and other
poems. By the Rev. Joseph H. Clinch,
A.M. Boston, J. Burns, 1840.
    4 p. 1., 115 p.   19 cm.

1903 Clingman, Thomas Lanier, 1812-1897.
    Letter of T.L. Clingman. [To the
editors of the Republic. Washington]
Gideon & co., printers [1850]
    4 p.   23 1/2 cm.

1904 [Clinton, De Witt] 1769-1828.
    An account of Abimelech Coody and
other celebrated writers of New-York.
In a letter from a traveller to his
friend in South Carolina. [New York]
January, 1815.
    16 p.   21 1/2 cm.

1905 Clinton, De Witt, 1769-1828.
    An address delivered before Holland
lodge, December 24, 1793, by De Witt
Clinton, master of said lodge, on the
evening of his installation. New-
York, Printed by F. Childs and J.
Swaine, 1794; republished by order
of the same Holland lodge, 1859.
    19 p.   16 cm.

1906 Clinton, De Witt, 1769-1828.
    Letters of Governor Clinton, and of

Colonel L. Baldwin ... improved as
evidence before the Joint committee
of the legislature of Massachusetts,
on the petition of Samuel Hinkley
and others, for the extension of the
Hampshire and Hampden canal. February, 1828. Boston, Dutton & Wentworth, state printers, 1828.
22 p.   23 1/2 cm.

1907   [Clinton, De Witt] 1769-1828.
Letters on the natural history and
internal resources of the state of
New-York. By Hibernicus [*pseud.*]
New-York, Sold by E. Bliss & E. White,
1822.
224 p.   18 cm.

1908   Clinton, De Witt, 1769-1828.
A memoir on the antiquities of the
western parts of the state of New-
York. Read before the Literary and
philosophical society of New-York.
By De Witt Clinton ... Albany:
Printed by E. & E. Hosford, 100 State-
street. 1820.
16 p.   22 1/2 cm.

1909   Clinton, De Witt, 1769-1828.
Remarks on the fishes of the western waters of the state of New-York,
in a letter to Samuel L. Mitchell ...
from the Hon. De Witt Clinton ...
Dated New-York, Feb. 1, 1815 ...
[New York, 1815]
8 p.   22 1/2 cm.

1910   [Clinton, De Witt] 1769-1828.
A vindication of Thomas Jefferson;
against the charges contained in a
pamphlet entitled, "Serious

considerations," &c. By Grotius ...
[*pseud.*] New York, Printed by D.
Denniston, 1800.
47 p.   22 1/2 cm.

1911 Clinton, George W[illiam] 1807-1885.
Preliminary list of plants of
Buffalo and its vicinity. By George
W. Clinton ... Buffalo, Young, Lock-
wood & co.'s steam press, 1864.
12 p.   23 cm.

1912 Clinton, Henry Lauren, 1820-1889.
Speech of Henry L. Clinton, esq.,
to the jury, on the part of the de-
fense, in the case of Andrew J. Mills-
paugh, against Seth Adams, 3d, in the
Supreme court, at a circuit holden
in the city of New York. Delivered
January 24th, 1865. New York, Baptist
& Taylor, printers, 1865.
53 p.   23 1/2 cm.

1913 Clippings from the California press in
regard to steam across the Pacific,
from March to November, 1860 ... San
Francisco, Towne & Bacon, printers,
1860.
104 p.   23 cm.

1914 [Clopper, Jonas]
Fragments of the history of Bawl-
fredonia: containing an account of
the discovery and settlement of the
great southern continent, and of the
formation and progress of the Bawlfredonian commonwealth. By Herman
Thwackius [*pseud.*] Tr. from the
original Bawlfredonian manuscript,
into the French language, by monsieur
Traducteur, and rendered into English,

by a citizen of America. [Baltimore?]
Printed for the American booksellers,
1819.
   2 p. l., 164 p. front.   22 cm.

1915 Clough, Simon.
     A candid appeal to the citizens of
the United States, proving that the
doctrines advanced and the measures
pursued by the abolitionists, relative to the subject of emancipation,
are inconsistent with the teachings
and directions of the Bible, and that
those clergymen engaged in the dis-
semination of these principles, should
be immediately dismissed by their respective congregations, as false teachers. By Simon Clough ... New York, A.
K. Bertron, 1834.
   39 p.   22 cm.

1916 Clubb, Henry Stephen, *b*. 1827.
     The Maine liquor law: its origin,
history, and results, including a
life of Hon. Neal Dow. By Henry S.
Clubb ... New York, Pub. for the
Maine law statistical society, by
Fowler and Wells, 1856.
   430 p. front, plates, ports.,
fold. map. 19 cm.

1917 Clubb, Stephen, *b*. 1762.
     A journal; containing an account
of the wrongs, sufferings, and neglect, experienced by Americans in
France. By Stephen Clubb ... Boston, 1809.
   1 p. l., ii, [5]-60 p. 23 cm.

1918 Cluseret, Gustave Paul, 1823-1900.
     Mexico, and the solidarity of

nations. By General G. Cluseret.
New York, Blackwell, printer, 1866.
 109 p.   23 cm.

1919 [Clymer, George] *d.* 1881-
       The principles of naval staff rank;
    and its history in the United States
    navy, for over half a century. By
    a surgeon in the U.S. navy. [Washing-
    ton?] 1869.
       240 p.   23 1/2 cm.

1920 The Coast survey. Reply to the official
    defence of its cost, abuses and power.
    [New York? 1858]
       36 p.   20 1/2 cm.

1921 Coates, Benjamin.
       Cotton cultivation in Africa. Sug-
    gestions on the importance of the
    cultivation of cotton in Africa, in
    reference to the abolition of slavery
    in the United States, through the or-
    ganization of an African civilization
    society. By Benjamin Coates. Phila-
    delphia, Printed by C. Sherman & son,
    1858.
       52 p.   22 1/2 cm.

1922 Coates, B[enjamin] H[ornor]
       Annual discourse, delivered before
    the Historical society of Pennsylvania,
    on the 28th day of April, 1834, on
    the origin of the Indian population
    of America. By B.H. Coates, M.D. ...
    Philadelphia, Printed for M'Carty &
    Davis, 1834.
       63, [1] p.   8 cm.

1923 Coates, Reynell, 1802-1886.

Oration on the defects in the present system of medical instruction in
the United States. Read before the
Philadelphia medical society, November
21, 1835. By Reynell Coates ... Philadelphia, J. Kay, jun. and brother,
[1835]
    32 p.   21 cm.

1924 Coats, William.
    The Geography of Hudson's bay: be-
ing the remarks of Captain W. Coats,
in many voyages to that locality,
between the years 1727 and 1751. With
an appendix, containing extracts from
the log of Capt. Middleton on his voyage for the discovery of the North-west
passage, in H.M.S. "Furnace," in 1741-
2. Ed. by John Barrow ... London,
Printed for the Hakluyt society, 1852.
    4 p. l., x, 147, [1] p.   22 cm.

1925 Cobb, Alvan.
    God's culture of his vineyard. A
sermon, delivered at Plymouth before
the Robinson congregation, on the 22d
of December, 1831. By Alvan Cobb ...
Taunton, E. Anthony, 1832.
    24 p.   22 cm.

1926 Cobb, Howell, 1815-1868.
    A Scriptural examination of the
institution of slavery in the United
States; with its objects and purposes.
By Howell Cobb. [Perry?] Ga., Printed
for the author, 1856.
    173 p.   19 1/2 cm.

1927 Cobb, Lyman, 1800-1864.
    The evil tendencies of corporal
punishment as a means of moral

discipline in families and schools,
examined and discussed. In two parts.
Pt. I.--Objections to the use of the
rod. Pt. II.--Substitutes for, and
preventives of, the use of the rod.
With an appendix ... By Lyman Cobb.
New York, M.H. Newman & co., 1847.
270 p. incl. front. 22 1/2 cm.

1928 Cobb, Sylvanus, 1798-1866.
Autobiography of the first forty-
one years of the life of Sylvanus Cobb,
D.D., to which is added a memoir, by
his eldest son, Sylvanus Cobb, jr.
Boston, Universalist publishing house,
1867.
552 p. front. (port.) 20 cm.

1929 Cobbe, Frances Power, 1822-1904.
The red flag in John Bull's eyes.
By Frances Power Cobbe ... London,
E. Faithfull, 1863.
24 p. 18 cm.

1930 Cobbett, James Paul.
Causes of the civil war in the Unit-
ed States. By James Paul Cobbett.
London, R. Hardwicke; Manchester, J.
Heywood, 1861.
16 p. 21 1/2 cm.

1931 [Cobbett, William] 1762-1835.
... A bone to gnaw, for the democrats; containing, 1st. Observations
on a patriotic pamphlet. Entitled,
"Proceedings of the United Irishmen."
2dly. Democratic principles exemplified by example. 3dly. Democratic
memoires; or An account of some recent
feats performed by the Frenchified
citizens of the United States of

442

America. 2d ed., with a new preface,
to which is subjoined a song, to be
sung by the democrats at their future
nocturnal meetings. By Peter Porcupine [*pseud.*] Philadelphia, Printed
& sold by T. Bradford, 1795.
  vii, [1], 66 p.   22 1/2 cm.

1932 [Cobbett, William] 1763-1835.
  A bone to gnaw for the democrats.
By Peter Porcupine [*pseud.*] ... To
which is prefixed A rod, for the backs
of the critics; containing an historical sketch of the present state of
political criticism in Great Britain;
as examplified in the conduct of the
Monthly, Critical, and Analytical reviews, &c. &c. Interspersed with anecdotes. By Humphrey Hedgehog [*pseud.*]
... London, Printed for J. Wright,
1797.
  2 p. l., xcv, [1] , v, [7] -175 p.
20 cm.

1933 Cobbett, William, 1763-1835.
  The emigrant's guide; in ten letters, addressed to the taxpayers of
England; containing information of
every kind, necessary to persons who
are about to emigrate; including sev
eral authentic and most interesting
letters from English emigrants, now
in America, to their relations in
England. By William Cobbett. London,
The author, 1829.
  153 p.   18 cm.

1934 [Cobbett, William] 1763-1835.
  French arrogance; or, "The cat
let out of the bag"; a poetical
dialogue between the envoys of

America, and X.Y.Z. and the lady.
Philadelphia: Published by Peter
Porcupine, opposite Christ-church,
and sold by the principal booksellers.
1798. [Price 25 cents.] [Copy-right
secured according to law.]
31 p. 20 1/2 cm.

1935 [Cobbett, William] 1763-1835.
A kick for a bite; or, Review upon
review; with a critical essay, on the
works of Mrs. S. Rowson; in a letter
to the editor, or editors, of the
American monthly review. By Peter
Porcupine [*pseud.*] ... Philadelphia,
Printed by T. Bradford, 1795.
31 p. 23 cm.

1936 [Cobbett, William] 1763-1835.
A letter to the infamous Tom Paine,
in answer to his letter to General
Washington. [Philadelphia, William
Cobbett, opposite Christ church, 1796]
18 p. 22 cm.

1937 Cobbett, William, 1763-1835.
Letters on the late war between the
United States and Great Britain: together with other miscellaneous writings, on the same subject. By William
Cobbett, esq. New-York: Published
by J. Belden and co., Van Winkle &
Wiley, printers . . . . . 1815.
vii, [9]-407 p. 22 1/2 cm.

1938 Cobbett, William, 1763-1835.
Life of Andrew Jackson, president
of the United States of America.
Abridged and comp. by William Cob-
bett, M.P. for Oldham ... London
[Printed by Mills, Jowett, and Mills]

1834.
2 p. 1., [iii]-x, [11]-142 p.
front. (port.)   18 cm.

1939   Cobbett, W[illiam] 1762-1835.
The life of W. Cobbett, esq.,
M.P. for Oldham.   Written by himself.
7th ed.   London, Pub. for the proprietor, by W. Strange [etc., 1835?]
32 p.   18 cm.

1940   Cobbett, William, 1763-1835.
Porcupine's works; containing
various writings and selections, exhibiting a faithful picture of the United
States of America; of their government,
laws, politics, and resources: of the
characters of their presidents, gover-
nors, legislators, magistrates, and
military men; and of the customs,
manners, morals, religion, virtues
and vices of the people: comprising
also a complete series of historical
documents and remarks, from the end of
the war, in 1783, to the election of
the President, in March, 1801.   By
William Cobbett.   In twelve volumes.
(A volume to be added annually.) ...
London, Printed for Cobbett and
Morgan, 1801.
12 v.   21 1/2 cm.

1941   Cobbett, William, 1763-1835.
The pride of Britannia humbled; or,
The queen of the coean unqueen'd, by
"the American cock boats," and the fir
built things, with bits of striped
bunting at their mast heads" ...   Illustrated and demonstrated by four
letters addressed to Lord Liverpool

on the late American war. By William
Cobbett, esq. To which is added, a
glimpse of the American victories, on
land, on the lakes and on the ocean.
With a persuasive to political moderation ... Published by T. Boyle, of
New York; Wm. Reynolds, of Philadelphia;
and J. Campbell, of Baltimore . . . . .
1815.
216 p. 19 cm.

1942 [Cobbett, William] 1762-1835.
A prospect from the Congress-gal-
lery, during the session, begun December 7, 1795. Containing, the President's speech, the addresses of both
houses, some of the debates in the
Senate, and all the principal debates
in the House of representatives ...
With occasional remarks, by Peter
Porcupine [pseud.] The 2d ed. Philadelphia, T. Bradford, 1796.
iv, 64 p. 22 1/2 cm.

1943 [Cobbett, William] 1763-1835.
The republican judge: or, The American liberty of the press, as exhibited, explained, and exposed, in the base
and partial prosecution of William Cobbett, for a pretended libel against
the king of Spain and his ambassador,
before the Supreme court of Pennsylvania. With an address to the people
of England. By Peter Porcupine [pseud.]
London, J. Wright, 1798.
1 p. 1., v, [7]-96 p. 21 cm.

1944 [Cobbett, William] 1763-1835.
The scare-crow; being an infamous
letter, sent to Mr. John Oldden, threat-
ening destruction to his house, and

violence to the person of his tenant, William Cobbett; with remarks
on the same. By Peter Porcupine
[*pseud.*] Philadelphia: Printed for,
and sold by, William Cobbett, North
Second street, opposite Christ church.
M.DCC.XCVI.
23 p.   20 cm.

1945   [Cobbett, William] 1762-1835.
Tit for tat; or, A purge for a pill:
being an answer to a scurrilous pamphlet, lately published, entitled, "A
pill for Porcupine." To which is added, A poetical rhapsody on the times.
Describing the disasters of an emigrant ... By Dick Retort [*pseud.*]
Philadelphia: Printed for the author
[1796]
v, [7]-34, 25 p.   22 cm.

1946   [Cobden, Richard] 1804-1865.
A friendly voice from England on
American affairs ... New York, W.C.
Bryant & co., printers, 1862.
30 p.   23 cm.

1947   Cobden, Richard, 1804-1865.
Political writings. London, W.
Ridgway; New York, D. Appleton &
co., 1867.
2 v.   22 cm.

1948   Cobden, Richard, 1804-1865.
Speech of Mr. Cobden, on the "Foreign enlistment act," in the House of
commons, Friday, April 24th, 1863.
London, W. Ridgway, 1863.
25 p.   20 1/2 cm.

1949 Cobden, Richard, 1804-1865.
     The three panics; an historical
     episode. By Richard Cobden ... 3d
     ed. London, Ward & co., 1862.
     2 p. l., 152 p. incl. tab.   21 cm.

1950 Cobleigh, Nelson E.
     Iniquity abounding. A sermon;
     preached at the Laurel street Method-
     ist Episcopal church, on Fast Day,
     April 10, 1851. By Rev. N.E. Cob-
     leigh ... Worcester, J. Burrill &
     co., 1851.
     16 p.   22 1/2 cm.

1951 Coburn, Edward Otis, b. 1830, defendant.
     ... Complete report of the trial of
     Edward O. Coburn, and Benjamin F. Dal-
     ton, for the manslaughter of William
     Sumner. By the reporter of the Times.
     Boston, Burnham, Federhen & co. [1856]
     58 p.   incl. 1 port.   27 cm.

1952 Cochrane, Clark Betton, 1815-1867.
     Address delivered at the centennial
     celebration of the incorporation of
     New Boston, New Hampshire, July 4,
     1863, by Clark B. Cochrane. Albany,
     N.Y., J. Munsell, printer, 1863.
     41 p.   24 cm.

1953 Cochrane, John, 1813-1898.
     Speech of Hon. John Cochrane, of
     New York, on the union and the Con-
     stitution. Delivered in the House
     of representatives, December 20,
     1859. [Washington, Printed by L.
     Towers, 1859]
     8 p.   22 cm.

1954 Cockayne, M   S.
       History and adventure; or, Stories
    of remarkable men of all nations.
    By M.S. Cockayne ... London, Binns
    and Goodwin, 1854.
       4 p. l., 344 p. front., plates.
    17 cm.

1955 Cockburn, *Sir* Alexander James Edmund,
    1802-1880.
       Nationality: or, The law relating
    to subjects and aliens, considered
    with a view to future legislation.
    By the Right Hon. Sir Alex. Cockburn
    ... London, W. Ridgway, 1869.
       1 p. l., 217 p.   22 1/2 cm.

1956 Cockburn, G.   F.
       Rapport sur les bassins proposés
    et l'extension du canal Lachine, à
    travers la cité de Montreal. Par
    G.F. Cockburn ... Juin 1854. Mon-
    treal, Impr. de La Minerve, 1854.
       7 p.   20 cm.

1957 Cockburn, John, *mariner*.
       A journey over land, from the Gulf
    of Honduras to the great South-Sea.
    Performed by John Cockburn, and five
    other Englishmen ... To which is add-
    ed ... A brief discoverye of some
    things best worth noteinge in the
    travells of Nicholas Withington, a
    factor in the East-Indiase. London,
    C. Rivington, 1735.
       viii, 349 p. fold. map.   20 cm.

1958 Cockburn, John, *mariner*.
       The unfortunate Englishmen: or, A
    faithful narrative of the distresses
    and adventures of John Cockburn, and

five other English mariners ... who
were taken by a Spanish guarda costa
in the John and Ann, Edward Burt,
master, and set on shore at a place
call'd Porto-Cavallo ... Containing
a journey over land from the Gulph of
Honduras to the great South Sea ...
As also an account of the manners,
customs, and behaviour of the several
Indians inhabiting a tract of land
of 2400 miles ... London, Printed and
sold by the booksellers of London and
Westminster, 1740.
     iv, 5-190 p.   17 cm.

1959   Cocke, Richard Ivanhoe.
          An address delivered before the
       Licivyronean society of William and
       Mary college, 15th May, 1847, the
       anniversary of the political indepen-
       dence of Virginia.   By Richard Ivan-
       hoe Cocke, of Fulvanna County.   Rich-
       mond, Printed by Shepherd and Colin,
       1847.
          22 p.   22 1/2 cm.

1960   Cocke, William Archer.
          The constitutional history of the
       United States, from the adoption of
       the Articles of confederation to the
       close of Jackson's administration.
       By William Archer Cocke.   In two
       volumes.   Vol. I.   Philadelphia, J.B.
       Lippincott & co., 1858.
          430 p.   22 cm.

1961   [Codding Milo Defonz]
          The issues of the hour, political
       and military: being reminiscences
       and conclusions ...   Rochester, N.Y.,

M. Defonz, 1863.
60 p. 19 cm.

1962 Coddington, David Smith, 1823-1865.
Eulogy on President Lincoln, by
David S. Coddington, delivered in
the Citadel square church, Charleston, S.C., May 6th, 1865, at the request of the officers and soldiers
in the Northern district, Department
of the South ... New York, Baker &
Godwin, printers, 1865.
2 p. l., [3]-30 p. 23 cm.

1963 Codman, John, 1782-1847.
The importance of moderation in
civil rulers. A sermon delivered
before His Excellency Edward Everett, governor, the honourable Council, and the legislature of Massachusetts, at the annual election,
January 1, 1840. By John Codman
... Boston, Dutton and Wentworth,
printers to the state, 1840.
32 p. 23 1/2 cm.

1964 [Coe, David Benton] 1814-1895.
Record of the Coe family. 1596-
1856. New York, J.A. Gray's printing
office, 1856.
14 p. 23 cm.

1965 [Coffey, W   A   ]
Inside out; or, An interior view of
the New-York state prison; together
with biographical sketches of the
lives of several of the convicts ...
By one who knows. New-York, Printed
for the author, and sold by J. Cos-
tigan, 1823.

xi, [13]-251 p.   17 1/2 cm.

1966   Coffin, Alexander, 1765?-1836.
The destructive operation of foul
air, tainted provisions, bad water
and personal filthiness upon human
constitutions; exemplified in the unparalleled cruelty of the British to
the American captives at New York during the revolutionary war, on board
their prison and hospital ships, in
a communication to Dr. Mitchill, dated
September 4, 1807. Also a letter to
the Tammany society, upon the same
subject, by Captain Alexander Coffin,
jun., one of the surviving sufferers,
with an introduction, by Charles I.
Bushnell. New York, Priv. print.,
1865.
   iv, [5]-28 p. front. (port.) pl.
25 1/2 cm.

1967   Coffin, Charles Carleton, 1823-1896.
Our new way round the world. By
Charles Carleton Coffin ...   Boston,
Fields, Osgood, & co., 1869.
   xviii, 524 p. front., illus.   20
1/2 cm.

1968   Coffin, Ebenezer, 1769-1816.
A sermon delivered February 22d,
1800, the day of national mourning,
recommended by the government of the
United States. For the death of General George Washington ... By the
Rev. Ebenezer Coffin, A.B., pastor of
a church in Brunswick. Portland [Me.]
Printed by Rand & Burdick, 1800.
   16 p.   21 cm.

1969   Coffin, James Henry, 1806-1873.

... Winds of the northern hemisphere.
By James H. Coffin ... [Washington,
Smithsonian institution, 1853]
vi, [5]-197, [1] p.   illus., VIII
pl. incl. maps (1 fold.)   32 1/2 cm.

1970   Coffin, John Gorham, 1770-1829.
An address delivered before the
contributors of the Boston dispen-
sary at their seventeenth anniversary, October 21, 1843. By John G.
Coffin ... Boston, Printed by J.
Eliot, 1813.
22 p.   21 cm.

1971   Coffin, Joshua, 1792-1864.
A list of some of the descendants
of Mr. Edward Woodman, who settled
at Newbury, Mass., 1635. Comp. by
Joshua Coffin. Newburyport, Mass.,
Printed for Cyrus Woodman, at the
Union job office, 1855.
16 p.   18 cm.

1972   Coffin, Joshua, 1792-1864.
A sketch of the history of Newbury,
Newburyport, and West Newbury, from
1635 to 1845. By Joshua Coffin ...
Boston, S.G. Drake, 1845.
viii, [9]-116 p.   illus. (incl.
plan) ports. (incl. front.) facsim.
24 cm.

1973   Coffin, Joshua, 1792-1864.
The Toppans of Toppan's lane, with
their descendants and relations.
Collected and arranged by Joshua
Coffin. Newburyport, W.H. Huse &
co., printers, 1862.
30 p. incl. mounted phot.   22 cm.

1974 Coffin, Nathaniel Wheeler, 1815-1869.
America, an ode: and other poems.
By N.W. Coffin ... Boston, S.G.
Simpkins, 1843.
viii, 124 p. 18 cm.

1975 Coffin, Robert Barry, 1826-1886.
Cakes and ale at Woodbine; from
Twelfth night to New Year's day.
by Barry Gray [*pseud.*] New York,
Hurd and Houghton, 1868.
vi, [7]-229 p. 18 cm.

1976 [Coffin, Robert Stevenson] 1797-1827.
The life of the Boston bard, written by himself ... Mount Pleasant,
N.Y., Stephen Marshall, Roscoe,
printer, 1825.
2 p. 1., 203 p. 20 1/2 cm.

1977 [Coffin, Robert Stevenson] 1797-1827.
Oriental harp. Poems of the Boston
bard ... Providence, R.I., Printed
and published by Smith & Parmenter,
agents for the sale of the Oriental
harp, 1826.
254 p. incl. front. (port.) 24
1/2 cm.

1978 Coffin, William Foster, 1808-1878.
1812; the war, and its moral: a
Canadian chronicle. By William F.
Coffin ... Montreal, Printed by J.
Lovell, 1864.
xvi, 17 -296 p. 22 1/2 cm.

1979 Coggeshall, George, *b.* 1784.
An historical sketch of commerce
and navigation, from the birth of
the Saviour down to the present
date (1860); with remarks on their

beneficial results to Christianity
and civilization ... By George Coggeshall ... New York, Printed by G.P.
Putnam, 1860.
    526 p. front. (port.) pl.   24
cm.

1980 Coggeshall, George, 1784-1861.
    History of the American privateers,
and letters-of-marque, during our war
with England in the years 1812, '13
and '14. Interspersed with several
naval battles between American and
British ships-of-war. By George
Coggeshall. New York, The author,
1856.
    liv p., 1 l., 438 p. front., pl.
22 cm.

1981 Coggeshall, George, b. 1784.
    Second series of voyages to various
parts of the world, made between the
years 1802 and 1841. By George Coggeshall. Selected from his ms. journal of eighty voyages. New York,
D. Appleton & company, 1852.
    335 p. front. (port.)   23 1/2 cm.

1982 Coggeshall, William Turner, 1824-1867.
    Lincoln memorial. The journeys of
Abraham Lincoln: from Springfield
to Washington, 1861, as president elect;
and from Washington to Springfield;
1865, as president martyred; comprising an account of public ceremonies
on the entire route, and full details
of both journeys. By William T.
Coggeshall. Columbus, Ohio state
journal, 1865.
    327 p. incl. front. (port.)   20 cm.

1983   Coggeshall, W[illiam] T[urner] 1824-1867.
The newspaper record, containing a
complete list of newspapers and per-
iodicals in the United States, Canadas,
and Great Britain, together with a
sketch of the origin and progress of
printing, with some facts about newspapers in Europe and America, by W.T.
Coggeshall. Philadelphia, Lay & brother, 1856.
xiv, 194 p. illus.   22 1/2 cm.

1984   Coggeshall, William Turner, 1824-1867.
The protective policy in literature.
A discourse on the social and moral
advantages of the cultivation of local literature. By William T. Coggeshall ... Delivered before the Beta
theta pi society of Ohio university
at the 54th commencement, June 22d,
1858. Columbus, O., Follett, Foster
and company, 1859.
29 p.   21 1/2 cm.

1985   Coggeshall, William Turner, 1824-1867.
The signs of the times: comprising
a history of the spirit-rappings, in
Cincinnati and other places; with
notes of clairvoyant revealments, by
William T. Coggshall ... Cincinnati,
The author, 1851.
144 p.   17 1/2 cm.

1986   Coghlan, *Mrs*. Margaret (Moncrieffe)
Memoirs of Mrs. Coghlan, (daughter
of the late Major Moncrieffe,) written by herself, and dedicated to the
British nation; being interspersed
with anecdotes of the late American
and present French war, with remarks

moral and political ... London, J.
Lane, 1794.
xv, 137 p. 17 1/2 cm.

1987 Cogswell, Elliott Colby, 1814-1887.
History of New Boston, New Hampshire. Comp. and written by Elliott
C. Cogswell ... Boston, Press of
G.C. Rand & Avery, 1864.
469, [1] p. front., plates, ports.
fold. map. 24 cm.

1988 Cogswell, Elliott Colby.
Memoir of the Rev. Samuel Hidden.
By E.C. Cogswell. Boston, Crocker
& Brewster, 1842.
xiii, 17 -332 p. front. (port.)
16 1/2 cm.

1989 Cogswell, Nathaniel, 1773-1813.
An oration, delivered before the
Republican citizens of Newburyport,
in the Rev. John Giles' meeting-
house, on the Fourth of July, 1808.
By Nathaniel Cogswell, esq. Newburyport, Printed by W. and J. Gilman,
Middlestreet. 1808.
19 p. 21 1/2 cm.

1990 Cohen, Myer M.
Notices of Florida and the campaigns.
By M.M. Cohen, (an officer of the
left wing.) Charleston, C.S., Burges
& Honour; New-York, B.B. Hussey,
1836.
240 p. front. (fold. map) pl.
18 1/2 cm.

1991 Cohoes, *N.Y. Charters.*
Laws relating to the incorporation

of villages, and the by-laws of the
village of Cohoes. Cohoes, J.H.
Masten, printer, 1855.
    68 p.   21 cm.

1992 Coke, Edward Thomas, 1807-1888.
    A subaltern's furlough; descriptive
of scenes in various parts of the United States, upper and lower Canada, New-
Brunswick, and Nova Scotia, during the
summer and autumn of 1832. By E.T.
Coke ... New-York, J. & J. Harper,
1833.
    2 v.   20 1/2 cm.

1993 Coke, Thomas, *bp.*, 1747-1814.
    A history of the West Indies, con-
taining the natural, civil, and ecclesiastical history of each island; with an
account of the missions instituted in
those islands, from the commencement
of their civilization; but more especially of the missions which have been
established in that archipelago by the
society late in connexion with the
Rev. John Wesley. By Thomas Coke ...
Liverpool, Printed by Nuttall, Fisher,
and Dixon, 1808-11.
    3 v. 5 pl. (4 fold., incl. front.,
v. 3) fold, map (front., v. 1)   21
1/2 cm.

1994 Coke, Thomas, *bp.*, 1747-1814.
    ... A journal, of the Rev. Dr.
Coke's fourth tour on the continent
of America. London, Printed by G.
Paramore, 1792.
    23 p.   19 cm.

1995 Coke, Thomas, *bp.*, 1747-1814.
    A statement of the receipts and

disbursements for the support of the
missions established by the Methodist
society, for the instruction and conversion of the Negroes in the West-
Indies, addressed to the subscribers.
By Thomas Coke, L.L. D.   London,
M,DCC, XCIV.
94 p.   19 cm.

1996   Colvin, John B.
Republican policy; or, The superiority of the principles of the present
administration over those of its
enemies, who call themselves Federal-
ists; exemplified in the late cession
of Louisiana.   By John B. Colvin ...
[Frederick-Town, Md., 1802]
23 p.   20 1/2 cm.

1997   [Colwell, Stephen] 1800-1871.
The five cotton states and New York;
or, Remarks upon the social and econ-
omical aspects of the southern political crisis.   [Philadelphia?] 1861.
64 p.   24 cm.

1998   [Colwell, Stephen] 1800-1871.
New themes for the Protestant clergy:
creeds without charity, theology without humanity, and Protestantism without Christianity: with notes by the
editor on the literature of charity,
population, pauperism, political economy, and Protestantism.   Philadelphia,
Lippincott, Grambo & co., 1851.
1 p. 1., v-xv, 5-383 p.   20 cm.

1999   [Colwell, Stephen] 1800-1871.
Politics for American Christians:
a word upon our example as a nation,
our labour, our trade, elections,

459

education, and congressional legislation. Philadelphia, Lippincott,
Grambo & co., 1852.
1 p. l., iv, [5]-134 p.   23 cm.

2000   Colwell, Stephen, 1800-1871.
The position of Christianity in the
United States, in its relations with
our political institutions, and spe-
cially with reference to religious
instruction in the public schools. By
Stephen Colwell. Philadelphia, Lippincott, Grambo & co., 1854.
viii, 9-175 p.   22 cm.

2001   Colwell, Stephen, 1800-1871.
The ways and means of payment; a
full analysis of the credit system,
with its various modes of adjustment:
By Stephen Colwell. Philadelphia, J.
B. Lippincott & co., 1859.
xii, 644 p.   23 1/2 cm.

2002   Colyer, Vincent, 1825-1888.
Report of the Christian mission to
the United States army, by Vincent
Colyer, presented To St. George's
church, New York, and other societies,
from April 1861 to August 1862, including the battles of Bull Run, Roanoke
Island and New-bern. New York, G.A.
Whitehorne, printer [1862?]
24 p.   22 1/2 cm.

2003   Combier, Cyprien, *b*. 1805.
Voyage au golfe de Californie ...
Nuits de la zone torride; par C.
Combier. Accompagné d'une carte
de la Sonora, dressée par M.V.A.
Malte-Brun ... Paris, A. Bertrand
[1864]

xvi, 544 p. fold. map. 22 cm.

2004 Combs, Leslie, 1793-1881.
Col. Wm. Dudley's defeat opposite
Fort Meigs. May 5th, 1813. Official
report from Captain Leslie Combs to
General Green Clay. Printed for Wil-
liam Dodge. Cincinnati, Spiller &
Gates, printers, 1869.
13 p. 24 cm.

2005 Comettant, Jean Pierre Oscar, 1819-1898.
Trois ans aux États-Unis; étude
des moeurs et coutumes américaines,
par M. Oscar Comettant. Paris, Pag-
nerre, 1857.
2 p. l., 364 p. 18 1/2 cm.

2006 Comfield, *Mrs.* Amelia Stratton.
Alida: or, Miscellaneous sketches
of incidents during the late American
war, Founded on fact. With poems.
By the unknown author of the former
editions, Mrs. Amelia Stratton Comfield ... 4th ed., with additions,
revised and improved. New York,
Printed for the author by Angell &
Engel, 1849.
ix, [1] p., 1 l., [13] 240 p.
incl. front. (port.) 20 cm.

2007 Commercial convention, *Detroit,* 1865.
Proceedings of the commercial
convention, held in Detroit, July
11th, 12th, 13th and 14th, 1865.
Pub. by order of the Convention.
Detroit, Advertiser and Tribune company print, 1865.
276 p. 22 1/2 cm.

2008 Commercial directory; containing, a

461

topographical description, extent
and productions of different sec-
tions of the Union, statistical information relative to manufactures, commercial and port regulations, a list
of the principal commercial houses,
tables of imports and exports, foreign and domestic; tables of foreign
coins, weights and measures, tariff
of duties.   Philadelphia, J.C. Kay-
ser & co., 1823.
  2 p. 1., [iii]-viii, 242 p., 1 1.,
41 p. front. (fold. Map) 6 pl.,
tables.   25 1/2 cm.

2009   A comparison between the British sugar
colonies and New England, as they
relate to the interest of Great Britain. With some observations on the
state of the case of New England. To
which is added A letter to a member
of Parliament. London, Printed for
J. Roberts, 1732.
  43 p.   19 cm.

2010   Compendio de la historia de los Estados
Unidos de America; puesto en castellan
Al que se han anadido la Declaración
de la independencia y la Constitución
de su gobierno. Nueva York, Impr.
de Tompkins y Floyd, 1825.
  2 p. 1., iv, 296 p., 1 1.   front.
(port.)   14 1/2 cm.

2011   Compendio del confesonario en mexicano
y castellano para que los que ignoren
el primero puedan á lo menos en los
casos de necesidad administrar á
los indígenas el sacramento de la
penitencia. Por un sacerdote del
obispado de Puebla. [Puebla]

462

Imprenta antigua en el portal de las
flores, 1840.
43 p.   14 cm.

2012   A complaint to the ____ of ____ against
a pamphlet intitled, A speech intended to have been spoken on the
bill for altering the charters of
the colony of Massachuset's Bay ...
London, Printed for B. White, 1775.
vii, 40 p.   20 cm.

2013   A complete practical guide to Her Majesty's civil service: containing (in
full) the examination papers for every department, used since the appointment of the commissioners; full
details of the limits of age and qual-
ification of candidates; hints to candidates for every office; and copious
tables of the emoluments and superann-
uation allowances of every civil servant in Great Britain, Ireland, India,
and the colonies. By a certificated
candidate, an officer of Her Majesty's civil service. London, J.
Blackwood [1860?]
250 p., 1 l., 107 p.   18 1/2 cm.

2014   Conant, Gaius, 1776-1862.
An oration pronounced at Franklin
on the Fourth of July, 1803. The
anniversary of the independence of
the United States of America. By
Gaius Conant. Printed at Providence,
by Nathaniel Heaton, jun. M,DCCC,III.
12 p.   20 1/2 cm.

2015   Conant, Sylvanus, 1720-1777.
The art of war, the gift of God.

463

A discourse delivered at Middlebor-
ough, before three military companies,
April 6, 1759. Being the day of gen-
eral muster in the Massachusetts Pro-
vince, for the Canada-expedition. By
Silvanus Conant, A.M., pastor of the
First church in said Middleborough ...
Boston: Printed by Edes and Gill in
Queen-Street, 1759.
16 p. 19 1/2 cm.

2016   [Conant, Sylvanus] 1720-1777.
A letter, occasioned by the death of
Mrs. Abigail Conant, late of Middleborough. New London, Conn., Printed
by T. Green, 1759.
8 p. 22 cm.

2017   Conciliator, *pseud.*
Why are we still at war? or the
American question considered; in a
series of essays rejected by the
journalists as unpopular; recommended to a candid perusal, by Conciliator ...
(*In* The Pamphleteer. London,
1814. 22 1/2 cm. v. 4, p. [551]-
575)

2018   A concise historical account of all the
British colonies in North-America,
comprehending their rise, progress,
and modern state; particularly of
the Massachusets-Bay, (the seat of
the present civil war,) together with
the other provinces of New-England.
To which is annexed, an accurate descriptive table of the several countries ... London, Printed for J.
Bew, 1775.
iv, 196 p. fold. tab. 22 1/2 cm.

2019   Conder, Josiah, 1789-1855.
        Wages or the whip. An essay on
        the comparative cost and productive-
        ness of free and slave labour. By
        Josiah Conder ... London, Hatchard
        and son [etc.] 1833.
        iv, 91 p.   21 cm.

2020   Condict, Ira, 1764-1811.
        A funeral discourse, delivered in
        the Presbyterian church of New-
        Brunswick, on the 31st of December,
        1799; the day set apart by the citi-
        zens for paying solemn honors to the
        memory of Gen. George Washington.
        By the Rev. Ira Condict ...   New-
        Bbunswick [!] New-Jersey, Printed by
        Abraham Blauvelt, 1800.
        iv, [5]-23 p.   21 cm.

2021   Condie, David Francis, 1796-1875.
        Annual oration delivered before the
        Philadelphia medical society, by ap-
        pointment, at the opening of its
        session of 1844-5. By D. Francis
        Condie ...   Published by order of the
        Society. Philadelphia, King and
        Baird, printers, 1845.
        24 p.   20 1/2 cm.

2022   Condie, Thomas, 1775?-1814.
        History of the pestilence, commonly
        called yellow fever, which almost
        desolated Philadelphia, in the months
        of August, September & October,
        1798. By Thomas Condie & Richard
        Folwell. Philadelphia, From the
        press of R. Folwell [1799]
        1 p. l., [5]-108, xxxii, [67] p.
        22 cm.

465

2023 Condit, Jonathan Bailey, 1808-1876.
      An address delivered before the
      literary societies of Dartmouth col-
      lege, July 28, 1841. By J.B. Condit.
      Portland [Me.] N.A. Foster, printer,
      1841.
      31 p.   22 cm.

2024 Condit, Jonathan Bailey, 1808-1876.
      Education at the West; in its
      claims on the church. A discourse,
      delivered before the Society for
      promoting collegiate and theological
      education at the West, in the Central
      church, New Haven, October 26, 1848,
      by J.B. Condit ... New York, M.W.
      Dodd, 1849.
      30 p.   21 1/2 cm.

2025 [Condorcet, Marie Jean Antoine Nicolas
      Caritat, *marquis* de] 1743-1794.
      Éloge de M. Franklin, lu à la
      séance publique de l'Académie des
      sciences, le 13 nov. 1790 ... Paris,
      Pyre [etc.] 1791.

2026 The conduct of the Dutch relating to
      their breach of treaties with Eng-
      land. Particularly their breach of
      the articles of capitulation, for
      the surrender of Surinam, in 1667;
      and their oppressions committed
      upon the English subjects in that
      colony. With a full account of the
      case of Jeronimy Clifford ... Lon-
      don, W. Bristow, 1760.
      1 p. 1., 220 p.   21 cm.

2027 The conduct of the ministry impartially
      examined. In a letter to the mer-
      chants of London. London, printed

for S. Bladon, 1756.
68 p.   20 1/2 cm.

2028 The conduct of the two b——rs vindicated;
      the examiner's numerous contradictions
      and inconsistencies exemplify'd; his
      false facts delineated. And his ro-
      mantic conjectures exploded ... Lon-
      don, Printed for M. Cooper, 1749.
          1 p. 1., 37 p.   19 1/2 cm.

2029 Condy, Jeremiah, d. 1768.
          Mercy exemplified, in the conduct
      of a Samaritan; and recommended to
      universal imitation. A sermon preached
      at Boston, in the province of the Massa-
      chusetts-bay. By Jeremy Condy, A.M.
      At Cambridge, in that province. [n.p.]
      Printed 1767.
          26 p.   19 cm.

2030 Cone, Andrew.
          Petrolia: a brief history of the
      Pennsylvania petroleum region, its
      development, growth, resources, etc.,
      from 1859 to 1869. By Andrew Cone
      and Walter R. Johns. Ed. by Walter
      R. Johns. New York, D. Appleton and
      company, 1870.
          iv p., 2 1., [9]-652 p.   12 pl.
      (incl. front.)   19 1/2 cm.

2031 Cone, David D.
          Letters relating to our agricultur-
      al, manufacturing, and commercial in-
      terests, and the action of Congress
      thereon, by D.D. Cone. 5th ed. Wash-
      ington, The United press association,
      1867.
          36 p.   22 1/2 cm.

2032   Cone, David D.
        Washington letters to the Vermont
        journal, Connecticut courant, N.Y.
        tribune, Iron age ... by D.D. Cone,
        president of the United press asso-
        ciation. 8th ed. Washington, The
        United press association, 1867.
        48 p.   23 cm.

2033   Confederate States of America. *Army.*
        Dept. of Mississippi and east
        Louisiana.
        Report of General Joseph E. John-
        ston of his operations in the depart-
        ments of Mississippi and east Lousi-
        ana, together with Lieut. General
        Pemberton's report on the battles of
        Port Gibson, Baker's creek, and the
        siege of Vicksburg. Pub. by order
        of congress. Richmond, R.M. Smith,
        public printer, 1864.
        213 p.   23 1/2 cm.

2034   Confederate States of America. *Army.*
        Dept. of Northern Virginia.
        Report of General Robert E. Lee,
        and subordinate reports of the bat-
        tle of Chancellorsville; also, re-
        ports of Major General J.E.B. Stuart
        and Brigadier General Fitz Lee, of
        cavalry engagements at Kelleysville.
        Also, report of Brigadier General
        W.H.F. Lee, and subordinates, of
        cavalry operations of the 14th and
        15th of April, 1863. Pub. by order
        of Congress. Richmond, R.M. Smith,
        public printer, 1864.
        144, [5] p.   23 1/2 cm.

2035   Confederate States of America. *Army.*
        Dept. of northern Virginia.

Report of General Robert E. Lee,
of operations at Rappahannock bridge;
also, report of Lieut. Gen. E.K.
Smith, of operations in lower Louisiana, and report of Major General Jones,
of engagement at Rogersville, Tennessee. Published by order of Congress.
Richmond, R.M. Smith, public printer,
1864.
61 p.   23 1/2 cm.

2036   Confederate States of America.   *Army.*
       Dept. of northern Virginia.
       Reports of the operations of the
army of northern Virginia, from June
1862, to and including the battle at
Fredericksburg, Dec. 13, 1862. Richmond, R.M. Smith, public printer, 1864.
2 v.   23 cm.

2037   Confederate States of America.   *Army.*
       Dept. of South Carolina, Georgia and
       Florida.
       Report of General G.T. Beauregard
of the defence of Charleston. Pub.
by order of Congress. Richmond, R.M.
Smith, public printer, 1864.
91, [2] p.   23 cm.

2038   Confederate States of America.   *Army.*
       Dept. of south-western Virginia.
       Report of Brigadier General Echols,
of the battle of Droop Mountain. Pub.
by order of Congress. Richmond, R.M.
Smith, public printer, 1864.
16 p.   23 cm.

2039   Confederate States of America.   *Army.*
       Dept. of Tennessee.
       Official report of the battle of
Chickamauga. Pub. by order of

Congress.   Richmond, R.M. Smith, 1864.
234 p.   23 cm.

2040   Confederate States of America. *Army.*
Trans-Mississippi dept.
Report of Major General Hindman,
of his operations in the Trans-
Mississippi district. Published by
order of Congress. Richmond, R.M.
Smith, public printer, 1864.
26 p.   24 cm.

2041   Confederate States of America. *Bureau*
of exchange.
Official correspondence between
the agents of exchange, together with
Mr. Ould's report. Richmond, Sentin-
el job office, 1864.
1 p., 1., p. [63] -149.   23 cm.

2042   Confederate States of America. *Congress.*
Address of Congress to the people
of the Confederate States. [Rich-
mond, 1864]
8 p.   23 cm.

2043   Confederate States of America. *Congress.*
Congress of the Confederate States.
Proceedings on the announcement of
the death of Hon. John Tyler, January 20, 1862. Published by order of
Congress, by J.J. Hooper, secretary.
Richmond, Enquirer book and job press,
1862.
54 p.   21 1/2 cm.

2044   Confederate States of America. *Congress.*
Conference committees.
Report of the Conference committee
on the Exemption bill. [Richmond,
1863?]

1 1.   23 1/2 cm.

2045   Confederate States of America. *Congress.*
       House of representatives.   Committee
       on claims.
          Report of Committee on claims.   In
       the case of Mary Clark.   [Richmond?
       1863]
          4 p.   24 cm.

2046   Confederate States of America. *Congress.*
       House of representatives.   Committee
       on Quartermaster and Commissary depart-
       ments.
          ... Report of the Committee on
       Quartermaster and Commissary depart-
       ments.   [Richmond, 1864]
          3 p.   23 cm.

2047   Confederate States of America. *Congress.*
       House of representatives.   Committee
       on ways and means.
          ...   Minority report of the Com-
       mittee on ways and means on the tax
       bill.   [Richmond, 1864]
          4 p.   23 1/2 cm.

2048   Confederate States of America. *Congress.*
       House of representatives.   Committee
       to enquire into the treatment of
       prisoners at Castle Thunder.
          Evidence taken before the Committee
       of the House of representatives, ap-
       pointed to enquire into the treatment
       of prisoners at Castle Thunder.   [n.p.,
       1863?]
          58 p.   22 1/2 cm.

2049   Confederate States of America. *Congress.*
       House of representatives.   Roanake

island investigation committee.
Report of the Roanoke island investigation committee. Richmond, Enquirer book and job press, Tyler,
Wise, Allegre & Smith, 1862.
14 p.   21 cm.

2050   Confederate States of America. *Congress.*
House of representatives. Special
committee on the recent military dis-
asters.
Report of the Special committees,
on the recent military disasters at
Forts Henry and Donelson, and the
evacuation of Nashville ... Richmond, Enquirer book and job press,
1862.
178 p.   21 cm.

2051   Confederate States of America. *Congress.*
Senate. Committee on foreign rela-
tions.
... Report of the Committee on foreign relations, on the resolution of
the Senate asking for the facts in
relation to the lawless seizure and
capture of the Confederate steamer
Florida in the bay of Bahia, Brazil,
and what action should be taken by
the government to redress the outrage. [Richmond, 1864]
8 p.   25 cm.

2052   Confederate States of America. *Congress.*
Senate. Committee on the judiciary.
... Report of the Committee on the
judiciary, on Senate bill, no. 150.
[Richmond, 1864]
11 p.   24 cm.

2053   Confederate States of America. *Congress.*

Senate. Select committee on a portion of the Message of the president of the 13th instant [March, 1865]
... Report of the Select committee to whom was referred that portion of the Message of the president of the Confederate States, of the 13th instant, relating to the action of Congress during the present session. [Richmond, 1865]
8 p.   25 cm.

2054 Confederate States of America. *Dept. of justice.*
Report of the attorney general. Department of justice, Richmond, November 18, 1863. [Richmond, 1863]
15 p.   23 cm.

2055 Confederate States of America. *Dept. of justice.*
Report of the attorney general. Department of justice, Richmond, April 25, 1864. [Richmond, 1864]
2 p.   24 cm.

2056 Confederate States of America. *District courts. Alabama.*
Rules of practice under the sequestration act for the District courts Confederate States, for the district of Alabama. Adopted, November, 1861. Mobile, By S.H. Goetzel & co., 1861.
19 p.   21 1/2 cm.

2057 Confederate States of America. *Laws, statutes, etc.*
Acts and resolutions of the first session of the Provisional congress of the Confederate States, held at

Montgomery, Ala. Richmond, Enquirer
book and job press, by Tyler, Wise,
Allegre & Smith, 1861.
(*In* Provisional and permanent con-
stitutions, of the Confederate States.
Richmond, Tyler, Wise, Allegre and
Smith, printers, 1861. 159 p. 22
cm. p. [33]-159)

2058 Confederate States of America. *Laws,
statutes, etc.*
... A bill to be entitled An act
extending the privilege of purchas-
ing clothing at government cost, to
all persons in its employment, who
have been discharged for the army on
account of wounds received or disease contracted whilst in the service. [Richmond, 1864]
[2] p. 23 1/2 cm.

2059 Confederate States of America. *Laws,
statutes, etc.*
... A bill to provide for the
safe and expeditious transportation
of troops and munitions of war by
railroads. [Richmond, 1863]
8 p. 22 1/2 cm.

2060 Confederate States of America. *Laws,
statutes, etc.*
Compilation of the tariff act, of
the Confederate States of America,
approved May 21st, 1864, showing the
rates of duties payable on imported
goods, wares and merchandise, from
and after September 1st, 1861, alpha-
betically arranged; also containing
recent acts of Congress and circulars
of the Treasury department, relative

474

to commerce, navigation and the
revenue; together with the warehouse
system ... Arranged by P.E. Walden,
deputy collector, custom house, port
of New Orleans. New Orleans, Corson
& Armstrong, 1861.
1 p. l., vii, [3]-282 p. incl.
tables, forms. 23 cm.

2061 Confederate States of America. *Laws,
statutes, etc.*
Private laws of the Confederate
States of America, passed at the
first-   session of the First
Congress; 1862-   Carefully collated,
with the originals at Richmond. Edited by James M. Matthews ... Richmond,
R.M. Smith, printer to Congress, 1862-
v.   23 1/2 - 25 1/2 cm.

2062 Confederate States of America. *Laws,
statutes, etc.*
Public laws of the Confederate
States of America, passed at the first-
session of the First Congress;
1862- Carefully collated with the
originals at Richmond. Edited by
James M. Matthews ... Richmond,
R.M. Smith, printer to Congress,
1862-
v.   23 1/2 - 25 1/2 cm.

2063 Confederate States of America. *Laws,
statutes, etc.*
... The statutes at large of the
provisional government of the Confederate States of America, from the
institution of the government, February 8, 1861, to its termination,
February 18, 1862, inclusive.

Arranged in chronological order. Together with the constitution for the provisional government, and the permanent constitution of the Confederate States, and the treaties concluded by the Confederate States with Indian tribes. Ed. by James M. Matthews ... Richmond, R.M. Smith, printer to Congress, 1864.
xv, [1], 411, xiviii p.   24 cm.

2064   Confederate States of America. *Laws, statutes, etc.*
Tariff (of 1857) made of force by act of Congress of the Confederate States of America, 9th February, 1861. With additional free list under act 18th February, 1861. Charleston, Steam-power presses of Evans & Cogswell, 1861.
40 p.   23 cm.

2065   Confederate States of America. *Navy dept.*
Register of the commissioned and warrant officers of the navy of the Confederate States, to January 1, 1863. [Richmond? 1863]
14 p.   23 cm.

2066   Confederate States of America. *Navy dept. Office of ordnance and hydrography.*
Regulations of the Confederate States school-ship Patrick Henry. [Richmond, 1863]
30 p.   21 1/2 cm.

2067   Confederate States of America. *War dept.*

Army regulations, adopted for the use of the Army of the Confederate States, in accordance with late acts of Congress. Revised from the Army regulations of the old U.S. Army, 1857; retaining all that is essential for officers of the line. To which is added, An act for the establishment and organization of the Army of the Confederate States of America. Also, Articles of war, for the government of the Army of the Confederate States of America. New-Orleans, Bloomfield & Steel, 1861.
1 p. l., 198 p., 1 l.   21 1/2 cm.

2068   Confederate States of America. *War dept.*
Official reports of battles, embracing the defence of Vicksburg, by Major General Earl Van Dorn, and the attack upon Baton Rouge, by Major Geneal [!] Breckenridge, together with the reports of the battles of Corinth and Hatchie Bridge; the expedition to Hurtsville, Tennessee; the affair at Pocotaligo and Yemassee; the action near Coffeeville, Mississippi; the action and casualties of the brigade of Colonel Simonton, at Fort Donelson. Richmond, Va., Smith, Bailey & co., printers, 1863.
170 p.   23 1/2 cm.

2069   Confederate States of America. *War dept.*
Official reports of battles. Published by order of Congress. Richmond, Va., Enquirer book and job press, 1862.
571 p.   23 cm.

477

2070 Confederate States of America. *War dept.*
Official reports of battles. Pub. by order of Congress. Richmond, R.M. Smith, public printer, 1864.
96, [2] p.   23 cm.

2071 Confederate States of America. *War dept.*
Official reports of battles. Published by order of Congress. Richmond, R.M. Smith, public printer, 1864.
98 p.   23 cm.

2072 Confederate States of America. *War dept.*
Proceedings of the Court of inquiry, relative to the fall of New Orleans. Pub. by order of Congress. Richmond, R.M. Smith, public printer, 1864.
206 p.   23 cm.

2073 Confederate States of America. *War dept.*
Report of Lieutenant General Holmes of the battle of Helena; also, a report of Lieutenant General A.P. Hill of the battle of Bristoe station; also, report of Major General Stevenson of expedition into east Tennessee. Pub. by order of Congress. Richmond, R.M. Smith, public printer, 1864.
63, [1] p.   22 1/2 cm.

2074 Congar, Obadiah, 1768-1848.
The autobiography and memorials of Captain Obadiah Congar. For

fifty years mariner and shipmaster
from the port of New York. By Rev.
Henry T. Cheever ... New York,
Harper & brothers, 1851.
xii, [13]-266 p. 17 cm.

2075 Congdon, Charles Taber, 1821-1891.
Flowers plucked by a traveller
on the journey of life. By Charles
T. Congdon ... Boston, G.W. Light,
1840.
2 p. 1., [7]-72 p. 19 cm.

2076 Congressional address ... Washington,
D.C., 1864.
32 p. 24 cm.

2077 Congressional total abstinence society,
Washington, D.C.
Proceedings of the Congressional
total abstinence society, at a meeting held in the hall of the House of
representatives, Friday, February
25, 1842. New York, American temperance union, 1842.
39 p. 21 1/2 cm.

2078 Conkling, Alfred, 1789-1874.
A discourse commemorative of the
talents, virtues and services of
the late De Witt Clinton; delivered
at Schenectady, before the Society
of the Phi beta kappa, July 22d, 1828.
By Alfred Conkling. Albany, Printed
by Websters and Skinners, 1828.
31 p. 22 1/2 cm.

2079 Conkling, Edgar.
Benton's policy of selling and
developing the mineral lands, and

the necessity of furnishing access
to the Rocky mountains by the con-
struction of the Northern and Central Pacific railroads ... By Edgar Conkling ... Cincinnati, C.
Clark, printer, 1864.
16 p.   22 1/2 cm.

2080 [Conkling, Edgar]
Exposition of Mackinaw city and
its surroundings. [Cincinnati,
O., C. Clark, printer, 1866?]
23 p.   illus. (maps)   22 cm.

2081 Conkling, Frederick Augustus, 1816-
1891.
Promotion of medical science.
Remarks of Mr. F.A. Conkling, on
the bill for the promotion of medical science. In Assembly, February 28, 1854. Albany, Weed, Parsons and company, 1854.
13 p.   23 1/2 cm.

2082 Conkling, Henry.
... An inside view of the rebellion, and American citizen's text-
book. By Henry Conkling ... Cincinnati, O., C. Clark, 1864.
23 p.   22 cm.

2083 Conkling, Margaret Cockburn, "Mrs.
Albert Steele," 1814-1890.
Memoirs of the mother and wife of
Washington, by Margaret C. Conkling
... Auburn [N.Y.] Derby, Miller &
co., 1850.
xiii, [15]-190 p.   front. (port.)
17 cm.

2084 Conkling, Roscoe, 1829-1888.

Argument of Hon. Roscoe Conkling,
June 26, 1866, before a special committee of the House of representatives,
raised to investigate the administration of the Bureau of the provost
marshal general, and also the act of
James B. Fry, the head of the said
bureau, in sending to the House a
letter libelling the character of
one of its members, and also the truth
of said letter. [Washington? 1866]
37 p.   22 1/2 cm.

2085 Conkling, Rocoe, 1829-1888.
Privileges of the House of repre-
sentatives. Battle of Ball's Bluff.
Speech of Hon. Roscoe Conkling of
New York. Delivered in the House
of representatives, January 6, 1862.
[Washington, Scammell & co., 1862]
7 p.   24 cm.

2086 Connecticut. *Governor, 1858-1866 (W.A.*
Buckingham)
Message to the Legislature of the
State, May session, 1862. New Haven,
Babcock & Sizer, printers, 1862.
24 p.   23 cm.

2087 Curtiss, *Mrs.* Abby (Allin)
Home ballads: a book for New Eng-
landers. In three parts. By Abby
Allin ... Boston and Cambridge,
J. Munroe and company, 1851.
238 p.   17 cm.

D

2088 Davis, George Lynn-Lachlan.

The day-star of American freedom;
or, The birth and early growth of
toleration, in the province of Maryland ... By George Lynn-Lachlan
Davis ... New York, C. Scribner;
Baltimore, J. Murphy & co., 1855.
xiv, [15]-290 p.   18 cm.

2089 Dean, John, 1679-1761.
A narrative of the shipwreck of
the Nottingham galley, in her voyage
from England to Boston. With an account of the miraculous escape of
the captain and his crew, on a rock,
called Boone-Island; the hardships
they endured there, and their happy
deliverance. By John Deane, then
commander of the said galley ...
5th ed. [London?] Printed in the
year 1762.
2 p. l., 28 p.   19 1/2 cm.

2090 Dean, John Ward, 1815-1902.
A brief history of the New England historical & genealogical register, being the preface to the seventeenth volume of that work. By John
Ward Dean. [Boston, 1865]
8 p.   23 1/2 cm.

2091 [Dean, John Ward] 1815-1902.
The story of the embarkation of
Cromwell and his friends for New
England. [Reprinted from the New
England historical and genealogical
register] Boston, D. Clapp & son,
1866.
11 p.   25 cm.

2092 Dearborn, Nathaniel, 1786-1852.
Dearborn's reminiscences of

Boston, and guide through the city
and environs. Boston, Printed by
N. Dearborn [1851]
    xii, 13 -180 p. front., illus.,
plates, port., map, plans (1 fold.)
fold. facsim.   15 1/2 cm.

2093 De Costa, Benjamin Franklin, 1831-1904.
      A narrative of events at Lake
George, from the early colonial
times to the close of the revolution.
By B.F. De Costa. New York, 1868.
    74 p.   front.   28 cm.

2094 De Fontaine, Felix Gregory, 1832-1896.
      History of American abolitionism;
its four great epochs, embracing
narratives of the ordinance of 1787,
compromise of 1820, annexation of
Texas, Mexican war, Wilmot proviso,
negro insurrections, abolition riots,
slave rescues, compromise of 1850,
Kansas bill of 1854, John Brown
insurrection, 1859, valuable statistics, &c., &c., &c., together with a
history of the southern confederacy.
(Originally published in the New
York Herald) By F.G. De Fontaine.
New York, D. Appleton & co., 1861.
    66 p.   23 cm.

2095 Des Essarts, Alfred Stanislas Langlois,
      1811-1893.
      La guerre des frères, par Alfred
Des Essarts. A l'Amérique. Paris,
Poulet-Malassis, 1861.
    30 p.   24 1/2 cm.

2096 A detail of some particular services
      performed in America, during the
years 1776, 1777, 1778, and 1779.

Compiled from journals and original
papers, supposed to be chiefly taken
from the journal kept on board of
the ship Rainbow, commanded by Sir
George Collier, while on the American
station during that period: giving
a minute account of many important
attacks on towns and places, expeditions sent up rivers, skirmishes, ne-
gotiations, etc. ... Printed for
Ithiel Town, from a manuscript obtained by him, while in London, in
the summer of 1830. New York, 1835.
ix, 117 p. 20 cm.

2097 A detection of the proceedings and practices of the directors of the Royal
African company of England, from
their first establishment by charter
in the year 1672, to the present
year 1748. With remarks on the use
and importance of the British forts
and settlements on the coast of
Guiney ... London, T. Warner, 1749.
viii, 51 p. 19 cm.

2098 Detroit. Public Library.
Catalogue of the Public library of
the city of Detroit; with the rules
concerning its use ... Detroit, The
Free press steam book and job printing establishment, 1865.
100 p. 21 1/2 cm.

2099 Detroit young men's society. *Library*.
Act of incorporation, by-laws and
standing rules of the Detroit young
men's society with the names of regu-
lar and honorary members ... and a
catalogue of books in the library ...

Detroit, M. Bates, printer, 1842.
43 p.   21 1/2 cm.

2100   Detroit young men's society. *Library*.
Catalogue of the library of the
Detroit young men's society, with
a historical sketch.   Detroit, O.S.
Gulley's steam power presses, 1865.
x, [11]-169 p.   23 cm.

2101   [Devens, Samuel Adams]
Sketches of Martha's Vineyard,
and other reminiscences of travel
at home, etc.   By an inexperienced
clergyman.   Boston, J. Munroe &
co., 1838.
viii, 207, [1] p.   18 cm.

2102   DeVoe, Thomas Farrington, 1811-1892.
The market book, containing a historical account of the public markets
in the cities of New York, Boston,
Philadelphia and Brooklyn, with a
brief description of every article
of human food sold therein, the in
troduction of cattle in America, and
notices of many remarkable specimens,
by Thomas F. De Voe ...   In two volumes.   Vol. I.   New York, Printed
for the author, 1862.
xiv, [15]-621 p.   23 1/2 cm.

2103   Dew, Thomas Roderick, 1802-1846.
The great question of the day.
Letter from President Thomas R.
Dew, of William and Mary college,
Virginia, to a representative in
Congress from that state; on the sub-
ject of the financial policy of the
administration ...   Washington, T.

Allen, 1840.
16 p.   26 cm.

2104   [Dexter, Franklin] 1793-1857.
       A letter to the Hon. Samuel A.
Eliot, representative in Congress
from the city of Boston, in reply
to his apology for voting for the
fugitive slave bill.   By Hancock
[pseud.]   Boston, W. Crosby, H.P.
Nichols, 1851.
       57 p.   24 cm.

2105   [Dexter, John Haven] 1791-1876.
       Mercantile honor, and moral hon-
esty ...   Boston, Printed for the
publisher, 1856.
       20 p.   19 cm.

2106   Dialogue between a one thousand dollar clerk and a member of Congress.
Washington, J. Gideon, jr., printer,
1836.
       12 p.   24 1/2 cm.

2107   A dialogue, between a southern delegate, and his spouse, on his return from the grand Continental congress.   A fragment, inscribed to
the married ladies of America, by
their most sincere, and affectionate
friend, and servant, Mary V.V.
[*pseud*.]   [New York] Printed [by
James Rivington?] in the year 1774.
       14 p.   20 cm.

2108   A diary of the wreck of His Majesty's
ship Challenger, on the western
coast of South America, in May,
1835.   With an account of the
subsequent encampment of the

officers and crew, during a period
of seven weeks, on the south coast of
Chili. London, Longman, Rees, Orme,
Brown, Green, & Longman, 1836.
    2 p. 1., 160 p. fold. front., fold.
pl., fold. map, plan.   22 cm.

2109   Dix, John Adams, 1798-1879.
    Address at the laying of the cor-
ner-stone of the Douglas monument
at Chicago, September 6, 1866. By
Major-General John A. Dix. New York,
E.F. Crowen, 1866.
    35 p.   22 1/2 cm.

2110   Dix, William Giles, *d.* 1898.
    The University of the South.   An
address, delivered at Beersheba
Springs, Tenn., August 19th and
22d, 1859, and also, by invitation
of the Historical society of Tennessee, at the Capitol, Nashville,
Sept. 8th, 1859. By William Giles
Dix. Nashville, Tenn., W.T. Berry
& company, 1859.
    32 p.   21 cm.

2111   Dixon, James, 1814-1873.
    American labor: its necessities
and prospects. Address of the Hon.
James Dixon ... delivered before
the American institute ... Oct. 2,
1852. New-York, Printed by Mann &
Spear, 1852.
    23 p.   22 cm.

2112   Dobbs, Arthur, 1689-1765.
    Remarks upon Capt. Middleton's
defence: wherein his conduct during his late voyage for discovering

a passage from Hudson's-Bay to the
South-Sea is impartially examin'd
... whereby it will appear, with the
highest probability, that there is
such a passage as he went in search
of. With an appendix of original papers ... By Arthur Dobbs, esq. London, Printed by the author's appointment, and sold by J. Robinson, 1744.
6 p. 1., 171 p. fold. map. 22
1/2 cm.

2113   Dodge, Jacob Richards, 1823-1902.
Red men of the Ohio valley: an
aboriginal history of the period
commencing A.D. 1650, and ending at
the treaty of Greenville, A.D. 1795;
embracing notable facts and thrilling incidents in the settlement by the
whites of the states of Kentucky,
Ohio, Indiana, and Illinois. By J.R.
Dodge ... Springfield, O., Ruralist
publishing company, 1860.
[iii]-x, 13-435 p. front., illus.
19 cm.

2114   [Dodge, Mary Abigail] 1833-1896.
Country living and country think-
ing, by Gail Hamilton [*pseud.*]
Boston, Ticknor and Fields, 1862.
vi p., 1 1., 461 p. 18 1/2 cm.

2115   [Dodge, Robert] 1820-1899.
A book for every soldier's knap-
sack. Tracts for the war. Secession: the remedy and result. New
York, J. Miller, 1861.
2 p. 1., [7]-71 p. 15 1/2 cm.

2116   Dodge, William Earl, 1805-1883.

Influence of the war on our national prosperity. A lecture delivered
in Baltimore, Md. ... March 13th,
1865, by William E. Dodge ... New
York, W.C. Martin, printer, 1865.
29 p. 23 cm.

2117 Donaldson, Thomas, 1815-1877.
American colonial history: an address made by Thomas Donaldson, esq.
before the Maryland historical society. Baltimore, March 29, 1849. ...
Baltimore, Printed for the Society
by J. Murphy & co., 1849.
28 p. 22 1/2 cm.

2118 Douglas, John, *surgeon in British army*.
Medical topography of Upper Canada.
By John Douglas ... London, Printed
for Burgess and Hill, 1819.
2 p. l., 126 p. 22 cm.

2119 Douglass, William, 1691-1752.
The practical history of a new
epidemical eruptive miliary fever,
with an angina ulcusculosa which prevailed in Boston, New-England, in
the years 1735 and 1736. By William
Douglass, M.D. Boston, N.E., T.
Fleet, 1736.
2 p. l., ii, 18 p. 18 1/2 cm.

2120 Dow, Lorenzo, 1777-1834.
Analectic history; touching nulli-
fication, northern and southern: the
last warning of Lorenzo Dow ...
Washington, 1834.
36 p. 19 1/2 cm.

2121 Dowdell, James Ferguson, 1818-1871.

The Kansas issue. Remarks of Hon.
James F. Dowdell, of Alabama, in the
House of representatives, March 10,
1858, advocating the necessity of
additional guarantees for the protection of southern rights. [Washington,
Printed at the Congressional globe office, 1858]
7 p.   23 cm.

2122 Downing, Andrew Jackson, 1815-1852.
The fruits and fruit trees of
America; or, The culture, propagation,
and management, in the garden and
orchard, of fruit trees generally;
with descriptions of all the finest
varieties of fruit, native and foreign, cultivated in this country.
By A.J. Downing ... New York &
London, Wiley and Putnam, 1845.
xix, 504 p.   illus.   20 1/2 cm.

2123 Downing, Clement.
A compendious history of the Indian wars; with an account of ...
Angria the pyrate. Also the transactions of a squadron of men of war under Commodore Matthews, sent to the
East-Indies to suppress the pyrates.
To which is annex'd, an additional
history of the wars between the Great
Mogul, Angria, and his allies. With
an account of the life and actions
of John Plantain, a notorious pyrate
of Madagascar ... By Clement Downing
... London, Printed for T. Cooper,
1737.
iv, 238 p.   16 cm.

2124 Dox, Peter Myndert, 1813-1891.
Restoration of Georgia--The true

condition of the South--Universal
amnesty the remedy.   Speech of Hon.
Peter M. Dox, of Alabama, in the House
of representatives, June 6, 1870.
[Washington, D.C., Printed by H.
Polkinhorn & co., 1870]
    8 p.   23 1/2 cm.

2125 Drake, Samuel Gardner, 1798-1875, *ed*.
    The old Indian chronicle; being a
collection of exceeding rare tracts
written and published in the time of
King Philip's war, by persons residing in the country: to which are now
added marginal notes and Chronicles
of the Indians from the discovery of
America to the present time.   By S.G.
Drake.   Boston, Antiquarian institute,
1836.
    3 p. 1., [5]-208 p.   front., plates,
ports., plan.   16 cm.

2126 Draper, John William, 1811-1882.
    The indebtedness of the city of
New-York to its university.   An address to the alumni of the University
of the city of New-York, at
their twenty-first anniversary, 28th
June, 1853.   By Professor J.W. Draper, M.D.   New York, Pub. by the Association, 1853.
    2 p. 1., [9]-30 p.   22 1/2 cm.

2127 Draper, Lyman Copeland, 1815-1891.
    Madison, the capital of Wiscon-
sin; its growth, progress, condition, wants and capabilities.   Comp.
by Lyman C. Draper ...   Prepared and
printed by order of the Common council of the city of Madison.   Madison,

Calkins & Proudfit, printers, 1857.
48 p.   21 cm.

2128   Dring, Thomas, 1758-1825.
Recollections of the Jersey pri-
son-ship; taken, and prepared for
publication, from the original manuscript of the late Captain Thomas
Dring ... one of the prisoners. By
Albert G. Greene ... Providence, H.H.
Brown, 1829.
xvi, [17]-167 p. fold. front.   17
1/2 cm.

2129   Drinkwater, D   F.
Letters to the Connecticut courant, Pennsylvania independent republican, Washington chronicle, North
Carolina union banner, Nemaha cour-
ier, Pittsburg commercial, and Topeka
record, by D.F. Drinkwater, secretary
of the United press association. Washington, United press association,
1867.
40 p.   22 1/2 cm.

2130   Duane, William, 1807-1882.
Canada and the Continental congress, delivered before the Historical society of Pennsylvania, as their
annual address, on the 31st of January, 1850. By William Duane. Philadelphia, E. Gaskill, 1850.
20 p.   23 1/2 cm.

2131   Dudley, John, 1805-1898.
Shall we save our country, or, The
duty of prayer for rulrrs [!], as a
means of self preservation. A sermon, delivered at Quechee village,
Thanksgiving day, by Rev. John

Dudley. November 28, 1845. Wood-
stock [Vt.] Printed at the Mercury
office, 1845.
12 p.   23 1/2 cm.

2132 Dumas, Alexandre, 1802-1870.
Un Gil-Blas en Californie, par
Alexandre Dumas. Paris, Michel
Lévy frères, 1861.
2 p. l., 323, 1 p.   17 cm.

2133 Dunant, Jean Henri, 1828-
L'esclavage chez les musulmans et
aux États-Unis d'Amérique, par J.
Henry Dunant ... Genève, Impr. J.G.
Fick, 1863.
58 p.   18 cm.

2134 Dunham, Josiah, 1769-1844.
An answer to the "Vindication of
the official conduct of the trustees
of Dartmouth college," in confirmation of the "Sketches": with remarks
on the removal of President Wheelock.
By Josiah Dunham ... Hanover, Printed by D. Watson, jun., 1816.
94 p., 1 l.   24 cm.

2135 Dunlap, William, 1766-1839.
History of the rise and progress
of the arts of design in the United
States. By William Dunlap ... New
York, G.P. Scott and co., printers,
1834.
2 v. facsim.   25 cm.

2136 Dunlap, William, 1766-1839.
Yankee chronology; or, Huzza for
the Constitution! A musical inter-
lude, in one act. To which are
added, the patriotic songs of The

freedom of the seas, and Yankee tars.
By W. Dunlap, esq. New-York: Published by D. Longworth, at the Dramatic repository, Shakspeare-gallery.
Dec.--1812.
   16 p.   14 cm.

2137 Dunlevy, A   H.
      History of the Miami Baptist asso-
ciation; from its organization in
1797 to a division in that body on
missions, etc., in the year 1836.
With short sketches of deceased pastors of this first association in
Ohio. Prepared, at request of the Association, at their session at Lebanon, Oct., 1855, by A.H. Dunlevy ...
Cincinnati, G.S. Blanchard & co.,
1869.
   iv p., 2 l., [7]-193 p. front.
17 cm.

2138 Dunn, Ballard S   1829-1897.
      Brazil, the home for southerners:
or, A practical account of what the
author, and others, who visited that
country, for the same objects, saw
and did while in that empire. By
Rev. Ballard S. Dunn ... New York,
G.B. Richardson [etc.] 1866.
   1 p. l., iv, [3]-272, [23] p.
incl. tab. front. (port.)   19 1/2
cm.

2139 Dunn, Thomas, 1761?-1833.
      A discourse, delivered in the New
Dutch church, Nassau street, on Tuesday, the 21st of October, 1794, before the New York society for the
information and assistance of persons

emigrating from foreign countries.
By Thomas Dunn, an emigrant ... New
York; Printed for L. Wayland; with the
priviledge of copy.--1794. [Price,
One and Sixpence.]
2 p. l., 28 p.   20 cm.

2140   Dunning, Homer N   1827-
Providential design of the slavery
agitation. A sermon preached to the
Congregational church of Gloversville
on the national fast day, January 4th,
1861. By the Rev. Homer N. Dunning
... Gloversville [N.Y.] A. Pierson,
printer, 1861.
18 p.   20 cm.

2141   Dunshee, Henry Webb.
The Knickerbocker's address to
the Stuyvesant pear tree: respectfully dedicated to the Knickerbockers
of Manhattan island, by Henry Webb
Dunshee. [New York, Pettiner & Gray,
printers, 1857?]
19 p.   23 cm.

2142   Du Pont, Samuel Francis.
Report on the national defences, by
Commander S.F. Du Pont, U.S. navy.
Washington, Printed by Gideon & co.,
1852.
28 p.   22 cm.

2143   [Dutton, George]
The present crisis, or The currency; a tract of the times, for
every man who can read: by Bank
Crash, esq. [pseud.] [Rochester]
1857.
25 p.   22 cm.

2144   Dwight, Edward Strong, 1820-1890.
        An address delivered in Saco, Oct.
12, 1862. On the one hundredth anniversary of the organization of the
First church in Saco, Me., by Rev.
Edward S. Dwight ... Saco, W. Noyes,
printer, 1862.
27 p.   23 cm.

2145   Dwight, Theodore, 1764-1846.
        The character of Thomas Jeffer-
son, as exhibited in his own writings. By Theodore Dwight. Boston,
Weeks, Jordan & company, 1839.
xi, [1], [13]-371 p.   19 cm.

2146   Dwight, Theodore, 1764-1846.
        An oration, spoken before the Socie-
ty of the Cincinnati, of the state of
Connecticut, met in Hartford, on the
4th of July, 1792. By Theodore Dwight,
esquire. Printed at Hartford, by Hudson and Goodwin. 1792.
18 p.   20 1/2 cm.

2147   Dwight, Theodore, 1796-1866.
        The northern traveller; containing
the routes to the Springs, Niagara,
Quebec, and the coal mines; with the
tour of New-England, and brief guide
to the Virginia springs, and southern
and western routes. By Theodore
Dwight, jr. 6th ed., with eighteen
maps, and nine landscapes. New-York,
J.P. Haven [1841]
    iv p., 2 l., [7]-50 (*i.e.* 250) p.
front., plates, maps (1 double)
16 cm.

2148   [Dwight, Timothy] 1752-1817.

496

The true means of establishing public happiness. A sermon, delivered
on the 7th of July, 1795, before the
Connecticut Society of Cincinnati, and
published at their request. New-
Haven: Printed by T. & S. Green, and
sold by I. Beers, at his book-store
[1795]
   3 p. l., [5]-40 p.   21 cm.

2149   Dye, John Smith.
   The adder's den; or, Secrets of the
great conspiracy to overthrow liberty
in America. Depravity of slavery: two
presidents secretly assassinated by
poison. Unsuccessful attempts to murder three others.--The evidence con-
clusive, and the facts established.
Together with the dying struggles of
the great southern rebellion. By John
Smith Dye. New York, The author,
1864.
   128 p.   20 1/2 cm.

2150   Dyer, David,
   A discourse, on the characteristics
of the Puritans, delivered in Dorchester, December 21, 1845. By David
Dyer ... Boston, Press of T.R. Marvin, 1846.
   24 p.   23 1/2 cm.

2151   Dymond, Jonathan, 1796-1828.
   An inquiry into the accordancy of
war with the principles of Christianity; and an examination of the philosophical reasoning by which it is
defended; with observations on the
causes of war and some of its effects:
by Jonathan Dymond. With a dedication

497

to Sunday School teachers and scholars, and notes, by Thomas Smith
Grimké ... Together with an appendix ... Philadelphia, Printed by I.
Ashmead & co., 1834.
  xx, [13]-300 p. 19 cm.

E

2152 Earle, Pliny, 1809-1892.
    History, description and statis-
tics of the Bloomingdale asylum
for the insane. By Pliny Earle ...
New-York, Egbert, Hovey & King,
printers, 1848.
    2 p. l., [3]-136 p. front. 23
cm.

2153 Early, Jubal Anderson, 1816-1894.
    A memoir of the last year of the
war for independence, in the Confederate States of America, containing
an account of the operations of his
commands in the years 1864 and 1865,
by Lieutenant-General Jubal A. Early
... [2d ed.] Lynchburg, C.W. Button,
1867.
    xii, [13], 135, [1] p. 23 cm.

2154 An earnest address to such of the people
called Quakers as are sincerely desir-
ous of supporting and maintaining
the Christian testimony of their
ancestors. Occasioned by a piece,
intituled. "The testimony of the
people called Quakers, given forth
by a meeting of the representatives
of said people, in Pennsylvania and
New-Jersy, held at Philadelphia the
twenty-fourth day of the fifth month,

1775." ... Philadelphia, Printed for
John Douglas M'Dougal, 1775.
iii, 4-56 p.   17 cm.

2155 East Haven, Conn. Congregational church.
A confession of faith, covenant,
constitution and rules of practice;
adopted by the Congregational church
in East Haven. To which is added a
catalogue of the officers and members
of the church, from the year 1755, to
December, 1833. New Haven, Printed by
H. Howe & co., 1833.
24 p.   18 1/2 cm.

2156 East Tennessee relief association at
Knoxville.
Report to the East Tennessee relief
association at Knoxville; with tabu-
lar statements from the general agent,
etc. by Thomas W. Humes, chairman of
the committee. To which are appended
the proceedings commemorative of the
death of Edward Everett. Knoxville,
Printed for the Association, 1865.
50 p.   23 cm.

2157 Eastburn, James Wallis, 1797-1819.
Yamoyden, a tale of the wars of King
Philip: in six cantos. By the late
Rev. James Wallis Eastburn, A.M., and
his friend ... New-York: Published
by James Eastburn. Clayton & Kings-
land, Printer. 1820.
3 p. 1., [v]-xii, 339, [1] p.
front.   19 cm.

2158 Eastburn, Robert, 1710-1778.
A faithful narrative, of the many
dangers and sufferings, as well as

wonderful deliverances of Robert Eastburn, during his late captivity among
the Indians: together with some remarks upon the country of Canada,
and the religion, and policy of its
inhabitants; the whole intermixed
with devout reflections. By Robert
Eastburn. Pub. at the earnest request of many friends, for the benefit of the author. With a recommendatory preface, by the Rev. Gilbert
Tennent ... Philadelphia: Printed
by William Dunlap. 1758.
45 p.   18 1/2 cm.

2159 Eastman, Hubbard, *d*. 1891.
Noyesism unveiled: a history of
the sect self-styled Perfectionists;
with a summary view of their leading
doctrines. By Rev. Hubbard Eastman
... Brattleboro, The author, 1849.
xii [13]-432 p.   18 1/2 cm.

2160 Eastman, John Robie, 1836-1913.
Discussion of the West India
cyclone of October 29 and 30, 1867.
Prepared by order of Commodore B.F.
Sands, U.S. navy, superintendent
U.S.N. observatory, by J.R. Eastman,
prof. of mathematics, U.S. navy.
Washington, Govt. print. off., 1868.
17 p.   fold. map.   22 1/2 cm.

2161 Eastman, Lucius Root, 1809-1892.
Genealogy of the Eastman family,
for the first four generations. Comp.
by Rev. Lucius Root Eastman ... Reprinted from the New England hist.
and gen. register, for July, 1867.
Boston, D. Clapp & son, 1867.
11 p.   24 1/2 cm.

2162   Eastman, *Mrs*. Mary (H[enderson]) 1818-
        The American aboriginal portfolio.
        By Mrs. Mary H. Eastman. Illustrat-
        ed by S. Eastman, U.S. Army. Phila-
        delphia, Lippincott, Grambo & co.
        [^{C}1853]
            1 p. l., v, [6]-34 p. front.
        (port.) 25 pl.   33 cm.

2163   Eastman, Mary (Henderson) *b*. 1818.
        Dahcotah; or, Life and legends of
        the Sioux around Fort Snelling. By
        Mrs. Mary Eastman, with preface by
        Mrs. C.M. Kirkland. Illustrated from
        drawings by Captain Eastman. New
        York, J. Wiley, 1849.
            xi p., 1 l., xxxi, [33]-268 p. front.
        illus., plates.   19 1/2 cm.

2164   [Eastman, Samuel Coffin]
        The White Mountain guide book. Con-
        cord [N.H.] E.C. Eastman, 1858.
            2 p. l., 152 pp. illus.   12 cm.

2165   Easton, Hosea.
        A treatise on the intellectual
        character, and civil and political
        condition of the colored people of
        the U. States; and the prejudice ex-
        ercised towards them: with a sermon
        on the duty of the church to them.
        By Rev. H. Easton. ... Boston, I.
        Knapp, 1837.
            54, [2] p.   23 cm.

2166   Easton, James.
        Human longevity; recording the
        name, age, place of residence, and
        year of the decease, of 1712 per-
        sons who attained a century, & up-
        wards, from A.D. 66 to 1799. By

501

James Easton ... Salisbury [Eng.] J.
Easton; [etc., etc.] 1799.
   xxxii, [60], 292 p.   22 1/2 cm.

2167 Easton, John, 1617-1705.
      A narrative of the causes which
led to Philip's Indian war, of 1675
and 1676, by John Easton, of Rhode
Island. With other documents concerning this event in the office
of the secretary of state of New York.
Prepared from the originals, with
an introduction and notes. By Franklin B. Hough. Albany, N.Y., J. Munsell, 1858.
   4 p. l., [v]-xxiii, 207 p. front.
(fold. map)   21 1/2 cm.

2168 Eaton, Amos, 1776-1842.
      An index to the geology of the
nothern states, with a transverse
section from Catskill mountain to
the Atlantic. Prepared for the
geological classes at Williams
college, Northampton, Belchertown,
Leicester and Worcester, (Mass.) By
Amos Eaton ... Leicester [Mass.]
Printed by Hori Brown. Sold by Websters and Skinners, Albany; by
Simeon Butler, Northampton; and by
Cummings and Hilliard, Boston. 1818.
Price, coloured 75 cents, plain 62
cents.
   52 p. fold. pl.   23 x 13 1/2 cm.

2169 Eaton, Jacob.
      Memorial of Marvin Wait (1st
lieutenant Eighth regiment C.V.,)
killed at the battle of Antietam.
September 17th, 1862. Written by

Jacob Eaton ... New Haven, T.J.
Stafford, printer, 1863.
16 p.   23 cm.

2170   Eaton, Rebecca.
A geography of Pennsylvania for
the use of schools and private families. 2d ed., with corrections and
additions. By Rebecca Eaton ...
Philadelphia, E.C. Biddle, 1837.
viii, [5]-282 p. incl. front.,
illus. fold. map.   18 cm.

2171   Eaton, Samuel John Mills, 1820-1889.
Petroleum; a history of the oil
region of Venango County, Pennsylvania. Its resources, mode of development, and value: embracing a discussion of ancient oil operations ...
By Rev. S.J.M. Eaton ... Philadelphia, J.P. Skelly & co., 1866.
x, 11-200 p. front. (fold. map)
illus., plates.   19 cm.

2172   Eaton, William, 1764-1811.
Interesting detail of the operations of the American fleet in the
Mediterranean. Communicated in a
letter from W.E., esq., to his
friend in the county of Hampshire.
Springfield, Mas. [Blliss & Brewer,
printers] [1805]
31 p.   21 1/2 cm.

2173   Eckfeldt, Jacob Reese, 1803-1872.
New varieties of gold and silver
coins, counterfeit coins, and bul-
lion; with mint values. 2d ed., re-
arranged ... By Jacob R. Eckfeldt
and William E. Du Bois ... To which
is added A brief account of the

503

collection of coins belonging to the
Mint. 2d ed., enl. By William E.
Du Bois. New York, G.P. Putnam,
1851.
  3 p. 1., 72 p., 1 1. 5 pl. 23
cm.

2174 Eckley, Joseph, 1750-1811.
  A discourse before the society for
propagating the Gospel among the
Indians and others in North America,
delivered Nov. 7, 1805. By Joseph
Eckley, D.D., minister of the Old
South church in Boston. Boston:
Printed by E. Lincoln, Water street.
1806.
  36 p. 22 cm.

2175 The eclipse. [Boston] M,DCC,LIV.
  8 p. 20 cm.

2176 [Eddowes, Ralph] 1751-1833.
  The unity of God, and the worship
that is due to Him alone. A discourse delivered at the opening of
the church erected by the First society of Unitarian Christians in the
city of Philadelphia, on the 14th
February, 1813. Philadelphia: Published by Thomas Dobson, at the
Stone house, no. 41, South second
street. William Fry, printer, 1813.
  39 p. 23 1/2 cm.

2177 [Eddy, Caleb]
  Historical sketch of the Middlesex
canal, with remarks for the consideration of the proprietors. By the
agent of the corporation. Boston,
S.N. Dickinson, printer, 1843.

53 p.   23 cm.

2178   Eddy, Daniel Clarke, 1823-1896.
        Liberty and union. Our country:
        its pride and its peril; a discourse
        delivered in Harvard street Baptist
        church, Boston, Aug. 11, 1861, on
        the return of the pastor from Syria.
        By Daniel C. Eddy, D.D. Boston, J.M.
        Hewes, 1861.
        32 p.   23 1/2 cm.

2179   Eddy, Robert Henry, 1812-1887.
        Report on the introduction of
        soft water into the city of Boston.
        By R.H. Eddy.   ... Boston, J.H.
        Eastburn, city printer, 1836.
        40 p. fold. map.   23 1/2 cm.

2180   [Eddy, Thomas] 1758-1827.
        An account of the State prison
        or penitentiary house, in the city
        of New-York. By one of the inspec-
        tors of the prison ... New-York:
        Printed by Isaac Collins and son.
        1801.
        94, 83-97 p. incl. tables (part
        fold.) fold. pl., fold. plan.   23
        cm.

2181   Eden, John,
        The Mt. Holyoke hand-book, and
        tourists' guide; for Northampton,
        and its vicinity, by John Eden.
        Northampton, Mass., Hopkins, Bridg-
        man & co., 1851.
        72 p.   14 1/2 cm.

2182   Edmonds, Francis William, 1806-1863.
        Defence of Francis W. Edmonds, late

505

cashier of the Mechanics' bank,
against the charges preferred against
him by its president and assistant
cashier. New York, McSpedon & Baker, printers, 1855.
   55 p.   21 1/2 cm.

2183 Egan, Charles, 1807 *or* 8-1869.
      The law of extradition, comprising
the treaties now in force between
England and France, and England and
America, for the mutual surrender,
in certain cases, of persons fugitive
from justice; with the recent enact-
ments and decisions relative thereto. By Charles Egan. ... London,
W.W. Robinson, 1846.
   viii, 62 p.   21 1/2 cm.

2184 Egar, John Hodson, 1882-
      The martyr-president. A sermon
preached in the Church of St. Paul,
Leavenworth, on the first Sunday
after Easter, and again by request
on the national fast day, June 1st,
1865. By the Rev. John H. Egar ...
Leavenworth, Printed at the Bulle-
tin job printing establishment, 1865.
   16 p.   21 1/2 cm.

2185 Egleston, Thomas, 1832-1900.
      ... Catalogue of minerals, with
their formulas, etc. Prepared for
the Smithsonian institution. By
T. Egleston. Washington, Smithsonian institution, 1863.
   xiii, 42 p.   23 1/2 cm.

2186 Egloffstein, F   W   von, *baron,*
      ed.
      Contributions to the geology,

and the physical geography of Mexico, including a geological and topographical map, with profiles, of some of the principal mining districts; together with a graphic description of an ascent of the volcano Popocatepetl. Ed. by Baron F.W. von Egloffstein. New York, D. Appleton & company, 1864.

40 p. 2 pl., 2 fold. maps. 27 cm.

2187 Ekins, *Sir* Charles, 1768-1855.
Naval battles, from 1744 to the peace in 1814, critically reviewed and illustrated. By Charles Ekins ... London, Baldwin, Cradock, and Joy, 1824.

xxix, [1] p., 1 1., 425, 2 p. illus., plates. 28 cm.

2188 Ela, Jacob Hart, 1820-1884.
Radical common sense--the President and Congress. Speech of Hon. Jacob H. Ela, of New Hampshire, in the House of representatives, December 13, 1867. [Washington, D.C., Printed at the Great republic office, 1867?]

7 p. 24 1/2 cm.

2189 Elder, William, 1806-1885.
Debt and resources of the United States: and the effect of secession upon the trade and industry of the loyal states, by Dr. William Elder ... Philadelphia, Ringwalt & Brown, printers, 1863.

cover-title, 32 p. 22 1/2 cm.

2190 The election of president of the

United States, considered. Addressed to the people. By a citizen. Boston, Printed for the author
by True and Greene, 1823.
27 p. 22 1/2 cm.

2191 Elegiac epistles on the calamities of
love and war. Including a genuine
description of the tragical engagement between his Majesty's ships
the Serapis and the Countess of
Scarborough, and the enemy's squadron under the command of Paul Jones,
on the twenty-third of September,
1779. London, Printed for the authors, 1780.
iv, [5]-[70] p. 18 1/2 cm.

2192 [Elwyn, Thomas]
A letter to a Federalist, in reply
to some of the popular objections
to the motives and tendency of the
measures of the present administration. February, 1805. [Portsmouth,
N.H., From the Chronicle-office,
1805]
31 p. 20 1/2 cm.

2193 Emery, Joshua, *jr.*, 1807-1882.
A discourse delivered in the
North church. Weymouth, January 5,
1851. By Joshua Emery, jr. ... Boston, Press of T.R. Marvin, 1851.
18 p. 23 cm.

2194 Emigration, emigrants and Know-nothings.
By a foreigner ... Philadelphia,
Pub. for the author, 1854.
47 p. 18 cm.

2195 Emigration. Practical advice to

emigrants, on all points connected
with their comfort and economy, from
making choice of a ship, to settling
on and cropping a farm ... London.
E. Wilson, 1834.
120 p.   23 cm.

2196   Emmons, Richard, *b*. 1788.
Defence of Baltimore, and death
of General Ross. By Richard Emmons, M.D. Fredoniad.--Canto XXXIX.
--3d ed. Washington, W. Emmons,
1831.
48 p. front. (port.)   18 cm.

2197   Emmons, Richard, *b*. 1788.
Tecumseh: or, The battle of the
Thames, a national drama, in five
acts. By Dr. Emmons. New York,
Eltor & Harrison, 1836.
36 p.   19 cm.

2198   Evans, E   Clinton, *tr*.
General legislation, supreme
decrees, laws, resolutions, and
regulations. Referring to employ-
ees and workers. Regulation of the
work of women and minors. Translated by E. Clinton Evans ... Lima,
Peru, Imp. Segrestán, 1937.
cover-title, 155, 151, [3] p.   17
1/2 cm.

2199   Eyre, Edward John, 1815-1901, *defendant*.
Report of the case of the Queen
v. Edward John Eyre, on his prosecution, in the Court of Queen's
bench, for high crimes and misde-
meanours alleged to have been com-
mitted by him in his office as
governor of Jamaica; containing the

509

evidence, (taken from the depositions), the indictment, and the charge
of Mr. Justice Blackburn. By W.F.
Finlason ... London, Chapman and
Hall [etc.] 1868.
    2 p. l., xi, 111 p. 22 1/2 cm.

2200   Eyre, John.
      The European stranger in America.
By John Eyre ... New York, Sold
at Folsom's book store, 1839.
    iv, [5]-84 p. 19 cm.

F

2201   Fabens, Joseph Warren.
      Resources of Santo Domingo. A
paper, read before the American
geographical and statistical society
of New York. By Joseph Warren Fabens ... New York, Carleton, 1863.
    32 p. map. 8 cm.

2202   Fabre, Hector, 1834-1901.
      Esquisse biographique sur Chevalier
de Lorimier. Par Hector Fabre ...
Montréal, Impr. du "Pays," 1856.
    15 p. 26 cm.

2203   [Fahnestock, George Wolff] 1823-
      A centennial memorial of Chris-
tian and Anna Maria Wolff, March
twenty-fifth, 1863: with brief
records of their children and relatives ... Philadelphia, 1863.
    [iii]-viii, [9]-113 p. ports.
27 cm.

2204   Fairbanks, Charles, 1821-

The American conflict as seen from
a European point of view. A lecture
delivered at St. Johnsbury, Vt., June
4, 1863, by Charles Fairbanks. Boston, Press of G.C. Rand & Avery,
1863.
44 p.   23 1/2 cm.

2205 Fairbanks, George Rainsford, 1820-1906.
The early history of Florida. An
introductory lecture, delivered by
George R. Fairbanks, esq., before the
Florida historical society, April 15,
1857. With an appendix containing the
constitution, organization, and list
of members of the society. St. Augustine, Florida historical society,
1857.
31, [1] p.   23 cm.

2206 Fairbanks, George Rainsford, 1820-1906.
History of Florida from its discovery by Ponce de Leon, in 1512,
to the close of the Florida war, in
1842. By George R. Fairbanks. Philadelphia, J.B. Lippincott & co.;
Jacksonville, Fla., C. Drew, 1871.
xii, 13-350 p.   20 cm.

2207 Fairchild, James Harris, 1817-1902.
Woman's right to the ballot. By
James H. Fairchild ... Oberlin,
G.H. Fairchild, 1870.
67 p.   17 1/2 cm.

2208 Fairholt, Frederick William, 1814-1866.
Tobacco; its history and associations; including an account of the
plant and its manufacture; with its
modes of use in all ages and countries

By F.W. Fairhold ... With 100 illustrations by the author ... London,
Chapman and Hall, 1859.
   vi p., 1 l., 332 p. front., illus.
19 cm.

2209 Falconbridge, Alexander, *d.* 1792.
   An account of the slave trade on
the coast of Africa. By Alexander
Falconbridge ... London, Printed by
J. Phillips, 1788.
   iv, 5-55 p. 20 cm.

2210 Fales, William R 1820-1850.
   Memoir of William R. Fales, the
Portsmouth cripple ... Philadelphia,
Lindsay & Blakiston, 1851.
   1 p. l., [xi]-xii, [13]-151 p.
16 cm.

2211 Falsehood and forgery detected and
exposed, or The conduct of Thomas
Jefferson, James Madison, James
Monroe ... Andrew Gregg, and other
distinguished Democarts [!] in relation to the right of suffrage in
Mississippi, vindicated against the
slanders & misrepresentations of John
Binns, Stephen Simpson & John Nor-
vel ... Philadelphia, Printed at
the office of the People's advocate,
1823.
   16 p. 20 1/2 cm.

2212 A familiar conversational history of
the evangelical churches of New-
York. New York, R. Carter, 1838.
   222 p. front. 15 1/2 cm.

2213 Famin, Stanislas Marie César, 1799-
1853.

Chili, Paraguay, Uruguay, Buenos-
Ayres, par m. César Famin ... Pata
gonie, Terre-du-Feu et archipel des
Malouines, par m. Frédéric Lacroix.
Îles diverses des trois océans, et
regions circompolaires, par m. le
commandeur Bory de Saint-Vincent ...
et par m. Frédéric Lacroix. Paris,
Firmin Didot frères, 1840.
   2 p. l., 96, 64, 91, 328 p.
plates, maps (part fold.)   21 cm.

2214 Fanaticism, and its results: or, Facts
      versus fancies. By a southerner.
      Baltimore, Printed by J. Robinson,
      1860.
         36 p.   22 cm.

2215 Fancourt, Charles Saint John.
         The history of Yucatan, from its
      discovery to the close of the seven-
      teenth century. By Charles St. John
      Fancourt ... London, J. Murray,
      1854.
         xvi, 340 p. fold. map.   22 cm.

2216 Fanning's illustrated gazetteer of the
      United States ... with the popula-
      tion and other statistics from the
      census of 1850. Illustrated with
      seals and thirty-one state maps in
      counties, and fourteen maps of ci-
      ties. New York, Phelps, Fanning &
      co., 1853.
         490 p. illus. (incl. maps, plans)
      23 1/2 cm.

2217 Faribault, Georges Barthélemi, 1789-
      1866.
         Catalogue d'ouvrages sur l'histoire

513

de l'Amérique, et en particulier sur
celle du Canada, de la Louisiane, de
l'Acadie, et autres lieux, ci-devant
connus sous le nom de Nouvelle-
France; avec des notes bibliographiques, critiques, et littéraires.
En trois parties. Rédigé par G.B.
Faribault, avocat. Québec, W. Cow-
an, 1837.
　　2 p. l., 207 p.　　21 cm.

2218　Farmer, Daniel Davis, 1793-1822.
　　Trial of Daniel Davis Farmer, for
the murder of the widow Anna Ayer,
at Goffstown, on the 4th of April,
A.D. 1821. Reported by Artemas
Rogers & Henry B. Chase ... Concord,
Hill and Moore, 1821.
　　72 p.　　22 cm.

2219　Farmer, John, 1789-1838.
　　A genealogical register of the
first settlers of New England ...
To which are added various genealogical and biographical notes, collected from ancient records, manuscripts
and printed works. By John Farmer
... Lancaster, Mass., Carter, Andrews & co., 1829.
　　viii, 9-351, [1] p.　　25 cm.

2220　[Farmer, John] 1789-1838, *comp.*
　　The new military guide; containing, extracts from the Constitution
of the United States and of New-
Hampshire; organization of the
militia of New-Hampshire; duty of
officers, non-commissioned officers
and privates; miscellaneous rules
for the observance of officers; a
system for forming, inspecting,

organizing and reviewing a regiment;
extracts from Gen. Scott's military
institutes; object, general powers
and duties of courts martial, courts
of inquiry, &c., acts of Congress
relating to the militia; the order
of uniform for the infantry established by the commander in chief; different forms used by the militia with
instructions for filling them up;
form of keeping a regimental roster,
and directions for keeping records.
Comp. for the use of the militia.
Concord N.H. Printed by Hill and
Moore, 1822.
    vi, [7]-144 p., 1 l. incl. forms.
18 cm.

2221 Farmer, Miles, *plaintiff*.
        Reports of a trial: Miles Farmer,
      versus Dr. David Humphreys Storer,
      commenced in the Court of common
      pleas, April term, 1830, from which
      it was appealed to the Supreme judi-
      cial court, and by consent of par-
      ties, referred to referees, rela-
      tive to the transactions between
      Miss Eliza Dolph and George Washing-
      ton Adams ... Reported by the plain-
      tiff. Boston, Printed for the re-
      porter, 1831.
        44 p. 21 1/2 cm.

2222 Farnham, Thomas Jefferson, 1804-1848.
        Mexico: its geography, its peo-
      ple, and its institutions: with a
      map, containing the result of the
      latest explorations of Fremont,
      Wilkes, and others. By Thomas J.
      Farnham ... New-York, H. Long &
      brother [c 1846]
        3 p. l. 5 -80 p. illus., 2

515

fold. maps (incl. front.)   22 1/2
cm.

2223   Farrar, C   C   S.
          The war, its causes and consequen-
       ces. By C.C.S. Farrar, of Bolivar
       County, Miss. Cairo, Ills., Memphis,
       Tenn. [etc.] Blelock & co., 1864.
          260 p.   19 cm.

2224   Farrar, Eliza Ware (Rotch) "*Mrs*. John
       Farrar," 1791-1870.
          Recollections of seventy years.
       By Mrs. John Farrar ... [2d ed.]
       Boston, Ticknor and Fields, 1866.
          viii, 331 p.   18 cm.

2225   [Farrar, Timothy] 1788-1874.
          Memoir of the Farrar family. By a
       member of the N.E. hist. gen. socie-
       ty. [Boston, Printed for private
       distribution at the press of T.
       Prince, 1853]
          45 (*i.e.* 55) p.   illus.   25 cm.

2226   Farrar, Timothy, 1788-1874.
          Report of the case of the trustees
       of Dartmouth college against William
       H. Woodward. Argued and determined
       in the Superior court of judicature
       of the state of New Hampshire, Novem-
       ber 1817. And on error in the Supreme
       court of the United States, February
       1819.   By Timothy Farrar ... Ports-
       mouth, N.H., J.W. Foster; [etc., etc.,
       1819]
          2 p. l., 406 p.   21 1/2 cm.

2227   Farrow, Henry Pattillo.
          The status of Georgia. Letter to

516

Hon. John B. Dickey, senator forty-
first senatorial district, upon the
status of Georgia, by Hon. Henry P.
Farrow, attorney general of Georgia.
Washington city, M'Gill & Witherow,
printers, 1869.
cover-title, 8 p.   23 1/2 cm.

2228   A farther examination and explanation
of the South-sea company's scheme.
Shewing, that it is not the interest of the South-sea company to offer
the annuitants such terms as may in-
duce them to come in; and that the
proposal of the bank is more likely
to be accepted by the annuitants,
and the publick not disappointed.
London, Printed, and sold by J.
Roberts, 1720.
39 p.   20 cm.

2229   Farwell, W   B.
Letter to the Hon. Hugh McCulloch,
secretary of the Treasury, from W.B.
Farwell, revenue agent, in reply to
the report of Messrs. Hulburd,
Rollins, and Broomall, of the Committee on public expenditures of the
House of representatives of the
Thirty-ninth Congress. [New York,
1867]
cover-title, [3]-15 p.   22 1/2
cm.

2230   Fast day sermons: or, The pulpit on
the state of the country. New
York, Rudd and Carleton, 1861.
viii, [9]-336 p.   19 1/2 cm.

2231   Fast, Edward Gustavus.
Catalogue of antiquities and

517

curiosities collected in the territory of Alaska by Edward G. Fast ...
consisting of more than 2000 most
valuable and unique specimens of an-
tiquity ... also a collection of
fire arms, a large geological collection, etc., etc. Now on exhibition
at the Clinton hall art galleries
... [New York] Leavitt, Strebeigh
& co. [1869]
32 p. front., illus. 21 cm.

2232 Fauche, Pierre François.
Réflexions sur la cession de la
Guadeloupe à la couronne de Suède.
Par Pierre François Fauche. Lon-
dres, J.C. de Boffe, 1813.
20 p. 19 cm.

2233 Faulkner, Thomas C
Faulkner's history of the revolution in the southern states; including the special messages of President Buchanan--the ordinances of
secession of the six withdrawing
states and etc. New York [J.F.
Trow, printer] 1861
94 p., 1 1. 22 1/2 cm.

2234 Faux, William.
Memorable days in America: being
a journal of a tour to the United
States, principally undertaken to
ascertain, by positive evidence,
the condition and probable prospects of British emigrants; including accounts of Mr. Birkbeck's
settlement in the Illinois ... By
W. Faux ... London, W. Simpkin and
R. Marshall, 1823.

xvi, 488 p. incl. front.   22 cm.

2235 Fay, Cyrus H.
        An address on the changes of a
      century, delivered before the mem-
      bers of Norwich university, at their
      annual commencement, Aug. 21, 1839.
      By Rev. Cyrus H. Fay ... Newport,
      N.H., Argus and spectator office,
      1839.
        31 p.   22 cm.

2236 Fay, Heman Allen, 1779-1865. *ed.*
        Collection of the official accounts
      in detail, of all the battles fought
      by sea and land, between the navy
      and army of the United States, and
      the navy and army of Great Britain,
      during the years 1812, 13, 14, & 15.
      By H.A. Fay ... New-York: Printed
      by E. Conrad, 1817.
        295 p.   23 cm.

2237 Featherstonhaugh, George William, 1780-
        1866.
        A canoe voyage up the Minnay
      Sotor; with an account of the lead
      and copper deposits in Wisconsin;
      of the gold region in the Cherokee
      country; and sketches of popular
      manners; &c. &c. &c. By G.W.
      Featherstonhaugh ... London, R.
      Bentley, 1847.
        2 v. fronts., illus., 2 fold.
      maps.   23 cm.

2238 Featherstonhaugh, George William,
        1780-1866.
        Geological report of an examina
      tion made in 1834 of the elevated

country between the Missouri and
Red rivers. By G.W. Featherstonhaugh, U.S. geologist ... Washington, Printed by Gales and Seaton,
1835.
    97 p.   front. (fold. profile)
23 cm.

2239   Featherstonhaugh, George William,
       1780-1866.
          Report of a geological recon-
       noissance made in 1835, from the
       seat of government, by way of Green
       bay and the Wisconsin territory to
       the Coteau de Prairie, an elevated
       ridge dividing the Missouri from
       the St. Peter's river. By G.W.
       Featherstonhaugh, U.S. geologist. ...
       Washington, Printed by Gales and
       Seaton, 1836.
          168 p.   4 pl., 2 fold. maps.   22
       1/2 cm.

2240   Felch, Alpheus, 1806-1896.
          Speech of Mr. Felch, of Michigan
       on ceding the public lands to the
       states in which they are situated.
       Delivered in the Senate of the Unit-
       ed States, January 13, 1851. Wash-
       ington, Printed at the Congressional
       globe office, 1851.
          20 p.   22 cm.

2241   Fellows, John, 1759-1844.
          An exposition of the mysteries; or,
       Religious dogmas and customs of the
       ancient Egyptians, Pythagoreans, and
       Druids. Also: an inquiry into
       the origin, history, and purport of
       freemasonry. By John Fellows ...
       New-York, Printed for the author,

and sold by Gould, Banks and co.,
1835.
    xvi, 403, 8 p. incl. front.,
illus.   22 1/2 cm.

2242   Felsenhart, Jacques, 1826-
    Les colonies anglaises de 1574
à 1660, d'après les State papers,
et épisode de l'émigration belge
en Virginie, par J. Felsenhart ...
Gand, Impr. de L. Hebbelynck, 1867.
    viii, 94 p.   23 cm.

2243   Felt, Joseph Barlow, 1789-1869.
    The annals of Salem, from its
first settlement. By Joseph B.
Felt ...   Salem, W. & S.B. Ives,
1827.
    611 p.   22 1/2 cm.

2244   Felt, Joseph Barlow, 1789-1869.
    The customs of New England. By
Joseph B. Felt ... Boston, Press
of T.R. Marvin, 1853.
    1 p. l., 268 p.   23 1/2 cm.

2245   Felt, Joseph Barlow, 1789-1869.
    An historical account of Massa-
chusetts currency. By Joseph B.
Felt ... Boston, Printed by Perkins & Marvin, 1839.
    2 p. l., [9]-259 p. plates.
23 1/2 cm.

2246   Felt, Joseph Barlow, 1789-1869.
    History of Ipswich, Essex, and
Hamilton. By Joseph B. Felt ...
Cambridge [Mass.] Printed by C.
Folsom, 1834.
    xv, 1 , 304 p.   23 cm.

2247 Felt, Joseph Barlow, 1789-1869.
Who was the first governor of Massachusetts? By Joseph B. Felt ... Boston, Press of T.R. Marvin, 1853.
17 p.   23 cm.

2248 Feltman, William.
The journal of Lieut. William Feltman, of the First Pennsylvania regiment, 1781-82. Including the march
into Virginia and the siege of York-
town. Philadelphia, Pub. for the Historical society of Pennsylvania, by
H.C. Baird, 1853.
48 p.   24 1/2 cm.

2249 Felton, Cornelius Conway, 1807-1862.
An address delivered at the dedication of the new building of Bristol
academy in Taunton, August 25, 1852,
by C.C. Felton ... With an appendix, containing an historical sketch
of the academy, an account of the
festival, and a list of the trustees
and preceptors. Cambridge [Mass.]
Metcalf and company, printers to the
University, 1852.
54 p.   24 cm.

2250 Felton, Franklin Eliot.
The purification and reconstruction of the American union. An oration delivered at Vallejo, July IV,
1867. By Franklin Eliot Felton ...
San Francisco, E. Bosqui & company,
1867.
22 p.   21 1/2 cm.

2251 [Field, David Dudley] 1781-1867, *ed*.
A history of the county of Berk-
shire, Massachusetts; in two parts.

The first being a general view of
the county; the second, an account of
the several towns. By gentlemen in
the county, clergymen and laymen.
Pittsfield, Printed by S.W. Bush,
1829.
    iv p., 1 l., [7]-468 p. front.
(fold map) plates (1 fold.) ports.,
fold. col. chart.   19 x 10 1/2 cm.

2252 Flinter, George Dawson.
    An account of the present state of
the island of Puerto Rico. Comprising numerous original facts and documents illustrative of the state of
commerce and agriculture, and of the
condition, moral and physical, of the
various classes of the population in
that island, as compared with the
colonies of other European powers;
demonstrating the superiority of the
Spanish slave code,--the great advantages of free over slave labour, &c.
By Colonel Flinter ... London, Longman, Rees, Orme, Brown, Green, and
Longman, 1834.
    xii, 392 p.   22 cm.

2253 Florida. *Commissioner of lands and
    immigration.*
    Florida: its climate, soil, and
productions, with a sketch of its
history, natural features and social
condition: a manual of reliable information concerning the resources of
the state and the inducements to immi-
grants. Jacksonville, Printed by E.M.
Cheney, 1869.
    iv, 151 p.   22 cm.

2254 Florida. *Constitution.*

Constitution or form of government
for the people of Florida, as revised
and amended at a Convention of the
people begun and holden at the city
of Tallahassee on the third day of
January, A.D. 1861, together with the
Ordinances adopted by said Convention.
Tallahassee, Office of the Floridian
and Journal, 1861.
68 p.   24 cm.

2255   Florida. Historical society.
Historical society of Florida. Organized in St. Augustine, 1856. New-
York, Printed by J.A. Gray, 1856.
9, [2] p.   14 1/2 cm.

2256   The Florida pirate, or, An account of a
crime in the schooner Esparanza, with
a sketch of the life of her commander ... New-York, W. Borrsdaile, 1823.
24 p. col. front.   19 1/2 cm.

2257   Flournoy, John Jacobus.
An essay on the origin, habits, &c.
of the African race; incidental to
the propriety of having nothing to
do with Negroes: addressed to the
good people of the United States. By
J. Jacobus Flournoy. New-York, 1835.
56 p.   21 1/2 cm.

2258   Flower, Richard, 1761?-1829.
Letters from Lexington and the Illinois, containing a brief account of the
English settlement in the latter
territory, and a refutation of the
misrepresentations of Mr. Cobbett.
By Richard Flower. London, J. Ridgway, 1819.
iv, [5]-32 p.   22 cm.

2259 Flynt, Henry, 1675-1760.
A caution to sinners against abus-
ing the patience of God, by a progress
in sin. A sermon preach'd to the
scholars in the college hall, February 8th, 1735, 6: And published at
the desire of many of them. By Henry
Flynt Fellow of Harvard college in
Cambridge ... Boston, Printed and
Sold by S. Kneeland and T. Green, in
Queen-street, 1736.
2 p. l., 20 p. 18 cm.

2260 Foley, Fanny, *pseud*.
Romance of the ocean: a narrative
of the voyage of the Wildfire to California. Illustrated with stories,
anecdotes, etc. By Fanny Foley ...
Philadelphia, Lindsay and Blakiston,
1850.
2 p. l., [ix]-xii, [18]-218 p.
18 1/2 cm.

2261 Follen, Eliza Lee (Cabot) *"Mrs*. C.T.C.
Follen," 1787-1860.
The liberty cap. By Eliza Lee
Follen. Boston, L.C. Bowles, 1846.
36 p. 16 cm.

2262 Folsom, James Madison, 1838-
Heroes and martyrs of Georgia.
Georgia's record in the revolution
of 1861. By James M. Folsom. Macon, Ga., Burke, Boykin & company,
1864.
164 p. 22 cm.

2263 Fontaine, Jacques, *b*. 1658.
A tale of the Huguenots; or,
Memoirs of a French refugee family.
Tr. and comp. from the original

manuscripts of James Fontaine, by one
of his descendants [Ann Maury] With
an introduction, by F.L. Hawks ...
New York, J.S. Taylor, 1838.
    xii, [13]-266 p.   18 1/2 cm.

2264   Foot, George, 1800?-1867.
    An address embracing the early his-
tory of Delaware, and the settlement
of its boundaries, and of the Drawyers congregation, with all the churches since organized on its original
territory: delivered in Drawyers
church, Del., May 10, 1842, being one
hundred and thirty-one years since the
site of the present house of worship
was purchased. By Rev. George Foot.
Philadelphia, Printed at the office
of the Christian observer, 1842.
    68 p.   20 cm.

2265   Foote, Andrew Hull, 1806-1863.
    The African squadron: Ashburton
treaty: consular sea letters. Reviewed, in an address, by Commander
A.H. Foote, U.S.N. Philadelphia, W.F.
Geddes, printer [1855]
    16 p.   22 cm.

2266   Foote, Henry Wilder, 1838-1889.
    Memorial lessons. A sermon preach-
ed at King's chapel, Boston, on
Sunday, May 29th, 1870, with a list
of the sons of the church who entered
the service of the country. By Henry W. Foote ... Boston, Barker,
Cotter & co., printers, 1870.
    28 p. fold. tab.   24 cm.

2267   Foote, John Parsons, 1783-1865.

The schools of Cincinnati, and its
vicinity, by John P. Foote ... Cincinnati, C.F. Bradley & co.'s power
press, 1855.
vi, [2] p., 1 1., 232 p. front,
3 pl., port.   23 cm.

2268   Foote, Thomas Moses, 1809-1838.
National characteristics. An address delivered before the literary
societies of Hamilton college, July
24, 1848. By Thomas M. Foote ...
Buffalo, Steam press of Jewett,
Thomas & co., 1848.
38 p.   23 1/2 cm.

2269   Forbes, Abner.
The rich men of Massachusetts:
containing a statement of the reput-
ed wealth of about fifteen hundred
persons, with brief sketches of more
than one thousand characters. By A.
Forbes and J.W. Greene. Boston,
Fetridge and company, 1851.
viii, [9]-208 p.   22 1/2 cm.

2270   Forbes, James Grant.
Sketches, historical and topographical, of the Floridas; more particularly of East Florida. By James
Grant Forbes. New-York, C.S. Van
Winkle, 1821.
viii, [9]-226 p. fold. pl. (map
and plan)   24 1/2 cm.

2271   Forbes, Robert Bennet, 1804-1889.
On the establishment of a line of
mail steamers from the western coast
of the United States, on the Pacific,
to China. By Robert B. Forbes. Boston, Boston journal office, 1855.

16 p.   23 1/2 cm.

2272   Force, Peter, 1796-1868.
        The Declaration of independence;
        or, Notes on Lord Mahon's History of
        the American Declaration of indepen-
        dence. By Peter Force ... London,
        G. Willis, 1855.
        66 p.   22 cm.

2273   Force, Peter.
        Register of the army and navy of
        the United States. No. 1, 1830.
        By Peter Force. Washington, P.
        Force, 1830.
        204 p.   18 cm.

2274   Ford, Henry Allen.
        The history of Putnam and Marshall
        counties, embracing an account of
        the settlement ... of Bureau and
        Stark counties. With an appendix,
        containing notices of old settlers
        .. lists of officers ... By Henry
        A. Ford ... Lacon [Ill.] The auth-
        or, 1860.
        vii, [1] 100 p.   15 cm.

2275   [Forman, Jacob Gilbert]
        The Western sanitary commission;
        a sketch of its origin, history,
        labors for the sick and wounded of
        the western armies, and aid given to
        freedmen and Union refugees, with
        incidents of hospital life. St. Lou-
        is, Pub. for the Mississippi valley
        sanitary fair, R.P. Studley & co.,
        1864.
        144 p.   front., pl.   23 cm.

2276   Forster, William Edward, 1818-1886.

Speech of Mr. W.E. Forster, M.P.,
on the slaveholders' rebellion; and
Professor Goldwin Smith's letter on
the morality of the Emancipation proclamation. Manchester, Union and
emancipation society's depot, 1863.
15, [1] p. 21 1/2 cm.

2277 "Fort-La-Fayette life." 1863-64, in extracts from the "Right flanker," a
manuscript sheet circulating among
the southern prisoners in Fort-La-
Fayette, in 1863-64 ... London,
Simpkin, Marshall & co.; Liverpool,
E. Howell, 1865.
1 p. 1., v, [7]-102 p. fold facsim. 16 cm.

2278 Forward, Walter.
Speech of Walter Forward to the
association of the Pittsburgh Board
of trade, on the occasion of the
fifth anniversary. Pittsburgh,
Printed at the Advocate office, 1840.
16 p. 21 1/2 cm.

2279 Fosgate, Blanchard.
Crime and punishment. By Blanchard
Fosgate ... Auburn, N.Y., W.J. Moses,
1866.
48 p. 18 1/2 cm.

2280 Foster, Benjamin Franklin.
Education reform. A review of Wyse
on the necessity of a national system of education, comprising the substance of that work, so far as relates to common school and popular
education. By B.F. Foster. New-
York, Wiley and Putnam, 1837.
iv, [5]-108 p. 23 cm.

2281   Foster, C.
An account of the conflagration of
the principal part of the first ward
of the city of New-York. Illustrated
with numerous etchings, and a plan
showing the state of the ruins, to
which is added a list of names of
the persons burnt out, and of remov-
als, forming a concise but useful supplement to the New-York directory,
&c. &c. &c., by C. Foster, 183 Broadway. [New York, 1835?]
54 p. front. (map) plates.   20
cm.

2282   Foster, Daniel.
Our nation's sins and the Christian's duty. A fast day discourse,
by Daniel Foster, minister in charge
of the Congregational church of Concord, Mass., delivered April 10th,
1851.   Boston, White & Potter, 1851.
34 p.   22 cm.

2283   Foster, Edmund, 1752-1826.
The works of God declared by one
generation to another. A sermon,
preached at Littleton, Dec. 4, 1815.
On the completion of a century from
the incorporation of that town. By
Edmund Foster ... Concord, Mass.,
Printed by Joseph T. Peters [1815]
2 p. l., 28 p.   21 cm.

2284   Foster, Ephraim Hubbard, 1795?-1854.
Funeral oration, by Ephraim H.
Foster; delivered in the McKendree
church, Nashville, Tennessee, on
the occasion of the celebration of
the obsequies of Henry Clay: July
28th, 1852. Nashville, Tenn., W.F.

Bang & co., printers, 1852.
21 p.   21 cm.

2285   Foster, Ethan.
        An examination of E.L.'s "Review
of the causes and course of the division in the Yearly meeting of Ohio."
By Ethan Foster. Boston, Press of T.R.
Marvin, 1855.
        26 p.   24 cm.

2286   Foster, Lillian.
        Way-side glimpses, north and south.
By Lilliam Foster. New York, Rudd &
Carleton, 1860.
        xi, [13]-250 p.   18 1/2 cm.

2287   [Foster, William] 1772-1863.
        A society for the special study of
political economy, the philosophy of
history, and the science of government,
proposed by a citizen of Boston. Boston, Printed by A. Mudge & son, 1857.
        19 p.   23 1/2 cm.

2288   [Fothergill, John] 1712-1780
        Considerations relative to the North
American colonies. London, Printed by
H. Kent, 1765.
        48 p.   21 1/2 cm.

2289   Foulke, William Parker.
        Considerations respecting the policy
of some recent legislation in Pennsylvania. By William Parker Foulke ...
Philadelphia, 1861.
        35 p.   22 1/2 cm.

2290   The fountain and the bottle; comprising
        thrilling examples of the opposite

531

effects of temperance and intemper-
ance. Ed. by a son of temperance.
Hartford, Case, Tiffany and co., 1850.
  xii, 8-448 p. incl. illus., plates.
22 1/2 cm.

2291 The four kings of Canada. Being a
succinct account of the four Indian
princes lately arrivd from North
America. With a particular description of their country, their strange
and remarkable religion, feasts, mar-
riages, burials, remedies for their
sick, customs, manners, constitution,
habits, sports, war, peace, policy,
hunting, fishing, utensils belonging
to the savages, with several other
extraordinary things worthy observation, as to the natural or curious
productions, beauty, or fertility of
that part of the world ... London,
Printed: and sold by J. Baker, 1710.
[Reprinted by J.E. Garratt & co.,
1891]
  47 p.   20 cm.

2292 Fournel, Henri Jérôme Marie, 1799-1876.
  Coup d'oeil historique et statistique sur le Téxas, par Henri
Fournel ... Paris, Delloye, 1841.
  57 p. fold. map.   25 1/2 cm.

2293 Fowler, Reginald.
  Hither and thither; or, Sketches
of travels on both sides of the
Atlantic. By Reginal Fowler ... London, F.R. Daldy, 1854.
  viii, 272 p.   22 cm.

2294 Fowler, William Chauncey, 1793-1881.
  Conditions of success in genealogical investigations, illustrated in

the character of Nathaniel Chaun-
cey ... By William Chauncey Fowler,
LL. D. Boston, Published by the
Society, 1866.
    28 p.   26 cm.

2295 Fowler, William Worthington, 1833-1881.
    Ten years in Wall street; or,
Revelations of inside life and experience on 'change ... By Wm. Worthington Fowler ... Illustrated by Arthur
Lumley. Hartford, Conn., Worthington, Dustin & co.; New York, J.D.
Denison; [etc., etc.] 1870.
    3 p. 1., v -xx, 19 -536 p. incl.
illus., plates. front. (4 port.)
22 1/2 cm.

2296 Fox, Charles.
    A portrait of George Washington,
from an original drawing, as he appeared while reviewing the Continental army on Boston Common, in 1776;
a history of the portrait, and docu-
mentary evidence in proof of the
correctness of the likeness. By
Charles Fox ... Boston, Crocker &
Brewster, 1851.
    37 p. front. (port.)   24 1/2
cm.

2297 Fox, Charles James, 1811-1846.
    History of the old township of
Dunstable: including Nashua, Nashville, Hollis, Hudson, Litchfield,
and Merrimac, N.H.; Dunstable and
Tyngsborough, Mass. By Charles J.
Fox. Nashua, C.T. Gill, 1846.
    xiv, 278 p. front., plates, map.
20 cm.

2298   Fox, George, 1624-1691.
            Cain against Abel, representing
        New-England's church-hirarchy, in
        opposition to her Christian protes-
        tant dissenters. By George Fox.
        London?   Printed in the year 1675.
        48 p.   19 1/2 cm.

2299   Fox, George, 1624-1691.
            An epistle to all professors in New-
        England, Germany, and other parts of
        the called Christian vvorld. Also
        to the Jews and Turks throughout the
        world. That they may see who are
        the true worshippers of God, that He
        seeks, and in what He is worshipped
        ... [By] George Fox. [London?] 1673.
        16 p.   18 1/2 cm.

2300   Fox, George, 1624-1691.
            Gospel family-order, being a short
        discourse concerning the ordering of
        families, both of whites, blacks and
        Indians. By G.F. [Philadelphia] 1701.
        23 p.   18 cm.

2301   Fox, Luke, 1586-1635.
            North-west Fox or, Fox from the
        north-west passage. Beginning with
        King Arthvr, Malga, Octhvr, the two
        Zeni's of Iseland, Estotiland, and
        Dorgia; following with briefe ab-
        stracts of the voyages of Cabot,
        Frobisher, Davis, Waymouth, Knight,
        Hudson, Button, Gibbons, Bylot, Baf-
        fin, Hawkridge: together with the
        courses, distance latitudes, longi-
        tudes ... M^r. Iames Hall's three
        voyages to Groynland, with a topo-
        graphical description of the coun-
        tries, the salvages lives and

treacheries ... Demonstrated in a
polar card, wherein are all the maines,
seas, and ilands, herein mentioned.
With the author his owne voyage, being
the XVIth. with the opinions and collections of the most famous mathema-
ticians and cosmographers ... By Captaine Luke Foxe ... Printed by His
Majesties command. London, Printed
by B. Alsop & T. Favvcet, 1635.
    5 p. l., 269, [3] p.   front., illus.
(map) fold. map.   19 x 14 cm.

2302   Fox, Thomas Bayley, 1808-1876.
    Memorial of Henry Ware Hall, adju-
tant, 51st regiment, Illinois infantry volunteers.   An address delivered in the First church, Dorchester,
Mass., Sunday, July 17, 1864.   By
Thomas B. Fox.   With an appendix.
Printed by request for private circu-
lation.   Boston, Printed by J. Wilson and son, 1864.
    35 p.   22 1/2 cm.

2303   Foxcroft, Thomas, 1697-1769.
    The earthquake, a divine visita-
tion.   A sermon preached to the Old
church in Boston, January 8, 1756.
Being a day of publick humiliation
and prayer, throughout the province of
the Massachusetts-Bay in New-England:
upon occasion of the repeated shock
of an earthquake on this continent,
and the very destructive earthquakes
and inundations in divers parts of
Europe, all in the month of November last.   By Thomas Foxcroft ...
Boston, Printed and sold by S. Kneeland, and T. Rand, 1756.
    2 p. l., 51 p.   20 cm.

2304 Foxcroft, Thomas, 1697-1769.
        God the judge, putting down one,
    and setting up another. A sermon
    upon occasion of the death of our
    late Sovereign Lord King George, and
    the accession of his present Majesty,
    King George II. to the British throne.
    By Thomas Foxcroft, A.M., minister of
    the Old church in Boston. Boston in
    New-England: Printed for S. Ger-
    rish, at the lower end of Cornhil.
    MDCCXXVII.
        2 p. 1., v (*i.e.* iv), 39 p.   19
    1/2 cm.

2305 Foxcroft, Thomas, 1697-1769.
        Grateful reflexions on the signal
    appearances of divine providence for
    Great Britain and its colonies in
    America, which diffuse a general joy.
    A sermon preached in the Old church
    in Boston, October 9. 1760. Being
    the thanksgiving-day, on occasion
    of the surrender of Montreal, and the
    complete conquest of Canada, by the
    blessing of heaven on His Britannic
    Majesty's brave troops, under the
    auspicious conduct of that truly great
    and amiable commander, General Am-
    herst. By Thomas Foxcroft ... Bos-
    ton, N.E., Printed and sold by S.
    Kneeland, 1760.
        2 p. 1., 36 p.   20 cm.

2306 Foxcroft, Thomas, 1697-1769.
        Observations historical and practi-
    cal on the rise and primitive state
    of New-England. With a special ref-
    erence to the old or first gather'd
    church in Boston. A sermon preach'd
    to the said congregation, Aug. 23.

1730. Being the last Sabbath of the
first century since its settlement. By
Thomas Foxcroft ... Boston, N.E.,
Printed by S. Kneeland and T. Green,
for S. Gerrish, 1730.
4 p. 1., 46 p.   20 cm.

2307   ... Fox's martyrs; or, A new book of the
sufferings of the faithful ... The
3d ed. ... London, J. Whitaker, 1784.
1 p. 1., vi, 70 p. front.   21 cm.

2308   [Fracker, George]
A voyage to South America, with an
account of a shipwreck in the river
La Plata, in the year 1817. By the
sole surviver. Boston, Printed by
Ingraham and Hewes, 1826.
vi, [7]-128 p.   17 1/2 cm.

2309   Francis, Convers, 1795-1863.
An historical sketch of Watertown,
in Massachusetts, from the first settlement of the town to the close of
its second century. By Convers Francis ... Cambridge, E.W. Metcalf
and company, 1830.
151 p.   22 1/2 cm.

2310   Francis & Haley.
Trotting record for 1869. Containing a complete and reliable record of
all the trotting events of the past
season, compiled and arranged with
great care, and respectfully dedicated to American turfmen by Francis &
Haley. New York [Torrey bros., 1870]
3 p. 1., [3]-142 p.   19 1/2 cm.

2311   Francis, James Bicheno, 1815-1892.
Lowell hydraulic experiments, being

a selection from experiments on hydraulic motors, on the flow of water
over weirs, and in canals of uniform
rectangular section and of short
length. Made at Lowell, Massachusetts. By James B. Francis ... Boston, Little, Brown and company, 1855.
xi, 156 p. xv fold. pl., tables.
32 cm.

2312 Francis, Samuel Ward, 1835-1886.
Biographical sketches of distinguished living New York surgeons. By Samuel W. Francis ... New York, J. Brad-
burn, 1866.
viii p., 1 1., 15-220 p. front.
(port.) 1 illus. 19 cm.

2313 Francis, Samuel Ward, 1835-1886.
Memoir of the life and character of
Prof. Valentine Mott, facile princeps.
By Dr. Samuel W. Francis ... New York,
W.J. Widdleton, 1865.
32 p. front. (port.) 24 cm.

2314 Francis, Valentine Mott, 1834-1907.
The fight for the Union. A poem.
By Valentine Mott Francis, M.D. New
York, J.F. Trow, printer, 1863.
14 p. 22 cm.

2315 Franklin, A   W   ed.
American cottage library; or, Useful facts, figures, and hints, for
everybody ... Edited by A.W. Franklin. New York, Burgess, Stringer,
& co.; Cincinnati, Burgess & Aker-
man, 1848.
2 p. l., 3-190 p. front., plates.
19 1/2 cm.

2316 Franklin, Benjamin, 1706-1790.
          Information to those who would re-
      move to America. By Dr. Benjamin
      Franklin. London, M. Gurney [etc.]
      1794.
          23 p.   22 cm.

2317 [Franklin, Benjamin] 1706-1790.
          A narrative of the late massacres,
      in Lancaster County, of a number of
      Indians, friends of this province, by
      persons unknown. With some observa-
      tions on the same. [Philadelphia,
      Printed by Anthony Armbruster] 1764
          31 p.   19 cm.

2318 [Franklin, Benjamin] 1706-1790.
          Plain truth: or, Serious Considera-
      tions On the Present State of the City
      of Philadelphia, And Province of
      Pennsylvania. By a Tradesman of
      Philadelphia ... [2d ed.] [Philadel-
      phia] Printed in the year MDCCXLVII.
          22, [2] p.   20 1/2 cm.

2319 [Franklin, Benjamin] 1706-1790.
          Proposals relating to the Education
      of Youth in Pensilvania. [Ornament]
      Philadelphia: Printed [by B. Franklin
      and D. Hall] in the Year, M.DCC.XLIX.
          32 p.   19 cm.

2320 Franklin, Benjamin, 1706-1790.
          Rules for reducing a great empire
      to a small one. By the late Benja-
      min Franklin, L.L.D.F.B.S. Dedicated
      to the Right Honorable Alexander,
      lord Loughborough. To which is sub-
      joined the Declaration of independence
      by the representatives of the United
      States of America in general Congress

assembled. London. Printed for
J. Ridgway, 1793.
16 p.   21 cm.

2321   Franklin and Marshall college, *Lancaster, Pa.*
Formal opening of Franklin and
Marshall college, in the city of
Lancaster, June 7, 1853: together
with addresses delivered on the occasion, by Hon. A.L. Hayes, Rev. J.W.
Nevin, D.D., and Right Rev. Alonzo
Potter, D.D. Lancaster, Pa., Pub.
by order of the Board of trustees,
1853.
44 p.   22 1/2 cm.

2322   Franklin Institute, *Philadelphia.*
Report. 1824/25- Philadelphia.
v. illus. 22-28 cm. annual.

2323   Frazier, Thomas Neil, *d.* 1887, *defendant.*
Proceedings of the High court of
impeachment, in the case of the people of the state of Tennessee, vs.
Thomas N. Frazier, judge, etc. Begun and held at Nashville, Tennessee,
Monday, May 11, 1867. Nashville,
S.C. Mercer, printer to the state,
1867.
124, 8 p., 1 1., 207 p.   22 1/2
cm.

2324   A free and impartial examination of the
preliminary articles of pacification,
signed at Paris, on the 20th of
January, 1783; by the respective
plenipotentiaries. With a retrospective view of the rise and various
stages of the war, to the time of

540

the present crisis. In which the treaties of 1674, and Utrecht, with those
of Aix-la-Chapelle, are occasionally
adverted to. By a member of Parliament. London, Printed for J. Fielding, 1783.
2 p. l., 50 p.   21 1/2 cm.

2325 Free trade and sailors' rights. American glory. The victories of Hull,
Jones, Decatur, Bainbridge; as detail-
ed in their official letters and the
letters of other officers. Together
with a collection of the public testi-
monials of respect; and the songs
and odes written in celebration of
those events. Illustrated with engravings of the actions. Philadelphia,
Pub. by the proprietor, D. Heartt,
printer, 1813.
58 p. pl.   21 1/2 cm.

2326 Freeman's address to the North Americans; proving that their present
embarassments are owing to their
federal union, their sovereign states,
their constitutions and their statesmen; and containing some propositions
for relief ... [n.p., 1846?]
29 p.   24 1/2 cm.

2327 Freeman, Frederick, 1799-1883.
Religious liberty. A discourse
delivered in the Congregational
church at Hanson, on the Fourth of
July, 1832. By F. Freeman ... Plymouth, Mass., Printed by B. Drew, jr.,
1832.
32 p.   25 cm.

2328 [Freeman, James] 1759-1835.

A description of the eastern coast
of the county of Barnstable, from Cape
Cod, or Race-Point, in latitude 42°
5'. to Cape Malebarre, or the sandy
point of Chatham, in latitude 41°
33'. pointing out the spots, on which
the trustees of the Humane society
have erected huts, and other places
where shipwrecked seamen may look for
shelter. October, 1802. By a member
of the Humane society. Boston:
Printed by Hosea Sprague, No. 44 Marl-
boro' Street. 1802.
15 p.   22 cm.

2329   Freese, Jacob R   1826-1885.
... Report on school houses, and
the means of promoting popular education, by J.R. Freese ... Washington,
Govt. print. off., 1868.
13 p.   24 cm.

2330   Frelinghuysen, Frederick, 1753-1804.
An oration on the death of Gen.
George Washington; delivered in the
Dutch church in New-Brunswick, on the
22d of February, 1800. By Major-
General Frederick Frelinghuysen ...
New-Brunswick, N.-J., Printed by
Abraham Blauvelt, 1800.
23, [1] p.   21 cm.

2331   Frelinghuysen, Theodore, 1787-1862.
Speech of Mr. Frelinghuysen, of
New Jersey, delivered in the Senate
of the United States, April 6, 1830,
on the bill for an exchange of lands
with the Indians residing in any of
the states or territories, and for
their removal west of the Mississippi.
Washington, Office of the National

542

journal, 1830.
44 p.   23 1/2 cm.

2332 French, Benjamin Franklin, 1799-1877,
      ed.
      Historical collections of Louisi-
ana and Florida, including transla-
tions of original manuscripts relating to their discovery and settlement,
with numerous historical and biographical notes. By B.F. French ... New
series. New York, J. Sabin & sons,
1869.
      4 p. l., 362 p.   facsim.   25 cm.

2333 French, Benjamin Franklin, 1799-1877.
      History of the rise and progress
of the iron trade of the United
States, from 1621 to 1857. With
numerous statistical tables, relating to the manufacture, importation,
exportation, and prices of iron for
more than a century. By B.F. French
... New York, Wiley & Halsted,
1858.
      xvi, 179 p.   23 cm.

2334 [French, Benjamin Franklin] 1799-1877.
      Memoirs of eminent female writers,
of all ages and countries. Philadelphia, T. Desilver and Towar & Hogan,
1827.
      2 p. l., [iii]-vii, 183 p.   front.
14 1/2 cm.

2335 French, Jonathan, 1740-1809.
      A sermon preached before His Ex-
cellency Samuel Adams, esq., governour; His Honor Moses Gill, esq.,
lieutenant-governour; the Honourable
the Council, Senate, and House of

representatives, of the commonwealth
of Massachusetts, May 25, 1796. Being the day of general election. By
Jonathan French, A.M., pastor of a
church in Andover. Boston, at the
State press, by Adams & Larking, printers to the Honourable the General
court, 1796.
   23 p.   21 1/2 cm.

2336 Frick, William, 1790-1855.
    An address preparatory to opening
the department of the arts and sciences in the University of Maryland.
Delivered on behalf of the trustees,
by Wm. Frick. Pub. at the request
of the Board. Baltimore, Printed by
J.D. Toy, 1831.
   37 p.   23 cm.

2337 Fries, John, 1764?-1825, *defendant*.
    The two trials of John Fries, on
an indictment for treason; together
with a brief report of the trials
of several other persons, for treason
and insurrection, in the counties of
Bucks, Northampton and Montgomery,
in the circuit court of the United
States, begun at ... Philadelphia,
April 11, 1799; continued at Norristown, October 11, 1799;--and concluded at Philadelphia, April 11, 1800;
before the Hon. judges, Iredell,
Peters, Washington and Chase. To
which is added, A copious appendix
... Taken in short hand by Thomas
Carpenter ... Philadelphia: Printed
and sold by William W. Woodward, No.
17, Chesnut near Front street. 1800.
   4, 226, 50 p.   20 cm.

2338 Friese, Philip C.
      An essay on wages, discussing the
      means now employed for upholding
      them, and showing the necessity of
      a workingman's tariff, founded on
      the principle of graduating import
      duties in inverse proportion to the
      rate of wages paid in the manufac-
      ture of the imported goods. By Phil-
      ip C. Friese. New York, Boston [etc.]
      Fowler & Wells, 1853.
      iv, [5]-35 p.   19 1/2 cm.

2339 Frieze, Jacob.
      A concise history, of the efforts
      to obtain an extension of suffrage
      in Rhode Island; from the year 1811
      to 1842. By Jacob Frieze. Provi-
      dence, B.F. Moore, printer, 1842.

2340 [Frieze, Jacob]
      Facts for the people: containing
      a comparison and exposition of votes
      on occasions relating to the free
      suffrage movements in Rhode-Island.
      Providence, Knowles & Vose, printers,
      1842.
      12 p.   20 cm.

2341 Frisbie, Barnes.
      The history of Middletown, Vermont,
      in three discourses, delivered be-
      fore the citizens of that town, Feb-
      ruary 7 and 21, and March 30, 1867,
      by the Hon. Barnes Frisbie ... Pub-
      lished by request of the citizens
      of Middletown. Rutland, Vt., Tuttle
      & company, printers, 1867.
      130 p.   22 1/2 cm.

2342 Frost, John, 1800-1859.

Illustrated historical sketches of
the Indians: exhibiting their manners and customs on the battle field
and in the wigwam. With numerous anecdotes and speeches, from the best
authorities. By John Frost, LL. D.
Hartford, L.E. Hunt, 1857.
1 p. l., viii, [9]-400 p. incl.
illus., pl., port. col. front. 20
cm.

2343 [Frost, John] 1800-1859.
Indian wars of the United States,
from the discovery to the present
time. From the best authorities.
By William V. Moore [*pseud.*] Philadelphia, R.W. Pomeroy, 1840.
321 p. incl. front., illus.
plates. 20 cm.

2344 Frost, John, 1800-1859.
The life of William Penn, with a
sketch of the early history of Pennsylvania. By John Frost. Philadelphia, O. Rogers, 1839.
xii, 239 p. incl. front., illus.
15 cm.

2345 Frothingham, Frank E.
The Boston fire, November 9th and
10th, 1872. Its history, together
with the losses in detail of both
real and personal estate. Also, a
complete list of insurance losses,
and an appendix containing the city
loan, insurance, and building acts,
by F.E. Frothingham ... Boston,
Lee & Shepard; New York, Lee, Shepard
& Dillingham, 1873.
115 p. fold. plan. 19 cm.

2346   Frothingham, Nathaniel Langdon, 1793-
          1870.
          A sermon on the death of General
          Lafayette, preached to the First
          church in Boston, on Sunday, the
          29th of June, 1834. By N.L. Froth-
          ingham ... Boston, Munroe & Fran-
          cis, 1834.
          16 p.   24 1/2 cm.

2347   Frothingham, Octavius Brooks, 1822-1895.
          The morality of the riot. Sermon
          of Rev. O.B. Frothingham, at Ebbitt
          hall, Sunday, July 19, 1863. New
          York, D.G. Francis, 1863.
          20 p.   14 1/2 cm.

2348   Frothingham, Octavius Brooks, 1822-1895.
          Seeds and shells: a sermon preached
          in New York, Nov. 17, 1861, by O.B.
          Frothingham. New York, Press of
          Wynkoop, Hallenbeck & Thomas, 1862.
          22 p.   24 cm.

2349   Frothingham, Richard, 1812-1880.
          The command in the battle of Bunk-
          er hill, with a reply to "Remarks on
          Frothingham's history of the battle,
          by S. Swett." By Richard Frothing-
          ham, jr. ... Boston, C.C. Little
          and J. Brown, 1850.
          56 p.   23 cm.

2350   Frothingham, Richard, 1812-1880.
          The history of Charlestown, Massa-
          chusetts. By Richard Frothingham,
          jr. ... Charlestown, C.P. Emmons;
          Boston, C.C. Little and J. Brown,
          1845 49.
          cover-title, 368 p. illus.,
          plates (1 fold.) port., maps (1

fold.) fold. facsims. 23 cm.

2351 Fry, Edmund, 1754-1835.
Pantographia; containing accurate
copies of all the known alphabets
in the world; together with an English explanation of the peculiar
force or power of each letter: to
which are added, specimens of all
well-authenticated oral languages ...
By Edmund Fry ... London, Printed
by Cooper and Wilson, for J. and A.
Arch [etc.] 1799.
2 p. l., xxxvi, 320 p. 25 cm.

2352 A full and particular account of all the
circumstances attending the loss of the
steamboat Lexington, in Long-island
sound, on the night of January 13, 1840;
as elicited in the evidences of the
witnesses examined before the jury of
inquest, held in New-York immediately
after the lamentable event ... Providence, H.H. Brown and A.H. Stillwell,
1840.
32 p. incl. front. 22 cm.

2353 A full answer to the King of Spain's
last manifesto, respecting the bay
of Honduras, and the Mosquito shore:
in which all the accusations brought
against the subjects of Great Britain settled in the bay of Honduras;
and against the ancient British settlement in the free and independent dominions of the Mosquito shore; are
candidly stated and refuted; and the
importance of the Mosquito shore to
Great Britain, delineated and ascer-
tained ... London, Printed for T.
Cadell, 1779.

75 p.   20 1/2 cm.

2354 Fullarton, William, 1754-1808.
      A statement, letters, and documents,
      respecting the affairs of Trinidad:
      including a reply to Colonel Picton's
      address to the Council of that island
      ... By Colonel Fullarton. London,
      Printed by B. McMillan, 1804.
      1 p. l., 201, 25-46, 81-94 p.
      27 cm.

2355 Fuller, Daniel.
      A familiar exposition of the con-
      stitution of Pennsylvania. For the
      use of schools, and for the people.
      By Daniel Fuller. Philadelphia, U.
      Hunt, 1840.
      iv, [5]-105, [1] p.   19 cm.

2356 [Fuller, Henry Weld] 1810-1889.
      The Woodlawn cemetery in North
      Chelsea and Malden ...   Boston,
      Higgins and Bradley, 1856.
      viii, 9 -125 p. front., illus.,
      plates.   22 cm.

2357 [Fuller, Hiram] 1814?-1880.
      Belle Brittan on a tour, at New-
      port, and here and there ...   New
      York, Derby & Jackson, 1858.
      vii, [13] 359 p.   19 cm.

2358 Fuller, Richard Frederick, 1824-1869.
      Chaplain Fuller: being a life
      sketch of a New England clergyman
      and army chaplain. By Richard F.
      Fuller ... Boston, Walker, Wise,
      and company, 1863.
      vi, 342 p. front. (port.)   19
      1/2 cm.

2359 Fuller, Robert, *b*. 1795?
          An account of the imprisonment and
      sufferings of Robert Fuller, of Cam-
      bridge ... Boston, The author, 1833.
      30 p.   22 1/2 cm.

2360 Fullonton, Joseph.
          The history of Acton, Me. By Jos-
      eph Fullonton ... [Dover] N.H. W.
      Burr, printer, 1847.
      iv, [5]-36 p.   18 1/2 cm.

2361 Fulton, Alexander R   1825-1891.
          The free lands of Iowa. Being an
      accurate description of the Sioux
      City land district. A general re-
      view of Iowa: her resources and ad-
      vantages; with reliable information
      relative to the vacant lands for all
      who are seeking homes in the West,
      and full directions for obtaining
      homesteads and pre-emptions. By
      A.R. Fulton ... Des Moines, Ia.,
      Mills & co., 1869.
      44 p.   32 1/2 cm.

2362 Fulton, Robert, 1765-1815.
          Torpedo war, and submarine explo-
      sions. By Robert Fulton ... New-
      York, Printed by W. Elliot, 1810.
      57, 3 p.   5 pl.   21 x 27 cm.

2363 [Furness, William Henry] 1802-1896.
          A sermon occasioned by the destruc-
      tion of Pennsylvania hall, and deliv-
      ered the Lord's day following, May
      20, 1838, in the First Congrega-
      tional Unitarian church, by the
      pastor. Printed, not published.
      Philadelphia, Printed by J.C. Clark,
      1838.

12 p.   23 1/2 cm.

2364 Further and still more important sup-
        pressed documents. [Boston, Russell
        & Cutler, printers, 1808?]
        24 p.   23 cm.

                              G

2365 Gabb, William More, 1839-1878.
        Catalogue of the invertebrate
        fossils of the Cretaceous formation
        of the United States, with references.
        By Wm. M. Gabb ... [Philadelphia,
        1859]
        29 p.   22 1/2 cm.

2366 Gage, Thomas, 1603?-1656.
        The English-American, his travail
        by sea and land: or, A new survey
        of the West-India's, containing a
        journall of three thousand and three
        hundred miles within the main land
        of America ... With a grammar, or
        some few rudiments of the Indian
        tongue, called, Poconchi, or Pocoman.
        By the true and painfull endevours
        of Thomas Gage ... London, Printed
        by R. Cotes, 1648.
        5 p. l., 220, [12] p.   28 1/2 cm.

2367 Gage, Thomas, 1721-1787.
        The letters of the two commanders
        in chief; Generals Gage and Washing-
        ton, and Major Generals Burgoyne and
        Lee; with the manifesto of General
        Washington to the inhabitants of Can-
        ada. New-York: Printed by James
        Rivington. 1775.
        8 p.   20 1/2 cm.

2368 Gagern, Carlos de.
        Apelación de los mexicanos a la
      Europa bien informada de la Europa
      mal informada. Por el ciudadano
      Carlos de Gagern ... Mexico, Impr.
      de I. Cumplido, 1862.
        xi, 86 p. pl.   22 1/2 cm.

2369 Gagnon, Ernest, 1834-1915, *comp*.
        Chansons populaires du Canada,
      recueillies et publiées avec anno-
      tations, etc., par Ernest Gagnon.
      Québec, Bureaux du "Foyer canadien,"
      1865.
        viii, 375, [1] p.   23 cm.

2370 Gaines, Edmund Pendleton, 1777-1849.
        To the young men of the states
      of the American union, civil and
      military. [n.p., 1838]
        88 p. illus. (plan)   23 1/2 cm.

2371 [Gale, Benjamin] 1715-1790.
        The present state of the colony of
      Connecticut considered. In a letter
      from a gentleman in the eastern part
      of said colony, to his friend in the
      western part of the same. [New Lon-
      don] 1755.
        1 p. l., 21 p.   20 1/2 x 16 cm.

2372 Gale, George, 1816-1868.
        The Gale family records in Eng-
      land and the United States: to
      which are added some account of the
      Tottingham family of New England,
      and Bogardus, Waldron, and Young
      families of New York. By George
      Gale ... Galesville, Wis., Leith
      & Gale, 1866.

254 p. front. ports. 19 1/2 cm.

2373 [Gale, Samuel] *d*. 1826.
        An essay on the nature and princi-
     ples of public credit. London, B.
     White, 1784.
        vi, 234 p. 22 cm.

2374 Gales, Joseph, 1786-1860.
        A sketch of the personal character
     and qualities of General Zachary Tay-
     lor. By Joseph Gales ... [Washing-
     ton, Towers, printer, 1848]
        8 p. 24 1/2 cm.

2375 Gall, James, 1784?-1874.
        The first initiatory catechism; by
     James Gall; with the Ten commandments
     and the Lord's prayer in the Ojibwa
     language: translated by Rev. P.
     Dougherty, aided by D. Rodd. Printed
     for the Board of foreign missions of
     the Presbyterian church. Grand Tra-
     verse bay, 1847. J. Westall and co.,
     printers, New York.
        69 p. incl. front. 19 cm.

2376 [Gallagher, William Davis] 1808-1894,
        ed.
        Selections from the poetical lit-
     erature of the West ... Cincinnati,
     U.P. James, 1841.
        204 p. front. (port.) 19 cm.

2377 Gallatin, Albert, 1761-1849.
        The right of the United States of
     America to the north eastern boundary
     claimed by them. Principally extract-
     ed from the statements laid before
     the King of the Netherlands, and re-
     vised by Albert Gallatin, with an

appendix and eight maps. New York, S. Adams, printer, 1840.

x, 179, [1] p. 8 maps on 6 fold. pl. 22 cm.

2378   Gallatin, Albert, 1761-1849.
Suggestions on the banks and currency of the several United States, in reference principally to the suspension of specie payments. By Albert Gallatin. New York, Wiley and Putnam, 1841.

2 p. 1., [9]-124 p. 23 cm.

2379   Gallatin, James.
The national debt, taxation, currency and banking system of the United States. With some remarks on the report of the secretary of the Treasury. By James Gallatin. New York, Hosford & Ketcham, printers, 1864.

61 p. 22 cm.

2380   Gallatin, James, 1796-1876.
The national finances, currency, banking, &c., by James Gallatin, being a reply to a speech in Congress, by Hon. Samuel Hooper. New York, Clayton & Medole, 1864.

34 p. 21 cm.

2381   Gallaudet, Thomas Hopkins, 1787-1851.
Gallaudet's Picture defining and reading book: also, New-Testament stories, in the Ojibua language. Boston, American board of commissioners for foreign missions, 1835.

123 p. illus. 18 cm.

2382   [Galloway, Joseph] 1731-1803.
A candid examination of the mutual

claims of Great-Britain, and the
colonies: with a plan of accommoda-
tion, on constitutional principles.
By the author of Letters to a noble-
man on the conduct of the American
war. New-York: printed by James
Rivington, early in MDCCLXXV. London Republished by G. Wilkie and R.
Faulder, 1780.
　　vi, [7]-116 p.　　21 1/2 cm.

2383　[Galloway, Joseph] 1731-1803.
　　　The claim of the American loyal-
ists reviewed and maintained upon
incontrovertible principles of law
and justice ... London, Printed for
G. and T. Wilkie, 1788.
　　viii, 138 p.　　21 cm.

2384　[Galloway, Joseph] 1731-1803.
　　　A letter to the Right Honourable
Lord Viscount H——e, on his naval
conduct in the American war. 2d
ed., cor. London, Printed for G.
Wilkie, 1781.
　　2 p. 1., 50 p.　　21 1/2 cm.

2385　Galt, *Sir* Alexander Tilloch, 1817-1893.
　　　Canada; 1849 to 1859. By the
Hon. A.T. Galt ... Quebec, Printed
at the Canada gazette office, 1860.
　　44 p.　　22 cm.

2386　Galt, *Sir* Alexander Tilloch, 1817-1893.
　　　Speech on the proposed union of
the British North American provinces, delivered at Sherbrooke,
C.E., by the Hon. A.T. Galt, minister
of finance, 23rd November, 1864 ...
Montreal, Printed by M. Longmoore &
co., 1864.

24 p.   25 1/2 cm.

2387   Galt, John, 1779-1839.
The life and studies of Benjamin
West, esq., president of the Royal
academy of London, prior to his arrival in England: compiled from materials furnished by himself, by John
Galt. Philadelphia: Published by
Moses Thomas. J. Maxwell, printer,
1816.
iv, 3, [9] -196 p.   22 cm.

2388   Galt, John Minson, 1819-1862.
Essays on asylums for persons of
unsound mind. By John M. Galt ...
Richmond Va. H.K. Ellyson's power
press, 1850.
22 p.   22 cm.

2389   Gamage, William, 1780-1818.
Some account of the fever which
existed in Boston during the autumn
and winter of 1817 and 1818. With a
few general remarks on typhus fever.
By W. Gamage, jr. ... Boston: Printed by Wells and Lilly. 1 18.
86 p.   23 cm.

2390   Garay, José de, 1801-1858.
An account of the isthmus of
Tehuantepec in the republic of Mexico; with proposals for establishing a
communication between the Atlantic
and Pacific oceans, based upon the surveys and reports of a scientific commission, appointed by the projector,
Don José de Garay. London, Printed
by J.D. Smith and co., 1846.
viii, [9]-128 p.   fold. maps.   23
cm.

2391   García y García, Aurelio.
        Peruvian coast pilot. By Captain
      Aurelio García y García ... New
      York, E. & G.W. Blunt, 1866.
        2 p. l., [3]-112 p. front. (fold.
      chart) 24 cm.

2392   Garden, Alexander, 1757-1829.
        Anecdotes of the American revolu-
      tion, illustrative of the talents and
      virtues of the heroes and patriots,
      who acted the most conspicuous parts
      therein. By Alexander Garden ...
      Second series ... Charleston [S.C.]
      Printed by A.E. Miller, 1828.
        ix, [1] p., 1 l., 240 p. 20 1/2
      x 11 1/2 cm.

2393   Garden, Alexander, 1757-1829.
        Anecdotes of the revolutionary war
      in America, with sketches of charac-
      ter of persons the most distinguished,
      in the Southern states, for civil and
      military services ... Charleston
      [S.C.] Printed for the author, by A.
      E. Miller, 1822.
        xi, 459 p. 21 1/2 cm.

2394   Gardette, Charles Desmarais.
        The fire-fiend, and other poems.
      By Charles D. Gardette. New York,
      Bunce and Huntington, 1866.
        104 p. 21 cm.

2395   Gardiner, David, 1784-1844.
        Chronicles of the town of East-
      hampton, county of Suffolk, New York.
      By David Gardiner. New York [Browne
      & co., printer] 1871.
        4 p. l., 121 p. 24 1/2 cm.

2396   Gardiner, George A.
       A brief and correct account of an
earthquake which happened in South
America, by which upwards of eighty
thousand persons perished! Together
with an account of the weather for a
month previous and subsequent to this
phenomenon. To which is added, an
allegorical description of the present state of the Royalists in that
country. By G.A. Gardiner ... Pough-
keepsie, Printed by P. Potter, 1820.
       24 p.   21 cm.

2397   Gardiner, Lion, 1599-1663.
       A history of the Pequot war, or, A
relation of the war between the power-
ful nation of Pequot Indians, once
inhabiting the coast of New-England,
westerly from near Narraganset bay,
and the English inhabitants, in the
year 1638. Written and left in manuscript by Lieutenant Lion Gardiner,
an actor in that war who resided in
the midst of those Indians. Cincinnati, Printed by J. Harpel for W.
Dodge, 1860.
       1 p. l., 36 p.   25 x 20 1/2 cm.

2398   Gardiner, Oliver Cromwell.
       The great issue: or, The three
presidential candidates; being a
brief historical sketch of the free
soil question in the United States
from the Congresses of 1774 and '87
to the present time. By O.C. Gardiner ... New-York, W.C. Bryant &
co.; Boston, B.B. Mussey & co.,
1848.
       176 p.   22 1/2 cm.

2399   Gardiner, Richard, 1723-1781.
          An account of the expedition to
       the West Indies, against Martinico,
       Guadelupe, and other of the Seeward
       Islands; subject to the French king,
       1759, by Richard Gardiner, esq., cap-
       tain of marines on board His Majesty's
       ship Rippon, on the expedition ...
       London, Printed for Z. Stuart, 1769.
          2 p. l., vi, [7]-75 p. 1 illus,
       map, plan.   24 x 18 1/2 cm.

2400   Gardiner, William Howard, 1797-1882.
          An address, delivered before the
       Phi beta kappa society of Harvard
       university, 28 August, 1834, on
       classical learning and eloquence. By
       William Howard Gardiner ... Cambridge,
       J. Munroe and company, 1834.
          1 p. l., 68 p.   23 1/2 cm.

2401   Gardner, Charles Kitchell, 1787-1869,
          defendant.
          Court martial. Proceedings of a
       general court martial, held at Fort
       Independence, (Boston Harbor,) for
       the trial of Major Charles K. Gard-
       ner, of the Third regiment infan-
       try. Upon charges of misbehavior,
       cowardice in the face of the enemy,
       &c., preferred against him by Major
       General Ripley. [Boston] Printed
       ... 1816.
          157 p.   20 1/2 cm.

2402   Gardner, Charles Kitchell, 1787-1869.
          A dictionary of all officers, who
       have been commissioned, or have been
       appointed and served, in the army of
       the United States, since the inaugura-
       tion of their first president in 1786,

559

to the first January, 1853,--with every commission of each:--including the
distinguished officers of the volunteers and militia of the states, and
of the navy and marine corps, who have
served with the land forces ... By
Charles K. Gardner ... New-York, G.
P. Putnam and company, 1853.
   587 p.   20 cm.

2403 Gardner, Daniel.
      Institutes of international law,
public and private, as settled by
the Supreme court of the United
States, and by our republic. With
references to judicial decisions. By
Daniel Gardner ... New York, J.S.
Voorhies, 1866.
   xix, 719 p.   24 cm.

2404 Gardner, Daniel.
      A treatise on international law,
and a short explanation of the juris-
diction and duty of the government of
the republic of the United States.
By Daniel Gardner ... Troy, N.Y.,
Press of N. Tuttle, 1844.
   xii, [13]-315 p.   19 cm.

2405 [Gardner, John Lane] 1793-1869.
      Military control, or Command and
government of the army. By an officer of the line. Washington, Printed
by A.B. Claxton & co., 1839.
   82 p.   18 1/2 cm.

2406 Garfield, James A[bram] *pres. U.S.*,
      1831-1881.
      The currency. Speech of Hon.
James A. Garfield ... in the House
of representatives, May 15, 1868

... Washington, F. & J. Rives & G.A.
Bailey, 1868.
cover-title, 16 p.   23 cm.

2407 Garfield, James Abram, *pres. U.S.*,
          1831-1881.
      Free commerce between the states.
Speech of Hon. James A. Garfield, of
Ohio, delivered in the House of representatives, March 24th and 31st,
1864, the House having under consideration the bill to declare the Rari-
tan and Atlantic railroad, a legal
structure for commerce between New
York and Philadelphia. New York,
1864.
      15 p.   23 cm.

2408 Garfielde, Selucius, 1822-1883.
      The north-west coast: a lecture
delivered in Lincoln hall, Washington city, on Monday, November 15th,
1869 ... by Hon. S. Garfielde ...
Washington, J.L. Pearson, 1869.
      cover-title, 26 p.   23 1/2 cm.

2409 Garlick, Theodatus, 1805-1884.
      A treatise on the artificial propa-
gation of certain kinds of fish, with
the description and habits of such
kinds as are the most suitable for
pisciculture, by Theodatus Garlick ...
Giving the author's first experiments
contained in a paper read before the
Cleveland academy of natural science.
Also directions for the most successful modes of angling for such kinds of
fish as are herein described. Cleveland, T. Brown, 1857.
      142 p. incl. illus., 4 pl.   21 cm.

2410   Garrard, Lewis Hector, 1829-1887.
           Chambersburg in the colony and
       the revolution. A sketch. By Lewis
       H. Garrard ...   Philadelphia, J.B.
       Lippincott and co., 1856.
           16, v. p., 1 l., 60 p.   22 1/2 cm.

2411   Garrard, Lewis Hector, 1829-1887.
           Wah-to-yah, and the Taos trail;
       or, Prairie travel and scalp dances,
       with a look at los rancheros from
       muleback and the Rocky mountain camp
       fire. By Lewis H. Garrard. Cincin-
       nati, H.W. Derby & co.; New York,
       A.S. Barnes & co., 1850.
           vi p., 1 l., 349 p.   18 1/2 cm.

2412   [Garrison, Wendell Phillips] 1840-1907.
           The Benson family of Newport, Rhode
       Island. Together with an appendix
       concerning the Benson families in
       America of English descent. Private-
       ly printed. New York, The Nation
       press, 1872.
           65 p. geneal. tab.   24 cm.

2413   Gasparin, Agénor Étienne, *comte* de,
           1810-1871.
           ... Reconstruction. A letter to
       President Johnson, by Count A. de
       Gasparin. Tr. by Mary L. Booth ...
       2d ed. New York, 1865.
           70 p.   22 cm.

2414   Gasparin, Agénor Étienne, *comte* de,
           1810-1871.
           ... Réponse de mm. de Gasparin,
       Laboulaye, Martin et Cochin, à la
       Ligue loyale et nationale de New
       York. New York, Impr. de W.C. Bry-
       ant & co., 1864.

20 p.   22 1/2 cm.

2415 [Gassett, Henry] 1813-1886.
        Catalogue of books on the Masonic
    institution, in public libraries of
    twenty-eight states of the Union;
    anti-Masonic in arguments and conclu-
    sions. By distinguished literary
    gentlemen, citizens of the United
    States. With introductory remarks,
    and a compilation of records and re-
    marks, by a member of the Suffolk com-
    mittee of 1829. Boston, Printed by
    Damrell & Moore, 1852.
        xi, 270 p.   22 1/2 cm.

2416 Gaston, William, 1778-1844.
        Speech of Hon. William Gaston of
    North Carolina, on the bill to author-
    ise a loan of twenty-five millions of
    dollars. Delivered in the House of
    representatives. February, 1814.
    Georgetown: Printed by Robert Alle-
    son. 1814.
        36 p.   21 1/2 cm.

2417 Gay, Ebenezer, 1696-1787.
        The old man's calendar. A dis-
    course on Joshua xiv. 10. Delivered
    in the First parish of Hingham, on
    the Lord's day, August 26, 1781, the
    birth day of the author, Ebenezer
    Gay ... Salem Mass. Re-printed by
    J.D. Cushing and brothers, 1822.
        36 p.   22 cm.

2418 Gayley, James Fyfe, 1818-1894.
        A history of the Jefferson medical
    college of Philadelphia. By James
    F. Gayley, M.D., with biographical
    sketches of the early professors ...

Philadelphia, J.M. Wilson, 1858.
2 p. 1., 11-59 p. front., plates,
ports. 28 x 22 cm.

2419 Gaylord, William L.
The soldier God's minister. A discourse delivered in the Congregational
church, Fitzwilliam, N.H., Sabbath
afternoon, October 5, 1862, on the occasion of the departure of a company
of volunteers for the seat of war, by
William L. Gaylord ... Fitchburg,
Printed at the Rollstone job printing office, 1862.
21 p. 21 1/2 cm.

2420 The general register of politics and
literature in Europe and America, for
the year 1827. Preceded by a memoir
of the Right Honourable George Can-
ning. Edinburgh, Printed for Consta-
ble & co.; [etc., etc.] 1828.
5 p. 1., [7]-335 p. 16 cm.

2421 Goddard, Samuel Aspinwall.
Reply to Mr. Lindsay's speech at
Sunderland, August, 1864, on the
American question, by S.A. Goddard.
Birmingham, E.C. Osborne, printer
[1864]
16 p. 18 cm.

2422 Goddard, Thomas H
A general history of the most prominent banks in Europe: particularly
the banks of England and France; the
rise and progress of the Bank of
North America; a full history of the
late and present Bank of the United
States. To which is added, a statistical and comparative view of the

564

moneyed institutions of New York, and
twenty-four other principal cities
of the United States ... Also, A.
Hamilton's report to Congress on currency, presented while secretary; and
McDuffie's report on currency, presented to the last Congress. By
Thomas H. Goddard ... New-York, H.C.
Sleight [etc.] 1831.
vi p., 1 1., [9]-254 p.   21 1/2 cm.

2423   [Goddard, William] 1740-1817.
The prowess of the Whig club, and
the manoeuvres of Legion ... Baltimore: Printed for the author [1777]
16, 4, 4 p.   17 cm.

2424   Goddard, William Giles, 1794-1846.
An address to the people of Rhode-
Island, delivered in Newport, on
Wednesday, May 3, 1843, in presence
of the General assembly, on the occasion of the change in the civil government of Rhode Island, by the adoption
of the constitution, which superseded
the charter of 1663. By William G.
Goddard. Providence, Knowles and
Vose, printers, 1843.
80 p.   23 cm.

2425   Goddard, William Giles, 1794-1846.
Memoir of the Rev. James Manning,
D.D., first president of Brown University, with biographical notices of
some of his pupils. By William G.
Goddard ... Originally published in
the American quarterly register.
Boston, Printed by Perkins & Marvin,
1839.
24 p.   22 1/2 cm.

2426 Godet, Theodore L.
Bermuda: its history, geology,
climate, products, agriculture, commerce, and government, from the earliest period to the present time; with
hints to invalids. By Theodore L.
Godet, M.D. London, Smith, Elder
and co., 1860.
xv, 271, [1] p. incl. tables (1
fold.) 20 1/2 cm.

2427 Godfrey, Thomas, 1736-1763.
Juvenile poems on various subjects.
With The prince of Parthia, a tragedy.
By the late Mr Thomas Godfrey, jun.^{r}
... To which is prefixed, Some ac-
count of the author and his writings
... Philadelphia, Printed by Henry
Miller, in Second-street. M DCC
LXV.
xxvi p., 1 l., 223 p. 23 cm.

2428 Godfrey, William C
Godfrey's narrative of the last
Grinnell Arctic exploring txpedi-
tion [!] in search of Sir John Franklin, 1853-4-5. With a biography of
Dr. Elisha K. Kane ... By Wm. C.
Godfrey ... Philadelphia, J.T. Lloyd
& co., 1857.
267 p. incl. front., plates.,
ports. 19 cm.

2429 Godwin, Morgan, *fl.* 1685.
Trade preferr'd before religion, and
Christ made to give place to Mammon:
represented in a sermon relating to
the plantations. First preached at
Westminster-Abby, and afterwards in
divers churches in London. By Morgan Godwyn ... London, B. Took, 1685.

3 p. l., 12, 34 p.   22 cm.

2430   Godwin, Parke, 1846-1904.
        Political essays. By Parke Godwin
        ... New York, Dix, Edwards & co.,
        1856.
        3 p. l., 345 p.   18 cm.

2431   Godwin, William, 1756-1836.
        Lives of the necromancers. Or, An
        account of the most eminent persons
        in successive ages, who have claimed
        for themselves, or to whom has been
        imputed by others, the exercise of
        magical power. By William Godwin ...
        New York, Harper & brothers, 1835.
        xii, [25]-307 p.   19 cm.

2432   Godwin, William, 1756-1836.
        Of population; an enquiry concern-
        ing the power of increase in the num-
        bers of mankind, being an answer to
        Mr. Malthus's essay on that subject.
        By William Godwin ...   London, Printed
        for Longman, Hurst, Rees, Orme, and
        Brown, 1820.
        xvi, [17]-22, 626 p.   22 cm.

2433   Goethe, *Mme*. Louise.
        Les esclaves, étude de moeurs con-
        temporaines, par Mme Louise Goethe;
        ouvrage précédé d'une lettre de M.
        Victor Hugo. Paris, Chez tous les
        libraires, 1862.
        360 p.   18 1/2 cm.

2434   Goldsmith, Oliver, 1794-1861.
        The rising village, with other
        poems. By Oliver Goldsmith, a
        descendant of the author of "The de-
        serted village." Saint John, N.B.,

Pub. for the author by J. McMillan, 1834.
x, [11]-144 p.   14 cm.

2435 Golovin, Ivan Gavrilovich, *b.* 1816.
Stars and stripes, or American impressions. By Ivan Golovin ... London, W. Freeman: New York, D. Appleton & co., 1856.
viii, 312 p.   20 cm.

2436 González de Agüeros, Pedro.
Descripción historial de la provincia y archipielago de Chilóe, en el reyno de Chile, y óbispado de la Concepción: dedicada á nuestro católico monarco Don Cárlos IV. (que Dios guarde), por el padre fray Pedro González de Agüeros ... [Madrid] Impr. de B. Cano, 1791.
4 p. 1., 318 p. pl., fold. map.
21 cm.

2437 González y Montoya, José.
Rasgos sueltos para la Constitución de América, anunciados por el intendente de exército Don Josef González y Montoya ... Cadiz, En la impr. de la Junta superior, 1811.
16 p.   20 1/2 cm.

2438 Goodale, Ebenezer, *defendant*.
Record of the proceedings of a general court martial, holden at the court-house in Salem, in the county of Essex, Monday, Sept. 28, 1812, by order of His Excellency Caleb Strong ... on the complaint of Lieut. Col. Samuel Brimblecom and others against Ebenezer Goodale, major general of the second division of the

militia. Cambridge: Printed by Hilliard and Metcalf. Sold at no. 1,
Cornhill, Boston, and by Cushing and
Appleton, Salem. 1812.
80 p.   23 cm.

2439 [Goodloe, Daniel Reaves] *b*. 1814.
The marshalship in North Carolina,
being a reply to charges made by
Messrs. Abbott, Pool, Heaton, De-
weese, Dockery, Jones, Lash and
Cobb, senators and representatives
of the state. [Washington? 1869]
12 p.   22 1/2 cm.

2440 Goodrich, Frank Boott, 1826-1894.
The tribute book, a record of the
munificence, self-sacrifice and
patriotism of the American people
during the war for the union ... By
Frank B. Goodrich ... New York, Derby & Miller, 1865.
3 p. l.,   3 -512 p.   illus.   plates.
27 1/2 cm.

2441 Goodrich, John Z   *b*.
A reply to the statements of Hon.
Samuel Hooper, in a pamphlet fanci-
fully entitled "A defence of the merchants of Boston," which justify the
wine frauds of J.D. & M. Williams and
the official misconduct of Timothy
B. Dix, and asperse the character of
"John Z. Goodrich, ex-collector of
customs." By J.Z. Goodrich. Boston,
Rockwell & Rollins, printers, 1867.
44 p.   24 cm.

2442 Goodrich, Samuel Griswold, 1793-1860.
History of the Indians of North
and South America, by the author

of Peter Parley's tales. Boston, G.C.
Rand, 1855.
iv, 320 p. illus., ports. 18 cm.

2443 Goodrich, Samuel Griswold, 1793-1860.
Lives of celebrated American Indians. By the author of Peter Parley's
tales. Boston, Bradbury, Soden, 1843.
315 p. illus. 18 cm.

2444 Goodwin, Hermon Camp, 1813-1891.
Ithaca as it was, and Ithaca as it
is; with thoughts suggestive of the
future. By H.C. Goodwin. Ithaca,
N.Y., Andrus, Gauntlett & company,
printers, 1853.
64 p. 21 1/2 cm.

2445 Goodwin, Isaac.
An oration, delivered at Lancaster.
February 21, 1826. In commemoration
of the one hundred and fiftieth anniversary of the destruction of that
town by the Indians. By Isaac Goodwin. Worcester, Rogers & Griffin,
printers, 1826.
15 p. 24 cm.

2446 Goodwin, Nathaniel, 1782-1855.
Descendants of Thomas Olcott, one
of the first settlers of Hartford,
Connecticut. By Nathaniel Goodwin ...
Hartford, Press of Case, Tiffany &
Burnham, 1845.
xii, [13]-63, [1] p. 22 1/2 cm.

2447 Goodwin, Nathaniel, 1782-1855.
The Foote family: or, The descendants of Nathaniel Foote, one of the
first settlers of Wethersfield, Conn.,
with genealogical notes of Pasco Foote,

who settled in Salem, Mass., and John
Foote and others of the name, who
settled more recently in New York.
By Nathaniel Goodwin ... Hartford,
Press of Case, Tiffany and company,
1849.
    2 p. 1., [iii]-xivi, [47]-360 p.
ports.   22 1/2 cm.

2448 Goodwin, Nathaniel, 1782-1855.
        Genealogical notes, or Contribu-
      tions to the family history of some
      of the first settlers of Connecticut
      and Massachusetts. By the late Na-
      thaniel Goodwin. Hartford, F.A.
      Brown, 1856.
        xx, 362 p.   23 cm.

2449 Gordon, Adoniram Judson, 1836-1895.
        The service of a good life. A dis-
      course commemorative of the life and
      character of Hon. Richard Fletcher,
      delivered by request in the Clarendon
      street Baptist church, Boston, July
      11, 1869. By Rov. A.J. Gordon. Bos-
      ton, Gould & Lincoln, 1869.
        24 p.   23 cm.

2450 Gowinius, Sven.
        ... Enfaldiga tankar om nyttan som
      England kan hafva af sina nybyggen
      i Norra America, med philosophiska
      facult. tillständ under ... Herr
      Pehr Kalms inseende ... Åbo, Johan
      Chrisopher Frenckell [1763]
        22 p.   22 1/2 cm.

                    H

2451 Hale, Edward Everett, 1822-1909.

A sermon delivered before His Excellency Nathaniel P. Banks, governor, His Honor Eliphalet Trask, lieutenant-governor, the honorable Council, and the General court of Massachusets, at the annual election, Wednesday, Jan. 5, 1859. By Edward E. Hale ... Boston, W. White, printer to the state, 1859.
37 p.   23 1/2 cm.

2452 Hale, Mercy, *b.* 1805.
A genealogical memoir of the families of Lawrences, with a direct male line from Sir Robert Lawrence of Lancashire, A.D. 1190; down to Robert Lawrence of Watertown, A.D. 1636: with notices of others of same name in different states. By Mercy Hale, Stowe, Mass. Boston, Printed for the author, 1856.
20 p.   21 1/2 cm.

2453 [Hale, Nathan] 1784-1863.
The American system, or the effects of high duties on imports designed for the encouragement of domestic industry; with remarks on the late annual treasury report. Boston: From Nathan Hale's press, 1828.
86 p.   21 1/2 cm.

2454 [Hale, Nathan] 1784-1863.
Notes made during an excursion to the highlands of New Hampshire and lake Winnipiseogee. By a gentleman of Boston. Andover, Printed by Flagg, Gould, & Newman, 1833.
184 p.   20 cm.

2455 Hale, Salma, 1787-1866.

Annals of the town of Keene, from
its first settlement, in 1734, to the
year 1790 ... By Salma Hale ... Concord [N.H.] Printed by J.B. Moore,
1826.
69 p.   24 cm.

2456   [Hale, Salma] 1787-1866.
... History of the United States,
from their first settlement as colonies, to the close of the war with
Great Britain in 1815.   To which is
added Questions, adapted to the use of
schools ... New-York, Collins and
Hannay, 1830.
298, 24 p.   15 1/2 cm.

2457   Hale, *Mrs.* Sarah Josepha (Buell) 1788-
1879.
Liberia; or, Mr. Peyton's experiments.   Edited by Mrs. Sarah J. Hale
... New Yor, Harper & brothers, 1853.
iv, [5]-304 p.   19 1/2 cm.

2458   Hale, *Mrs.* Sarah Josepha (Buell) 1788-
1879.
Traits of American life.   By Mrs.
Sarah J. Hale ... Philadelphia, E.L.
Carey & A. Hart, 1835.
298 p.   18 1/2 cm.

2459   Hale, Sarah Josepha (Buell) 1788-1879.
Woman's record; or, Sketches of all
distinguished women, from the crea-
tion to A.D. 1868.   Arranged in four
eras.   With selections from authoresses
of each era.   By **Mrs.** Hale ...   Illustrated by two hundred and thirty portraits, engraved on wood by Lossing
and Barritt.   3d ed. rev., with additions.   New York, Harper & brothers,

1870.
    4 p. 1., vii-xiviii, 17-918 p.
front. (port.) illus.   27 cm.

2460 Hall, Clayton Colman, 1847-1916, ed.
        ... Narratives of early Maryland,
1633-1684, ed. by Clayton Colman
Hall ... with a map and two fac-
similes. New York, Charles Scribner's
sons, 1910.
        ix p., 2 1., 3-460 p. front. (fold.
map) 2 facsim. (1 fold.)   22 1/2
cm.

2461 [Hickey, William] 1787?-1873.
        Hints on emigration to Upper Cana-
da; especially addressed to the middle and lower classes in Great Britain and Ireland. By Martin Doyle
[*pseud*.] ... 2d ed. enl. Dublin, W.
Curry, jun. and co.; [etc., etc.] 1832.
        2 p. 1., [iii]-vi, 92 p. front.
(fold. map)   19 1/2 cm.

2462 Hollberg, Esaias.
        Norra Americanska färge-örter ...
under ... Pehr Kalms inseende ...
I Åbo Academies öfre   Iäro-sal ...
26 Nov. 1763. Åbo, Jon. Christ.
Frenckell 1783
        4 , 8 p.   21 cm.

2463 [Howard, Frank Key] 1826-1872.
        Fourteen months in American bas-
tiles ... Baltimore, Kelly, Hedian
& Piet, 1863.
        89 p.   23 cm.

                    I

2464 Indrenius, Andreas Abraham.

Specimen academicum de esquimaux,
gente americana, quod in regio fen-
norum lycaeo, consent. ampliss.
facult. philos. viri ampliss, atque
celeberrimi Dn. Petri Kalm ...
submittitur ... ad diem XIX. Junii
... MDCCLVI ... Aboae, Jacob Merckell [1756]
    23 p.   22 1/2 cm.

J

2465   James, Edwin, 1797-1861, comp.
    Account of an expedition from Pitts-
burgh to the Rocky mountains, performed in the years 1819 and '20, by order of the Hon. J.C. Calhoun, sec'y
of war: under the command of Major
Stephen H. Long. From the notes of
Major Long, Mr. T. Say and other gentlemen of the exploring party. Comp.
by Edwin James, botanist and geologist
for the expedition ... Philadelphia,
H.C. Carey and I. Lee, 1822-23.
    2 v.   23 cm.

2466   Jesuits. Letters from missions.
    Lettres édifiantes et curieuses,
écrites des missions étrangères.
Nouv. ed., ornée de cinquante belles
gravures ... Lyon, Chez J. Vernarel
[etc.] 1819.
    14 v. plates (part fold.) ports.,
fold. maps.   21 1/2 cm.

L

2467   Leonardo [y] Argensola,   Bartolomé
    [Juan] 1562-1631.

Conqvista de las islas Malvcas al
rey Felipe III. nº. s.er Escrita por
el Licen.do Bartolome Leonardo de
Argensola ... Madrid, A. Martin,
1609.
6 p. l., 407 p. 29 cm.

2468 Leonardo [y] Argensola, Bartolome,
[Juan] 1562-1631.
The discovery and conquest of the
Molucco and Philippine islands. Containing their history ... description
... habits, shape, and inclinations
of the natives ... Written in Spanish by Bartholomew Leonardo de Argensola ... Now translated into English: and illustrated with a map
and several cuts. London, 1708.
3 p. l., 260, [8]p. plates, map.
21 x 16 cm.

2469 Lord, George A   1820-1888.
A short narrative and military experience of Corp. G. A'Lord, formerly
a member of Co. G. ... 125th reg't
N.Y.V. ... Containing a four year's
history of the war, the Constitution
of the United States in full, a correct list of stamp duties, and also
patriotic songs of the latest selection ... [n.p., 186-?]
80 p.   15 cm.

2470 [Lyttelton, George Lyttelton, *1st baron*] 1709-1773.
Farther considerations on the
present state of affairs, at home
and abroad, as affected by the late
convention, in a letter to the minister: with an appendix; containing
a true state of the South-Sea company's

affairs in 1718 ... London, Printed
for T. Cooper, 1739.
  2 p. 1., 66 p.   20 cm.

N

2471 National ship-canal convention, *Chicago,*
        1863.
          Memorial to the president and Con-
        gress of the United States, by the
        National canal convention, assembled
        at Chicago, June 2, 1863. Chicago,
        Tribune company, printers, 1863.
          cover-title, 24 p.   22 1/2 cm.

P

2472 Paris. Muséum national d'histoire na-
        turelle. Archives. t.1-10. Paris,
        1839-61.
          10 v. illus. (part col.)   32 cm.

2473 Pons, François Raymond Joseph de, 1751-
        1812.
          Travels in parts of South America,
        during the years 1801, 1802, 1803 &
        1804; containing a description of
        the captain-generalship of Carraccas,
        with an account of the laws, com-
        merce, and natural productions of that
        country; as also a view of the cus-
        toms and manners of the Spaniards and
        native Indians. By F. Depons ...
        London, R. Phillips, 1806.
          iv, 5 -137, 3 p. front. (fold.
        map) fold. plan.   22 cm.

2474 The Pro-slavery argument; as maintained
        by the most distinguished writers

of the southern states, containing
the several essays on the subject,
of Chancellor Harper, Governor Hammond, Dr. Simms, and Professor Dew.
Charleston, Walker, Richards & co.,
1852.
  1 p. 1., 490 p.   18 1/2 cm.

2475 The pro-slavery argument; as maintained
by the most distinguished writers of
the southern states; containing the
several essays, on the subject, of
Chancellor Harper, Governor Hammond,
Dr. Sims, and Professor Dew. Philadelphia, Lippincott, Grambo, & co.,
1853.
  1 p. 1., 490 p.   20 cm.

                    R

2476 [Rede, Leman Thomas] *d*. 1810.
    Bibliotheca americana; or, A chron-
ological catalogue of the most curious and interesting books, pamphlets,
state papers, &c. upon the subject of
North and South America, from the
earliest period to the present, in
print and manuscript; for which re-
search has been made in the British
Musaeum, and the most celebrated
public and private libraries, reviews,
catalogues, &c. With an introductory
discourse on the present state of
literature in those countries. London, 1789.
    271 p.   27 cm.

2477 Republican party. *National convention.*
2d, Chicago, 1860.
    Proceedings of the Republican

national convention held at Chicago,
May 16, 17, and 18, 1860. Albany,
Weed, Parsons, and company, printers,
1860.
   cover-title, 153 p.   23 cm.

2478 The Rush-light.   v. 1-2, no. 1 (no. 1-7);
      Feb. 15, 1800- [1801?] New York, W.
      Cobbett.
         2 v. in 1.   22 cm.   irregular.

                         S

2479 [Sangston, Lawrence]
         The bastiles of the North. By a
      member of the Maryland legislature
      ... Baltimore, Kelly, Hedian & Piet,
      1863.
         136 p.   22 1/2 cm.

2480 [Scoville, Joseph Alfred] 1815-1864.
         The old merchants of New York city.
      By Walter Barrett, clerk [pseud.]
      [First-fourth series] ... New York,
      Carloton, 1863--
         v.   19 1/2 cm.

2481 [Strong, George Crockett] 1832-1863.
         Cadet life at West Point. By an of-
      ficer of the United States army. With
      a descriptive sketch of West Point, by
      Benson J. Lossing. Boston, T.O.H.P.
      Burnham, 1862.
         xvii, [2], [9]-367 p. front.
      18 1/2 cm.

2482 Stryker's American register and magazine
         ... Conducted by James Stryker. v.
      1-6; May 1848-1851. Philadelphia [etc.,
      1848-53]

6 v.   illus.   22 1/2 cm.

T

2483 [Tennant, Charles] 1796-1873.
        The American question, and how to
      settle it ...   London, S. Low, son,
      and co., 1863.
        2 p. 1., 313 p.   19 1/2 cm.

W

2484 Westman, Georgius A
          ... Itinera priscorum scandianorum
      in Americam ...   praeside ...   Dn.
      Petro Kalm ...   Aboae, Jacob Merckell
      [1757]